Craig S. Galbraith, Alex F. DeNoble
Technology Development and Commercialization

Craig S. Galbraith, Alex F. DeNoble

Technology Development and Commercialization

Concepts, Tools and Best Practices

DE GRUYTER

ISBN 978-3-11-168378-2
e-ISBN (PDF) 978-3-11-168442-0
e-ISBN (EPUB) 978-3-11-168556-4

Library of Congress Control Number: 2025942336

Bibliographic information published by the Deutsche Nationalbibliothek
The Deutsche Nationalbibliothek lists this publication in the Deutsche Nationalbibliografie;
detailed bibliographic data are available on the internet at http://dnb.dnb.de.

© 2026 Walter de Gruyter GmbH, Berlin/Boston, Genthiner Straße 13, 10785 Berlin
Cover image: your_photo/iStock/Getty Images Plus
Typesetting: Integra Software Services Pvt. Ltd.

www.degruyterbrill.com
Questions about General Product Safety Regulation:
productsafety@degruyterbrill.com

Acknowledgments

In preparing this book, we were fortunate to interview many highly accomplished professionals working across the spectrum of technology development and commercialization. These individuals generously shared their expertise and real-world perspectives from university technology transfer offices and startup ventures to global corporations and investment firms. Their insights shaped our understanding of the commercialization process and enriched the practical relevance of this book.

We are especially grateful to Marc Sedam (NYU Langone Health), Tommy Martindale (SDSU), Justin Streuli (UNC Wilmington), James Zanewicz (Tulane University School of Medicine), Michael Rondelli (University of North Texas), Paul Roben (UC San Diego), Kirsten Leute (Osage University Partners), Brad Chisum (Eyepop.ai, Lumedyne Technologies), Eric Aguilar (Omitron Sensors), Darrel Drinan (RayBalance, Inc.), Napoleon Monroe (New Directions Technology Consulting), Michael Mesa (Mesa Science Associates), Richard Sudek (CEO Coach), Molly Cernicek (Los Alamos National Laboratory), and Steve Fontana (Fontana International).

We also wish to thank the many other entrepreneurs, engineers, IP experts, investors, and tech transfer professionals who spoke with us and chose to remain anonymous. Additionally, we are grateful to the presenters at the 2025 California Entrepreneurship Educators Conference and the 2024 North Carolina Entrepreneurship Educators Conference for their invaluable insights into the topics explored in this book.

In addition, we extend sincere thanks to the following individuals who provided early reads and constructive feedback on draft chapters of this manuscript: Scott Galbraith, John York, Ray Combs, Lily Davidov, Fabian Eggers, Lois Shelton, Laura Buffard, Jamey Darnell, Jim Dovey, Ami Doshi, Anthony Sawh, Connor Nielsen, Rachel DeNoble, and Oliver Galbraith IV.

Finally, we offer special thanks to the late Brian Dovey, Senior Partner at Domain Associates. His enduring wisdom and partnership had a profound impact on Alex DeNoble's thinking and continues to influence how we approach the topics of entrepreneurship and technology commercialization.

https://doi.org/10.1515/9783111684420-202

Contents

Introduction

Why Study Technology Development and Commercialization?

Taking an idea to the marketplace is one of the most fundamental concepts in any economy. New ideas, innovations, and technologies fuel the advancement of societies, create wealth for populations, and motivate entrepreneurial expression. Past innovations like the water wheel, steam engine, light bulb, and integrated circuit changed the world, and oftentimes provided the technological push for industrial revolutions on a global scale. Other technologies, such as the invention of the first commercial typewriter by Sholes and Glidden in 1866 not only changed the way people communicated but also created a whole new profession of typists and office workers that brought working women into white-collar jobs for the first time in history.[1] Today we still use the QWERTY keyboard. Other, more modern technologies such as artificial intelligence, nano-science and biotechnology are already making huge impacts on industry and society.

While it is fun to discuss and use such examples, these paradigm-busting innovations are actually quite rare. Most commercialized technologies are incremental in nature, involving slight improvements that still create value in the minds of customers. The average person has never heard of the vast majority of successful technologies. These are the technologies that are ultimately integrated as critical components into much larger systems, which, in turn, become the automobiles we drive, the aircraft we fly in, and the phones we use to communicate. All of these technologies, large and small, revolutionary and incremental, need to be properly developed, effectively engineered, sufficiently financed, carefully managed, and produced in order to create value for both the individual customer and society in general.

But the numbers are not positive. A number of research studies have investigated the percentage of ideas that actually make it to the marketplace.[2] One study, for example, found an average of only a single commercial success out of every 3,000 early innovations.[3] Other studies might be a little more positive but still report success rates in the 1% to 2% range depending on the industry. Perhaps only 5% of modern patents ever produce revenues. Many innovations are simply not ready for the market or don't create much value. More often there might be competitive technologies that are simply better for the target applications.

In many examples, however, the development and commercialization processes were simply botched. Attempting to commercialize a poor technology is a waste of time, effort and money. But not properly managing the development and ultimate commercialization of a promising technology also represents a huge cost since needs are not met, resources are squandered, systems can fail, and ultimately missed opportunities create losses for everybody involved.

https://doi.org/10.1515/9783111684420-001

This book attempts to fill an important gap. The word "technology" is actually derived from two ancient Greek words, *technie* and *logos*. *Technie* signifies the method or manner by which something is achieved. It includes understanding both the theoretical foundation and the practical applications of this knowledge. *Logos* describes the organization of the body of knowledge or discourse. It is this combination of *technie* and *logos* that has created the focus for this book. It is specifically designed as a practical textbook for classes in technology management, commercialization, and entrepreneurship. It can also be used in courses related to engineering and the applied sciences that focus more on the transitional process of bringing discovery to the market.

The book also may be useful to professionals in technology development and commercialization. Corporate R&D managers, technology transfer officers, and commercialization consultants will all find many of the topics, concepts, tools, and best practices covered in this book useful in their professional practice. The book focuses on managing technologies, whether they are being developed by innovative and entrepreneurial start-ups or through the R&D and design efforts of larger corporations. The end target is the same.

Structure of the Book

This book is designed to help bring promising technologies to market more effectively by addressing the critical management processes required at various stages in the technology's development. In addition to guiding technology developers, it serves as a valuable resource for readers learning about technology commercialization and innovation management. The book not only helps to identify technologies with strong market potential but also highlights when a project should be reconsidered or abandoned before excessive resources are invested. Furthermore, it offers insight into recognizing key moments for strategic pivots that can keep a technology viable and advancing toward commercialization, and how managers can both understand and influence this process.

The first part of the book primarily addresses the underlying key concepts of technology development and commercialization. These discussions provide the necessary foundation for later, more management-oriented chapters.

The second part of the book delves deeply into the management of technology development and commercialization. These chapters not only cover concepts but also focus on the managerial tools and "best practices" that are used in the modern world of technology development and commercialization. These more practical chapters are presented as somewhat stand-alone topics but also build upon prior chapters and concepts in the book. The book is designed as a progressive process, from the first chapter to the last chapter. However, certain chapters could be taken out of order or even skipped if not relevant to the reader's interest.

We also provide a number of examples. Some examples are short descriptions, others longer. By design, some of these examples are very modern technologies, while others are somewhat older technologies. Regardless of the age of the technologies, we have tried to pick examples that both underline and illustrate the topics in the book and are interesting. All of our examples are real technologies, although occasionally we had to eliminate the developer's name due to confidentiality issues. Some examples are well known to readers. Many examples come from the experiences of the authors' professional backgrounds in technology development and commercialization, while other examples were provided by the many technology experts that we interviewed for this book.

We believe a book on technology development and commercialization needs to provide both a good foundation in the underlying concepts and theories, as well as focusing on the tools for specific topic areas and problems. A good analogy is medicine. Before physicians pick a medical specialty, they must all completely understand the basic, but still complex foundational material. All physicians must have a strong grounding in anatomy, pathology, pharmacology, genetics, physiology, and medical microbiology. These areas represent the preclinical foundational material that medical schools teach and the medical licensure exams cover. Taking a foundational understanding is also our approach in this book. Understanding this foundational material will hopefully guide the entrepreneurial minded student, the technical professional, and commercialization consultant as they focus on their particular area of specialization.

However, professionals need to also specialize. Whether in medicine, science, architecture, engineering, or business, this is where the professional learns the tools and methods they will actually use in practice. Certainly, each stage of technology development, each entity that is involved in technology development, and each slice of science and engineering has its own unique characteristics. We have found that both the foundations and tools tend to be universal. That is the orientation of this book – a focus on "best practices".

Given this focus, the book should be of interest to seven broad groups of readers, whether they are students learning about the fascinating topic of technology development and commercialization or active practitioners involved with some aspect of technology development and commercialization:

1) Students taking classes in technology commercialization, entrepreneurship, technology management or product innovation. This book is designed as a core resource for classes in technology management and commercialization, or as a supplemental book to general entrepreneurship classes.

2) Entrepreneurship start-ups and development firms that often acquire a technology, through a licensing arrangement and then manage the development of that technology closer toward the market. Many of these firms are founded by scientists, technology developers, and engineers, who often want to understand a little more about the business side of commercialization.

3) Technology transfer agencies (TTOs) at universities, government R&D laboratories, and contract technology transfer agencies. While most TTOs focus on patenting and licensing early-stage technologies, managing these strategies effectively requires a clear understanding of the entire commercialization spectrum.

4) Immersive technology entrepreneurship training programs, such as the NSF I-Corps™ and start-up accelerators. These programs can use the book as a supplemental resource to help participants navigate commercialization challenges such as IP strategy, market validation, customer discovery, and business model development.

5) Larger corporations and other system developers that often acquire technologies as well as internally developing innovations. These organizations then integrate these technologies into effective packages, which are subsequently commercialized into the marketplace.

6) Private equity investors, such as angel groups and venture capitalists, will need to perform comprehensive due diligence reviews prior to investing in early-stage firms driven by underlying technologies.

7) Government granting agencies that target technology development. Agencies such as the National Science Foundation (NSF), National Institutes of Health (NIH), and the Department of Energy (DOE) all offer Small Business Innovation Research (SBIR) grants and Small Business Tech Transfer (STTR) grants.

In this book we focus on the key takeaways and thus keep the book at a reasonable length while still covering a vast topic. This is clearly a balancing act. We provide sufficient detail to establish the correct foundational material but also create a book that is both approachable and useful in practice.

Focus on Managerial Tools and Best Practices

What makes this book unique? Combined, the authors of this book have over 80 years of experience teaching technology development and commercialization at both the graduate and undergraduate university levels. The authors also have extensive professional and personal experience in the actual process of commercializing technologies. In addition, in preparing this book, we formally interviewed numerous technology professionals including university technology transfer officers, technology entrepreneurs, private equity investors, and corporate R&D and product management directors from across the globe. Their important contributions are fully incorporated into the book.

We believe in a holistic view of commercialization, not just the final stages of bringing a technology-driven product to the consumer market, or the very early process of licensing a recently patented technology to other developers. Individuals and organizations are often involved in only part of the technology development journey, and this typically becomes their perspective. But technology commercialization involves all of these areas. It represents a whole journey from beginning to end. We have been fortunate in our careers to have personal experience at all of these levels.

Two common themes from these experiences and interviews were uncovered. First, is the need to focus on "managerial tools" and "best practices". In the modern world, students need tools to take into the job market and their careers. We heard time and again that modern textbooks focus too much on theory, and not enough on the actual tools, concepts, and methods that can be put into practice. We strongly believe that a book on technology development and commercialization, while needing to cover basic concepts to provide a strong foundation, should also focus on managerial skills, tools, and processes that can lead to greater technology success. Second, everybody has their own perspective of the topic. The practice of technology development and commercialization is highly fragmented. There are technology transfer officers, IP attorneys, entrepreneurs, engineers, corporate RD managers, investors, and many other groups. They all have a unique perspective of the topic, based upon their own niche of experiences. We wanted to take a much broader and holistic view and include the full range of important experiences, tools, topics, and best practices at all stages in the technology development and commercialization process. These two perspectives make this book unique in the field.

Finally, we try to use the actual terminology and nomenclature of the technology development and commercialization community. Learning the proper language of the field is particularly important for students. While we tend to use primarily U.S. examples, we regularly reference the organizations, institutions, rules, and perspectives of other countries and cultures.

At the beginning of each chapter, we identify some of the important managerial tools covered in the chapter. These are the systems, applications, and methods for calculating solutions and acquiring best practices that readers should know when venturing into the ever-changing field of technology development and commercialization.

It should be noted that we purposely did not spend a lot of time on entrepreneurial finance or funding issues. While certainly recognizing the importance of different forms of funding, particularly for early-stage technology start-ups, we felt that the detailed topics of funding are generally well covered in entrepreneurship programs by either separate courses in entrepreneurship finance or modules that discuss funding in introductory entrepreneurship courses. However, when appropriate we provide extensive references to critical funding issues, such as the different stages of private-equity funding, including the various players such as pre-seed funding, angel investors, venture capital firms, and corporate partnership support. We also identify various granting opportunities for technology, such as SBIR/STTR grants, and the timing of such events.

The Role of AI in Commercialization

Artificial intelligence (AI) has taken the world by storm. It is no different in technology development and commercialization. While AI has been around for decades, new advances in web search processes and learning programs have made AI a very powerful tool. There are some areas where AI has made a significant impact on the study of technology development and commercialization, particularly in performing technology commercialization and feasibility studies. New AI applications targeted specifically to technology commercialization have only recently emerged, while various generalized AI applications can also be effectively used. When appropriate, we identify those areas where AI applications have become important. The inevitable march of more advanced AI systems in the future will likely make it even more important in the field of technology commercialization. However, AI is only a tool, albeit a powerful one. In other areas, humans must still make the strategic decisions of which markets to target, how to target them, how to manage the technology development process, when to commit scarce resources, and when to pivot to new markets and technological variations if necessary.

Getting Started

Whether you are a student stepping into this field for the first time, a scientist eager to see your breakthrough reach the world, or a seasoned professional looking for sharper tools and strategies, we wrote this book with you in mind. Technology development and commercialization is not just about invention. More importantly, it is about judgment, timing, communication, and execution. As you move through these chapters, you will gain the frameworks, vocabulary, and real-world insights to guide technologies from the lab bench or whiteboard to the marketplace. So let us begin this journey together and explore what it really takes to bring great ideas to life.

Chapter 1
Stages of Technology Development

This Chapter

- Introduces the stages of technology development and highlights key decisions at each stage.
- Presents common managerial models – such as Technology Readiness Levels (TRLs) – used to assess and communicate commercialization progress.
- Explores the systems nature of technology, emphasizing how most innovations are built from bundles of interrelated technologies.

Key Management Tools and Best Practices

- Stages of technology development
- Technology Readiness Levels (TRLs)
- Manufacturing Readiness Levels (MRLs)
- System Readiness Levels (SRLs)
- Interface and Integration Readiness Levels (IRLs)

! INSIGHT

All technologies go through an evolutionary process of development, from early stages of idea generation to the final stage when the improved technology is introduced into the market. Understanding the stage that a technology is currently in becomes one of the most critical aspects of managing technology development. Each stage of a technology's development is associated with a different set of management decisions. Investment decisions differ by the stage of technology development. The stage of development also becomes critical when communicating the technology to potential customers, investors, and system designers. It becomes important to obtaining patents, grants, and partnerships. Not surprising, there have been efforts to develop formal classifications of the key technology development stages.

Introduction

The most common definition of technology commercialization is taking an idea or innovation from the research lab, then turning it into a design, technology, or product that is sold to customers. But this process ultimately involves many different steps and phases of technology development along the way.

Oftentimes, technology commercialization begins as a search for the right application. It is less about executing a fixed plan and more like a fishing expedition. Developers may start with a general target in mind but must remain open to pivoting when new evidence reveals a better market opportunity. In other cases, technology commercialization represents a highly structured process with a clear end target market in mind.

https://doi.org/10.1515/9783111684420-002

The path is straight, the customers are on board, and the developers just need to get the technology to a point where it can be incorporated into a larger system.

The market and customer base for a technology changes significantly, depending on its stage of development. One of the unique aspects of technology development is how fragmented the technology development process really is. Different entities often participate in different stages of a technology's development. For example, from the perspective of a university technology transfer officer, the primary focus is identifying potential value, early in the process. The typical goal of a technology transfer office is to quickly determine whether investing in a patent or another form of IP protection is worthwhile. Once the IP is protected, the next step is to license the technology to early-stage development firms or larger companies. Other enterprises will then take over these later phases of technology development and end-user commercialization.

In addition, one technology might be successfully commercialized, simply as a component in a much larger system, and this larger system might still need to go through additional development cycles in order to be commercialized into even other systems. Finally, the whole functional package needs to be commercialized into the final end-user market. In fact, most of the technologies that are sold into consumer markets, whether computers, phones, or automobiles, are bundles of technologies within systems. There are many players involved along the full path of developing a technology.

Stages of Technology Development

Like most things in the world, technologies also have a life cycle. New technologies always originate as an innovative idea, a thought on how something might be improved or a problem solved. This original idea then matures. With the application of knowledge, skill, design, and testing, this original idea might actually be turned into a technology or product with a potential for market acceptance and use.

Like most things in the world, technologies also have a life cycle.

In this chapter, we focus on how technologies tend to evolve through various, and somewhat predictable stages or phases, from the initial point in time when somebody has a brilliant idea for a new innovation to when the finished product or technology is finally launched into the marketplace. Research has shown that almost all technologies, regardless of what sector we are discussing, progress through identifiable phases in their development.[1]

Each phase also has its own set of decision points and issues. Is the technology at a point where it can be sold or licensed to an external customer or do I keep working at it internally to bring it closer to commercial viability? How do investors view a technology at this stage versus waiting to a later stage of development? How can I understand a complete system when the components are all in different stages of development? How can I communicate to others about what stage my technology is in? These are all critical questions.

Strategic decisions tend to be made at certain points in a technology's development. This is true whether the technology is being developed by a small entrepreneurial effort or a larger, technology-driven corporation. Most organizations involved with technology commercialization and development tend to have specific phases that they focus on. This focus becomes part of their overall corporate strategy. In addition, many funding organizations, whether in the private equity market, like venture capitalists or angel investors, or the various government granting programs, tend to focus on technologies at certain stages in their development.

This is true whether the technologies are computer hardware products, scientific instrumentations, advanced aircraft or auto parts, medical technologies, software and mobile apps, or drug and biopharmaceutical developments. Each category of technologies tends to follow a common pattern of development, although the phases might be somewhat different between these broad categories of technologies.

Descriptive Phases of Technology Development

What are the phases or stages that a technology progresses through during its evolution? In general, we can talk about eight basic phases.

Phase 1: Idea generation. Idea generation is the first stage in a technology's life. This is when the inventor starts to get the idea for a new invention, or a method to improve an older technology. In some respects, this can be considered the "light-bulb" moment. In this phase, the inventor might put together some very preliminary sketches of the innovation and start talking with other technology developers. Ideas are a very unique human characteristic. We have all probably been in an idea generation phase at some point in our lives, particularly when we get frustrated at something not working right. Some truly creative individuals, or perhaps just people with more persistent personalities, might try to push the idea forward a bit harder.

Phase 2: Proof-of-Concept. This stage is called the "Proof-of-Concept" or PoC phase. People have a lot of innovative ideas; however, at some point, these brilliant ideas need to be shown as having the potential of actually working. The proof-of-concept phase is when the original idea that springs from Phase 1 can actually be shown to work in practice or theory. Using a galactic space travel analogy, Phase 1 might be the idea of "Warp Drive Engines", or a propulsion system that can move a spaceship many orders faster than the speed of light – great idea, and the basis of many science fiction stories and movies. However, can it be shown to actually be workable in the real world? Not at the present time. This is the proof-of-concept phase. The proof-of-concept phase is focused on demonstrating an idea's feasibility in the real world. Depending on the technology, a proof-of-concept might be accomplished using mathematical theories or engineering principles. In other cases, proof-of-concept can be shown with experimental and lab results, such as in biological studies. In many cases, proof-of-concept can be shown with detailed sketches, or even an original crude model of the technology.

⚡ Critical Decision Points with Phase 2, Proof-of-Concept

There are a number of key decisions that are often made in the proof-of-concept phase.

First, in order to obtain a patent (Phase 3), you generally have to show proof-of-concept to the patent office.

Second, once a proof of concept is achieved, an organization reaches a critical decision point. This decision point involves whether or not future funding will be needed in order to apply and obtain a patent or some other type of intellectual property around the technology. Developers or their sponsors need to make a formal decision whether to continue funding the development in technology. It is difficult, for example, for organizations to justify continued funding of a technology when there is little movement toward developing a solid proof of concept, regardless of how excited the inventors are about the idea.

Third, after a proof of concept is reasonably established, many organizations will perform a "quick-look" commercialization study in order to obtain an idea of market feasibility and success. This is important since continuing to fund a technology through its patent or intellectual property phase will be largely determined by whether the funding organizations see a potential market for the technology. This market needs to be of sufficient size and profitability to justify the future investments in the technology. However, a preliminary or first-cut commercialization study almost always needs a proof of concept established for the technology in order to assess the market feasibility and get feedback from potential customers or partners.

Phase 3: Intellectual Property Protection. This phase is when the intellectual property embodied in the technology is formally protected. The World Intellectual Property Organization (WIPO) defines intellectual property, or IP, as "creations of the mind".[2] But what makes creations of the mind into intellectual property is the associated "property right". Hard assets, such as real estate, machines, or cars are regularly called "property". In most societies, this means somebody can own them. It is the same with IP. With IP, somebody can own this right of creation; they can sell it, license it, or use it as collateral. Just like real property, this right of ownership is ultimately established by the laws of society, through governmental action.

The most obvious method of protecting intellectual property is via the patent process. We discuss the patent process in much more detail later in the book. However, when applying for a patent, inevitably, the governmental entity responsible for issuing patents will always expect proof-of-concept to be demonstrated. There are, of course, a number of other elements required in order to obtain a patent, but a well-documented, clear proof-of-concept is a major requirement. This proof-of-concept needs to be clear enough to be put down on paper in the patent application. Copyrights might also be a component of phase 3 for certain types of innovations, such as software.

⚡ Critical Decision Points with Phase 3, IP Protection

Intellectual property protection establishes formal ownership of a technology. Just like any other type of property, where ownership can be identified, the owner of that property can transfer ownership, rent or lease the property, donate or give the property away, or use the property as collateral for loans. These are the key elements of "property rights", one of the most critical components of modern economic institutions.

The strategic thinking of most government and university laboratories is to take their technologies through the intellectual property protection phase. The technology transfer offices (TTOs) of these laboratories, once their technologies have achieved a patent or some other form of intellectual property protection, will then seek to license or sell these technologies to other entities.

Upon completion of the IP protection phase, this is also when many early-stage entrepreneurial firms are created. These firms will seek out and license technologies from university and government labs as the starting point for their new venture. Some of these licenses will be issued to the inventers as university "spin-outs", while other licenses will be made to independent entities. This is probably the most common type of technology-oriented entrepreneurial effort – license a Phase 3 technology coming out of the lab, and then attempt to develop it further, ultimately to the point of commercialization. One study of angel group investors showed that over 90% of the funded early-stage entrepreneurial firms had licensed their technologies from university or government laboratories.

Phase 3 is important to private equity investors. venture capitalists and angels. Investors will almost always want some type of strong intellectual property wrapped around the technologies for the firms they are investing in. The analogy is obvious – who would invest in a real estate deal when there is no clear title to the property?

Phase 3 is also a stage when larger corporations will look to in-license technologies that might enhance their own product portfolio, either as a new product line or more often, to improve their existing products and technological base. If developing the technology internally, Phase 3 is the point when larger corporations might initiate an internal venture within their corporation. These internal ventures will essentially operate as entrepreneurial entities, but within the existing corporate structure.

Other types of intellectual properties, however, may not be patentable or copyrighted in a formal manner. In these cases, the associated intellectual property can often be protected through a trade-secret process. Trade secrets are when an organization makes a coordinated, clear and specific effort to keep the relevant intellectual property confidential. Only certain individuals have access to the underlying components or ingredients that comprise the technology. Trade secrets are a particularly important method of protecting intellectual property when the technology is more formulaic or process in nature, such as the ingredients for Coca Cola's flavor, or the unique formulation of WD-40's lubricant. Oftentimes, the intellectual property protection phase of technology development is a combination of patentable components and trade-secret components.

Phase 4: Dummy/Low-Fidelity Prototypes. The next stage is developing a "dummy prototype". Dummy prototypes are sometimes called "low-fidelity" prototypes. For most tangible technologies, a dummy prototype could be a constructed presentation model or 3-D printed representation of the technology. For mobile app designers, phase 4 might involve a mockup or wireframe effort, where the sketches of the various mobile app screens are drawn and the overall structure between the screens are defined.

Dummy, or "low-fidelity" prototypes generally do not work. The purpose of a dummy prototype is to show people what the possibilities are. Dummy prototypes are often used in focus groups to get early feedback from potential customers about technological ideas. Dummy prototypes can also be used internally to show around the organization.

Since dummy prototypes have minimal, if any, functionality when demonstrating a dummy prototype, the proposed future functionality will need to be described. It is much easier, however, to describe a technology's functionality when having something in hand as a visual prop. The advantage of a dummy prototype is that customer and user feedback will often include recommendations for required functionality and preferred design elements, thus allowing the designers to fine-tune their thinking about the future technology.

A classic example of a dummy, or low-fidelity, prototype is Douglas Engelbart's original conception of a computer mouse, shown in Figure 1.1. Developed in 1964, the prototype was simply a formed piece of wood with a light, and some connected wires that could be connected to a computer.[3] Though non-functional, it helped demonstrate the core concept of user-controlled cursor movement, during early presentations.

Figure 1.1: Dummy prototype of the computer mouse. Source: Computer History Museum.[4]

Phase 5: Lab Prototypes. After a dummy, or low-fidelity prototype is created, engineers and technology developers will start to incorporate critical functionalities into their designs. They will start transforming the idea into a working product. A lab prototype is usually built to see if, in fact, the target functionalities can be obtained. Since functionality is the key objective at this point, lab prototypes are often called "ugly prototypes". Lab prototypes start to make the transition from "low-fidelity" to "high-fidelity" designs. Lab prototypes can also provide initial performance data. This performance data can then be compared against competitive technologies, and be incorporated into communications with potential customers, licensees, or investors. In essence, lab prototypes work with basic functionality, but are not close to being a final, "high-fidelity" technology that one can take into the field. Lab prototypes are not intended to be presented to the market as a viable product, but rather to show the technology actually works. In software development, this stage is sometimes called the "pre-alpha test". While lab prototypes are primarily intended for internal use, they can still be shown to others, typically demonstrating the primary functionality, even if secondary features are not yet incorporated.

⚡ Critical Decision Points with Phase 5, Lab Prototype

Oftentimes, after a lab prototype is built, there are other decision points to be considered.

As a specific strategy, there are many small, entrepreneurial development companies that take a technology to the lab prototype stage and then sell or license it to larger corporations to bring to market. This is their business model.

This is particularly true when bringing a product to the final market requires government approvals and/or significant investment for final technology development, marketing, and distribution. An example of this approach is seen in the medical instrument industry. It is common, for example, where very small medical instrument development companies, many of them owned by physicians and surgeons who are also inventors, will see a need for a new instrument in their field of medicine, design it, and bring the technology to the lab prototype phase. At this point, they can demonstrate the advantages of their technology, then sell or license that technology to larger, well established medical tool and instrument companies for final product engineering, commercialization, and distribution into the marketplace.

Phase 6: Field Prototype. The next stage of technology development is to build a prototype product or technology that can withstand actual field applications. This represents a true "high-fidelity" prototype. The technology should look and perform somewhat like what is anticipated for the final product. In the entrepreneurship literature, if the field prototype has just the most critical functionalities, this is sometimes referred to as a "minimum viable product" (MVP) design stage.

A field prototype is a version that: a) has a solid working primary functionality, b) has incorporated additional features that may be desired by the marketplace, c) looks somewhat like the expected final product design, and d) is sufficiently sturdy to operate in actual field conditions. A well-designed field prototype incorporates the insights from prior focus groups and customer feedback studies regarding the key functionality and design features needed for market success. The field prototype is not expected to be the final product, but of sufficient design and functionality to be given to some early customers. These customers can then use it in the "field" or start interfacing with the technology in ways that can provide feedback to the developers about improvements. Customer feedback from a field prototype is often considered "initially verified", since these early customers are using a product that is close to the final design.

Phase 7: Beta Testing. Beta-Testing, sometimes called "acceptance testing", is the process of placing the field prototype with selected customers for a period of time in order to obtain feedback under continuous field conditions. Customer feedback from a field prototype is often considered "fully verified", since these beta-test customers are using a product that is close to the final design, and they are using it in a normal field or integrated manner. Beta-testing for technology-based products must be considered strategically. Beta-testing can occur with end-users, such as putting a new auto license plate scanning technology with a major parking enforcement service provider, or for intermediate technologies, by providing the technology as a working component with a major system developer for testing and review. Beta testing is almost a required step in the software, mobile app, and game development industries, but is commonly used in all technology sectors.

Some firms also use the concept of "alpha" testing. Alpha testing is done before a full-blown beta-test, and often uses a group of internal personnel to formally use the technology rather than seeking out external, potential customers as in a beta test. A full-blown beta test would then follow a successful alpha test.

Critical Decision Points with Phase 7, Beta Testing

Beta testing must always be considered strategically.

In order to get a full range of verified feedback regarding market potential and any possible final recommendations for design changes or functionalities, the beta-test customers must be very familiar with the technological space, the competitive products in the market, and interested in using the beta-test technology on a regular basis.

Beta-test customers are also a very important source of recommendations regarding the quality of the technology. You need to pick a beta-test customer that has significant legitimacy in the market. They need to be considered a thought or opinion leader in that particular market space. For example, while there are many crime labs in the United States, generally the Los Angeles County Crime Lab is considered one of the largest and most experienced crime labs in the world, often utilizing the most current technologies. If developing a technology targeted toward the crime lab market, using the Los Angeles Country Crime Lab would be much better for a beta-test than a small crime lab located in a rural area.

If the beta-test is successful, beta-test participants often become the first revenue-generating customers.

Phase 8: Commercialization into the Market. This phase represents the final commercialization or launch of the technology into its target market. This is true whether that final target market consists of system developers or end-use consumers. It is at this point when the technology can start producing revenues on a regular basis.

Readiness Levels: Key Managerial Tools

While the stages of technology development in the previous sections provide a good understanding of how technologies evolve, it soon became obvious that more defined methods of identifying and measuring technologies at their different levels of maturity was needed. This was particularly evident in working with various subcontractors, engineers, and companies involved in highly complex system designs, such as putting spacecraft on Mars or developing complex defense systems.

Technology Readiness Levels (TRLs)

In the 1970s, the National Aeronautics and Space Agency (NASA) took the lead in developing the idea of Technology Readiness Levels (TRLs) to numerically identify what phase a technology was in. By the late 1980s, the notion of TRLs had started to gain traction in other branches of the U.S. government. In 1995, NASA published their 9-point scale, which has become the base standard for TRL identification in the United States and most of the world.[5] In 2001, the U.S. Department of Defense started requiring the use of TRLs in their acquisition and procurement programs. The use of TRLs has now become almost universal in the technology work environment.

> The use of Technology Readiness Levels, or TRLs, has now become almost universal in the technology work environment.

TRLs can be considered a sequence of carefully defined levels of technology maturity, with two objectives in mind: a) communicate the development status of technologies, and b) draw attention to the risks associated with emerging technologies as they need to evolve into subsequent levels.

A general TRL 9-point model is outlined in Table 1.1. While the 9-point TRL doesn't typically include a TRL 0, some governments use a TRL 0 level in their TRL format.

Table 1.1: Technology Readiness Levels.

TRL level	Category	Description
TRL 0	Idea	Unproven concept; just an idea with no proof or testing.
TRL 1	Basic research	Basic principles observed. Starting to do research. Technologies are in very early stages of development; just starting to get data.
TRL 2	Technology formulation	Concept and application formulated; getting better data. The goal of this stage is to start conducting studies to examine the feasibility of the technology.
TRL 3	Proof-of-concept	Laboratory tests completed; theoretical or experimental aspects proven; applying for patent protection.
TRL 4	Validation in lab. Small-scale/ Lab prototype	Work on validating the technology in a laboratory environment; possible development of an "ugly prototype". Goal is to start obtaining data and functionality parameters.
TRL 5	Large-scale prototype	Can be tested and demonstrated in the intended environment, field prototype. Goal is to show that the technology works as intended, although perhaps the technology is not ready for the rigors of actual field testing.

Table 1.1 (continued)

TRL level	Category	Description
TRL 6	Final prototype system	Can be used extensively in relevant field environments, near-final functionality. This is really the demonstration stage. The technology can be incorporated into larger systems and shown to end-users.
TRL 7	Demonstration technology or system	Operating as intended; pre-commercialization scale. Technology could be in beta-testing environments.
TRL 8	Commercial first of kind	System is complete and qualified. Production issues solved. Can start producing in significant qualities at an efficient cost structure.
TRL 9	Commercial application	Technology is complete; available for large-scale commercial purchase.

TRLs have been specifically developed for a number of different industries, but they all share the same progressive levels of technological maturity. While the descriptive components of each stage might be somewhat different for each industry, the nine levels showing the evolution of a technology from idea to final commercialization are consistent between the different industry TRL models.

Three Development Stages

While the TRL system of classifying technologies is universally used, there are broader technology development categories that are often discussed from a management perspective. In each of these categories, or combinations of TRL phases, there is generally a broader set of players and investors involved.

Knowledge Development Stage. TRL1 to TRL3 is often called the "knowledge development" stage. This stage is the primary orientation for university and government laboratories, as well as corporations that have a strong early R&D focus.

Entrepreneurial Investment. The knowledge development phase is when the earliest seed funding generally takes place. In the earliest TRL phases, funding for entrepreneurial efforts is likely to be the founders, combined with family and friends. This is often called "pre-seed" funding. Entrepreneurs will be looking for small amounts of funding to get through the proof-of-concept/patent application period and building out an initial understanding of the commercial potential. Once some form of IP protection is obtained, then many entrepreneurs will start to look for private equity investment, or seed funding, from angel groups. Private equity investors, such as angels, will almost always want to see some form of IP protection before investing. The knowledge development stage is also where the earliest government grants take place, such as Phase

1 of the Small Business Innovation Research (SBIR) grants. Larger R&D corporations will also view this phase as knowledge development, with internal funding focused on moving the technologies to later phases.

Technology Development Stage. TRL4 to TRL6 are the next levels that are often strategically combined. This is often called the "technology development" stage. This is considered the entrepreneurial part of the process. The focus becomes putting together the team, obtaining some serious financing, fleshing out the designs, and expanding the team's knowledge of how to ultimately bring the technology to the market. This process also takes place within a project management orientation in larger corporations. Early-stage entrepreneurial start-ups that license technologies from other R&D labs and universities, as well as the internal venturing efforts of larger corporations tend to work in this range.

Entrepreneurial Investment. TRL4 to TRL6 is also where there is significant investment activity, particularly by private equity investors such as angel groups and early-stage venture capital firms. All of the stakeholders want to see the technology move aggressively toward the commercialization end of the spectrum, and this takes money. While many angel investment groups look at this stage for funding opportunities, this is also when early-stage venture capitalist firms might get involved. For these venture capitalists, investment in the technology development stages will normally be a first-round type of funding, or a Series A funding event. This stage is also the period when governments become interested in supporting technology development for targeted industries. For example, SBIR Phase 2 grants are generally focused on entities in the technology development stage. The technology development stage is when larger corporations might form and fund "internal ventures" around a particular promising technology.

Business Development Stage. TRL7 to TRL9 is the "business development" end of the spectrum. This is when the focus is on the marketplace, and what the customers demand in terms of bells and whistles. Fine-tuning the technology, beta-testing, and planning for the final market launch are the common business activities during this time. This is also when manufacturing and distribution needs to be incorporated into the process to make sure that there are no difficulties or delays.

Entrepreneurial Investments. By the TRL7 to TRL9 phase, the nature of investment activities changes. Funding is needed to build out the organization at all levels, beta-test the technology, and successfully implement the final commercialization plan. This is the stage when entrepreneurs may seek follow-up rounds of funding from venture capitalists, oftentimes called Series B and Series C funding. The purpose of this investment is really on commercialization. Governments also want to help at this stage. Phase 3 of SBIR grants, for example, focuses on the business development phase. At the point of actual commercialization (TRL9), revenues are starting to be realized. This is when many entrepreneurial organizations will start to think about an IPO or being acquired by a larger firm in order to "monetize" or generate a return on all of their earlier investments. At this stage, larger corporations funding of the technology project will also refocus on bringing the technology to market, including harnessing the resources of other departmental activities, such as marketing, production, and distribution, to become activity-involved. Figure 1.2 provides a visual summary of these three strategic stages - knowledge development, technology development and business development - mapped across TRL levels 1 through 9.

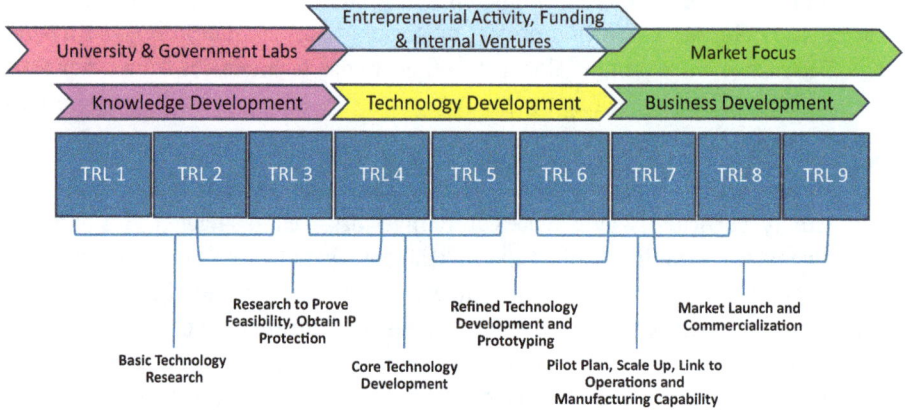

Figure 1.2: Integrated view of technology and commercialization readiness.

Manufacturing Readiness Levels (MRLs)

How ready the production or manufacturing process is to implement an effective technology commercialization process is also important. Similar to the TRL categories, some large organizations have started using a "manufacturing readiness level" (MRL) scale as a way to ensure that manufacturing and quality risks are identified and managed throughout a program's life cycle.[6] The MRL model represents a concurrent way of identifying the readiness to commercialize technologies from an operational point of view. For example, a technology may be an excellent prototype, with customers excited about the prospects; however, if the production kinks aren't worked out at the same time, the technology might fail upon market launch due to quality issues. Below is an example of a MRL system that could be used concurrently with TRLs (see Figure 1.3).

The Manufacturing Readiness Level, or MRL model represents a concurrent way of identifying the readiness to commercialize technologies from an operational point of view.

Manufacturing Readiness Levels (MRLs)		
Materials Solutions Analysis	1	Basic manufacturing implications identified
	2	Manufacturing concepts identified
	3	Manufacturing proof-of-concept (PoC) developed
	4	Capable of producing technology in laboratory setting
Technology Development	5	Capable of producing prototype components in a production relevant setting
	6	Capable of producing systems/sub systems in a production relevant setting
Engineering and Production Development	7	Capable of product all system components in a production representative setting
	8	Pilot line demonstrated with low-rate production
Production Deployment	9	Low-rate production is established. Capable to begin full rate production
Operations in Place	10	Full rate production with lean practices in place

Figure 1.3: Manufacturing Readiness Levels.

While the MRL model can be used simultaneously with the TRL model, it is important to note that the individual categories of the MRL model do not necessarily line up with the same TRL category. Thus, an MRL 6 does not necessarily correspond to a technology at the TRL 6 stage. While organizations can connect the MRL and TRL models internally in a broader "commercialization readiness" model (discussed in a later chapter), they tend to be considered independent models, except at the end when MRL 10 needs to line up with TRL 9 in order to have a successful market launch. However, some organizations create internal mappings between MRL and TRL levels to ensure that manufacturing readiness is in step with technology development.

Technology System Readiness Levels (SRLs)

While the TRL model, with the underlying stages of technology evolution, is used extensively in governments, granting institutions, funding organizations, and corporations, there are some challenges to the TRL model.

By itself, the TRL model focuses on a single technology and its level of maturity. Most technologies and products in development, however, are bundles of technologies, each possibly at a different TRL. Consider the electric car, which is a complex bundle of hundreds of different technologies, all interconnected with each other. How do we manage the complexity of interconnected technologies within the development of a new electric car? This is especially concerning when some components are being developed by external providers, others can be purchased off the shelf, some are carried over from earlier car generations, and still others are being developed in-house.

To address this concern, some system developers are now using tools to help them assess the readiness of the whole system. These represent structured approaches to assessing not only the maturity of individual technologies, but also their integration within a larger system, thus offering a more holistic view of overall system readiness.[7] There are two basic approaches to this problem: the "Weakest Link" model and a full "System Readiness Level" (SRL) model.

Weakest Link Model. Some organizations, when considering the appropriate readiness levels for a bundle of technologies (such as the electric car example), use the "weakest link" model. This approach, originally developed at NASA, considers that for a system, or sub-system, readiness is simply the lowest TRL of any component within the system. For example, a product being developed might have sixty different technologies ranging from TRL6 to TRL9 that will all need to be integrated into the final product. Under the weakest link model, the system readiness is a "6", reflecting the lowest TRL within the system at that particular point in development. Additional resources may then be allocated to the weakest link component.

System Readiness Levels (SRLs). Other organizations have developed more complex SRLs for large-scale technologies. One approach to visually understanding a system's readiness is using a spreadsheet that captures both the TRLs of the various technologies embedded into a larger system and the future development difficulty for each of the component technologies. Using this approach, it is possible to see where potential future bottlenecks might occur. In this case, additional resources and development efforts would be directed toward the lower-TRL technologies that present greater challenges. If these components are being developed by subcontractors, it may be necessary to explore alternative technologies as substitutes (see Figure 1.4).

Technology Integration Readiness Levels (IRLs)

In larger systems, individual components and subsystems need to interface with each other. When integrating a new technology into a larger system, we need to understand not only the TRL phases of individual technologies, but also how advanced the integration is between the technologies. Sometimes, the interface between technologies is as difficult as the development of individual component technologies. Any organization managing the development of a technological system involving two or more technologies needs to map and understand the problem of integration.

System Readiness Levels

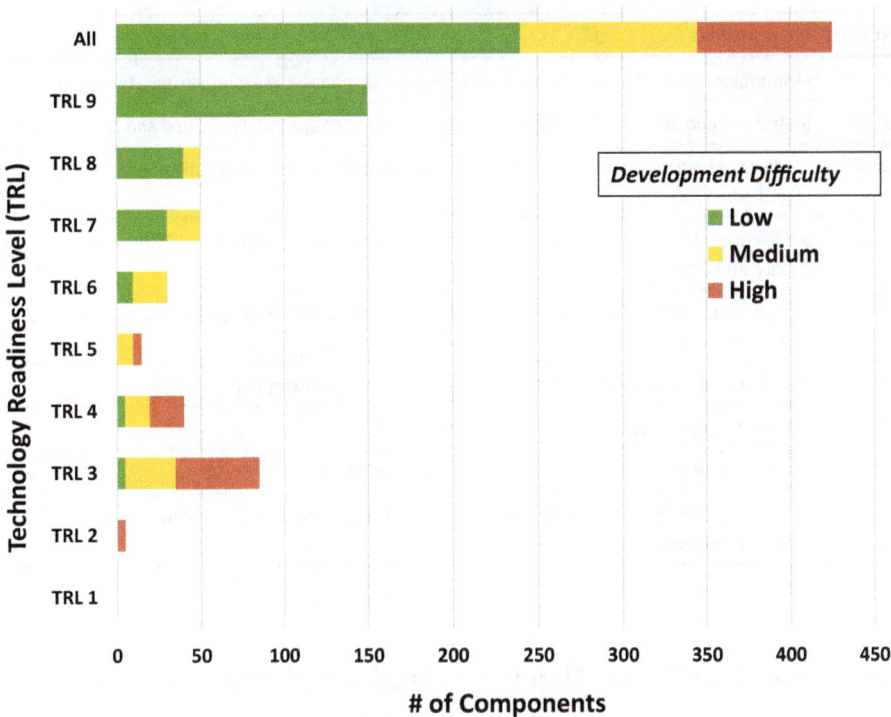

Figure 1.4: Example of System Readiness Levels (SRL).

When integrating a new technology into a larger system, we need to understand not only the TRL phases of individual technologies, but also how advanced the integration is between the technologies.

Interface/Integration Readiness Levels (IRLs). Some organizations have also developed models to capture "Interface Readiness Levels" or IRLs. Similar models are called "Integration Readiness Levels". IRLs are now being used by many large system developers, particularly in the defense, space, auto, and aircraft industries where systems might take years to develop. Formalizing system integration should also be a focus for all complex system developers, large or small, where components need to interface with each other in order to achieve a workable technology for the market. Table 1.2 illustrates a typical IRL, designed along the same lines of TRLs:[8]

Table 1.2: Example of Interface/Integration Readiness Level (IRL).

IRL level	IRL principles
IRL 1	All interface requirements (systems, subsystems, components, and expertise) have been identified.
IRL 2	Interaction and interfaces between components have been specifically defined and characterized.
IRL 3	Specific compatibilities and incompatibilities between components and subsystems have been identified.
IRL 4	Sufficient detail in defining incompatibilities have been developed in terms of requirements, quality, and assurance.
IRL 5	Design plans from sub-system developers are delivered to obtain compatibility and proper interfaces.
IRL 6	Proposed compatibility plans and designs are accepted and executed.
IRL 7	Interfaces and integration are verified and validated.
IRL 8	The total system is "mission-qualified" and ready for market.
IRL 9	All items, interfaces, sub-systems and the complete system are proven to achieve market-commercialization without risk.

Technology Readiness: Biopharmaceutics and Drug Development

While the TRL, and other readiness level models discussed so far in this chapter cover the majority of cases we might see, the technologies of biopharmaceuticals, drug development and biotechnology-related products tend to go through levels of development that do not exactly fit into the typical TRL models. This is partly due to the different nature of biological and pharmaceutical development and research, and partly due to the impact of government regulations. For these technologies, the actual creation, and ultimately commercialization, of a therapeutic molecule tends to involve different distinct stages, each with its own descriptive name[9] (see Figure 1.5).

In these markets, much of the time involved with moving a potential technology toward the marketplace involves the different levels of testing for efficacy and safety, with increasingly complicated and expensive phases. Many of these phases are defined by government regulators, and vary by industry sector (human drugs, animal drugs, genetically modified foods or agricultural products, etc.). These phases might also vary by country, where different countries will establish the stages, approval processes, and speed for bringing a product to market. A typical pharmaceutical model of drug evolution is shown below, with an approximation of the time it takes in each phase.

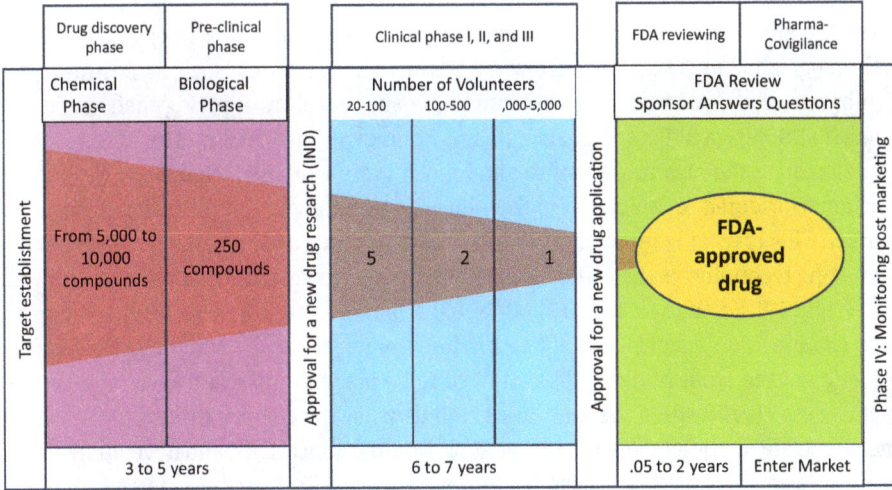

Figure 1.5: Biopharma innovation: Readiness and regulatory stages.

In cases when a technology falls within the phases of drug development and mandatory approval, the industry will generally use this model to define the level of "technology readiness", rather than the traditional TRLs used in other industries. Thus, a drug development company will generally refer to their vaccine or therapeutic technology as being in the early "preclinical" stage, "pre-clinical animal testing" phase, or "phase 1 of human testing", for example, rather than use a TRL format.

Concluding Insights

One of the core principles of technology commercialization is recognizing that all technologies follow an evolutionary development process. This process begins with idea generation and progresses through stages of improvement until the final product or system is ready to launch into the market. Understanding the stage of technology development becomes critical when communicating to potential customers, granting agencies, investors, and system designers. Each stage of a technology's development is also associated with a different set of strategic and management decisions. This is the purpose of this chapter, to assist readers in understanding not only the levels of technology maturity, but the different readiness models that are available to assist in understanding this process.

Commercialization of technologies does not always mean bringing a product to the final, end-user market. Generally, there are different players, designers, companies, funding mechanisms, customers, and partners at each level of the technology development process. In this context, technology commercialization really means moving a technology toward the final consumer, from one stage to another stage. It is a process of moving forward, of advancing to the next level of technology development. Thus, a small technology development company, which might have a strategy of licensing technologies in the TRL3 stage from top research universities, such as Purdue, MIT, Cambridge, or Barcelona, might be immensely successful by applying their entrepreneurial and design skills to advance this technology to the TRL6 or TRL7 levels. They can then, pass the now more mature, and much more valuable, technology to another consumer-oriented organization to fine-tune the technology, and ultimately bring it to market. This is what commercialization actually means – applying the necessary skills in moving technologies through its stages of maturity, toward the end user.

While TRLs, and the associated MRLs, SRLs, and IRLs are all very useful and important classification models to help technology managers and technology developers understand the types of decisions that need to be made at different stages of development, these classification systems do not tell us what the correct strategies are. These include strategic choices, managerial actions, funding allocations, and development priorities. However, the TRL framework, along with MRLs, SRLs, and IRLs, do underline the key stages where these decisions become most important and need to be considered.

Chapter Example: Technology Evolution through Different Stages – Crime Scene Sample Collection

Problem

Blood splatter and other liquid evidence collected at crime scenes, need to be carefully managed. When a crime scene investigation (CSI) team goes on site, the samples need to be collected according to certain, and very detailed protocols. The evidence and specific location of the sample needs to be photographed and documented, with appropriate labels put on every sample collected at the crime scene. There are protocols as to how much of the fluid or secretion is swabbed and how many samples are required for each spot of evidence. There are other protocols for collecting dry secretions.

Any confusion can result in evidence being challenged and possibly excluded from trial. Cross contamination needs to be minimized. Upon delivery to the crime lab for DNA analysis, the sample, along with its documentation and labeling, must all be carefully tracked to establish a chain of custody. For these reasons, collecting blood and other secretion samples at a crime scene most often involves two individuals, one person collecting and bagging the sample according to evidence protocols, while the other person photographs, labels, and documents each sample. The multiple samples are then taken to the crime lab, where all the information is hand entered into the computer.

Technological Solution

HazMat engineers at the Los Alamos National Laboratory in New Mexico developed a technology that combined a sampling device (spring-loaded to minimize cross contamination), with a camera, laser location finder, GPS, label maker, and small, and portable phone-sized computer, all interconnected into one system. This required only one person, rather than the normal two-person team to collect and document crime scene samples. The computerized handheld device can also then upload all the necessary documents and information directly into the crime-lab computer rather than entering data by hand, thus saving time and reducing possible entry errors.

Early focus groups showed strong interest in the technology. This technology is a good example of progressing through the different phases of development, from the original idea to solve a problem, to patents (US Patent 6,947,866 B2), to 3D printing of a dummy prototype, to constructing a working lab prototype. After the development of the working lab prototype, the technology was licensed by Los Alamos National Laboratory to a private sector company for final design development and beta-testing with crime labs. Figure 1.6 shows the prototyping progression from dummy prototype to lab prototype to beta prototype.

| 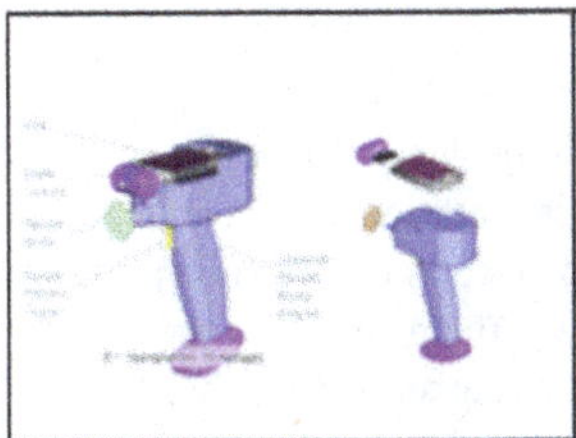 Dummy Prototype: 3-D printed to use in focus groups with U.S. Crime labs to determine size of market, functionality requirements, and possible pricing. | 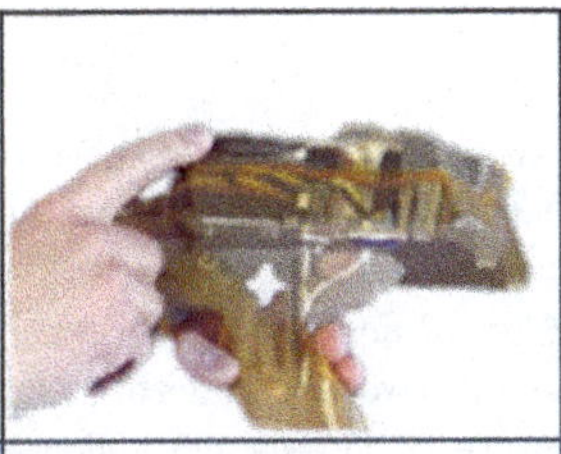 Lab Prototype: Almost complete functionality. Used to demonstrate to Press, potential licensees, and used in TV shows such as CSI and Court TV. |  Field Prototype: Licensed and developed by *Digital Forensic, Inc.* Used for Beta-Testing with various crime labs. |

Figure 1.6: Prototyping progression of a forensic field tool.

Chapter 2
The Driving Forces of Technology Markets: The Three Technology "Curves"

This Chapter

– Introduces the concepts of market S-curves, technology S-curves, and experience curves.
– Highlights the strategic implications of these models for understanding and navigating technology markets.

Key Management Tools and Best Practices

– Market S-curves
– Stages of technology adoption
– Market penetration curves
– Technology substitution
– Technology S-curves
– Experience curves

INSIGHT

Technologies need to be commercialized into the market. While each technology is unique in its own way, all technology markets do share many common characteristics. These characteristics are often illustrated by three different types of mathematical curves or models. These models are commonly called the "market S-curve", the "technology S-curve", and the "experience curve". These three different curves show important relationships about market growth, the nature of customers for technology-based products, the limits of technological performance, technology substitution, and the forces behind decreasing costs over time.

Introduction

Technologies ultimately need to be introduced into the market. That is the whole purpose of a technology commercialization effort. In some cases, technology commercialization means introducing the product into the retail, or end-user market. In many other cases, however, the target market for technologies designed by early-stage developers are the system-level integrators that take a variety of different input technologies and bundle them into more fully developed products.

https://doi.org/10.1515/9783111684420-003

Setting the Stage: The Evolution of Data Storage Technology

Consider the fast-moving market for data storage. One approach to both internal and removable data storage is, of course, the classic hard disk drive (HDD). HDDs have been around for decades. And while the "cloud" has taken over some of the storage requirements in the modern world, HDD technologies remain an integral part of almost every consumer electronics sold, including computers, medical instruments, mobile phones, and game consoles. Even "cloud" providers use large scale HDDs for their archival storage. Current projections are that the HDD global industry will be over $100 billion (USD) by 2032.[1]

Like most technologies, HDDs are actually bundles of other technologies and components that have been integrated into a final workable and efficient product. As a system of embedded technologies, there are always advancements taking place. For some HDDs, one of these embedded technologies might be the "microwave-assisted magnetic recording" or MAMR technology. MAMRs are a way of using microwaves to efficiently write data onto high-capacity disks.

Suppose you are a small, early-stage start-up company developing a new approach that might significantly enhance MAMR technology. What is your market? It is certainly not the final, end-user retail market. There is no retail market for just the MAMR technology. Instead, the market for the MAMR technology will most likely be the large, HDD manufacturers such as Western Digital, Seagate, and Toshiba. These HDD vendors are essentially systems developers using a variety of components and technologies, some licensed from other sources, some purchased through a subcontract process, and many developed internally by the R&D departments within these manufacturers.

As is typical in most markets, there are different market stages in the overall production chain, as products are developed from the raw material side to the final end user. It is no different in the HDD market, or any technology-driven industry. After bundling and manufacturing their HDD product using different technologies, interfaces, and components, the large HDD companies will then sell their products to both computer manufacturers, such as Dell, Apple, Acer, and HP or directly into the consumer retail market, where the end user can buy a new HDD off the shelf or through an online source.

But the HDD market is highly competitive at each stage in this process. Just within the MAMR market there are possibly a number of developers, each offering slightly different approaches to the MAMR technology. In fact, engineers and scientists have been playing with MAMR technologies for decades. Then of course, there are different competing technical approaches of writing data onto disks. Some of these approaches are newer and some more established. These competitive approaches might include heat-assisted magnetic recording (HAMR), perpendicular magnetic recording (PMR), and shingled magnetic recording (SMR) to name a few, all with the potential to increase the storage capacity and speed of hard-drives.

HDD technologies also need to compete with other data storage technologies, such as the solid-state drives (SSDs) we use when plugging in a flash drive. SSDs, however, have their own multiple sets of advanced internal technological approaches, such as multi-level cell (MLC), triple-level cell (TLC), and quad-level cell (QLC) technologies. In addition, there will likely be future developments in non-volatile random-access memory (NRAM). Finally, data storage devices such as HDDs and SSDs now need to compete with various cloud services. There will certainly be even more technologies in the future.

Within the removable computerized data storage market, there are fundamentally different approaches, such as hard disk drives (HDD) versus solid-state drives (SSD), each built from a mix of legacy components, recently developed technologies, and emerging innovations. In addition, the different manufacturers of HDD and SSD technologies need to sell into both the computer assembly market and the retail market, competing with other manufacturers and technologies in the same space.

Compounding this challenge, reverse engineering and intellectual property theft are rampant in this market. Clone products from China and other regions with reputations for IP theft often flood the market at significantly lower price points. As a result, sustaining success in this space becomes a constantly shifting issue.

During an interview with one of the authors, the senior management of a large HDD company revealed they have a specific product commercialization strategy of introducing new, improved HDD designs to the marketplace no longer than every six months just to stay competitive.

The rapid speed of technological development and commercialization requires sophisticated management. As with most technology-based products, the HDD and SSD are bundles of technologies where each component and its interfaces are going through evolutionary changes such as described in Chapter 1. Some of the new component technologies are already in use by HDD and SSD manufacturers. Others are nearing implementation, while some may still be years away from commercial viability, if they ever reach it at all. That is simply the nature of technology markets.

Certainly, every technology is unique, with its own set of success parameters, technical requirements, market forces, and design hurdles. However, there are some basic concepts that allow us to understand how technology markets work in general. Understanding these basic industry structure characteristics allows technology directors, product development managers, and commercialization officers to develop coherent strategies within the seemingly chaotic and the always-changing nature of technology markets. Some technologies move very quickly through the different phases of the market, while other technologies will survive much longer. Regardless of the speed of market transition, these structural characteristics seem fairly consistent across all technologies.

There are three major forces that influence the nature of industry structure in technology-oriented markets. Each of these forces can be illustrated graphically, although there are certainly underlying forces that can be much more complicated to understand. Government regulations and influence might be another force, but we concentrate on market driven forces in this chapter.

Technology Adoption: The "Market S-Curve"

It has long been recognized, in both the study of the natural world and the study of societies, that many growth-related phenomena tend to follow an "S-shape pattern". Sociologists, geographers, and anthropologists, going back to the nineteenth century, started formally investigating how ideas and innovations are adopted by societies.

By the 1920s and 1930s, university researchers observed a trend among independent farmers in the U.S. These farmers were adopting new hybrid seeds, innovative farming equipment, and modern crop management techniques. Notably, this adoption occurred without direct influence from outside forces, such as the government. The pattern of adoption appeared to follow a fairly predictable course. Researchers found that almost always, the adoption of innovations typically starts slowly, then quickly accelerates as the word gets out, and then slows down as market saturation is approached. This research laid the foundation for the S-curve model of technology adoption or diffusion.[2]

Technology Adoption and Market S-Curves

In 1962, Dr. Evertt Rogers, a professor at Ohio State University, published a book titled *Diffusion of Innovations*.[3] In this highly cited work, Rodgers summarized hundreds of previously published studies of technologies across a wide range of sectors. He found that the S-shaped curve of market diffusion was an almost universal characteristic describing how new technologies and ideas enter and then expand both in the marketplace and in societies.

While modern academic research has fine-tuned our understanding of how and why innovations are adopted, it has also consistently confirmed the importance of the S-shaped model of diffusion and adoption.[4] For our purposes, we call this the "market S-curve".

The "Market S-curve" refers to the rate that a new technology is adopted by users.

The market S-curve refers to the rate that a new technology is adopted by users. It is most often used to describe the rate of technology adoption by the end-user market, such as consumers, but it also applies to the adoption of new technologies by system developers.

When discussing the diffusion and adoption of innovations, one of the most important contributions deals with the psychology of individual customers. Some customers adopt or purchase a new innovation or technology early in the life cycle. Others, consciously wait until later in the life cycle to make a purchase. In its simplest, but still highly effective form, Dr. Rodgers classified these groups of individuals (or organizations) as "innovators, early adopters, early majority, late majority, and laggards". This model, of course, was quickly adopted by the marketing field, and is now commonly called the "product life cycle", a topic covered in any basic marketing college course.

The "market S-Curve" is often presented in two different ways, as shown below in Figure 2.1. The yellow line, which has an "S" shape represents the cumulative sales, or total market share, of the product, slowing down as the market reaches maturity. The blue line, which has a "bell-shape", represents the new sales or new market share captured over time. The two lines present the same information, but with a different axis.

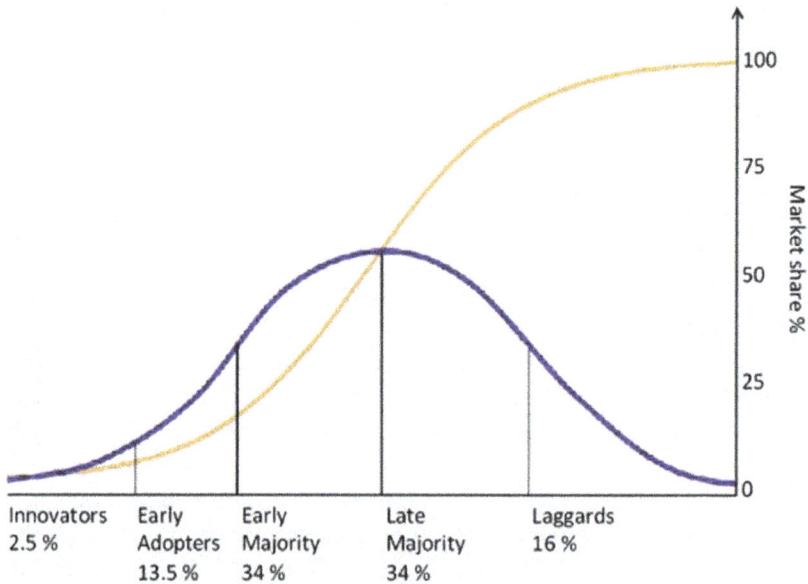

Figure 2.1: Market S-curve and technology adoption: From innovators to laggards.

The Psychology of Technology Markets

The psychology and culture of different groups of technology adopters has been studied extensively, from a number of different perspectives and theories.[5] Each adopter group has its own motivations, price sensibility, risk profile, and sense of gratification. The following presents typical profiles for the different groups.

Innovators. Innovators are often called "Tech Enthusiasts". These customers are the most risk-oriented. They obtain gratification from being the first to try a new product. They are typically not price sensitive. Tech Enthusiasts can also become "influencers" for later groups of users, although that is not the reason for purchasing the technology. Tech Enthusiasts are risk-takers and accept that they are purchasing a technology that might fail. They obtain delight in being the first to try a new innovation.

Early Adopters. This group is sometimes called "Visionaries". Like the "Tech Enthusiasts", customers in this group are risk-takers. They generally are not overly price-sensitive. Unlike the "Tech Enthusiasts", however, early adopters tend to wait until they are convinced the technology will likely become the dominant technology. They are active in judging the technology and influencing others. They enjoy becoming a central part of the networking community and will often post their opinions about a technology on the web.

Early Majority. In the tech community, these are called the "Pragmatists". Less risk-taking than earlier groups, and certainly more price-sensitive. Pragmatists will often read and study other people's opinions. They will wait until a particular technology appears to be an industry standard, but then they quickly enter the market. They possess a strong sense of practicality. Pragmatists entering the market stimulate the bulk of product sales.

Late Majority. These are the "Conservatives". The Late Majority are not risk-takers. They definitely wait until a technology becomes a standard, is used extensively, and is readily available. This group will be aggressive price-shoppers.

Laggards. These are the "skeptics" of the group. Many people in this group will enter the market only because they need to join. There is nothing else available. Their old TV, car, or computer breaks, and they need to buy another.

The Technology Acceptance Model (TAM)

There are a number of psychological dimensions that influence when somebody adopts a technology. These are generally examined using Rodger's original "diffusion of innovation" model or the more recent "Technology Acceptance Model".

The Technology Acceptance Model, or TAM, introduced by Fred Davis in 1989 has become one of the most influential models when examining the personal adoption of technologies. TAM specifically incorporates psychological behaviors by looking at two dimensions – perceived usefulness and perceived ease of use. The original TAM approach is shown in Figure 2.2:

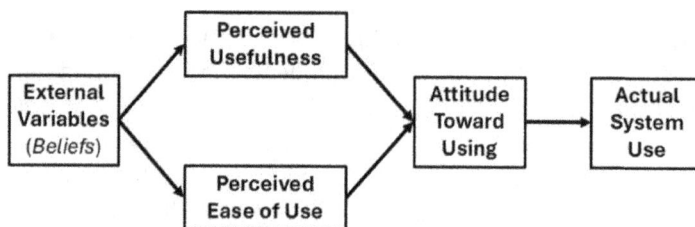

Figure 2.2: Technology Acceptance Model (TAM): Framework for user adoption.

There have been a number of extensions of the original models over the years, including TAM2, TAM3, and the more recent "Unified Theory of Acceptance and Use of Technology (UTAUT). While they are interesting, in general, these extensions involve simply adding additional variables or directional arrows to the original model. The key underlying basis of all of technology adoption models, however, is found in a combination of the customers' psychological dimensions with other variables, such as knowledge, resources, and culture.

The most common psychological dimensions found to be important in explaining technology adoption behaviors include risk aversion, attitudes toward innovation, personal trust, and self-efficacy.

The most common psychological dimensions found to be important in explaining technology adoption behaviors include risk aversion, attitudes toward innovation, and personal trust. More recently, there has been an emphasis on the psychological dimension of "self-efficacy". Self-efficacy, or the confidence that an individual has in their decisions, also impacts technology adoption. Individuals with high self-efficacy tend to adopt technologies earlier. This same sense of confidence is also a defining psychological trait of entrepreneurs – "I'm simply confident I will not fail."

Cultural Differences in Technology Adoption

A number of studies have also investigated cultural and international differences related to technology adoption. Many of these studies have found that different cultures, indeed, have different risk-taking behaviors, which impacts their rate of technology adoption. A common approach to this type of research uses the different cultural dimensions developed by the Dutch social psychologist, Geert Hofstede. [6]

Hofstede worked with the IBM corporation from 1967 to 1973 to develop a better understanding of managerial behaviors in different countries, and why some expatriate managers fail when they are transferred to a factory in a different culture. Using a large sample of workers, Hofstede found four key dimensions that characterize different international cultures: individualism v. collectivism, masculinity v. femininity, uncertainty avoidance v. risk taking, and power distance (how people adapt to differ-ent levels of power within their society and institutions). Later Hofstede added two other dimensions of culture, long-term v. short-term orientation and indulgence v. restraint. Hofstede's work remains the most recognized model of characterizing cul-tures. Using the Hofstede model, for example, some studies of technology adoption classified cultures or countries as being a Type 1 culture or a Type 2 culture.[7] Type 1 cultures, such as the United States, tend to have a more short-term orientation, higher risk-taking behaviors, and a greater sense of individualism than Type 2 cultures, such as South Korea.

Type 1 cultures are more likely to exhibit early adoption behaviors, whereas Type 2 cultures tend to adopt technologies later or follow more imitative patterns. Many other studies have supported the idea that different cultures adopt technology differently, and that cultural dimensions such as individualism, risk-taking, and time-orientation tend to be important predictors.[8]

However, there needs to be caution in interpreting the impact of culture on tech-nology adoption. First, some studies have not found a strong relationship between all the dimensions of culture and technology adoption. Second, many countries, such as the United States, have multiple sub-cultures within the country, all with different char-acteristics. Third, culture is considered one of the most difficult things to measure, and there is concern that the dimensions commonly used in technology adoption studies do not accurately reflect the full nature of country culture.

Sequential Adoption Behavior in Intermediate Markets and by Market Segments

While often applied to the retail market, the life cycle model is also highly relevant to how organizations adopt innovations. For example, when the target is the interme-diate market, such as systems developers and manufacturers, some companies are indeed early adopters of new innovations, while others tend to be laggards. This is true whether the organization is adopting an end-user technology for their use, such as a new computer system, or whether the organization is adopting components for the products they are manufacturing.

How soon a company adopts new innovations is often a function of a number of things. Is the internal corporate culture innovative or traditional? Companies are like any consumer. Some are early adopters while others are laggards. Are the R&D and engineering employees risk takers or risk adverse? Are the company's products or systems targeted to the early adopters in their particular market, or more toward the established product design market? Is the new technology or component more expen-sive than the old technology, and thus less likely to be adopted by companies selling their system into a price-sensitive end market than a higher end competitor? For these reasons, the market S-curve appears to apply equally well in describing both end-user and intermediate market adoption.

Example of Sequential Technology Adoption in System Components

A classic example is the late adoption of electronic watches by the traditional mechanical watch industry. But even within the market for the individual components that go into the modern electronic watch, there is often the same type of sequential adoption behavior. For example, over the years there have been several different technologies that regulate timing in electronic watches. Originally the timing device was a metal tuning fork, which vibrated at a low frequency, about 360 cycles per second. Integrated circuits then took this oscillation into 1-second impulses, thus capturing the movement of time. This metal oscillator was quickly replaced by various quartz crystal designs, each with different oscillation speeds. Finally, a fourth generation XY flexure was developed. The XY flexure was a small strip of quartz crystal that was vacuum sealed, with two wires. When electronically stimulated (by the watch battery), the XY flexure technology vibrated at a remarkably accurate 32,768 cycles per second, which was then stepped down to 1-second impulses by the watch's integrated circuits. This XY flexure design became the standard for electronic watches for years. At its peak use, the XY flexure was sold to electronic watch manufacturers for about $1.50 each.

Like all technologies, there is always the potential for better technologies on the horizon. In this case, the new oscillator design for watches was the tuning-fork (TF) crystal (see Figure 2.3). Rather than a strip of crystal, like the XY flexure, the tuning-fork crystal looked like a tuning fork, but still made with quartz crystal. It had several advantages; it was adjustable and had better temperature and shock characteristics. Whenever a new technology is introduced, such as the most modern adjustable tuning-fork quartz crystal oscillator, it is often significantly higher priced than the existing technology. With the watch tuning-fork crystal, it was introduced to the market at about triple the cost of the XY flexure at the time.

At the beginning, only the higher-end, more expensive watch manufacturers adopted the new tuning-fork crystal technology. Most lower-priced watchmakers, who were under much more severe price competition in the retail market, continued using the older, traditional, and far less expensive XY technology. Slowly, the newer technology captured different market segments as the component price of the tuning-fork technology decreased, until finally the whole watch industry completely adopted the new tuning-fork technology.

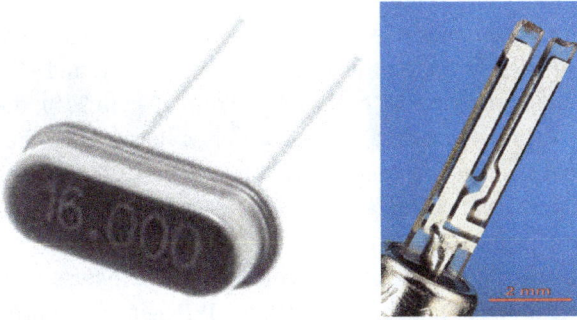

Figure 2.3: XY Flexure and Tuning Fork Crystal Oscillator: Advancing timekeeping accuracy.

Example of Sequential Technology Adoption by Market Segments

The sequence of market adoption is not always just price-driven as in a commodity type product such as watch crystals. Many markets are not uniform but rather made up of different market segments. Technologies tend to enter different market sectors at different times, even with the same or similar technologies. Take for example, the history of global positioning technologies. All GPS systems rely on satellites. The earliest GPS systems were based on a "Doppler" effect of radio signals being sent from satellites coming over the horizon. These early GPS systems were called "transit" systems and introduced in the 1960s for the U.S. Navy. Transit systems, while not very accurate by modern standards, were still a major development since prior ocean navigation was either by the ancient traditional method of celestial navigation, or if close to shore, by radio direction finders (RDF) or LORAN stations. Depending on the satellite locations and availability, these early transit systems provided at best, an accuracy of about 200 meters. But it was still much better, and more reliable than prior methods of navigation. By the 1970s, transit systems were available for the commercial market and used primarily by commercial freighters, cruise liners, and deep-sea cruising yachts.

With the development of solid-state circuitry, by the late 1970s, the first Navstar/GPS satellites were being launched, which provided a much more accurate location based on the triangulation of signals from several satellites. Accuracy was within a few feet of location. The new GPS technology was both expensive and used almost exclusively by the U.S. Military. In 1983, President Ronald Regan authorized the use of Navstar/GPS for the civilian commercial market. The first commercially available, handheld GPS system was introduced in 1989 by the Magellan Corporation (Figure 2.4). The cost was $3,000 or about half the price of a 1989 Honda Civic car. It was also awkward to use, about the size of a brick. In addition, the U.S. military demanded that the signal be degraded for commercial versions due to fear of its use by military adversaries. The Magellan system was used almost exclusively by larger ships at this time.

During the 1990s, GPS technology continued to improve. New satellites were launched. In 2000, the U.S. government ended the "selective" availability, and GPS immediately became 10 times more accurate for civilian use. From 1990 to 2010, the price of GPS chips also dropped from approximately $2,000 to less than $2 (another predictable force that we discuss later in this chapter). All of a sudden, GPS systems were affordable, conveniently sized, and accurate enough to be used in civilian cars and trucks, private airplanes, and farming equipment.

During this time, Garmin, Ltd, became the dominant provider of GPS products, with multiple new models (originally the *StreetPilot*, followed by the *NAVI*) being introduced every year (Figure 2.5).

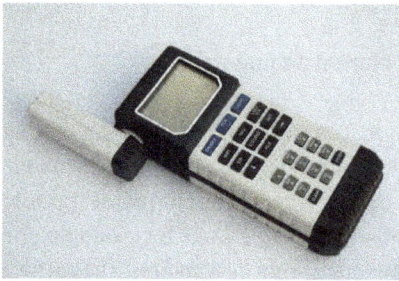

Figure 2.4: 1989 Magellan NAV 1000.

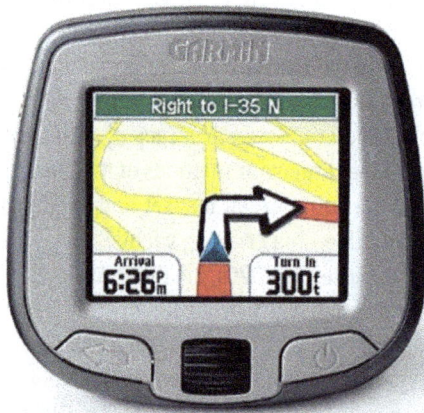

Figure 2.5: Garmin Street Pilot.

But the dominance of satellite GPS systems in the consumer market lasted only so long. Now cell-based phone and car navigation apps, such as Google Maps, have almost completely replaced the need for satellite-based GPS products for the average person.

But not completely – while the general market for satellite-based GPS has declined dramatically in the modern world, there are still some critical market segments (outside cell-tower range or when there is risk of cell signal disruption, such as during armed conflicts) where GPS system demand is rapidly expanding. Satellite systems are increasingly relied upon for a range of applications, including defense, disaster relief, and tracking of ocean shipping containers. The global market for satellite-based GPS systems is projected to exceed $150 billion by 2030.[9]

Lessons in Technology Adoption

This history of GPS, watch crystals, and numerous other technologies indicates several important facts about the nature of technology markets:
1. Technology adoption tends to follow an S-shaped curve process.
2. Technologies often penetrate different market segments somewhat sequentially.
3. Technologies are always improving over time, from crude designs to more sophisticated designs.
4. The cost/price of a technology always decreases over time.
5. There is always a substitutable technology that will ultimately replace, or significantly impact, the old technology.
6. After a new technology replaces an older technology, there still might be niche markets where the old technology can be successful.
7. Government rules can impact technology adoption.

The Big Picture of Technology Adoption and Market S-Curves

A market S-curve only illustrates a single technology, and its rate of adoption. We can also take a longer-term view of technology adoption. We look at the "big picture" from two perspectives. First, from the perspective of an overall market penetration curve, and second from the idea of technology substitution.

The Market Penetration Curve. We have already seen that technologies often penetrate different submarkets in an approximate sequential process. Not all markets for technology products have distinct sub-markets, but some do have clear sub-markets. In markets where there are distinct submarkets a new technology might enter a particular submarket and be successfully adopted before another submarket opens up. What is interesting is that each of the individual sub-markets is often characterized by an "S-shaped" curve as well as the overall market penetration of the larger market that includes all the sub-markets.

The sequences of different market adoption can be illustrated by an overall "market penetration" curve (Figure 2.6). In these cases, the "market penetration" curve acts as an envelope for the individual sub-markets that sequentially adopt a technology with each of these individual sub-markets also showing an S-shaped characteristic of adoption.

Market S-Curve Development

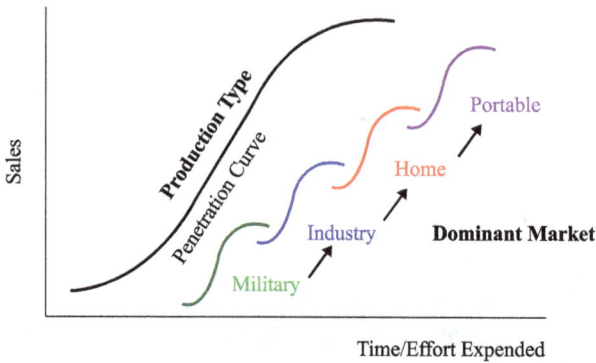

Figure 2.6: Market Penetration Curve: Sequential S-curves across submarkets.

Technology Substitution Curves. All technologies will be replaced by newer technologies. This is almost a law of nature for the modern world. But inevitably this replacement process will be gradual in nature. There will be a period when the old technology is still dominant, but the newer technology is starting to make inroads. In fact, this is one of the basic assumptions of the life cycle concept. Early adopters start using a new technology while later adopters are still using the older technology. The rate of substitution is different, of course, depending on the technology. Some substitution rates are fast, while in other cases it takes years or even decades before the new technology makes serious inroads.

All technologies will be replaced by newer technologies. This is almost
a law of nature for the modern world.

Technology substitution curves attempt to model this process of how newer technologies substitute for older technologies, and how fast this substitution is taking place. Almost all technology substitution models assume an "S-shaped curve" process for both the old and the new technologies.

One of the most commonly used models to predict the rate of technology substitution is called the Fisher-Pry model. The Fisher-Pry model was developed in 1971 as a simple model that can be used to predict the future rate of substitution.[10] The Fisher-Pry model has been widely used over the decades to forecast the rate at which new technologies replace older ones. Remarkably, it can generate fairly accurate predictions based on early market penetration, often using data from when the new technology has captured less than 5% of the market. The Fisher-Pry model is illustrated in more detail in our appendix on technology forecasting.

Technology Performance: The "Technology S-Curve"

While the market S-curve, and the associated notion of the product life cycle, are important to understand for all types of products, technology oriented or not, another S-curve is critical to understanding technology markets. This is called the "Technology S-curve" (Figure 2.7).

While the illustrative curve takes the same "S-looking" shape, the critical difference is that while the "market S-curve" is a relationship between sales, the number of users, or market share against time, the technology S-curve is the relationship between a measure of technological performance and time.

Thus, the technology S-curve focuses exclusively on the performance of the technology, not on the sales or adoption of technologies. An example of a technology S-curve is shown below.

Technology S-Curve Development

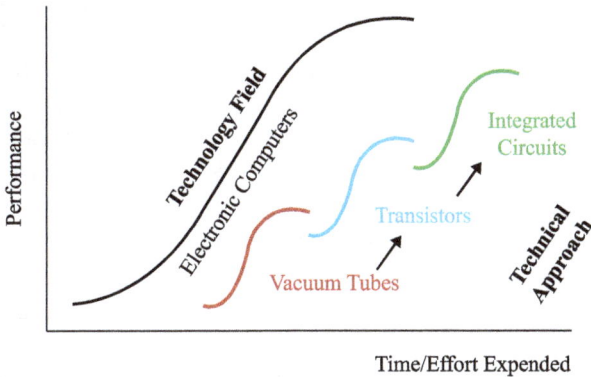

Figure 2.7: Technology S-curve: Mapping performance progression.

There are several critically important lessons illustrated by the above figure.

Key Lessons from Technology S-Curves

Technology Performance Follows an S-Curve Shape. Technology performance for a particular technological approach almost always follows an "S-shaped" pattern. At the beginning, the performance of a new technology is relatively low. Then as more development takes place, the technology's performance rapidly improves over time. Then at some point, the rate of performance improvement for a particular approach starts to slow down and ultimately stops. This creates the S-shape of the technology S-curve.

Technology Improvements Are Ultimately Limited by the Laws of Science. While the limit to the "market S-curve is essentially determined by the size of the market, or market saturation, the performance limits in the technology S-curve are determined by the laws of physics, nature, science, or engineering that are relevant to that particular technological approach.

The performance limits in the "Technology S-curve" are determined
by the laws of physics, nature, science, or engineering.

Performance can only go so far with a particular technology, no matter how hard people try. For example, in Figure 2.7, early vacuum tubes, while creating the technological foundation for early radios, computers, and TVs, had limits no matter how advanced the design became. The basic science behind vacuum tubes is to heat up a piece of metal called the cathode. This thermal energy would then knock some electrons loose, which would then flow across a gap to the anode. The level of electron flow could be controlled by a control grid. Finally, all this action had to take place within a vacuum in order for the electrons to flow easily.

The limitations of vacuum tubes are well-documented. They are not solid-state switching and amplification devices, like transistors. Normally vacuum-sealed in glass, they also break easily. The transistor technology has some advantages that no advancement in vacuum tubes can ever overcome, no matter how much time and money is invested. Transistors were a fraction of the size of vacuum tubes, more efficient, and took less energy, and since transistors were solid-state, they were much more durable. This allowed the overall speed and durability of computers, TVs, and radios to increase dramatically. Once the transistor solid state technology was introduced, vacuum tubes were destined to be replaced.

However, transistors were also replaced over time due to their design limitations. Transistors tend to be "single-switches" and can handle only a certain amount of power until they overheat. These are the theoretical limits to transistor designs. The replacement for the transistor technology was the integrated circuit, which started to be commercially viable by the mid-1960s when Fairchild Semiconductor started marketing their version of the integrated circuit. The integrated circuit essentially places multiple solid-state switching circuits onto a single component. The race was on. How many switching circuits can one cram into a small component? Multiple technological approaches, such as SSI, MSI, LSI, VLSI, and ULSI, started to develop over time, a technological rivalry that continues to the present. At the beginning, an integrated circuit had fewer than 100 switches. Now, there are billions of switches on a single chip. The introduction of the integrated circuit changed everything. New markets exploded for technologies such as personal computers, digital watches, calculators, medical instruments, mobile phones, and everything that is computerized in the modern world.

Another example of this "law of limits" is the history of self-propelled aircraft. The Wright Flyer, which first flew at Kitty Hawk, North Carolina in 1903, had a speed of less than 10 miles per hour. By World War 1, the French-designed SPAD fighter biplane could go about 120 miles per hour. The U.S. Mustang P-51 in World War 2 could reach a speed of around 400 miles per hour. Pretty dramatic improvements over time, but a regular propeller driven aircraft can only go so fast, about 500 mph, due to the laws of physics. They simply cannot break the sound barrier, with maximum straight-line speeds in the Mach 0.7 range, and this is for specialized racing aircraft. To go faster simply required a new technology, jet engines.

Technologies Have Sub-technologies with Their Own S-Curves. Just as the market S-curve indicates that technologies can penetrate different dominant markets sequentially as the functionalities and cost of the technologies change, the technology S-curve also shows that there are sub-technologies or technical approaches that anchor the performance improvements of the overarching technology field.

New Technologies Often Have Lower Initial Performance. Almost always, new technologies are introduced into the marketplace at a lower level of performance and higher costs than the older, more developed technologies. Over time, the new technology will ultimately surpass the performance of the old technology. This might happen very quickly, but in other cases it might take some time. It really depends on the technology and the market characteristics.

Old Technologies May Still Have Niche Markets. While rare, niche markets sometimes develop for older technologies. For example, although almost completely replaced by integrated circuits for modern electronic products, there are still small niche markets for vacuum tubes. Many music audiophiles and recording studios still prefer vacuum tube amplifiers due to the "warmness" or "pitch color" of the sound. There are still a few vacuum tube manufacturers supplying this market, and R&D continues. There are still fountain pens, steam engines, vinyl records, and mechanical watches even though these are old technologies. Oftentimes these niche markets are higher-end markets, such as the Rolex or Patek Philippe mechanical watches, or they might be for specialized markets where the older technology may have some advantages. Even the old Polaroid camera design popularized in the 1950s has been resurrected for the children's market, since it involves both entertaining steps and fast end products, such as stickers, that children appear to enjoy versus digital photography.

While these niche markets tend to be in retail markets, multiple components are still needed for the products that service these niche retail markets. Gears and springs are still needed for high-end mechanical watches, vinyl record pressing equipment is still being built and improved, and specialized film chemicals are needed for Polaroids. Also, of course, there is the whole collector market for older technologies, such as antique autos and slot machines. Components are always needed for the collector markets.

Technology Productivity: The "Experience Curve"

One well-established characteristic of technology-based products is that as performance improves over time, prices tend to decline. This trend holds true across a wide range of technologies. Think of TVs, computers, cell phones, printers, and electronic watches – better and better technologies, for less and less money. There are two basic reasons for this phenomenon. One is driven by increased competition as more "clone" competitors jump into the market, and the other is the law of experience curves. This is the third curve concept we discuss in this chapter.

What Are Experience Curves?

At the most fundamental level, the notion of an experience curve is simple: the more we do something, the better we get at it. This is true whether we are shooting free throws in basketball, playing the piano, or designing and producing technologically based products. Experience curves, sometimes referred to as learning curves or progress indices, simply show the relationship between a measure of productivity and the accumulated experience of making that effort.

The notion of an experience curve is simple: the more
we do something, the better we get at it.

Experience curves have been studied in thousands of technologies, and while there are many elegant formulas offered, the basic experience curve formula is often very accurate. The basic formula is $Y=ax^b$ where Y = measure of productivity and x=cumulative production experience. The parameters "a" and "b" are estimated from the data. In this formula, b is negative when the measure of productivity decreases with more experience, such as unit cost and b is positive when the productivity measure increases with experience such as yield rates or quality.

The equation of the experience curve also means that every time cumulative experience doubles, productivity improves by a constant amount, or cost decreases by a constant amount. This formula is found to apply in most situations, whether in athletic skills, practicing musical instruments, or manufacturing integrated circuits.

Steepness of Experience Curves

Some experience curves are steep. This means that as we accumulate experience, there is a lot of improvement in our productivity, as reflected by measures such as unit cost or yield rates. Other products and technologies tend to show more shallow experience curves.

Many technologies appear to operate in the 70% to 80% experience curve range.

This measure of steepness is often translated to statements such as a 90% or 70% experience curve. This refers to how much improvement there is every time cumulative experience doubles. For example, a 70% experience curve is steeper than a 90% curve, since this means (if our measure of productivity is unit cost) that every time we double our cumulative experience, our technology's unit cost goes down 30% (called a progress ratio) or we end up at 70% of the previous unit cost. Many technologies appear to operate in the 70% to 80% experience curve range. For example, studies have shown that photovoltaic cell development and manufacturing have an experience curve of approximately 75%. Thus, every time production experience doubles, the cost of photovoltaic cell modules should decrease by about 25%. This means that sometime in the future, the full energy costs (incorporating the initial investment, which is the major cost of generating solar-based electricity) from photovoltaic cell modules should be highly competitive with current, more traditional sources of energy production.

Figure 2.8 shows typical experience curves plotted on regular graph paper. When plotted on logarithmic paper, the experience curve becomes a straight line.

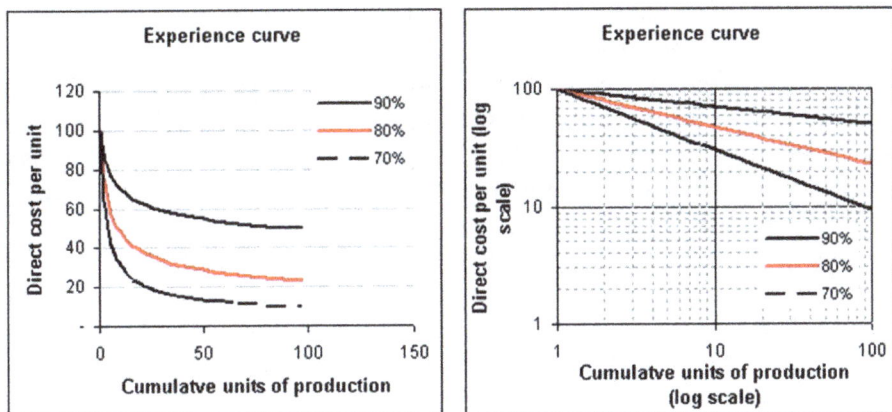

Figure 2.8: Visualizing experience curves: Standard vs. logarithmic scales.

What creates a steep experience curve? Generally, there are four requirements for a steep learning curve. First, are humans involved in the process. People tend to be the best at learning, although there are some indications that AI has now created machine learning that is beginning to rival the speed at which humans learn. However, human learning still tends to be much more inclusive of incorporating different elements and experiences, while machine learning is limited by the domain in its programming.

Second, are there good opportunities for "process innovation"? Process innovation is the ability to improve and innovate in the production process. Third, does the basic design stay relatively stable? As in music, a person needs to practice the piano for a relatively long period of time to get better, rather than constantly jumping to new musical instruments each week. Fourth, is the production process more like an assembly process? Experience comes from doing things over and over repetitively, like shooting free throws from the same location on the court, practicing hitting drives from a golf tee at a driving range, or manufacturing photovoltaic modules.

Importance of Understanding Experience Curves in Technology Markets

While R&D and engineering groups can develop experience in what they do, in general, experience curves tend to be applied to technologies that are either in production or as a forecast to understand the cost structure of new technologies that will be commercialized in the future.

In 1968, Bruce Henderson, the founder of the Boston Consulting Group (famous for their Dog-Cash Cow-Star-Question Mark or BCG Matrix), published a short book titled *Perspectives on Experience*.[11] In many ways, this changed the way that technology companies developed their strategy. We can paraphrase the strategic importance of Henderson's *Perspectives on Experience* for technology products by the following figure (See Figure 2.9).

By using the straight line on logarithmic paper, it is easier to show the strategic implications of experience curves. Suppose there is a steep experience curve in the industry, and there are three companies. Company A has a 50% market share, Company B has a 25% market share, and Company C has a 10% market share. This means that Company A accumulates experience twice as fast as Company B, and five times faster than Company C.

From a productivity point of view, Company A will drive down the experience curve and reduce their unit costs faster than Company B, and much faster than Company C. When an experience curve is steep, the market share leader (or company with the most cumulative experience) will always have an absolute advantage in cost and productivity.

Perhaps Company C, although it lags behind the other companies on cost, might be able to differentiate itself and charge a higher price. However, this will only generally work in retail markets where products can be differentiated by aggressive marketing or in markets where there are strong government regulations and patent protections.

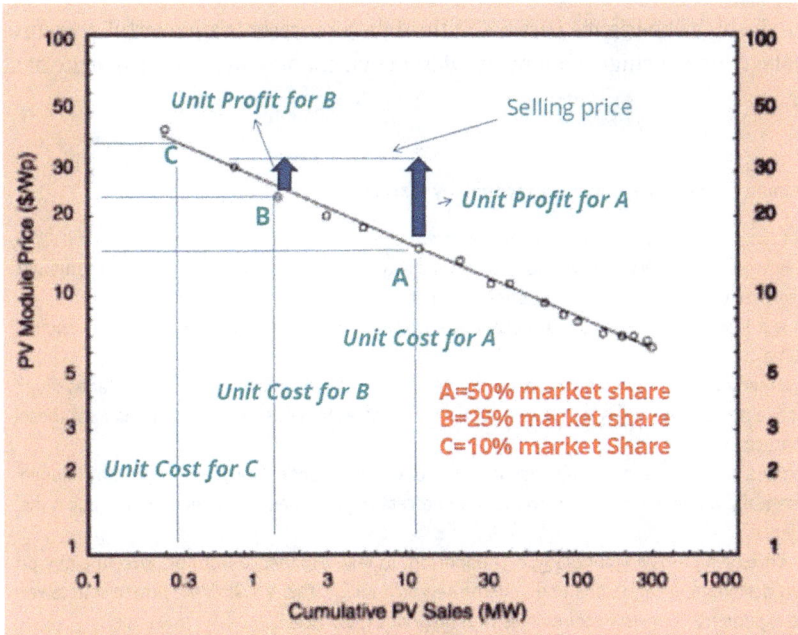

Figure 2.9: Strategic implications of experience curves for technology firms.

But what about intermediate markets? The majority of any developed country's economy related to technologies is seen in selling technologies and components into intermediate markets.[12] These are system assemblers that bundle technologies, interfaces, and components into an integrated product. Any laptop computer has hundreds of components and technologies embedded in the product.

In these intermediate markets, once a design standard is established (a topic in Chapter 3) what is most important are price, delivery, quality, and meeting the required specifications for that component. Marketing and advertising strategies that are so important for the retail and consumer markets are far less important in intermediate markets.

In fact, once a product's design is in its later stages of development, most of the input components and technologies are generally standardized. All the companies need to price their product the same in non-differentiated, commodity-type markets. In this case, as seen in the figure, the absolute advantage that Company A has on productivity and cost will ultimately translate into an absolute advantage in unit profit. Company B has less profit, while Company C might have a loss on each product sold since they are higher on the experience curve. This scenario is common in technology-driven markets, where companies with small market share often sell at a loss while trying to compete. Typically, they encounter one of three outcomes: they exit the market (the most frequent result), they land a major contract that accelerates their learning curve and improves cost competitiveness, or they launch a new, disruptive technology that resets the industry's experience curve. The third path represents a powerful entrepreneurial strategy-introducing an innovative design that enables them to become the next cost leader.

Critical Lessons – Experience Curves in Technology Markets

Our study of experience curves provides some important lessons.

1) Experience curves apply to overall industry productivity/cost as well as how an individual company will decrease costs. The impact of experience can be quantified.
2) There is a first mover advantage in experience. However, firms need to maintain this advantage over time.
3) Being a market leader generally creates absolute productivity advantages. These advantages often last until a new technology is introduced, which starts the experience curve all over again for these new participants.
4) Companies need to manage their cost structure down the experience curve. It does not happen automatically. Management needs to focus on process improvements and keep driving down the experience.
5) When developing a new technology, it is important to take experience from prior technology or product development, and transfer that to the new technology. This will allow the firm to start lower on the experience curve than companies with no prior experience.
6) When entering a market with a new technology, understanding the experience curve will allow the commercialization expert to determine what price points will need to be obtained in the future.
7) One can forecast a technology's likely cost structure at different times in the future based on anticipated sales and production orders, even before entering the market.
8) An experience curve might also tell a company if they are too late in entering the market, since they will not be able to obtain a cost structure relative to other firms with larger cumulative experience or market share. It can also provide data as to what their minimum acceptable market share or sales levels needs to be in order to be price competitive for a new entrant.
9) Many large companies that develop technology-based products will establish a target experience curve-based cost structure for their new products and expect product managers to meet those targets over time. They use the experience curve obtained on prior products as an analog to the new technology's future cost structure.

Concluding Insights

The starting point of understanding technology commercialization has to be in a broader understanding of how technology markets actually work. As seen in Chapter 1, technologies generally go through different levels of development from early idea generation, through prototyping to market commercialization. Moving through these levels of technology and integration is one key component of understanding the basics of technology management. The other key component is understanding the forces at work in technology markets. The markets for technologies and innovation are some of the most interesting and investigated topics of research. From this research, we have uncovered some basic forces at play.

Certainly, every different technology has its own characteristics. Engineers, scientists, programmers, and developers working on new technologies for computers or e-bikes are dealing with very different technical issues than teams working with a new technology for drug delivery or medical testing. Each technology is different. But regardless of the technology, there are common, foundational concepts that appear somewhat universal to almost all technology markets.

In this chapter, we examined three broad foundational concepts, the market S-curve, the technology S-curve, and the experience curve. Combined, these graphical concepts provide a good foundation to understand how technology markets work.

Although this chapter focuses on foundational concepts in technology development and commercialization, many of the models and curves discussed are mathematical in nature. As a result, organizations often seek to apply them to forecast future technology adoption or experience curve trends. For readers interested in these forecasting techniques, we provide more detailed guidance in the appendix on technology forecasting.

In the next chapter, we discuss some of the key stages of technology markets, the strategic decisions that need to be made during these stages, and the importance of understanding the technology standardization process.

Chapter Example: Corporate Responses to Technological Threats – Failures in the Mechanical Watch Industry

Problem

Mechanical watches have been around for centuries. Originally offered as pocket watches, by the 1930s most people had moved to wearing the more convenient wristwatch. These beautiful and highly crafted timekeeping devices of gears and springs dominated the world market. In the United States, there were a number of highly respected and traditional companies manufacturing mechanical watches. These included the Elgin Watch Company (founded 1864), Waltham Watch Company (founded 1850), and Bulova (founded 1875). A nice mid-priced new wristwatch in the mid-1960s might have cost $80. The Timex Corporation was a latecomer to the market, and focused on less expensive, mechanical watches. During this time, some Timex watches sold for about $20.

Everything changed in 1970. With the introduction of the integrated circuit in the 1960s, a number of new products were being developed, such as personal computers and calculators. The Hamilton Watch company developed the first fully electronic commercial watch, called the "Pulsar Time Computer" by combining integrated circuits, a battery, a quartz crystal oscillator, and a digital LED display. This was actually an inspiration that started a couple years earlier when film director Stanley Kubrick and science fiction writer Isaac Asimov asked the Hamilton Watch Company to make a futuristic watch for the now classic 1968 movie, *2001: A Space Odyssey* (see Figure 2.10).

By early 1970 the Pulsar was in prototype mode, and a full press campaign was started. The Pulsar prototype was first shown in May 1970 on the "Johnny Carson Show", with a price tag of $1,500. Johnny Carson threw the watch in the air and laughed at both the concept and the price tag. In spite of Johnny Carson's antics, several rich and famous people, including actors and royalty, started to place orders for the Pulsar. The Pulsar was fully commercialized by 1972. By the end of 1972, the electronic digital watch was selling for about $300. It was awkward to use the LED display, which needed to have a button pushed to light-up. It did not look very attractive by traditional watch standards since it was too futuristic. During this time, most traditional mechanical watch companies simply did not believe in the technology. Reading the annual reports in the early 1970s of traditional watch companies, almost universally these traditional watch companies saw the electronic watch as simply an expensive fad, with no possible future in the mass market. From the CEO down, nobody in these time-honored mechanical watch companies could embrace the new technology.

Shift forward by only four years. By 1976 one could buy a cheap electronic watch for about $20. The display problem had been solved by using LCDs rather than LEDs. About 90% of the market had shifted to electronic watches, many which were produced by U.S. and Japanese semiconductor firms such as Texas Instruments. Almost all the major traditional mechanical watch companies were going bankrupt, selling their brand names to electronic watch producers.

Lesson

The traditional, old-fashioned corporate culture of most mechanical watch companies in the late 1960s and early 1970s simply did not allow them to embrace the new electronic technologies on the horizon. It was just too much. Timex barely survived the transition, while the majority of old, traditional watch companies are gone. The traditional Swiss watch industry needed to be heavily subsidized by the government to survive. Seiko, as an early electronic timing and instruments company, was better able to make the transition, and actually become an early market leader.

The introduction of smart watches changed the market even more. Most of the watches sold from the end of the 1970s to the present time were, and still are, manufactured by players from completely different industries, such as Texas Instruments, Apple, Google, the Samsung Group, and Casio although there are a few survivors from the old industry. Company culture is often a powerful barrier to the adoption of radically new technologies. Clearly, when confronted with radically new technologies, most traditional companies simply cannot make the change. This has been shown to be true time and again, in many different technologies, the old players simply disappear when they cannot emotionally acknowledge the threat created by a new technology.

Figure 2.10: Hamilton watch developed for the 1968 movie, *2001: A Space Odyssey*.

Chapter 3
Key Industry Stages and Dominant Product Designs

This Chapter

- Examines the key stages that technology-intensive industries pass through and how the success factors and strategic priorities evolve across these stages.
- Explores the role of dominant product designs and how they are developed and established in the market.
- Highlights the importance of standard setting and how effective commercialization strategies can influence this process.
- Emphasizes the need for both technology designs and commercialization strategies to adapt as industries evolve.

Key Management Tools and Best Practices

- Utterback and Abernathy model of product and process innovation
- Develop strategies and key decisions appropriate to stage of development
- The need to understand, influence, and track the design standardization process
- Becoming involved in standard-setting organizations (SSOs)

! **INSIGHT**

This is our final chapter on industry structure in technology industries. Like any industry, technology-based industries go through stages. Some of these stages are driven by the S-curves and experience curves, discussed in Chapter 2. In most technology-driven industries, there are three key stages of industry evolution. Each stage takes a different form, with different key success factors at play. This means that firms must approach commercialization in different ways, depending on the stage they are entering the market. One of the most important driving forces that underlies the evolution in technology industries is the creation of a dominant product design.

Introduction

There are very powerful forces in technology-based industries. First, technologies and innovations tend to diffuse through the market in a somewhat predictable manner, often capturing different market segments and users in a sequential manner. Second, a particular technological approach will improve its performance over time, but is ultimately limited by the laws of nature, physics, and science. Once these limits are reached, performance improvements cease or, at best, slow dramatically, until a new and ultimately better technical approach to the problem enters the market, substituting the old technology. Finally, with most technology-based products, as the firms accumulate experience over time, the various measures of productivity, such as unit cost, error

https://doi.org/10.1515/9783111684420-004

rates and yield rates, will improve in a very predictable manner. In many industries with steep experience curves, this improvement can be quite dramatic, particularly in the early stages of a technology's life.

In this chapter, we explore how these forces come together to create three distinct phases in the market for technologies. In addition, in this chapter, we also discuss another powerful force, the establishment of a dominant product design. In many situations, firms can influence how dominant product designs and standards are set as part of their overall commercialization strategies.

Companies can commercialize their technologies at different times into the market, depending on their skills and overall strategic orientation. Some firms commercialize their designs early in the life cycle, while other firms may wait. But any commercialization and design strategy must consider the forces that drive the evolution of technology-based markets. Every technology-based industry evolves through fairly definable stages.

Utterback and Abernathy Model of Innovation

In 1975, James Utterback and William Abernathy published their seminal article, "A dynamic model of process and product innovation" in the journal *Omega*.[1] In this article, they argued that there are essentially two broad types of innovation: product innovation and process innovation. Product innovation represents improvements in the design of the technology, the product itself. Process innovation represents improvements in the manufacturing and delivery processes. Examining evidence from a number of prior studies and industries, they found the following relationship depicted in Figure 3.1.

Process and Product Innovation

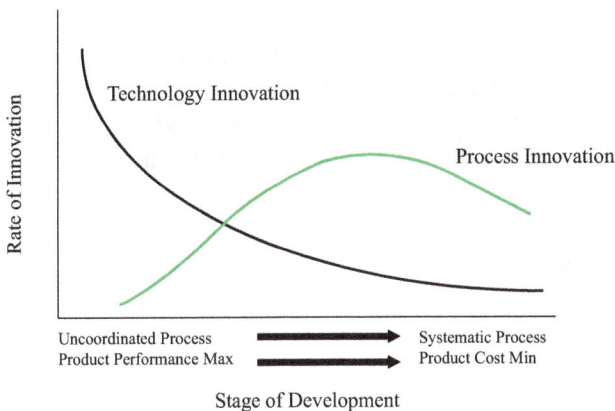

Figure 3.1: Process and product innovation. Source: Utterback & Abernathy (1975).

At the beginning, product innovation is high. The focus is on design developments, functionality, and performance improvements. Less effort is placed on process innovation early in the development cycle. Over time, however, the rate of product innovation decreases, while process innovation increases. At some point, process innovation becomes much more important in order to drive down the cost of production as markets become more price-sensitive. Then, at the end of the cycle, the rate of both product and process innovation declines. A key part of this Abernathy and Utterback model is to link competitive strategies to the different types of innovation over time.

There are essentially two broad types of innovation – product innovation and process innovation.

This early model of product and process innovation by Abernathy and Utterback became the foundation for later research, examining the relationship between managerial decisions, competitive strategies, research effort, and nature of innovation that technology-oriented firms need to consider. The importance of the early Utterback and Abernathy model of product and process innovation cannot be overstated and is taught in every technology management course throughout the world. The next sections in this chapter build on Utterback and Abernathy's early work and expand many of their points, considering the development of modern technologies and the concepts presented in our earlier chapters. However, we also focus on the nature of technology standardization, a critical development that drives much of what Utterback and Abernathy discuss.

Stage 1: The Early Growth Period

The early growth stage is when the Market S-curve, the Technology S-curve, and the Experience curve are all just starting for a particular technology. This is the period of rapid growth, as early adopters quickly enter the market and users are excited about the technology (see Figure 3.2). However, at this stage, there are often competing technical approaches that can accomplish the same objective. Nothing has really been standardized at this point, and users, customers, and potential partners often have many different technology design choices.

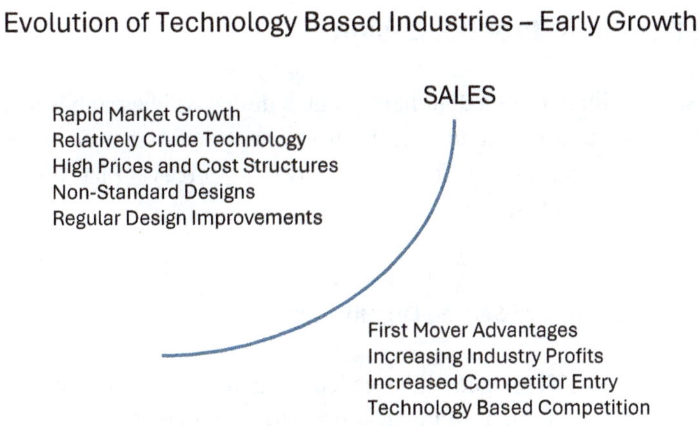

Evolution of Technology Based Industries – Early Growth

Rapid Market Growth
Relatively Crude Technology
High Prices and Cost Structures
Non-Standard Designs
Regular Design Improvements

SALES

First Mover Advantages
Increasing Industry Profits
Increased Competitor Entry
Technology Based Competition

Figure 3.2: Evolution of technology-based industries: Early growth.

The early growth phase of technology markets, whether for consumer products or intermediate components, often features relatively crude performance, compared to the older technologies they aim to replace. Prices also tend to be higher for these new technologies, particularly when compared to the older, more established technologies in the market.

The early growth period is when there are first-mover advantages of getting into the market quickly, getting your technical approach known to customers, and starting to drive down the experience curve.

The early growth period is when there are first-mover advantages of getting into the market quickly, getting your technical approach known to customers, and starting to drive down the experience curve. Profits increase as more customers start acquiring the technology. But this is also a period where competition is primarily based on a technology's approach and performance. Sales pitches to customers, for example, will tend to focus on a technology's solution or sophistication – "my technology is better than the competitors". At this stage, price or cost are almost secondary. Essentially, early adopter customers don't care that much about price.

If attempting commercialization at this point in the industry evolution, the commercialization strategy needs to have its primary focus on design. The emphasis needs to be on the technological advantages when compared to the competitor's designs, getting into the market quickly to gain first mover advantages, and attracting a customer base of early adopters. This is also a time when sophisticated commercialization strategies will attempt to influence the dominant design that will ultimately be established.

Establishing the Dominant Product Design

In every industry, at some point in time, a dominant product design will be established. Technology developers need to understand that the best science or design does not always translate into the dominant design. There are many other forces at play. Dominant product designs can be set in many ways.

Dominant Product Designs: Standard-Setting Organizations

Standard-setting organizations (SSOs), sometimes called standard-developing organizations (SDOs), are one of the most important mechanisms to address issues related to both the interoperability and safety of various technologies. Voluntary SSOs are most common since interested firms can freely negotiate among themselves in a formalized manner to set various technology standards. In essence, SSOs are networks for innovators and developers, large and small, to join in order to shape future technological development and markets through standards.

In every industry, at some point in time, a dominant product design
will be established.

SSOs are formed through a variety of ways. Often times, groups of early developers simply decide to form an alliance or SSO. Another method is when one of the larger standard-setting organizations sets up an affiliated SSO for a new, developing technology. Unless a government agency requires a certain standard, individual firms are not required to join an SSO nor are they bound by the SSO's decisions. But recommendations from influential SSOs often become the standards for many technologies.

Given the influence of SSOs, involvement in an SSO should be considered part of any commercialization strategy. But SSOs are not for everybody. The decision to become actively involved in a voluntary SSO or standards alliance is ultimately based upon a strategic analysis that weighs the benefits of alliance involvement (influencing global technology standards, finding potential customers or development partners, learning about new standards before others, tracking potential competitors' technologies, etc.) with the costs (possibly, exposing a firm's current R&D and designs to potential competitors, cost of membership, time and effort, etc.). These interests will likely vary between different firms within the same industry and become part of the decision to "join or not to join".

SSOs also vary in their influence, and sometimes, there are competing SSOs for the same developing technology. The most influential SSOs are ones that the major corporate players in the industry have either formed or become involved with at an early stage. Most SSOs require membership fees, but a few SSOs, working with "open-source" technologies, are free to everybody.

Every industry, and developing technologies within these industries, has SSOs. For example, the earliest standards for wireless power transmission technologies (transmitting power over a distance without having a cord plugged into the wall), were developed by the Alliance for Wireless Power (A4WP), a group with over a hundred firms, large and small, all interested in developing systems for wireless power. The A4WP ultimately merged with another SSO, the Airfuel Alliance, and this effort continues to this very day.

Typically, SSOs work through various sub-committees who then make recommendations for standards to the whole SSO, who then vote. Once adopted, this becomes a recommended standard or technical requirement for that technology.

SSOs can be very important, particularly for intermediate technologies that make up components and interfaces in a product, as well as many retail technologies. In these SSOs, the various member firms often compete with each other to convince the SSO to adopt their particular standard. After all, this will immediately give these developers an advantage in having their design accepted in the market. They can then start further down the experience curve since other competitors will need to change their products to conform to the new standard. These successful companies might even have their own intellectual property wrapped up in the final standard that other companies might have to license in the future.

But not all SSO members are developing early innovations. Other firms are sitting on the sidelines, seeing what standards will be developed, and them jumping into that particular standard with their own R&D and processes. Other firms in SSOs are customers of these technologies, who are watching carefully, since any new standard for a component will need to be integrated into their final designs. The stakes can be very high in SSOs.

Another advantage of being involved in an SSO for developers is that a company can keep track of what technologies are being developed by potential competitors. Are these other technologies better, or do we have an advantage? Are the competitor's technologies more developed or can we be the first to market? Having this inside information, developers can then design their technologies to conform to the standard that appears to be getting traction within the SSO's discussions, thus getting a first-mover advantage or foot in the door with potential customers and system designers.

Most of the larger technology corporations are involved in SSOs, so being active in an SSO also allows for excellent networking for a smaller early-stage technology developer. Oftentimes, larger firms will partner with smaller technology developers they met in the SSO. Finally, many SSOs offer training seminars and developer kits to their members.

Influencing the Standard-Setting Process. If joining an SSO, then become involved. There are several ways an early-stage technology developer can influence SSO decisions or benefit from SSOs. These include.

1) Being directly involved with the sub-committees, particularly the technology sub-committee that is working on the most important standard recommendations.
2) Attending all SSO meetings with multiple representatives rather than just waiting for the written minutes or summaries of the meetings. Many of the monthly meetings are video-based, with annual face-to-face meetings. Attend them.
3) Become involved very early in an SSO, as soon as one is formed in your technological space. The earlier a developer is involved in an SSO, the more influence they can often obtain.
4) If possible, become a sub-committee chairperson. Chairing a sub-committee can sometimes influence the SSOs recommendation for standards, but perhaps most importantly, allow for making friends with other SSO members.

Because SSOs often determine the prevailing standards for emerging technologies, companies should engage with them early as part of a proactive commercialization strategy. In other industries, SSOs may have less influence. It really depends.

Dominant Product Designs: Market Force Determination

While important in many developing technologies, SSOs certainly do not set all standards. SSOs tend to concentrate on individual technologies in fairly narrow markets that might end up as components or interfaces in larger systems. SSOs typically do not set standards for retail products or large integrated systems, except perhaps at the interface level. At this level, they are generally ineffective, where a single company holds dominant intellectual property rights, as such firms have little need for external standard setting.

Additionally, SSOs cannot always set a standard that everybody agrees upon. This can happen for a number of reasons. Perhaps an SSO has not been established; perhaps not enough large corporations have joined the SSO to make it influential. Since SSO recommendations are largely voluntary and not binding, companies with different technologies can still bring their own technology to the market. Some companies, such as Apple, have often developed their own internal standards as part of their corporate strategy rather than working with SSOs. In all of these cases, market forces will ultimately set a "standard" through a dominant product design.

History is full of examples where competing technologies were in the marketplace, and the market ultimately decided which standard or design it wanted. The classic example cited in many textbooks was the "video format war of the 1980s" between the competing technologies of Sony's Betamax versus Panasonic's VHS format for video tapes; a battle that ultimately the VHS format won when Sony finally gave up. The market decided they wanted the VHS even though many still argue the Betamax was a superior format.

It is important to remember, however, that the best science does not always win in the marketplace. The market often demands a whole list of performance requirements along various dimensions. Some performance requirements are readily apparent and tend to be the initial focus of early engineering efforts. However, many critical requirements are less visible, thus making it essential for a strong commercialization study to explore both the market structure and the often hidden needs of potential users. A technology that can best satisfy the complete bundle of requirements is likely to become a dominant player.

Design Complements and the Eco-system. A dominant design can also be established by a combination of the different requirements, segments and players within the larger system. Oftentimes, a technology's advantage comes from "design complements" with other technologies within the system's ecosystem. For example, most technologies are part of a larger system or at least require the support of a complex system. All of these supporting system technologies will have their own specifications, interfaces, and requirements. Combined, a technology needs to satisfy all of the requirements of the supporting system's technologies, although it might not be the optimum solution for any of the individual supporting technologies. In this case, a "satisficing solution" might become the dominant technology, at least until the requirements of the supporting technologies change.

Consider the dominant design for small satellites. For many years, the dominant design for small satellites was CubeSat (see Figure 3.3). The CubeSat is considered a relatively inexpensive "nano" satellite of a common size (10cm x 10cm x 10cm) and form factor. CubeSats are typically used for education and research purposes, since small experiments can be enclosed into this small space. CubeSats can also be used for more commercial purposes. The components to build a CubeSat can be purchased "off the shelf", and the designs are relatively simple. However, launching a satellite involves a number of different technologies, including the launch vehicle, satellite adaptors, and the multiple ways a satellite interfaces with other technologies on the vehicle. In addition, because of its small size, CubeSats often piggyback on larger loads or even human space flight operations.

Figure 3.3: CubeSat as dominant design.

The CubeSat was designed in 1999. When invented by university professors, the CubeSat was not the most cost effective; it did not have any major institutional supporters and was often ridiculed as a "toy" by the major satellite designers. CubeSat had its first launch in 2003. Nothing at the time would suggest that the CubeSat would become a dominant design. However, by 2013, CubeSats had become a dominant satellite design for small satellites, commanding over 50% of the market. Why? Because CubeSat's technology satisfied the requirements of all the different interfaces for satellites, including adaptors, deployers, launch vehicles, communication systems, and ground equipment. It was not the best solution for any of the individual requirements, but rather the best for the combination of all the different interface and launch requirements. After about a decade, as the technologies improved in the interfaces, adaptors and launch vehicles, the CubeSat started to lose its dominant position as heavier, larger, and more sophisticated satellites could be launched in the same cost-effective manner.[2]

Dominant Product Designs: Customer Influence

In some industries, a major customer can determine the dominant product design, simply by selecting that technology over competitors. This is true in the government procurement process. For example, if the U.S. Department of Defense defines a technology specification for a new, expensive system, technology developers will also work with these particular design standards for their general market technologies.

Dual-Use Technologies. Finding another commercial use for a technology developed specifically for the government, such as for the Department of Defense, NASA, or Department of Energy, is often called a "dual-use" technology. Can a technology developed internally by government R&D laboratories, or by the private sector under government contracts or grants also be used, perhaps with slight modifications, in the civilian market?

For example, a new water purification technology developed for use by the Army's special force units deep in enemy territory might have applications in the commercial backpacking and camping community. Dual-use technologies are a great way of finding other markets to commercialize a product, while letting the government pay for most of the original R&D and design efforts. Identifying a dual-use application offers greater return on the government's initial investment and provides developers with an opportunity to spread commercialization costs across multiple markets. Thus, the design for the original use will become the market standard for the private sector applications.

Large Standard-Setting Customers in the Commercial Market. Large buyers often exist in the commercial market. A good example is the selection by IBM to use the operating system (PC-DOS) developed by Microsoft for their desktop computers. PC-DOS was introduced with the new IBM PCs in August, 1981. At the time, there were actually many operating systems competing for the personal computer market, but when IBM entered the PC market in 1981 with the Microsoft developed operating system, all this changed. Immediately, all PC makers shifted to the Microsoft operating system (sold as MS-DOS). These "clone" companies even marketed their personal computers (with similar internal components) as "IBM compatible" for the first several years. Microsoft became the dominant operating system for personal computers (and larger systems) ever since.

Only Apple didn't follow suit. Apple had a specific strategy at the time of being different from IBM, targeting the educational market rather than the business or personal computing market, and not licensing their internal operating system called MacOS at the time. Thus, there were no Apple compatible PCs, only IBM compatible PCs in the early days of desktop computers.

Dominant Product Designs: Government Influence

Governments can certainly influence standards. In some cases, governments can simply order a particular design standard. Governments have the power to set the regulations, the specifications, and the design of a particular technology. If anybody wants to market in that particular technological space in that country, they must build their technology to that standard.

Most governments will take the recommendation of an SSO, but not always. A global organization called the Internal Organization for Standardization (ISO) exists to oversee global standard setting processes. Formed in 1947, the ISO also acts as an SSO in many areas, recommending standards in various technology sectors. However, unlike SSOs, which are usually made up of corporations and technology developments, the ISO members are representatives of different countries, with only one member per country. Years ago, the U.S. Government, along with several professional societies, formed a non-profit, non-government body, now known as the American National Standards Institute (ANSI). ANSI is the U.S. representative to the ISO. Individual governments will often take the recommendations of the ISO committees.

Some non-Western governments tend to be more aggressive in controlling standards in their countries. This is particularly true of governments that view setting a standard different from the U.S. or Europe as assisting their home-grown businesses. Sometimes, the governments are simply anti-West in their orientation. Thus, you often find different standards for the same technology in different parts of the world. Russia, China, and the European Union often encourage, if not require, different standards than what has been developed in the U.S. or recommended by SSOs that have a large U.S. presence.

The U.S Government, for example, has the National Institute of Standards and Technology (NIST). NIST has a specific national standards strategy for critical and emerging technologies. Most of the strategies developed by NIST involve following private sector standard-setting processes. NIST has identified several technologies that are important for U.S competitiveness and national security over the next 30 years. These include communication and networking, microelectronics, AI, biotechnology, navigation systems, distributed ledger technologies, clean energy and quantum information technologies. At the present time, the U.S. government is letting the SSOs and the market decide standards in these areas.

While typically not setting standards, the U.S. government will influence standards, particularly in areas that it considers of high interest to U.S. security. Much of the influence involves offering research grants and contracts to organizations that tend to work toward what the U.S. government sees as the appropriate standards.

While U.S. standards are almost always determined by SSOs or the marketplace, standards set by the government can occasionally be more direct. Through lobbying efforts, but more often based upon internal government offices or department recommendations, various government agencies can set standards. Oftentimes, before these standards are set by governments, there might be a period of obtaining public and stakeholder comment, but occasionally it is simply by order with no public comments. Recently, for example, we are starting to see more government rules (basically standards) in the areas of AI, cyber security, recombinant DNA, genetically modified foods, and crypto currencies. At the present time, in the U.S., most of these directives are more safety or security oriented, but they do limit the development of certain technological approaches.

The key issue when it comes to commercialization is to be not only aware but involved as much as possible in the standard-setting process relevant to your technology.

Stage 2: The Late Growth Period

Everything changes once a dominant product design is established. This is true whether an SSO sets the standard, or a large customer, the government, or simply the marketplace creates a dominant product. Once a dominant product design is set, the nature of competition, and the ability to commercialize a design, changes dramatically.

The late growth period is still a period of rapid growth (see Figure 3.4). In fact, once a dominant product design is established, this is when most of the customers, whether in the retail market or the secondary market of system development, will enter the market. This is the period of the "majority" – the full-blown market expansion. Customers and system developers, who didn't want to take a chance on the largely untested early technologies, will quickly contract, source, or buy technologies once it becomes the dominant design.

The late growth period still is a period of rapid growth. Once a dominant
product design is established, this is when most of the
customers enter the market.

Key Strategic Issues of the Late Growth Period

Several other forces start to become much more important at this time.

1) Once a dominant product design is established, companies need to move to this more standardized design, or variation of the standard, in order to stay in the market.
2) Once a dominant product design is established, prices become much more important since R&D effort on design issues will decline in the industry. Moving down the experience curve and developing efficient production systems becomes most important. Market share and cost controls become critical at this point.
3) Technology commercialization is still very possible at this point, but it needs to focus on designs that are within the standards set by the dominant product design, and it often needs to focus on outpricing the competitive technologies. There are a whole bunch of technology development companies that wait for a dominant product to be established, then they innovate and design slight variations of this dominant product design, even doing "work-arounds" of any patent protections.
4) Once a dominant product design is established for a system (such as an electronic watch, the computer, the electric car, the cell phone, etc.), immediately costs become much more important. Since market price is becoming more important for the end products, these end-product system developers will immediately also start looking for standardization and price advantages in most of their components, internal technologies, and interfaces.
5) Establishing a dominant design is what generally triggers the period of decreasing product innovation, and rapid increases in process innovation seen in the Utterback and Abernathy model of innovation.

In the late growth phase, technology commercialization is still important, but in two very different ways. First, commercialization tends to be around products that are variations of the dominant product design that make the technology less expensive, higher quality, and perform better. This is what the market is looking for.

The other strategy will focus on understanding that a new more radical design will ultimately replace the dominant product design. Thus, flash drives replaced CDs as portable data storage devices and tuning fork quartz crystals replaced XY flexure designs. This is the fact of the technology S-Curve. Coming up with a radically new technology to replace the old technology is the true innovative and entrepreneurial strategy, although it doesn't always work in practice. But sometime in the future, there will always be technology introduced that will become the new dominant product design – the key entrepreneurial success comes from being the one that actually innovates the new dominant technology.

As a technology strategy, many technology developments, particularly larger developers, will specifically work both strategies at the same time – tweaking and commercializing incremental improvements in the dominant product design while at the same time developing new, innovative technologies that will hopefully replace the old technology in the future. In other words, larger developers might be working simultaneously in all stages of development within the same market space as their specific corporate strategy.

Evolution of Technology Based Industries – Late Growth

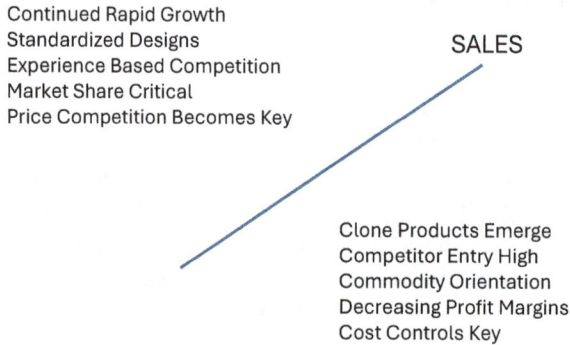

Continued Rapid Growth
Standardized Designs
Experience Based Competition
Market Share Critical
Price Competition Becomes Key

SALES

Clone Products Emerge
Competitor Entry High
Commodity Orientation
Decreasing Profit Margins
Cost Controls Key

Figure 3.4: Evolution of technology-based industries: Late growth.

Stage 3: Technology Maturity and Decline

The final stage in technology markets is maturity and decline. At this stage, the incremental improvements in the dominant product design have essentially stopped. The limiting nature of the laws of physics just won't allow designers to squeeze much more performance improvements out of the technology (see Figure 3.5).

During this final stage, most of the customers have already purchased or used the technology. There is simply not much left in terms of market growth or performance improvements. The weaker companies have already left the market, and there might only be a few survivors left.

At this stage, new and innovative technologies are likely emerging, with some potentially already entering the market. It is widely recognized that these newer technologies will eventually replace the older ones, particularly when they are based on fundamentally different physical or scientific principles. The key questions then become: how long will the transition take, and which of the new approaches will ultimately become the dominant design? This is when every technology company needs to make a decision. Do they jump into the new technology and shift their R&D efforts? Do they stay in the old technology market and ride it down, perhaps even surviving in some niche markets? Or do they attempt to do both?

Almost always, the maturity and decline phases of technology markets overlap with the early growth phase of the new, substitute technology. However, managing these emerging technologies often demands a fundamentally different organizational culture, investment strategy, R&D focus, and leadership approach. This is especially true when considering organizations accustomed to legacy technologies.

Almost always, the maturity and decline phases of technology markets overlap with the early growth phase of the new, substitute technology.

Players in old technologies generally do not do well in the new technologies. None of the floppy drive manufacturers were ever successful in the flash drive technologies. The global positioning system (GPS) developers never made the transition into cell-based location apps for phones. Most of the great mechanical watch companies went bankrupt. Baldwin Locomotive Works, the absolute leader in Steam Railroad Engines in the U.S. until the 1940s, was simply unable to transition to the more modern diesel-electric locomotive systems. Baldwin ultimately stopped producing railroad equipment in 1956, being acquired by Amour & Company. By 1990, even the last remnants of this famous brand name had disappeared.

The history books are full of the smoldering relics of failed technology companies that were unable to transition to newer, and more innovative technologies. Deciding whether to jump into the new, upcoming technologies, and when to make the jump is an important part of any technology developers' commercialization and design strategy.

Evolution of Technology Based Industries – Maturity

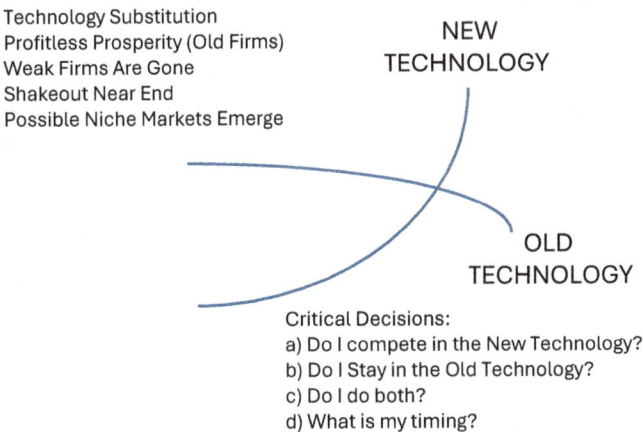

Technology Substitution
Profitless Prosperity (Old Firms)
Weak Firms Are Gone
Shakeout Near End
Possible Niche Markets Emerge

NEW
TECHNOLOGY

OLD
TECHNOLOGY

Critical Decisions:
a) Do I compete in the New Technology?
b) Do I Stay in the Old Technology?
c) Do I do both?
d) What is my timing?

Figure 3.5: Evolution of technology-based industries: Maturity.

Drug Development and Software

All technology-driven industries will move through distinct, and somewhat predictable phases, both before and after commercialization. But each industry also has its own unique characteristics and competitive quirks. Drug and software development are examples of this type of situation.

Strategies and the Stages of Drug Development

There are several radically different approaches to drug development, from traditional drug discovery and testing methods to more recent approaches such as messenger RNA (mRNA) that use biotechnology and recombinant DNA approaches to specifically target certain diseases and conditions. Unlike most industries, drug development is highly regulated by world governments at its various stages, including early-stage testing with animals, and particularly the different stages of human testing where potential therapies and vaccines are examined for both efficacy and safety with human samples.

Once a drug is patented, pharmaceutical companies are highly protective of their intellectual property, as the expiration of a patent allows competitors to produce and sell generic versions of the drug. However, clone or generic versions are often produced even for those drugs still under patent. These "illegal versions" are often distributed in less-restrictive countries, such as those in Africa, or through the mail from online sources. In addition, some countries have laws to shorten patent protections for pharmaceutical products, in order to allow new drugs to enter into their market sooner, and at a lower price.

In spite of these characteristics, drugs, whether developed for the human market (prescription or over the counter) or the animal/veterinarian market, still appear to progress through a series of somewhat predictable industry or life cycle stages after a drug in introduced to the market.

For example, the U.S. Food and Drug Administration (FDA) recently published their perspective of the life cycle of approved drug products.[3] As the FDA points out, "a quality product of any kind consistently meets the expectations of the user – drugs are no different". In this report, the FDA notes distinct periods of development, each with its own distinct stages (see Figure 3.6). As we discussed in the previous chapters, the first period represents the drug development process, from original idea to FDA approval. In this stage, there are distinct phases of development, typical of any technological development process, although somewhat more controlled by government testing and regulations.

Life Cycle of Approved Drug Products

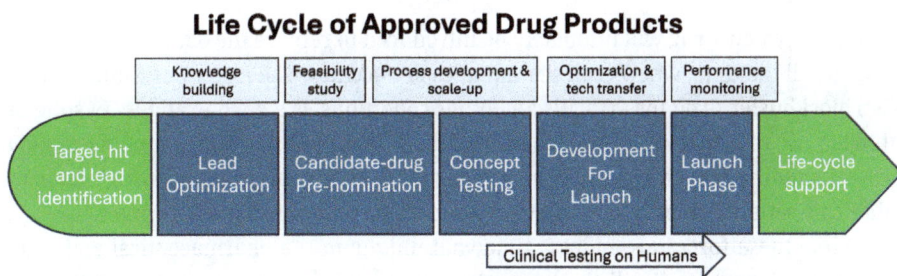

Figure 3.6: FDA perspectives of the life cycle of approved drug products. Source: FDA.

The second period is after commercialization, and most relevant to this chapter. This is the drug life cycle period. This is also a period of commercialization opportunities, but of a different nature. In this life cycle period, the drug does not necessarily stay constant. First, there is always competition from both the existing drugs and new drugs being developed by competitors. In fact, the product launch and commercialization success rate of branded pharmaceuticals is not high, only about 37%, similar to other technologies, such as medical devices.[4]

Like any technology, after initial commercialization, there are still incremental improvements and strategic decisions to be made. The FDA notes a number of the forces that occur after the initial FDA approval/commercialization period. These include manufacturing changes, changes to the formulation, changes to the container closure system, changes to the specifications, changes to the shelf-life, instructions of new strengths and new presentations. Drugs also need to go through a global registration process to be sold world-wide. In addition, packaging, marketing, and distribution change over time.

Some drugs can also shift from a prescribed medicine to an over-the-counter product. Some of the commonly used OTC medicines we use today, such as Allegra, Flonase, and Lumify were all prescribed drugs in their earlier life. Some of these changes might require government approval, while others do not. Essentially, the market for drugs after initial commercialization remains a dynamic battlefield.

In addition, like other technology-driven markets, oftentimes, one particular drug will become the dominant approach for a certain disease or condition. This is true whether the drug is prescribed or over-the-counter. Other drugs in the same space must then either differentiate themselves on some dimension, such as susceptibility to allergic reactions, or to withdraw from the market. Once a drug is off-patent, a new phase is reached where competition is almost always based on price as generic versions are created.

Once a dominant therapy or vaccine is introduced, competitors will also work to develop their own "copycat" drug or "biosimilar" product that does not violate the existing patent. This continuous tweaking of established and successful pharmaceutical products will create a multitude of opportunities for new drug commercialization until a completely new drug will ultimately be introduced to replace the old technology. This happens all the time, whether in therapeutics or vaccines. The history of Humira, AbbVie's blockbuster drug for arthritis and other conditions, is a good example. In spite of AbbVie's use of a "patent thicket" to protect their dominant position, a number of new drugs, including Amgen's recent commercialization of Amjevita and the introduction of other competitors' "biosimilars", have significantly eroded Humira's revenues.

While these forces are indeed somewhat unique to the pharmaceutical and drug development markets, it still results in a typical phased approach to understanding the industry[5] (see Figure 3.7).

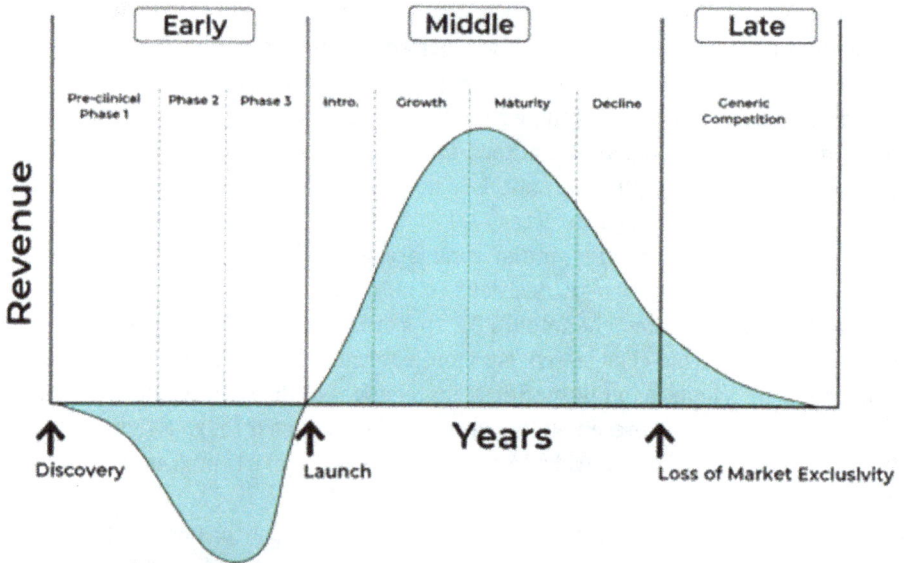

Figure 3.7: Pharmaceutical life cycle dynamics.

Regulatory Strategies for Medical Devices and Other Healthcare Technologies

This regulatory approval process is also required for almost anything associated with the medical field or healthcare, whether the technology is targeted toward the human market or animal applications. Approval of these technologies will look at a combination of safety and effectiveness. This includes medical instruments, drug delivery systems, medical devices, AI programs, and healthcare-related IT software; most likely require regulatory approval for use in medical applications. Even certain insects, such as leeches used in healthcare, are subject to a regulatory approval process. Mobile phone apps or wearable devices with a healthcare focus, such as diagnosing or recommending treatments for various health or medical issues, will likely need some type of regulatory approval. Within the U.S., the FDA is the primary regulatory agency for both human and animal applications. The responsibility of the FDA is to implement the rules and regulations often made by other agencies or offices in the government. Almost every country in the world has a similar regulatory approval agency, although some countries such as the U.S. and Europe may have stricter requirements than other countries, such as in Africa and Latin America.

Typically, the government regulatory agencies will classify the technology as low, medium, or high risk. This classification will then determine the type of approval, which agency needs to approve, and the speed of approval. One of the major mistakes that early technology developers make is not planning early enough for the approval process, collecting the necessary data early, keeping the appropriate documents or records, or even understanding which agencies and processes are needed for approval.

This tends to be a serious problem with smaller entrepreneurial enterprises that don't have an in-house regulatory committee. But even the smallest firm needs to have a regulatory strategy as part of the technology development strategy. A technology's regulatory strategy should be developed in concert with the overall commercialization plan, since there is nothing more frustrating than having a technology ready for launch but then prohibited until all the regulatory requirements are dealt with. Investors looking at technologies in these industries will often require a regulatory strategy to be explicit, prior to funding. In addition, bringing a product to market without proper regulatory approval can result in serious fines, and the withdrawal of the product from the market. One might think that the regulatory approval process is fairly "black and white"; however, it really depends on the technology. For a new drug, it is obvious; however, for a wearable fitness device or mobile app that has some health component to it, the requirements tend to fall in the gray areas.

For most of these technologies, the typical technology readiness (TRL) models can appropriately describe the technology's stages of development, but "regulation readiness" must always be considered concurrently with the actual technology being developed. Fortunately, there are several "compliance" software programs available. These compliance programs, often called GRC (government risk and compliance) software, are effective in both managing a regulatory strategy and reducing legal fees.

Some non-healthcare technologies may also need governmental and regulatory approval. These include technologies such as fuel cells, diesel alternatives, electric and hybrid-electric vehicles, and technologies for VOC reduction, or other technologies that are deemed to create potential risk. A clear regulatory strategy must all be concurrently developed for these types of technologies as the technology is being developed.

Strategies and the Stages of Software Development

The early stages of software development, often called the software development life cycle (SDLC), describe the same general stages of development, from initial idea to commercialization, as any other technology. The terms might be different for the different phases, such as "mockups", "wireframing" and "code development", to ultimately different types of testing near the end of the development cycle, such as "performance testing, functional testing, security testing, and acceptance testing", prior to final commercialization or "deployment".

After commercialization, software and mobile apps follow the same postlaunch trajectory as other technologies – starting with early adoption, followed by the emergence of a dominant design, and eventually evolving through improved technologies or adaptations for niche markets. For example, Facebook held the dominant product design in the social media space for many years; then, the market started to fragment into sub-markets based on both purpose of use and age group. These now include the video sub-market (dominated by TikTok), the social communication market (dominated by Instagram, although Facebook is still used by older generations), the news sub-market (originally dominated by Twitter, and now "X"), the text and video-live communication market (dominated by WhatsApp, Zoom or Snapchat, for younger generations interested in the video expiration characteristics) and the online sales market (originally dominated by Amazon, but now fragmented into various sub-markets such as Etsy for small businesses, or the shopping components of Facebook and TikTok). In spite of these well-known brands, all of these markets have a number of smaller competitors, each trying to develop a new technology that satisfies a different sub-market or rising generational age group.

What is interesting about the mobile application market, for example, is that many of these platforms can have multiple applications targeting different sub-markets on the same platform, such as the recently added sales components of both Facebook and Tik-Tok, which were not on the original platforms.

As in any technology market, dominant products eventually emerge; the landscape fragments into sub-markets, targeted by more specialized innovations; technologies continue to improve over time; and once-leading product designs are gradually replaced by newer, more advanced alternatives.

With the advent of AI approaches, a new generation of technologies is sure to emerge.

Concluding Insights

Understanding both the stages of technology development, whether talking about a single technology or a bundle of technology systems, as well as understanding the evolutionary process of technology-driven markets, provides the key foundation to any commercialization strategy. Any technology commercialization effort will always take place at a particular time in the development stage (what TRL or IRL are we at, and what TRL or IRL are we going to sell into) and at different times in the market evolution (do we commercialize a pre-dominant design technology, a post-dominant design variation, or do we develop and commercialize a paradigm busting innovation that will ultimately substitute for the old technology).

As we progress through the process of developing an effective commercialization strategy or learn how to organize and complete a high-quality technology feasibility study, understanding the nature of technologies and the evolutionary process that technology-driven markets go through will become key.

Every technology is certainly different. For some technologies, influencing the development of standards through an SSO might be an important part of a commercialization strategy. In other commercialization situations, SSOs are irrelevant. Likewise, every entity developing a technology has its special collection of abilities, skills, intellectual property, and resources. Some technology developers might be able to develop radically innovative technologies for the marketplace, while other entities prefer to only tweak and fine-tune existing technologies for commercialization. Both are perfectly good strategies, and necessary to the continuous improvement of technologies and the advancement of societies over time. However, entities need to always understand where they fit in the bigger picture of technology markets.

Some technologies are narrowly focused, while others are complex, integrated systems composed of multiple technologies that must be seamlessly interfaced with one another. In fact, by the time most products reach the retail market, they are actually bundles of other technologies, components, and interfaces that are designed to target the complex needs of the market segments – segments that often rapidly evolve over time as new generations of users enter or leave the marketplace.

This is what makes technology commercialization both intensely interesting, but also frustratingly confusing. However, much of the confusion can be initially focused by understanding the foundational points discussed in these first three chapters.

Chapter 4
Finding Opportunity and Need to Pivot

This Chapter

- Distinguishes between basic and applied research, highlighting their different objectives and roles in the innovation process.
- Explores how specific features of a technology's design can generate value across different market applications.
- Introduces the concepts of pivots and technology leveraging as strategies for adapting early-stage technologies to commercial opportunities.

Key Management Tools and Best Practices

- Developing and launching a Minimum Viable Product (MVP) to avoid feature creep and accelerate market entry.
- Identifying and managing strategic pivots – such as form, function, market, and revenue models – based on market feedback.
- Leveraging existing technologies or internal capabilities to expand into new applications and markets.
- Creating a compelling strategic narrative to connect technical capabilities with commercial value.

! INSIGHT

Most commercialized technologies today are rooted in basic research efforts by developers who were curious about the behavior of phenomena, without regard to how it might be used. They leave it up to others to explore if the unique properties of a phenomenon might be applied in various commercial applications. Applied researchers are focused on solving specific problems through product, technology, or process development. They begin to envision how to design features that could yield unique benefits based on their application focus. The path to commercialization is one of discovery and experimentation, with many pivots and new insights along the way.

Introduction

At the present time, a successful technology development effort almost always involves a combination of agility, mobility, and experimentation. Very few technologies end up at launch time looking exactly like it was envisioned during the earliest idea stages. Innovation, and movement toward the market requires finding the "white spaces" or niches in the marketplace, producing a technology that has better functionality than competitive technologies for this market, and being able to quickly bring that technology to commercialization before either the white space disappears, or a competitive technology occupies the niche. This is often called "pivoting". Pivoting can be examining

https://doi.org/10.1515/9783111684420-005

a whole new approach, or pivoting can mean tweaking the technology to open up new applications and marketing.

Basic Research

Human beings have always been curious about their environment and the forces that shape our world. The drive to understand why and how things work has fueled count-less efforts to uncover new insights into the behavior and properties of natural systems in fields such as biology, energy, physics, materials science, and chemistry. Humans, by their very nature, are innovators and pioneers.

Those involved in basic research are driven by their desire to understand and advance society's collective knowledge about a particular area of study. They uncover insights that can shed new light on complex questions about their subject area. They are typically less concerned with how their discoveries might ultimately be used in practical applications. Basic researchers can be found predominantly in university and government labs, in privately funded non-profit think tanks and even some larger cor-porations. Funding for basic research efforts comes from sources such as government agencies, philanthropic endowments, and industry partnerships.

Despite the fact that basic research has no immediate market applications, this work is essential for laying the foundation for future technological and market innovations. Take for example, the basic research efforts that led to numerous commercial applica-tions for laser technologies. In the early 1900s, scientists were curious about how light and matter interacted with each other. Based on principles of quantum mechanics (the study of how small particles like atoms and electrons interact), theorists such as Albert Einstein predicted that stimulated electrons could produce photons (light particles). He was not concerned with the practical applications of his theories nor were many of the basic researchers in physics labs, such as the Pupin Physics Laboratories at Columbia University, who continued to expand knowledge in this area.

But years later, Gordon Gould, a physicist and inventor, started exploring the fea-sibility of a Light Amplification by Stimulated Emission of Radiation (LASER).[1] Today, laser technologies have been used in fields such as communication (fiber optics for rapid data transmission over long distances), medical technology (surgical procedures in ophthalmology and dermatology), manufacturing (cutting, welding, and engraving) and consumer electronics (readers for CDs, DVDs, and Blue-ray players).

To bridge the gap between basic scientific knowledge and subsequent market applications, oftentimes, requires intermediaries such as tech transfer officers (TTO). Based in universities and other government and private institutions, these individuals play crucial roles in the technology commercialization process. TTOs work closely with faculty researchers within their organizations to begin thinking about possible market applications. They are responsible for protecting intellectual property associated with the work of basic researchers, identifying individuals and organizations who might be interested in using the technology in various market applications, and negotiating and brokering licensing and other types of deals with industry partners and entrepreneurs that would enable commercialization efforts to proceed.

Applied and Translational Research

As contrasted with the work of basic researchers, applied researchers and inventors are interested in figuring out how to solve real-world problems. Drawing on their understanding of basic scientific principles of how things work, they begin to imagine the creation of products and/or services that can be introduced into various market segments. Essentially, the focus is on translating basic research for the commercial market. This research translation is then picked up by engineers and developers, who create the form of the technology.

Applied researchers typically take one of two paths in channeling their efforts. First, these researchers and inventors can be driven by the challenge of solving a real-world problem. During the height of the COVID-19 pandemic, for example, researchers were frantically trying to develop a vaccine that could shield people from getting infected by the virus. Their focus was problem-driven. What scientific principles related to the virus could they draw upon to produce an effective solution? To address this issue, they had to first understand the behavior patterns of the virus (from basic research) in order to figure out effective ways to stop the spread. Then, they had to rapidly conduct tests for efficacy and safety, followed by the challenges of manufacturing the vaccine at a scale large enough to meet global demand. They also had to overcome regulatory hurdles, set up distribution systems for rapid deployment, and protect the intellectual property associated with these new discoveries. Clearly, when the focus of applied research is problem-driven, it involves more than just the technical development of a solution. Applied researchers must also take into account a host of other issues such as manufacturing, marketing, distribution, and regulatory compliance in order to reach the market.

Global upheavals often create a flurry of problem-driven applied research efforts. Armed conflict and wars, events like the 9/11 attack on New York's World Trade Center, plagues, and natural disasters, all seem to ignite the pressure for new and innovative technological solutions to different problems.

The second path that applied researchers can take is focused on figuring out what can possibly be done, given new insights about the capabilities of an emerging technology. In the laser example discussed above, the scientific principles yielded insights about how to control and focus light waves. By channeling the energy produced by light waves, researchers such as Gould began to ask questions related to how this capability can be used in various applications. Beyond just understanding light's behavior patterns, subsequent developers started to think about the question of how this new capability could be deployed in various new applications. If applied in new or existing markets and industries, what kinds of products or services can be developed in order to provide value to specific user segments? Could such new products provide incremental improvements in speed, accuracy, or quality over existing products or services? Or possibly, could new technologies yield products or services that enable users to do things that could never be done before?

Throughout history, there have been certain periods of intense technology improvements built upon the large-scale commercialization of certain foundational technologies. These historical periods are often called industrial revolutions. In the eleventh and twelfth centuries, for example, the combined large-scale innovations of efficient waterwheels, transom-located ship rudders, and improved yokes that dramatically increased the pull weight of horses and oxen laid the foundation for hundreds of new technologies that dramatically improved steel making, construction, agricultural yields, and ocean trade, leading to the greatest economic growth seen to date in Europe. Similarly, the steam engine innovations in the seventeenth and eighteenth centuries created the industrial revolution that gave us waves of new technologies, resulting in large factories, the mass production of products, railroads, and oceangoing steamships, technologies that changed society for ever. A couple hundred years later, the commercialization of the integrated circuit in the 1960s, and the modern technologies of AI and biotechnology are creating whole new classes of technologies, industries, and markets, allowing for space travel, mobile communication, and perhaps even cures for the most deadly cancers in the near future. This is the nature of applied and translational research. It is constant and continuous, but occasionally with historical waves of even greater productivity.

Technology Features and Benefits

As future developers of products based on emerging technological discoveries, one must be able to look both inward and outward. By focusing on the insights one can derive from science, developers must consider what technical features can be translated from emerging scientific discoveries into new product design. However, it is just as important to focus on the needs of your target market segment. As you envision emerging product design, you must also consider what benefits can be offered to future customers in your target market segment.

Technical Features

Product technical features represent key design elements that enable new capabilities and functionalities that can be incorporated into a product design. Product features define what a product can do and how effectively it can perform its desired functions. Features stem from scientific principles, engineering enhancements, and/or material innovations. Think of product features as enablers. Given unique design elements, how might a product feature enhance product performance? In addition to speed and accuracy, various product features might be designed to improve a user's interface, leading to an enhanced user experience. Alternatively, product features also may serve to facilitate system integrations. In intermediate technologies that are generally sold as components in larger systems, these technical features are often referred to as "functionalities".

Product's technical features represent key design elements that enable new capabilities and functionalities that can be incorporated into a product design.

One example of a product feature stemming from research in material science is carbon fiber.[2] Thomas Edison originally used carbonized bamboo for filaments in developing incandescent light bulbs. However, further explorations into the properties of carbonized fiber by researchers such as Roger Bacon, during the 1950s and 1960s, produced materials that were strong, yet lightweight and durable. Researchers began to apply these properties to military applications in aircraft and space exploration. But soon, carbon fiber material started to be applied in a wide range of commercial applications, including bicycles, golf clubs, and even prosthetic limbs. Thus, when a manufacturer of golf clubs incorporates carbon fiber materials into the club design, it represents a unique feature of the club as compared to competitor clubs made from different materials.

Most products on the market today incorporate many features emanating from prior scientific research. Take, for example, today's smart watches. By incorporating many types of sensing devices into a single product design, modern smart watches can provide a way to measure and monitor numerous key vital bodily functions. An Apple watch, for example, can monitor a person's heart rate by incorporating photodiodes as a feature in product design. Pulse oximetry sensors, also incorporated in a smart watch, can measure a person's blood oxygen levels. Additionally, ambient light sensors enable the watch to adjust the display's brightness based on prevailing lighting conditions. Each of these features, along with many others, enable today's smart watches to perform a wide array of different functions.[3]

Feature Creep. However, while envisioning an end product emanating from an emerging technology, developers must also be mindful of the tendency toward overdesign. During the development process, it can become tempting for developers to strive to add more and more features into an emerging new product. This phenomenon is commonly referred to as "feature creep",[4] or the tendency to continuously add new capabilities that, while impressive from an engineering standpoint, may not align with customer needs or market demand.

Feature creep is one of the most common challenges that can inhibit the technology commercialization process. Feature creep is essentially defined as adding excessive features or functionalities, beyond the original scope of the planned technology, or beyond what customers actually use in their decision-making process. Feature creep leads to technologies that are too complex, cost more than was planned, and adds additional development time to bring the product to market. Feature creep can even kill a perfectly good design.

An example of the feature creep phenomenon can be found in the development of smart refrigerators. While the main function of a refrigerator is the preservation of food, developers have continued to add new features such as touchscreens, cameras, inventory monitors, and communication systems. These additional features, while attractive to perhaps some small segments of the market, will most likely result in an end product that is more complex and pricier than required by the primary market.

Often feature creep is a result of "scope creep", which is, attempting to target multiple distinct sub-markets, each with different functionality requirements, but with the same product. That might have worked with Henry Ford's original mass-produced black Model-T in the early 1900s, but those days are long gone.

Feature creep is typically driven by three sources: marketing teams eager to expand into additional market segments, engineering teams motivated by the challenge of adding new functionalities, and flawed Voice of the Customer analyses that fail to prioritize which technical features truly matter to buyers. But in the end, feature creep is a management problem.

Clearly, while features emanating from prior scientific research provide the foundation of most commercialized products, they must be designed with the end-user in mind to ensure that they translate into tangible benefits that address real customer needs.

To avoid delaying market entry and risking the loss of white-space opportunities, developers often consider the concept of a minimum viable product (MVP) – a version of the product, with just enough features to satisfy early adopters. By focusing on core functionality and customer priorities, teams can streamline development and ensure the product reaches the market with maximum impact and minimal delay.

Product Benefits

The process of figuring out how scientific advances can benefit particular segments of customers, represents the essence or reason why we focus on efforts related to technology commercialization. For applied researchers and developers, it is critical that they visualize who would use their technology and how the technology might help them to better meet their needs.

Thus, if product features represent the enablers of product performance, then product benefits represent the "why". While the critical "why" for basic researchers is the advancement of knowledge within a field, the critical "why" for applied researchers and developers is based on how particular customer segments might use the technology for personal or commercial benefit.

This notion of product benefits is commonly referred to as "value proposition". The stronger the value proposition, the more compelling it is for developers and those stakeholders who support the developers, to pump additional time and resources into the commercialization effort. A clear and supportable value proposition is now almost a requirement for any development plan, whether for internal review by a major corporation or an entrepreneur pitching to a group of angel investors.

Value propositions represent the unique benefits a product or service offers to specific target market segments. For early-stage technology developers and innovators, the challenge lies in identifying market applications where their emerging technologies can deliver meaningful advantages to potential customers. Successfully defining a compelling value proposition requires aligning technological capabilities with actual customer needs, ensuring that the innovation provides clear, tangible benefits that make it attractive and market-ready.

Many such benefits offer incremental improvements over the value that customers are currently experiencing, based on the availability of existing products or services in the market. Incremental improvements might include speed, accuracy, lower cost, higher quality, or customer experience. An example of a new technology that offers incremental advantages over existing products and processes might include AI powered chatbots that can be used in customer service. Such bots can provide quicker response times to customer inquiries and lower operational costs to companies. Another example might be 5G wireless networks that can offer customers higher internet speeds and improved reliability.

Other emerging technologies might offer "brave new world" advantages to customers that enable them to do things that have never been done before. Examples of radical new technologies might include the emerging field of brain-to-computer interface (BCI) technologies.[5] Emerging technologies in this space have the potential of offering disabled individuals the ability to control devices and communicate with others using only their thoughts. Clearly, these types of applications represent advanced capabilities for users that could never have been imagined before.

Bridging Technology Development with Market Opportunity

For researchers and developers seeking to identify market applications for their emerging technologies, the journey from scientific discovery to market success requires more than just technical expertise. Just as important, this journey requires that the developer have a strategic vision for how the technology might be used in actual market applications. By identifying future applications for an emerging technology, developers can craft compelling narratives that attract funding and support, helping to advance the technology toward market readiness. Such narratives might be based around answering the following fundamental questions for a potential given market application:

- Who do you envision will benefit from having access to the features enabled by your technology?
- What problem will your technology features solve for them?
- Are there enough potential customers in the market space to make it worthwhile for the developers to continue investing time, energy, and resources into the commercialization effort?
- Will the improvement enabled by the technology be strong and compelling enough to entice customers to want to pay for it?
- How does the technology improve upon existing solutions, if any, in the market?
- What features are necessary to deliver the promised benefits?

A persuasive narrative, based on answers to the above questions, can help researchers to communicate the value of their work to potential stakeholders. An effective narrative can thereby demonstrate how technical features will create market impact. The ability to convey the idea through a story about the envisioned capabilities of a new technology is vital not only for securing funding but also for guiding strategic decisions throughout the product development life cycle.

Successful technology commercialization efforts always require a balance between technical innovation and the practicality of future customer needs and desires.

In general, successful technology commercialization efforts require a balance between technical innovation and the practicality of future customer needs and desires. It is important for developers to remain focused on technical innovations that mesh with identifiable market benefits.

Pivots and Technology Leveraging: The Need for Adaptability

Introducing a new technology or product to the market is rarely a smooth transition. Early-stage product introductions are built on a series of assumptions – about customer needs, market demand, and the effectiveness of the solution. While some assumptions may prove accurate, others may not resonate with customer needs or desires. Sometimes, the design team simply can't make the original vision of the technology work properly.

When market feedback runs counter to a developer's initial assumptions about anticipated buying and use behavior of target market customers, they must be willing to adapt. When the design team throws their hands up in frustration, saying the product can't be created with current knowhow, then applications and features may need to be reconsidered. This is where the concept of pivots becomes critical. A pivot is a deliberate shift in commercialization strategy, in response to new insights about the market, customers, or product performance.[6] It is the process of finding the "white space" in an oftentimes crowded market. Commercialization strategy pivots can take many forms, including but not limited to changes in product form and function, target market segments, value proposition, channels, and revenue streams.

Product Form Factor Pivots

A form factor pivot may be necessary when the physical design, shape, or structural features of an early-stage product are modified based on market feedback about usability concerns. This type of a pivot is often necessary when the original design proves too bulky, uncomfortable, impractical, or misaligned with user expectations. This is usually the case when developers first create a prototype of their envisioned product or service. They will have to continue to refine the product's form factor until it better aligns with the desired user experiences. Continued refinement in form factor is necessary in order to ultimately drive wider adoption. A form factor pivot is not about changing the core technology but rather adapting how it is packaged and delivered to better fit actual customer use cases.

An illustrative example of a form factor pivot is GoPro's early shift from helmet-mounted cameras designed for extreme sports to more compact, handheld, and stick-mounted devices.[7] While the original design targeted niche action sports users, broader adoption required a less cumbersome form that casual users could easily carry. This pivot in form factor opened up mass market appeal for travelers, vloggers, and everyday consumers, helping to establish GoPro as a global brand.

Product Function Pivots

When trying to assess performance requirements for an emerging technology, developers often must guess about the ideal speed, accuracy, and sensitivity of their product. Preliminary market research can offer insights into these requirements, helping developers compare customer expectations with the product's current capabilities. If significant gaps exist, a product function pivot may be necessary, requiring technical redesigns to better align performance with customer needs.

A classic example of a product function pivot involves Apple's introduction of SIRI into iPhones in 2011.[8] Among other technologies, SIRI was based on emerging voice recognition technology, designed for hands-free interaction between the user and a device. But as can be imagined, earlier versions of this service struggled with accuracy, speed, and adapting to different background noise. These issues led to much frustration among users experiencing the new technology. Post introduction, Apple continued to make improvements based on emerging machine learning and natural language technologies.

Clearly, early-stage technology developers cannot be expected to perfect a product's form and function from the outset. At some point in the development process, they must weigh the costs and benefits of when to introduce the product to the market. Should they wait until they achieve a "perfect" version, or should they launch earlier to gather real-world market feedback?

This decision is particularly challenging for perfectionists, who may be hesitant to release a product before it meets their ideal standards. However, waiting too long can increase development costs, delay revenue generation, and risk losing market opportunities. Alternatively, launching too soon may lead to poor user adoption if key functionalities are missing. Striking the right balance between early market entry and continued refinement is a critical aspect of successful product commercialization.

Target Market Segment Pivots

A target market segment pivot occurs when the initially envisioned customer base does not turn out to be the best fit for a product. While the product may gain some market traction with early adopters, further market insights may reveal that other customer segments derive greater value from the offering. In such cases, it may be more strategic and profitable to redirect product development and marketing efforts toward a more receptive segment or an entirely new industry application.

These pivots often stem from real-world customer feedback, sales data, or unexpected use cases that emerge after product launch. Sometimes, the original market proves too niche, with not enough upside potential to sustain future growth. Other issues such as cost sensitivity, or resistance to change, may encourage developers to explore new possible use cases. Successful companies continuously assess where their product generates the most value and shift focus accordingly. Clearly, understanding the true "sweet spot" in the market requires rigorous customer discovery, data analysis, and flexibility to adapt sales, marketing, and distribution strategies to the most promising opportunities.

An example of a target market pivot can be found in the case of the development of a drug called "Relaxin" by the biotech company Genentec.[9] The company's researchers focused on the challenges that women face during childbirth. The Genentech team thought that if they could develop a pharmaceutical compound that could relax the ligaments surrounding the muscle used in delivery, they could ease the birthing process.

But for a host of reasons, both technical and market related, this early-stage project was not enjoying any market traction. As a response, Genentech decided to license the rights to the technology to BAS Medical. The BAS Medical team believed that they could redefine the product as an orthodontic drug that could soften the ligaments around teeth, thus making it easier and faster for braces to move them. But again, this market application did not take off.

It wasn't until one of the founders hypothesized that there might be an application in treating heart failure patients during surgery. The drug could relax the heart muscles, thereby making it easier for surgeons to execute their procedures. Thus, it was not until this final pivot that the product finally found a pathway into the market. Based on this application, they renamed the effort "Corthera" and successfully developed the product; Corthera was finally sold to Novartis for a significant sum.

Value Proposition Pivots

A value proposition pivot occurs when a product developer revises their initial assumption about the primary benefit their target customers seek – and are willing to pay for. Early in the technology development process, this assumption is often just an educated guess. However, accurately identifying the value proposition is crucial for effective communication with the target market.

A common challenge arises when developers focus on the wrong perceived benefit. For example, they might assume that cost is the primary driver of customer decision-making and tailor their messaging accordingly. However, through customer feedback, they may discover that buyers are actually more concerned with speed, precision, or another performance attribute. By recognizing and adapting to these insights early in the product life cycle, developers can refine both the product and its positioning to better align with customer needs.

A well-executed value proposition pivot enhances not only product – market fit but also competitive advantage. It allows the company to allocate resources more efficiently, avoid wasted marketing efforts, and ultimately improve adoption rates. The key is to remain open to feedback, systematically test assumptions, and iterate quickly based on real customer data.

A classic example of a value proposition pivot can be found in the story of Slack. In 2011, the founder Stuart Butterfield put together a team to create a company called Tiny Speck. Their main product was a multiplayer online gaming platform called Glitch. The envisioned value proposition focused on offering a unique, non-violent gaming experience that emphasized creativity, exploration, and social interaction. As part of the offering, the game included an internal communication tool for team collaboration.

Unfortunately, the game did not gain significant traction in the market. However, the team noticed that the internal communication tool was highly effective and resonated with their customers. Believing that this feature constituted a new opportunity based on a completely different value proposition, they shifted the entire focus of the company, leading to a rebranding of the company to Slack.[10] The new value proposition focused on enhancing workplace productivity by offering a centralized hub where teams can communicate, share files, and collaborate efficiently. This pivot from a gaming product to a communication platform was driven by observing user behavior and identifying a more valuable application of their technology.

Channel Pivots

When launching a new product, developers typically have assumptions about the best way to reach their target customers. Channels refer to the pathways through which a company delivers its product or service and facilitates the exchange with customers. These channels significantly impact customer access, experience, and overall business model execution.

Examples of common channels for retail technologies include:

- Online stores – where the exchange occurs over the internet via e-commerce platforms, direct-to-consumer websites, or marketplaces like Amazon or Shopify.
- Brick-and-mortar locations – where customers visit a physical store to purchase the product.
- Direct sales teams – where a company's salesforce actively engages potential buyers, often in B2B or high-touch sales environments.
- Independent distributors or retail partnerships – where third parties handle product distribution and sales on behalf of the company.

However, companies often discover that their initially chosen channel is not the most effective way to reach their audience. A channel pivot occurs when a company shifts its primary distribution method to better align with customer behavior, preferences, and purchasing patterns.

Channel pivots may be required when a company that originally plans to sell exclusively through retail stores may find that customers prefer the convenience of direct online purchases. Alternatively, a startup that begins with a self-managed e-commerce approach might pivot to selling through third-party marketplaces after realizing that acquiring customers directly is too costly or inefficient.

The choice of channel for introducing an emerging technology into the marketplace has many important considerations that must be taken into account. Four critical areas to consider include ease of customer access, cost efficiency, scalability, and customer experience. Each of these considerations can significantly impact customer receptivity for new product introductions. A well-executed channel pivot can unlock new growth opportunities and significantly improve market penetration. The key is to remain agile, test assumptions early, and continuously evaluate how customers prefer to engage with the product or service.

An example of a channel pivot is captured in the Netflix story.[11] The company's original business model focused on providing a DVD rental service, whereby customers could place an order and receive DVDs via the mail. But this process was slow and cumbersome because of the time lag between ordering a movie and ultimately being able to watch it. However, as streaming technology advanced and customers began to demand instant content, the company needed to adapt its distribution strategy. By setting up a subscription-based streaming platform, the company now allows its customers to access their vast library online. This channel shift pivot enabled the company to position themselves as a leader in the digital entertainment industry.

Revenue Stream Pivots

A revenue stream represents the method by which a developer monetizes an innovative technology. At its core, a developer has several primary options for generating revenue:

- **Licensing:** The developer grants another company the rights to use the technology in a commercial application. This can involve a one-time licensing fee or an ongoing royalty structure based on product sales or usage. The licensing agreement may cover a broad market application or be restricted to a specific industry or geographic region.
- **Service-Based Model:** The developer introduces the technology as a service rather than a stand-alone product. Customers pay for access to the technology either as a one-time service fee or through a recurring subscription model (e.g., Software-as-a-Service or SaaS).
- **Product Commercialization:** The developer arranges for the manufacture, distribution, and sales of the product directly to customers. This approach involves handling production, supply chain logistics, sales, and customer support, making it more resource-intensive but potentially more lucrative.

Each of these revenue models carries significant implications for the overall business model, affecting factors such as capital requirements, scalability, and customer engagement. Early in the commercialization process, developers make assumptions about which revenue stream best aligns with customer preferences and business viability. However, real-world market feedback often reveals a more effective path. Accordingly, a revenue stream pivot occurs when a company shifts its primary method of monetization based on these insights.

A revenue stream pivot often overlaps with other types of pivots, such as market or channel pivots. For example, shifting from a B2B to B2C model often changes how the company earns revenue (i.e., moving from enterprise licensing to individual subscriptions) but it also impacts the target customer, delivery channels, and product support. In this case, it is the shift in monetization logic that defines the revenue pivot, even though it may be accompanied by broader strategic changes.

This pivot might also involve transitioning from a one-time product sale to a subscription-based model to generate more predictable recurring revenue. Or, the pivot might involve a shift from an upfront payment model to usage-based billing, in response to customer feedback. By remaining flexible and continuously assessing market feedback, developers can pivot to a more effective revenue strategy that maximizes customer adoption, competitive positioning, and long-term profitability.

A well-known example of a revenue stream pivot is the story of Duolingo, the language-learning platform.[12] In 2011, Duolingo began by offering free access to its courses to customers, while deriving revenue through advertisements. Over time, the company pivoted to an ad-free subscription-based model that proved to be more sustainable and profitable. As of June 2024, Duolingo reported having 8 million paying subscribers, contributing to revenue of $531 million in 2023, up from $250.77 million in 2021. The "freemium" model, where basic features are free but premium features require payment, has become a widely adopted strategy across digital platforms.

Technology Leveraging

Technology leveraging refers to the process of applying technological features and capabilities developed for one application to create or enhance related products, or even products in entirely different markets or industries. A key advantage of technology leveraging is that it can accelerate entry into new markets by repurposing existing technological advancements rather than developing new features from scratch. This approach not only reduces time and costs associated with R&D but also increases the return on investment for prior development efforts.

Technology leveraging refers to the process of applying technological features and capabilities developed for one application to create or enhance related products, or even products in entirely different markets or industries.

Technology leveraging differs from pivots, which are typically driven by unexpected challenges that force a shift in strategic focus. A pivot occurs when an initial market strategy is not gaining traction, prompting developers to explore alternative applications or business models, in search of a viable path to success.

By contrast, technology leveraging is additive. It involves expanding into new markets, without necessarily abandoning an existing one. Even when a technology is gaining traction in its initial target market, developers can explore ways to apply its core capabilities to unlock additional revenue streams in different industries. This strategic approach enables companies to diversify their market presence, reduce dependence on a single industry, and maximize the commercial potential of their technology.

One example of technology leveraging is the story of how the Black and Decker (B&D) company developed its very successful vacuum product known as the Dustbuster.[13] In the late 1960s, during NASA's preparation for landing a man on the moon, they had a need for a portable, wireless, and rechargeable drill that astronauts could use to gather moon samples to take back to earth. Since B&D was already working with General Electric on battery-powered technologies, they were awarded the contract from NASA to develop such a tool. To meet NASA's requirements, they accelerated their R&D

efforts to develop this tool. But beyond the space program, B&D began to explore other commercial applications for the underlying battery-powered technology they originally developed for the space drill. They ultimately developed the Dustbuster, a handheld portable and rechargeable vacuum for household use. They also used this same technology to create a variety of other products such as cordless drills and screwdrivers and battery-powered trimmers and leaf blowers.

Technology leveraging can also include leveraging the important asset of "experience". As a company starts producing a new technology, a key management question emerges – Is it possible to take a portion of the cumulative experience generated from a prior technological project and apply it to the new technology? Perhaps, a significant amount of design, engineering, prototyping, and production experience might transfer to the new technology. For a multiproduct development firm, transferring experience between projects needs to be a key focus of management. Experience can be transferred from prior projects, and between projects that are ongoing at the same time. If experience transfer or leveraging is possible, this means a new product will start lower on the experience curve, at a higher level of productivity, and at lower costs than competitive products, which cannot leverage the same amount of experience.[14] Figure 4.1 illustrates the cumulative advantage of technology leveraging.

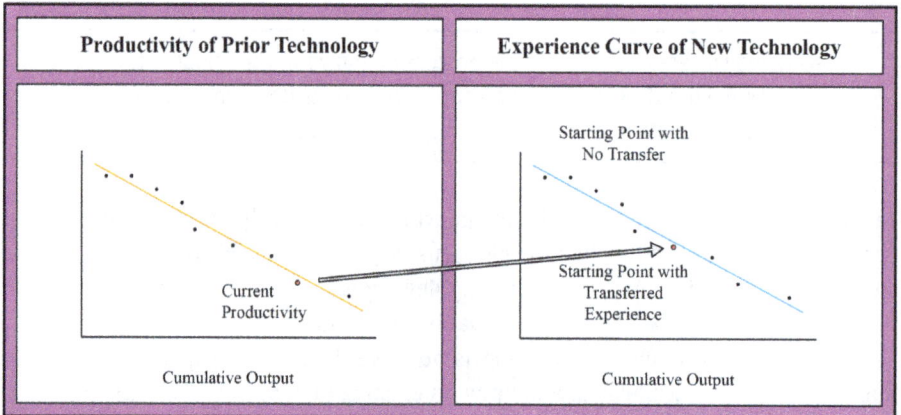

Figure 4.1: Cumulative advantage: How experience from one innovation drives success in another.

Best Practices for Pivoting

Every technology commercialization effort will assess the need to pivot at some time in the development process. Most pivots will likely be minor, but some might be major. Some pivots will be successful, and other pivots will fail. Oftentimes, pivoting means giving up what makes you good, to become even better. What are some of the best practices when considering the need to pivot?

Always Keep Pivoting in Mind. Don't get stuck in a typical narrow, myopic technology development process. Tunnel visioning is often an organizational mindset in the technology development process. Pivoting, however, is not an admission of failure, but rather seeking opportunity. Throughout the development process, senior managers need to keep asking, "what about a pivot?" Perhaps, they just need to keep the option open and in the conversation.

Pivot Sooner Rather Than Later. Pivoting means two things – the need to invest in a new direction, and the need to reduce investment in the old target. Much of the investment in the old approach needs to be considered a sunk cost. It is lost and there is nothing that can be done. But pivoting sooner than later saves money and creates opportunity sooner.

Leverage Prior Effort. Pivoting doesn't mean trashing all the prior time, effort, and investment. Not all prior investment needs to become a useless, sunk cost. Rather, create a formal strategy of leveraging as much prior knowledge, design, material, and experience as possible into the pivot.

Oftentimes, pivoting means giving up what makes you good, to become even better.

Validate the Need to Pivot. A pivot decision should not be made in a vacuum or by intuition. Validate the need to pivot through data, research, and talking with customers.

Develop a Formal Pivot Plan. The need to pivot can come from many different sources. But when it seems like a pivot might be necessary, create a formal plan. Initiate a new commercialization study or Voice of the Customer analysis. Hire outside consultants and analysts to look at the pivot opportunity to overcome any internal biases. Assign project responsibilities. Pivoting should be managed as a project, just like the original design path.

Develop Financial Models of the Pivot Strategy. Once a pivot decision is likely to be made, develop a financial model of the new approach. Make sure the revenue projections work and the cost of pivoting is incorporated.

Always Communicate Pivots. Customers, suppliers, internal management, consultants, and employees need to be informed about any pivots. They should not be caught by surprise after the fact.

Create Internal Pivot Incentives. Pivoting inevitably means changing directions. Some employees and stakeholders will celebrate the new opportunities. However, others might be emotionally tied to the old strategy. It is important to bring all stakeholders on board. This might involve creating incentives to change orientation and behaviors.

Don't Give Up Too Soon with the Old Approach. It is often easy to "abandon a sinking ship" and jump into a new direction, particularly if the old approach is having problems. But you always need to carefully understand whether the old approach is really a dead end, or perhaps it just wasn't being managed properly in the first place. Validate all decisions. Perhaps, both the old approach and the new pivot might work in conjunction with each other. This is always the tension with pivoting, finding the right balance between waiting too long, versus changing too soon before all options are tested.

Use Best Practices to Facilitate a Successful Pivot. A number of tools can be brought to bear to identify and validate the need to pivot. These are discussed throughout this book. Technology commercialization studies, Voice of the Customer analysis, project management risk analysis, phased-review processes, and pro forma development are just a few of the managerial tools that need to be used to identify the need to pivot and successfully manage moving into new directions.

Concluding Insights

This chapter explored the transition from basic research, which focuses on expanding scientific knowledge without immediate commercial intent, to applied research, where discoveries are transformed into real-world solutions. While basic research lays the foundation for innovation, applied researchers must determine how emerging technologies can be developed into products that deliver tangible benefits to specific market segments.

The commercialization journey involves balancing technical features (the enablers of functionality) with product benefits (the value delivered to customers). However, the path from idea to market success is rarely linear. Developers often need to pivot – whether by adjusting product design, refining the target market, rethinking the value proposition, or shifting distribution channels and revenue models based on real-world feedback. Additionally, technology leveraging offers opportunities to extend innovations into new markets, increasing their commercial potential beyond their initial intended use.

Ultimately, successful commercialization requires both adaptability and strategic foresight. Developers must continuously test their assumptions, listen to market feedback, and remain open to refining their approach. By combining scientific discovery with market-driven innovation, early-stage technologies can evolve into impactful, commercially viable products that shape industries and improve lives.

Chapter Example: Finding the Right Market and Partnering with a System Integrator – Lumedyne Technologies

The Challenge

Brad Chisum began his career as a Photolithography Process Engineer at San Diego-based Spawar, a Department of Defense (DoD) government laboratory, working on advanced sensor technologies.[15] While the work was cutting-edge, it was largely confined to research, with little consideration of commercialization outside of military applications. That changed when a colleague, Dr. Richard Waters, casually remarked that if a particular sensor product he was working on, succeeded, *"we'd all be millionaires"*.

At the time, Brad had no knowledge of technology transfer or how government-funded research could transition into commercial applications. His curiosity led him to chat with the Tech Transfer Office at Spawar, where he realized that turning a technology into a viable business would require identifying a promising market and securing industry partnerships.

The Solution

The first challenge was determining which industries would benefit most from the sensor technology. While aerospace and defense were obvious applications, those industries were dominated by well-established players with strong patent protections. After extensive research, Brad identified the oil and gas industry, where advanced seismic sensors were needed for exploration.

This industry posed a unique opportunity because:
- Oil and gas companies had a history of funding early-stage R&D.
- Existing solutions were locked under exclusive patents, leaving competitors searching for alternatives.
- A more advanced sensor could provide a competitive advantage in seismic imaging.

To validate his assumptions, Brad conducted extensive secondary research, utilizing Frost & Sullivan reports and industry publications. However, he quickly realized that real market insights would only come from direct conversations with potential customers and system integrators.

Early Interest, but a Setback

One of Brad's first major breakthroughs came when he secured early interest from a major player in the seismic imaging industry. The company saw potential in the sensor and agreed to a preliminary contract, giving Lumedyne Technologies an initial path to market.

However, despite the company's initial enthusiasm, the contract ultimately fell through due to internal corporate issues, unrelated to the technology or Brad's efforts. While disappointing, this setback forced Brad to find other avenues to ultimately gain entry into the market.

Breaking into the Market

One of the biggest hurdles in commercializing an emerging technology is getting the attention of system integrators (companies that design and build larger systems using multiple components). In Brad's case, seismic imaging companies were the key system integrators for his accelerometer technology.

Strategies for Market Entry

Networking through Business Plan Competitions:
> While working on his MBA at San Diego State University, Brad entered multiple university-based business plan and modeling competitions. At the Rice Business Plan Competition, he met an industry judge, who introduced him to key executives in the seismic imaging sector.

Leveraging Government Research Initiatives:
> He examined Small Business Innovation Research (SBIR) and Broad Agency Announcements (BAA) solicitations to understand funding opportunities and industry needs.

Gaining Credibility through a Research Institution:
> A research team at Lawrence Berkeley National Laboratory, was searching for a small-form-factor sensor, with the capabilities that Brad and Richard's technology could offer. This unexpected validation gave Lumedyne Technologies credibility and helped open doors to major industry players.

Building Strategic Relationships:
> Through persistent networking, Brad secured introductions to decision-makers at key system integrator companies, ultimately leading to fruitful strategic partner relationships.

Strategic Insights

Although Brad didn't pivot away from the seismic imaging market, his commercialization path involved channel and value proposition pivots. The early setback with a major corporate partner underscored the limitations of relying on a single customer channel, particularly when dealing with large, bureaucratic organizations. Brad's eventual success came from repositioning the technology as a modular, integratable solution that smaller system integrators and research labs could deploy with minimal barriers.

By shifting his strategy to focus on mid-tier integrators, research collaborators, and government-funded technical use cases, Brad opened new pathways to market validation. This pivot in engagement model allowed Lumedyne to gain traction and build the trust needed for broader commercial partnerships.

Actionable Steps

If you are a technology developer looking to commercialize a research-based innovation through system integrators, consider these steps:

Identify potential markets where your technology's features create clear value.

Conduct deep secondary research (market reports, industry publications, SBIR solicitations, etc.) to understand industry trends.

Engage directly with system integrators through competitions, networking, and warm introductions.

Leverage credibility-building opportunities (research partnerships, government programs, pilot projects, etc.) to gain trust.

Be ready to pivot when initial deals don't go through.

By following these steps, developers can navigate the commercialization process more effectively and successfully bridge the gap between innovation and market adoption.

Chapter 5
Intellectual Property: Why Is It Important?

This Chapter

- Highlights the importance of establishing and protecting intellectual property (IP) as a core component of the commercialization process.
- Outlines the major types of IP – including patents, trade secrets, trademarks and copyrights – and their relevance to technology ventures.
- Summarizes the basic steps for securing patent protection, both domestically and internationally.
- Introduces tools for safeguarding early-stage IP, such as non-disclosure agreements and provisional patent applications.

Key Management Tools and Best Practices

- Toolbox for protecting against misappropriation of trade secrets
- Best practice insight that intellectual property, and its protection, is developed all through the whole development process, not just once

! INSIGHT

Intellectual Property, or "IP", is at the foundation of any commercialization process. By its very nature, technologies inevitably involve discussions of ownership, how to establish ownership, and how to protect this ownership. These are the key issues of intellectual property. After all, ideas are what become innovations, and it is these innovations that ultimately become technologies. Just like any physical assets, before something can be commercially used, licensed, sold, or funded, ownership should be established. But not everything can be patented, so other strategies are often necessary.

Introduction

Technology inherently involves the concept of intellectual property, often referred to as "IP". Everybody understands the nature of ownership over physical assets. Houses, cars, and boats all have titles and deeds to indicate ownership. When somebody purchases machinery, equipment, or inventory, there is an assumption that the seller has ownership of these items, and the right to this ownership is transferred to the buyer. Nobody would purchase a car from somebody that did not have the right to sell that car. No bank is going to finance the purchase of a house without a clean title. It is theoretically no different in the world of technology. In practice, however, the ownership and protection of technologies, and the underlying intellectual property, is much more complicated.

While technologies, like a computer, phone, or tractor, are often seen as physical assets to the end user, the knowledge, innovations, programming, and designs that

https://doi.org/10.1515/9783111684420-006

are embedded in these technologies and make them work, are inevitably based on somebody's intellectual effort. This is the key to the notion of intellectual property. The U.S. State Department defines intellectual property as embodying "unique work reflecting someone's creativity". Similarly, the World Intellectual Property Organization (WIPO) defines intellectual property as "creations of the mind, such as inventions; literary and artistic works; designs; and symbols, names and images used in commerce".

In general, one can establish ownership of IP through patents, trademarks, copyrights, and trade secrets. However, not all creative ideas can be protected in this manner. In many situations, important innovations such as the logic behind a rule or a medical procedure cannot be formally protected by patents. In other situations, it might be too early to patent a design still undergoing development. In many cases, an entrepreneur might simply want to keep the creative backbone of their core technology a secret, hidden from their competitors. Of course, there is always the threat of intellectual property theft, where somebody reverse engineers a successful design that has been patented, and then markets their own version of the technology under their brand name.

Intellectual property is developed throughout the whole technology development process, not just as a one-time event.

All technology developers need to realize that intellectual property is developed throughout the whole technology development process, not just as a one-time event. This requires overlaying the technology development cycle with the different types of intellectual property, and the life cycle of each type of IP. It also requires constant communication with your IP team.

These issues are critical, and the focus of this chapter. We discuss three main methods of protecting intellectual property – patents, trademarks, and copyrights. We also discuss the notion of trade secrets, and how trade secrets can become an important component of protecting ideas in the highly competitive world of technologies. In addition, since patenting is often time-consuming and expensive, and many times, not even possible, it is also important to understand the use of other IP protection strategies, such as non-disclosure agreements and provisional patent applications.

Finally, the development and protection of intellectual property must always be considered strategically. For example, do we patent our technology in just one particular country, such as the United States, or do we want to obtain patent coverage for all countries? What are the strategic differences between platform technologies versus technologies with very narrow applications? How do I strategically consider the hazards of intellectual property theft? Can I, or a licensee, afford to enforce and protect patents?

An Important but Short History of IP Protection

Every country in the world now has mechanisms and institutions to protect intellectual property. For some countries, this protection dates back centuries, while for many other countries, IP protection is a relatively new concept.

The first modern patent appears to have been granted in Tuscany, in 1421, to an engineer who designed a crane system for moving marble blocks during the construction of a Florence cathedral. In England, the first recorded patent was granted in 1449 by King Henry IV. This patent gave John of Utynam, a 20-year monopoly for a technique to make stained glass.

During these earlier times, the granting of patents and copyrights was essentially an ad hoc activity, where various monarchs issued "letters" that granted monopolies related to new techniques to individuals or organizations. The Venetian Patent Statute of 1474 is often referred to as the earliest codified system of patent laws in the world. However, England's 1624 Statute of Monopolies, by defining the duration of patent protection, granting exclusive rights for "novel" inventions, and assigning those rights to the "true and first inventors", more closely reflects modern intellectual property principles. Similarly, the 1710 Statute of Anne, was the first comprehensive governmental statute for granting specific lengths of copyright protection to authors and publishers.

For the United States, protection of intellectual property is clearly laid out in the U.S. Constitution of 1788. James Madison, along with Charles Pinkney of South Carolina, was instrumental in addressing intellectual property during the writing of the U.S. Constitution. Their efforts resulted in Article 1, Section 8, Clause 8 of the U.S. Constitution, which specifically grants Congress the power "to promote the Progress of Science and useful Arts, by securing for limited times to authors and Inventors the exclusive right to their respective writings and discoveries".

This clause was adopted without objection, perhaps because many of the "Founding Fathers" in the United States were not only entrepreneurs and farmers, but also active inventors themselves. Thomas Paine, for example, developed a smokeless candle and made significant contributions to the design of iron bridges. Thomas Jefferson was a prolific inventor, which included a mechanical cipher wheel, swivel chairs, and many other gadgets. Benjamin Franklin, of course, designed the lighting rod and bifocal lenses for glasses. Even George Washington was known for architectural innovations to increase efficiency in processing grain.

Article 1, Section 8, Clause 8 is now known as the "intellectual property clause" in the U.S. Constitution. In response, the U.S. Congress passed the first patent statute in 1790, which designated a "Patent Board", made up of the Secretary of State, the Secretary of War, and the U.S. Attorney General, who had the responsibility to review and issue patents. Due to the increasing number of applications, in 1802, the U.S. established a separate patent office. Subsequent Congressional efforts, particularly the Patent Act of 1836, established the more modern process of examining prior inventions for originality and a patent numbering system, which continues to modern times.

While the U.S. established the first modern patent office in 1802, it has been well recognized throughout history that creators should be rewarded with some type of ownership over their intellectual property. Copyright protection, for example, has a much longer history, dating to Ancient Greece and Rome, where legal protections were sometimes granted for specific written items, such as food recipes and manuscripts.

Intellectual property disputes involving copyrights were also recorded during the Middle Ages, with one of the most notable conflicts between two important figures in the early Christian Church, St. Columba and St. Finnian in Ireland. Sometime around 560, St. Columba is reported to have copied a manuscript belonging to St. Finnian's monastery. The issue became who owned the copy – St. Columba, who put in the time and effort to hand copy the manuscript or St. Finnian, who created the original manuscript?

This ultimately required an arbitration hearing by Irish King Diarmait MacCerbhaill, who is reported to have said, "to every cow belongs her calf, therefore to every book belongs its copy", thus ruling in favor of St. Finnian. St. Columba evidently took issue with this ruling, and according to legend, instigated a successful rebellion of his clan members against the King. This ultimately resulted in the battle of Cul Dreimhne in 561, also known as the "Battle of the Books.[1]" While this story may be more legend than fact, it certainly underlines the interest in intellectual property issues during this time.

Patents and copyrights are, of course, obvious components of intellectual property. Other forms of intellectual property, such as trade secrets and trademarks, appeared later in development. By the mid-nineteenth century, the U.S. started to take the lead in developing modern IP standards.

After the Civil War, the United States underwent rapid industrialization and western expansion. During this period, the extraordinary productivity of nineteenth-century inventors such as Thomas Edison, Samuel Morse, Alexander Graham Bell, and Nikola Tesla, highlighted the growing connection between intellectual property and economic development. Courts and lawmakers in the U.S. quickly recognized the need to have broader definitions of intellectual property.

For example, in a series of cases in 1879, the U.S. Supreme Court fully recorded that Congress was authorized under the Copyright and Patent Clause to secure "the fruits of intellectual labor" in not only patents and copyrights, but also trademarks. These cases, now known as the "trademark cases", specifically extended the protection of intellectual property law to trademarks registered with the Patent Office. This was an important development, since unlike patents and copyrights, trademarks, according to the U.S. Supreme Court's opinions, "have no necessary relation to invention or discovery" (100 U.S. at 94), but they are "important instrumentalities, aids, or appliances by which trade, especially in modern times, is conducted" (100 U.S. at 9).

With respect to trade secrets, in the United States, both the *Vickery v. Welch* (1837) case involving a chocolate making formula and the *Peabody v. Norfolk* (1868) case, where an employee stole the process of making burlap in order to set up a competitive business, are cited as the key early court cases that established trade secrets as a form of

IP protection in modern terms. Protecting trade secrets became increasingly important in the nineteenth century as competitors started to "reverse engineer" successful inventions or copy designs, when they were published in patent applications. This encouraged many inventors and entrepreneurs to keep key parts of their formulas, designs, and processes a trade secret.

For example, the Coca-Cola formula was invented in 1886 by Dr. John S. Pemberton and has been kept as a trade secret under lock and key ever since. The QWERTY keyboard was designed around 1872 by the inventor of the typewriter, Christopher Sholes, but the real logic behind the QWERTY keyboard has been kept a secret until recently. Unlike most countries, in the United States, individual States regulate trade secret law independently, while patents, copyrights, and trademarks are generally covered more under Federal law.

By the end of the nineteenth century, both U.S. courts and the U.S. lawmakers saw intellectual property under a much broader definition, including not only patents and copyrights, but also trade secrets and trademarks, as having foundational economic, moral, and legal justification. This broader perspective of intellectual property has now been adopted by most countries throughout the world as well as by international institutions, such as the UN and the World Intellectual Property Organization (WIPO). This broader definition has become even more important, with the introduction of new technologies. These include biotechnology and recombinant DNA methods, pharmaceutical compounds, non-naturally occurring biological organisms, complex integrative computer code, and generative AI tools, all of which are now deeply embedded in modern society.

Patenting

A patent essentially represents a temporary ownership of an invention, combined with a monopoly right to exploit that invention. During the term of the patent, normally 20 years from the original filing date, the owner of the patent has the right to exclude the actions of others related to the protected subject described in the patent. These actions include the manufacturing, commercialization, and use of the described intellectual property. Since patents are issued by countries, this temporary right to exclude applies only within the country that issued the patent. It is important to note that patent offices do not investigate or prosecute patent violators; patent offices are not a police force. Instead, the right to exclude, granted by a patent, allows the patent holder to pursue their own legal remedies in court.

Each country has its own patenting process, with a specific governmental office responsible for reviewing and issuing patents. In the United Kingdom, the patenting office is called the Intellectual Property Office; in Japan, the office is titled the Japan Patent Office; and in Brazil, the office responsible for patenting is the National Institute of Industrial Property (INPI).

The patenting process developed in the United States by the United States Patent and Trademark Office (USPTO) has long been considered the template for other countries, and almost all countries now follow a similar process.

The general process of obtaining a process, using the USPTO model, is shown below in Figure 5.1.

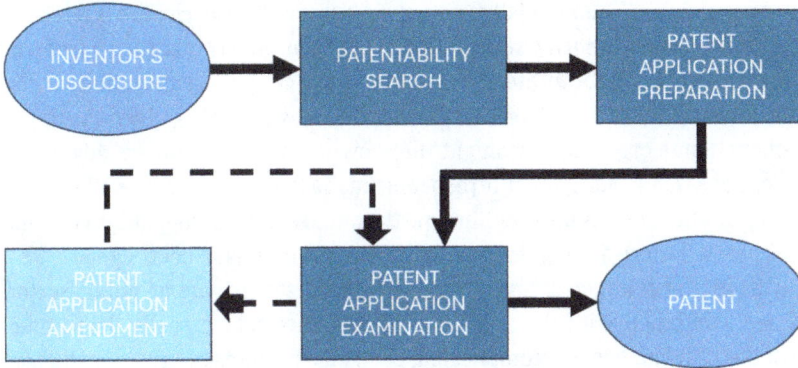

Figure 5.1: Basic steps for patent filing.

Inventor's Disclosure. Disclosure is not technically part of the governmental patenting process but still is an important step to understand. Anybody who is an employee, particularly technical employees, is likely to work under an employment contract. Almost always, these employment contracts state that the organization "owns", or at least has certain rights related to any intellectual property developed by somebody, while employed, provided the invention is related to the work an individual is hired to do.

It becomes a little more complicated for independent contractors. IP ownership might be spelled out in the contract. Without specific statements in employment or subcontractor contracts, there are general default rules. In the U.S., for copyrights, independent contractors typically own the rights to their copyrighted works, unless a written agreement states otherwise. In contrast, under the "work for hire" doctrine, employers generally own the copyright for works created by employees, provided the work was done within the scope of employment.

It tends to be a little different for patents, however. Absent any formal agreement, in the U.S., both independent contractors and employees would typically own the rights to their inventions. However, there are often exceptions to these general rules, such as when somebody is hired to solve a specific problem, uses the employer's resources, or develops a new technology using existing technology owned by the firm.

In other cases, the employee might own the IP, but the employer has a "shop right" to license the invention royalty-free. In addition, these rules can be different for different countries and often change as new laws are created, and new court decisions announced. This is why the vast majority of technology development firms, large and small, will (and should) have carefully crafted a specific IP ownership clause in their employment and contractor agreements. Given the complexity of IP ownership between employers, employees, and subcontractors in technology development firms, it is critically important to get advice from a qualified IP attorney when developing employment and contract agreements.

An inventor's disclosure is the process by which an employee or contractor reports a potentially patentable or commercially valuable invention. This disclosure is typically made to the appropriate authority, such as a university or government lab's technology transfer office (TTO), a corporate IP office, or, in the case of a small company, to senior management. The TTO or IP office can then decide what to do, given the applicable agreement. Some organizations might share ownership, while others might not. Some organizations might share the future income made from the patent, while others may not. Every organization is different in how they address this issue, but inventions should be disclosed if there are application IP agreements that have been signed.

When working for a larger organization, whether in the private or public sector, this is the step, combined with the applicable agreements, which really determines ownership of the IP. It can become complicated, particularly when an inventor changes employers midstream in the development process, when some of the development of the technology occurred at the earlier employer, and then is finished-up and patented at the new employer. Both parties might claim ownership. Inevitably, the technology transfer offices, IP offices, and attorneys will negotiate a shared agreement that defines ownership, the right to use the IP, and future royalties.

Patentability Search. In order to obtain a patent, there are some critical requirements. First, the invention must be "novel", or in other words, there is no "prior art" that discloses the exact same invention. Whether an invention is "novel", is open to a lot of debate. The word "art" is often used in the world of patenting, since specialized patent artists were often hired to draw the inventions for early patent applications. Second, the invention must be non-obvious to "one reasonably skilled" in the profession. Anybody can do a "keyword" search of the USPTO, or any other country's patent office website, to see if a design is unique enough, or if prior patents might have already covered the topic. Or, one can hire a specialized patent attorney to do the patentability search.

Patent Application. Patent applications can be complicated and need to follow the required strict formats. The keys to a patent application are the description of the invention and the claims that are made. Patent applications also reference prior patents that are relevant. There are also filing fees. Other than for very simple applications, specialized patent attorneys are generally employed at this stage.

Patent Application Examination. The patent office will then examine the patent application. In the modern world, patent offices are swamped with patent applications, many of which are highly complicated and technical in nature. In the United States, it generally takes 1 to 2 years for the patent office to respond. The patent office might accept the application as is, and issue a patent, but this is rare. In the United States, data over the years suggests that only about 10% to 20% of patent applications are accepted on the first round. More likely, the patent office will reject the application (with comments and reasons for the rejections). This is called an "office action". The two major reasons for rejections are that the invention is not considered new or novel, meaning prior patents or prior art already cover it, or that the invention is deemed obvious. About 20% of rejections are based on confusing or indefinite language. This type of rejection is probably the easiest to correct. It should be noted, however, that in general, only the claims can be changed, not the description. This is why it is important to have the patent application prepared by a qualified and experienced IP specialist.

Many entrepreneurs or technology developers might give up upon receiving their first "office action" rejection. After all, it is discouraging to be rejected. However, patent application rejections are very common in the world of patenting, and it simply means the applicant needs to address the issues identified by the office action.

Patent Application Amendments. The comments from the patent office might be addressed with simple changes, or more likely, they will require complex amendments. You have the right to respond, generally within a certain time limit, such as three months. If an Office Action is received, it is strongly advised to seek professional assistance in developing a response. There might be a number of reviews and subsequent amendments required in order to move the patent application through the process.

It can become complicated. For example, if there was subject matter that was taught in the original application but not claimed in the "allowed" application, the inventor/owner typically has a right in the U.S. to file a continuing application that would claim the previously unclaimed subject matter. However, a continuing application must be filed before the allowed claims are issued in a patent. But sometimes, it is simply a lost cause, and the patent application may ultimately need to be abandoned.

Patent Issue and Fees. Once the patent office is satisfied, the USPTO will issue a Notice of Allowance. This requires an additional fee, after which the patent will be issued. It is important to understand that most countries, including the U.S. require not only filing fees, but also maintenance fees at different intervals, such as 3.5, 7.5, and 11.5 years after the patent is granted. Small entities and businesses can often get a discount on fees. Many countries have annual payments.

Types of Patents

In the United States, there are three types of patents.

Utility Patents. Utility patents are what most people think of. These are for "inventing new or improved and useful processes, machines, articles of manufacture, or compositions of matter". The term of a utility patent in the U.S. is 20 years from the earliest filing date. This is typical of almost all countries. In general, patentable technologies fall under five categories

- Machines (something, using energy to complete a task)
- Process (a method of creating physical change in materials)
- Article of manufacture (physical objects that are created)
- Composition of matter (compound created by two or more elements)
- Improvements (new improvements of an existing invention)

In order to get a patent, ideas must be reduced to practice. However, modern technologies, such as computer programs, AI, and biotechnology have made the patentable v. non-patentable discussion very fuzzy, and patent offices and courts are constantly addressing these complex issues. While most patent rejections stem from the issue of originality, there are some categories of inventions that typically cannot be patented. These include:

- Laws of nature, such as gravity
- Abstract ideas, such as formulas or algorithms. However, applications of a formula or algorithm might be patentable. For example, the formula for creating specialized non-repeating patterns is not patentable; however, the paper product that uses this formula to prevent rolls from sticking to each other is patentable. This is also an issue with computer programs that use specialized algorithms. If the algorithm produces something usable, that might be patentable, even though the algorithm itself may not be patentable. However, software code that implements an algorithm can be protected by copyright.
- Using existing technologies, but simply presenting these technologies to the user in a new manner. For example, phone apps are sometimes difficult to patent. This is because many phone apps are not really new technologies but rather use existing technologies and spreadsheets to interface with users. Given their reliance on existing technologies and user interface conventions, simple phone apps are often rejected by the patent office due to the "novelty" and "obviousness'" requirements. However, some phone apps, or at least elements of them, can be patented. Patenting the different novel elements of a phone app appears to be the current strategy, rather than attempting to patent the complete app. For example, in 2022, Google patented their improved "drag and drop" feature used in many phone apps, while Zillow, Inc. has been very aggressive in filing, and very recently, receiving a number of patents, each for specific components and functions in their real estate phone app.
- Physical phenomena, even if newly discovered (e.g., the Northern Lights or a new type of magnetic field cannot be patented simply for being observed in nature).
- Naturally occurring products, such as minerals or plants. With the advent of modern biotechnology, this has created a lot of ambiguity. For example, discovering

a new plant that might have therapeutic properties may be difficult to patent since they are naturally occurring. However, using biotechnology to create new plants, animals, bacteria, or other biological components might be patentable. In addition, even if something is naturally occurring, such as a plant compound that has therapeutic value, if it needs to be specially purified to have value, or if the compound cannot survive in isolation, then it might be patentable.

– Inventions that have moral or ethical issues. Human cloning might fall under this restriction.

Design Patents. Design patents are for protecting new, original, and ornamental designs for articles of manufacture. For example, a design patent might be appropriate for a new design of an ornamental metal fence. The term of a design patent in the U.S. is 15 years from the grant date.

Plant Patents. Plant patents are for "inventing or discovering and asexually reproducing any distinct and new variety of plant". Thus, a new hybrid rose might be issued a plant patent. Plant patents are commonly used by breeders of flowers and agricultural products. The term of a plant patent in the U.S. is 20 years from the filing date.

First to Invent v. First to File

For hundreds of years, the overriding philosophy of intellectual property protection is that the first person to invent something should get the benefit of the patent. The "first-to-invent" concept is how the USPTO in the United States had been running for centuries. Over the past fifty years, as other countries attempted to catch up with the United States in technology development, many experts believed that a quicker path to economic growth could be obtained by a "first-to-file" patenting process.

These advocates argued that a "first-to-invent" process sounds good in theory but slows things down, as inventors "sit" on inventions and people end up fighting each other in court about who invented something first. The United States held out until 2013, when it finally changed to a "first-inventor-to-file" patent priority. A "first-inventor-to-file" process doesn't mean that somebody can steal, or otherwise illegally obtain an idea and then quickly file for a patent. Rather, it means that if people are working independently on a similar invention or discovery, the first inventor to file for the patent will generally be granted the patent.

A Freedom to Operate (FTO) Opinion

This is an important but often overlooked step in the early commercialization process. While a patent application is being developed or reviewed, an FTO can be performed by a qualified patent attorney. This provides an expert opinion about any potential infringement on other patents, and whether you can freely operate in the marketplace.

An FTO involves a complete search of prior or pending patents, and a careful analysis of their claims as to whether you have freedom to operate with your particular technology, and what the boundaries are. The FTO opinion is generally considered a "green light" to operate with the technology.[2] An FTO opinion is important when developing strategies around a key patent or attempting to license or commercialize your technology, prior to an actual patent being issued.

The "Freedom to Operate" opinion, or FTO is generally considered a "green light" to operate with the technology.

Patent attorneys that issue FTOs also use modern AI tools to constantly monitor patents, to see if any new developments might restrict your ability to operate with your technology. FTOs can also reduce exposures to certain liability costs if somebody sues. Many customers and integrators may require a FTO before they license or adopt a technology. Potential investors in start-up firms may also ask for an FTO if a patent has not yet been issued.

Global Variations and "Utility Model" Patents

While various international agreements on patents have tended to standardize the types and terms of patents, not all countries are the same. For utility patents, the World Trade Organization's (WTO) Agreement on Trade-Related Aspects of Intellectual Property Rights (TRIPs Agreement) specifies a 20-year term. All countries appear to use this 20-year term, although some countries have different rules for extending the term. Design patents, however, might have different terms and requirements, depending on the country.

In addition, some countries have different types of patents. One type, not seen in the United States and most developed countries, is the "utility model" patent. The idea of a utility model is to protect "incremental" or minor innovations. These are sometimes called "petty patents", "minor patents", "small patents", or "utility certificates".

Utility model patents have lower requirements for novelty and originality than regular patents but also come with a shorter life, typically between 6 years and 12 years. Currently, about 70 countries have some form of a utility model patent. In countries that offer utility model patents, it is generally not allowed to file for both a regular patent and a utility model patent. Utility model patents also only apply to the country that issues them.

Getting International Protection and the PCT

As previously discussed, patents are country-specific. Until recently, if somebody wanted to obtain patent protection in different countries, they would need to individually file in every country of interest. This was a very confusing and expensive process. In 1970, the Patent Cooperation Treaty (PCT) was developed and signed by 18 contracting countries, including the U.S. Currently, there are approximately 160 countries that operate under the PCT (see Figure 5.2).

Essentially, the PCT allows for the filing of a single patent application with a PCT member's country's patent office, declaring it as a PCT filing, and it will then be accepted as an application in the member countries (See Figure 5.3 for a map of the PCT member countries). There are several steps involved with a PCT filing.

1) International patent applications are initially filed with a "receiving office", which are typically the national patent offices, such as the USPTO. If not in violation with a country's security or export control requirements, a PCT application can also be filed directly with the World International Patent Organization (WIPO). In the U.S., if a technology falls under export control rules, you need to get an approval, called a "foreign filing license" before a PCT filing. Different countries have different rules regarding security and control issues, but it is very important to check. In some cases, such as with European Union members, a PCT application can be filed with a regional patent office that covers countries in that regional agreement.

2) An international search is completed by a designated international authority, which examines all the member countries' patent files and prior art, etc. This results in an opinion (called an international search report, or ISR) regarding patentability at the international level. Based upon this, the patent applicant can decide what countries to designate for the patent (and the associated fees). A search report won't affect or determine the choice of countries, but may influence your decision.

3) The PCT application and the ISR are transmitted to the World International Patent Organization (WIPO), who then publishes and communicates this information to the designated country patent offices. One advantage of the PCT is that many of the patenting offices of the designated countries will rely heavily upon the ISR opinion, and not spend time doing their own detailed patentability searches.

4) The individual country patent offices will then review the application. This is called the "national phase" of the PCT process. These national offices will then grant patents for the countries that are designated, and the different fees will need to be paid.

The advantage of the PCT process is that it simplifies the filing and review of patent applications in different countries and defers the payment of some fees.

Inventions

are the object of

International applications

filed with

Receiving Offices
(national or regional
patent Offices or
the International Bureau)

*transmit
applications to*

International
Authorities
(ISA, SISA and IPEA)

*Carry out search, prepare
written opinion and
transmit reports to*

WIPO

International
Bureau

publishes on

PATENTSCOPE *communicates to*

Designated Offices
(national and/or regional
patent Offices)

grant

Patents

**International
phase**

**National
phase**

Months from
priority date:

| 0 | 12 | 16 | 18 | 22 | 28 | 30 |

| Application filed with patent Office (priority date) | International application filed with PCT receiving Office | Transmittal of ISR & written opinion | Publication of international application ISR and written opinion | Applicant requests supplementary international search *(optional)* | Applicant files a demand for international preliminary examination *(optional)* | Transmittal of IPRP II or SISR *(optional)* | PCT national phase entry (where the applicant seeks protection) |

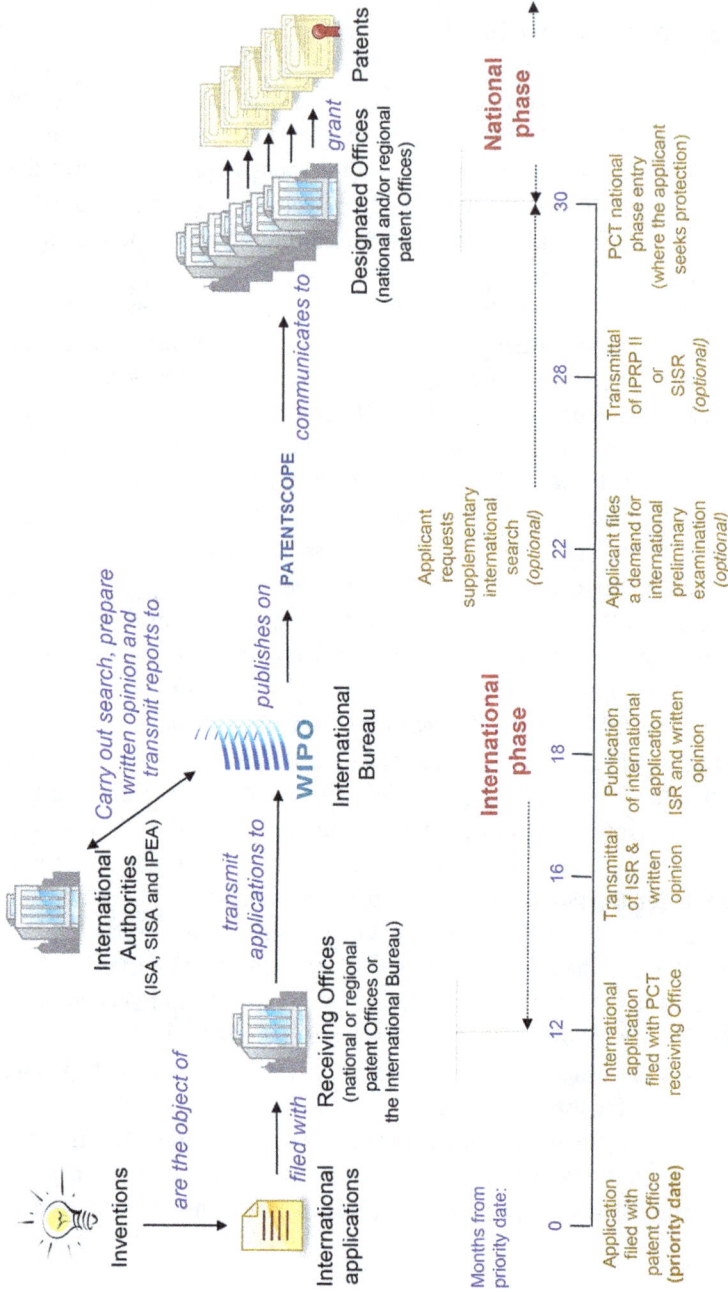

Figure 5.2: Overview of the patenting process using the PCT system.

China currently leads the filing of PCT applications, followed by the United States, Japan, Germany, and the Republic of Korea. Most PCT applications are filed by larger corporations, such as Qualcomm and Mitsubishi Electric. Remember, however, that individual country maintenance fees are generally required for the designated countries in a PCT filing, so holding a number of international patents can be expensive. The PCT process can also be used for countries that have "utility model patents" of shorter duration.

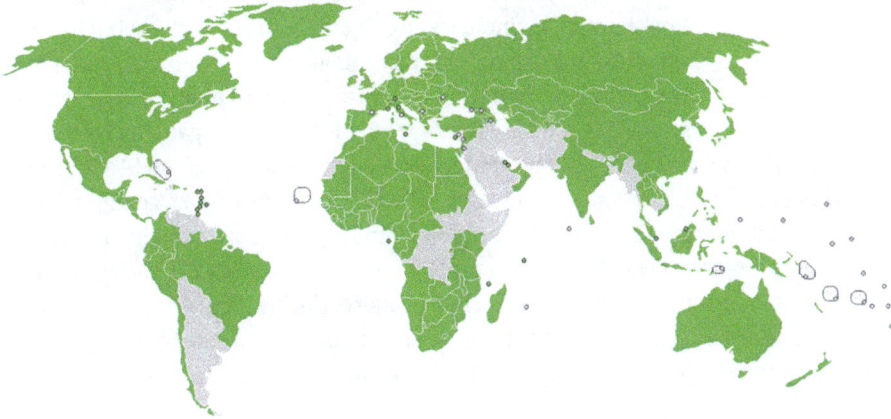

Figure 5.3: PCT member countries.

While the PCT process appears quite effective, some inventors prefer to file directly with specific countries, instead. This slightly reduces the risk of technology "leakages" to competitors since the publication of the patent application and patentability report is more restricted, although still published and available for competitors if they search hard enough. Furthermore, many inventors choose to first file in one or more countries, typically in the U.S., to establish an early priority date. This approach provides more time for development, while preserving that original filing date. They then submit a PCT application within one year of the original U.S. filing, still maintaining the U.S. priority date".

Like everything in the world of IP protection, rules are constantly changing as courts decide on cases, and governments create new laws.

Pre-patent Protections

An important part of the commercialization process of early-stage technologies is pre-patent protection. Many early-stage firms, R&D laboratories, and entrepreneurial developers can't spend a lot of money on patenting, so they need to be sure there is commercial potential first. They will often start demonstrating their non-patented technologies to potential users or licensees in order to see the level of interest.

An important part of the commercialization process of early-stage
technologies is pre-patent protection.

Caution must be exercised, however, since non-patented technology that is "sold" to another entity may result in a form of public disclosure or "prior art", and the loss of the ability to obtain a future patent. The U.S. generally has a one-year grace period. However, different countries may have different rules and time frames related to this rule of prior sale. Many European countries, for example, have an "absolute novelty rule", that means, once a product is offered for sale, it generally eliminates the right to file in that country. Thus, it is important that demonstrating a technology is considered just a review process, not for the actual sale of the technology. Again, as referenced many times in this chapter, it is important to get the advice of a qualified IP attorney.

Technology developers may also want to perform a "quick-look" commercialization study that involves showing the technology in focus groups or talking to experts. Without a specific strategy of pre-patent protection, this can be very dangerous. Diligent effort needs to be made to protect intellectual property during these early development stages. There are three basic approaches to pre-patent protection. Most early-stage technology developers will use a combination of these three methods in order to obtain the strongest protection.

Keep It Secret and the Danger of Public Disclosure

A major threat to getting something patented is "public disclosure" or "publication" of the know-how. Publication, from an intellectual property perspective, is simply letting other people, not legally bound to secrecy, have the critical know-how, technology, or designs in a way that somebody with normal knowledge in the field could recreate or use the technology. Publication is more than writing an article. Publication, or public disclosure, means any type of communication, whether it is in a speech, a conference presentation, an academic article, or even talking with a couple friends around a lunch meeting. In addition, offering for sale, selling, or licensing a technology, prior to getting a patent, even for beta-testing purposes, might be considered putting the technology into the public domain.

In the United States, if something is "published", then the inventor has only one year to file for a patent. In most other countries, however, if published, the inventor completely loses the right to a patent. The patent application examiner will also search the journal databases and internet to see if something is published. This is a major issue for research universities, where professors are rewarded for publications. Many inventors begin by filing in one or more countries – most often in the United States – to secure an early priority date. This initial step gives them additional time to refine their technology, while keeping that date intact. Within one year, they can submit a PCT application, which allows them to retain the original U.S. priority date across participating countries.

In addition, certain online postings and e-mails may seem to be confidential but actually constitute publication, if the critical know-how is communicated via these sites.

If the critical know-how is published, then the technology is considered in the "public domain". In addition, if somebody wants to challenge a patent, they might be able to show it was published prior to the one-year deadline for filing.

Essentially, the strategy is to treat all early-stage technologies like a "trade secret" – only authorized people have access, make an effort to keep it secret from other people, and use non-disclosure agreements when talking to other people. In some specialized cases, such as filling out a government grant application, communicating the technology on the application is not considered "publication" if certain measures are taken. The bottom line, however, is talk to your legal team or technology transfer office if you are communicating the technology to anybody, by any means.

For the reasons stated above, companies, government labs, and universities should maintain publication policies requiring any intended publication to be reviewed by IP counsel, prior to permitting the submission of a manuscript for publication. Depending upon the respective agency, this may also be true, prior to the submission of a grant application.

Non-disclosure Agreements

Non-disclosure agreements, or NDAs, are the go-to method to legally bind people and organizations to confidentiality. NDAs are legal contracts between parties that describe what is confidential, the know-how that is being shared, and the limits by which this knowledge can be shared with others. NDAs need to follow certain formats and are almost always written and approved by lawyers on both sides of the exchange. There are major sections in an NDA, such as the definition of the confidential information, the exclusions (such as know-how that is already in the public domain or previously known), the various obligations of the parties (who can be provided the information and for what purpose), and the time frame (usually until the time the know-how is no longer a trade secret or a specific length of time). Different types of technologies will have specific terminology in an NDA. Common uses for NDAs are when showing a pre-patent technology or trade secret to potential licensees or customers and when performing various market research activities, such as focus groups or talking with experts.

An NDA is often considered no stronger than the integrity of the companies signing.

There is always a risk of providing somebody an early-stage technology, even with an NDA. Some companies have been known to look at potential technologies, oftentimes under the guise of evaluating these technologies for potential future licenses, in order to simply gain information. After they get the technology, they give it to their technical team to reverse engineer, then improve and change the technology to a point where it is different enough to work around the NDA description. They then file for their own patent around the new and improved technology. Clearly, a strong and well-written NDA (or license agreement) is critical. As one well-known IP attorney noted, however, "an NDA is considered no stronger than the integrity of the companies signing.[3]"

Provisional Patent Applications

Provisional patent applications are often confused with a "real" or non-provisional utility patent. In the United States, the provisional patent application process is administered by the USPTO and can be filed for either utility or plant inventions. Many people argue that since a provisional patent application does not really provide normal patent protection, perhaps the name should be changed. Many countries, such as the UK and France, have similar provisional patent application processes, but many countries do not. Provisional patent applications are commonly used in the United States as a form of pre-patent protection.

In the United States, a provisional patent application is simply an application to the USPTO that describes the technology, and follows a certain format. A provisional patent application is not examined for prior art, and a patent examiner does not assess the technology's patentability. It also does not require formal claims and offers no guarantee of future patent protection.

A provisional patent application is really designed to establish a filing date for a technology with the anticipation of filing for a utility patent within a one-year period. It also provides pre-patent protection, since by establishing this filing date, other people cannot obtain their own patent around the covered technology.

A provisional patent application is really designed to establish a filing date for a technology with the anticipation of filing for a utility patent within a one-year period.

This filing date becomes particularly important in a "first-to-file" patent process. However, when filing within the allowed one-year period for a regular, non-provisional utility patent, the patent examiner will compare the new application with the provisional filing. They must ensure that the technology described is sufficiently similar and that the application meets the necessary description requirements.

This one-year window is critical. Somebody filing a provisional application must file for a regular, non-provisional utility patent within this one-year period. If they miss this deadline, even by one day, they lose the right to file for a patent around the defined technology.

The term "patent pending" can also be used when a provisional patent application is filed. Oftentimes, one hears of some inventors and entrepreneurs stating they have a "patent" during an investor pitch for funding, when in actuality it is only a provisional patent application. This is clearly misleading, since it implies a degree of IP ownership and protection that is not really there.

The advantages of a provisional patent application are numerous. It is significantly less expensive than a regular patent filing and can be submitted online. It also establishes a patent priority date that is recognized globally, including for PCT filings. Unlike regular applications, it is not published or made publicly available, helping preserve the secrecy of the technology. Finally, it gives inventors time to refine their technology before submitting a full utility patent application.

A provisional patent application, combined with an NDA, generally provides the best pre-patent protection when demonstrating a technology to potential customers/ licensees or when doing market research, where the technology is demonstrated or discussed in detail.

A product can also be sold after a provisional patent application has been filed. If there is little commercial interest in the technology, many inventors and developers simply allow the one-year term of the provisional patent application to expire. Similarly, if the technology undergoes significant changes that would require a new patent, they may choose to abandon the original application entirely. However, since provisional patent applications essentially establish the priority date, missing the one-year deadline may not be completely disastrous. You can still file for a non-provisional application; however, you risk losing priority to competing filings or any public disclosures that might have taken place.

Copyrights

The first evidence of copyright protection appears in ancient Greece and Rome, when kings and emperors allowed favored authors to have ownership over books, poems, and even food recipes. The introduction of the printing press in the late fifteenth century forced governments to start developing consistent copyright laws. In the U.S., the Copyright Act of 1790 set important standards. There have been a number of revisions and changes in copyright laws since this time, not only in the U.S. but throughout the world as technology changes.

The copyright law of 1976 currently governs copyrights in the U.S. In its basic form, copyright laws are designed to protect written or artistic expressions that are fixed in some type of tangible medium. This could include books, articles, poems, paintings, photographs, movies, songs, and the more modern mediums of blogs and various social media. Even less obvious works, such as class PowerPoint presentations and personal notes are protected. In essence, the idea of copyright is to protect an idea's expression, but not the idea itself.

According to the U.S. Copyright Office, copyrights are designed to, "protect original works of authorship, as soon as an author fixes the work in a tangible form of expression". This is quite different from patents, where applications need to be submitted and reviewed.

Copyrights are designed to, "protect original works of authorship as soon as an author fixes the work in a tangible form of expression".

The owner of a copyright has the right to reproduce the work, to make derivative works from it (such as a movie based on a book, or reproductions of art), to distribute these works, and to sell, perform, or display the protected work in public. Registration is not required to hold a copyright. In the U.S., for works created after January 1, 1978, copyright protection lasts to the death of the author plus another seventy years. Coauthored works, anonymous works, works for hire, and creations prior to 1978 have different time frames and rules. The commonly seen symbol, © can be used anytime to show copyright intent, but the symbol does not really add any additional protection.

To gain even more protection, it is possible to register the work. This is also required if an author or creator wants to enforce their exclusive rights through the courts. In the U.S., copyright registration is done only through the U.S. Copyright Office. This involves depositing the work, either on paper or online, and paying a fee. Digital works can also be uploaded.

Each country has its own copyright laws. This is critical in the modern world, since the Internet has made sharing protected material accessible within seconds. What can be protected, and for how long can vary.

For example, most countries, such as Canada and those in the European Union, use a 70-year life after the death of the author, or all coauthors, similar to the U.S. Mexico, however, has a 100-year period of protection after the death of the creator, while other countries such as China and Arab countries use only 50 years. A few countries have even lower time periods.

In certain situations, the ability to use indigenous created material, sacred objects, rituals, or other cultural elements might vary between countries, based upon different laws. However, most countries have signed various copyright treaties and conventions that attempt to harmonize copyright protection across the globe and provide a degree of standardized protection.

Copyright has become particularly relevant for many technology development firms since computer code, once written, is protected. Technology and scientific diagrams are also protected. Like patent protection, copyright allows for the right to exclude others from using that material.

All copyright lawsuits are based upon this fact. In reality, many software developers do not place a strong emphasis on copyright protection as part of their IP strategy. This is because it is relatively easy for others to develop "work-arounds" to existing code. Additionally, it is often very difficult to detect whether a competitor has used someone else's code in their product. Most of the litigation and complaints about copyright-related IP for technology-related efforts appear when an employee leaves one company, taking critical computer code to a competitor.

Most technology companies tend to treat computer code and other written technology documents more as trade secrets. Even this can create a problem. As mentioned above, in order to sue somebody for copyright infringement, it generally requires depositing or registering the code with the appropriate copyright office. Interestingly, this may constitute a "publication" of the code, thus eliminating trade secret protections. Fortunately, many copyright offices, including in the U.S., allow for the redaction of critical elements of the code when registering. Registering software code may be a smart strategy, but it requires professional expertise to effectively maintain the trade secret components.

AI is taking the world by storm. Generative AI-produced works, whether written or artistic, are generally not granted copyright protection. At the present time, these AI systems, including image and music generators, and text creators such as ChatGPT, are not considered "authors", since these systems essentially produce their output based on the culmination of human effort "scraped" from public sources. This can include AI-produced computer code and other technical material. However, in many cases, humans and AI collaborate on the production of works. This is where current laws become ambiguous and varies from country to country. Future case law will need to untangle the exact copyright issues related to joint works that have both AI and human input. Lawsuits are also appearing when the generative AI-produced work clearly utilizes already copyright-protected material as its source.

Trademarks

The third category of IP protection is Trademarks. The USPTO defines trademarks as, "any word, phrase, symbol, design, or a combination of these things that identifies the source of your goods or services". It's how customers recognize you in the marketplace and distinguish you from your competitors.

Oftentimes, the specific term "trademark" refers to identifying products or goods, while the term "service mark" references service providers, although both fall under the same IP category. Trademarks do not give complete ownership over a phrase or word, but rather how it is used.

For example, a similar identifying phrase could possibly be used by both a local coffee shop and a national computer company. The key is whether or not it creates confusion in the minds of the consumers. To obtain national protection over trademarks, it needs to be registered with the appropriate national office, such as the USPTO. Once registered, one can use the symbol ®. Alternate forms of registration identification might be statements such as "Registered in the U.S. Patent and Trademark Office". For unregistered trademarks, people often use "TM" (meaning trademark) or "SM" (meaning service mark) to show intent and claim "common-law" rights. In addition, sometimes, trademarks can be protected under common law when no trademark registration is filed.

Like other forms of IP protection, trademark rules and processes vary by country. While some countries will honor trademark registration from other countries, it is generally advised to register trademarks in all the countries you might be doing business in. The "Madrid System" has been established, so applicants can fill out a single trademark application, pay one set of fees, and apply for trademark protection in approximately 130 countries. Some regional agreements, such as the European Union and the African Regional Intellectual Property Organization, allow for a single trademark registration for the member countries.

Trade Secrets

The rate of technological innovations is rapidly increasing. At times, a technology can become obsolete even before a patent is granted. In addition, a lot of technological know-how cannot be formally protected through the specific requirements of patenting. Finally, the rate of IP theft is increasing dramatically, as is the difficulty and time it takes to prosecute IP theft cases in court. The combination of these forces has encouraged most technology developers, R&D labs, and companies to consider "trade secrets" their primary form of intellectual property protection through the whole commercialization cycle.

What Is a Trade Secret?

In the United States, the Uniform Trade Secrets Act (UTSA) was introduced to create a standardized definition of trade secrets and misappropriation, while also setting a consistent statute of limitations for states to adopt. The UTSA (Section 1:4) offers the following definition:

> *"Trade secret" means information, including a formula, pattern, compilation, program, device, method, technique, or process, that: (i) derives independent economic value, actual or potential, from not being generally known to, and not being readily ascertainable by proper means by, other persons who can obtain economic value from its disclosure or use, and (ii) is the subject of efforts that are reasonable under the circumstances to maintain its secrecy.*

Europe and other countries have very similar definitions, with the same three components – information that has been developed, keeping it a closely held secret, and it has independent value. The concept of trade secrets is fundamentally different from other types of IP protection. First, it does not require a formal filing or registration with a government office. Second, it requires diligent security measures and proper behavior on the part of the trade secret holders. Third, the threshold for a trade secret is much lower in terms of creativity and originality. The threshold is essentially that the know-how has independent economic value because it is unknown to others.

Trade secrets have three components – information that has been developed, keeping it a closely held secret, and it has independent value.

Trade secrets do not cover general knowledge, skill, or abilities. Thus, an employee who gains skills while working for an employer, even if exposed to that company's trade secrets, can generally take those skills to a new job with a competitor firm. But they cannot take or use any specific material and information that is protected as a trade secret by their previous employer. Likewise, a chef can move to another restaurant and use their acquired cooking skills and techniques, but they should not take specific recipes from the prior employer. This issue is constantly being debated in courts since programmers, scientists, engineers, and technicians regularly jump between employers in high-technology industries.

Well-known trade secrets include the formula for WD-40, formulas for famous perfumes, and the Coca Cola and Kentucky Fried Chicken recipes. However, in modern technology-based industries, almost everything can qualify as a trade secret. Examples include algorithms and software code, manufacturing processes for technologies like semiconductor chips and pharmaceutical delivery devices, and innovations in autonomous driving. Additional examples are the design and architecture of computer chip components, battery technologies, and cloud computing systems. Major technology firms, such as Apple, Samsung, IBM Google, Qualcomm, Microsoft, Tesla, and Uber have all been involved in recent trade secret lawsuits. Trade secrets are particularly important in the early stages of technology development, but can continue through the whole commercialization process into the marketplace.

Protecting against Misappropriation of Trade Secrets

Misappropriation of trade secrets can happen in many ways. Most common is outright theft, either by an employee or a competitor's efforts. Other methods of trade secret theft include a) misrepresentation, where a company might say they are interested in a joint venture but use this relationship only to obtain secrets, b) espionage by physical or electronic means, and c) breach of duty to keep secrets. Reverse engineering a technology, however, is not a violation of trade secrets if the original technology was obtained legally.

The USPTO Toolkit for Trade Secrets has a number of critical recommendations to protect intellectual property through trade secrets. These include:

a) Limit access to trade secrets only to employees who require it for their jobs.
b) Have employees sign work agreements that acknowledge the obligation to maintain secrecy.
c) Train employees regarding trade secrets.
d) Mark materials relevant to trade secrets as "confidential".
e) Control access to trade secrets, such as having locked rooms or safes.
f) Control digital access to trade secrets, such as computer logins with different levels of permission and specialized, encrypted data devices such as flash drives.
g) Ensure departing employees return or destroy trade secret materials.
h) Have outside individuals, including contracts, potential licensees, focus groups, vendors, potential investors, etc., sign confidentiality or non-disclosure agreements, if providing access to trade secrets.

One of the most difficult parts of litigating trade secret violations is the determination of economic damage and monetary loss. Courts often assess damages based on market value, estimating the economic worth by referencing comparable products or technologies, even if doing so requires examining unofficial or gray market transactions. However, a lot of trade secret know-how is embodied in early-stage technologies, where the economic value is primarily in the future income that might be obtained from the technology when it is fully developed at a later date. In these cases, U.S. Courts have generally allowed any reasonable method, such as determining the R&D costs to develop the technology, or possibly the present value of lost future income based on forecasts.

In the U.S., most trade secret laws fall under the individual states. Most states in the U.S., however, have adopted the Uniform Trade Secrets Act (UTSA). There is also some federal protection in the U.S. for certain types of trade secret violations.

As in all cases of IP protection, trade secret laws vary by country. Most countries currently have trade secret laws, although each country addresses it somewhat differently through statutes, common law, or case law. In some countries, such as India, trade secrets are enforced by related laws, such as laws of "equity" and "confidence". Although almost all countries have trade secret protection in theory, in practice, there is a huge degree of variation in the enforcement of trade secret laws.

In some countries, such as China and Russia, most experts consider it is very difficult to pursue a trade secret infringement lawsuit and difficult to even get a judgement if the violating firm is a local entity.

Concluding Insights

Intellectual property and technology commercialization must be considered hand in hand. Intellectual property, without commercialization, is a waste of time and money. Commercialization, without protecting the associated intellectual property, will likely fail in the long run, as clones and copycat products jump into the market. Establishing and protecting the know-how, designs, and knowledge embedded in a technology becomes critical at almost every step in the commercialization process.

Trade secrets need to be protected prior to a patent application, as well as through the whole commercialization process. Private equity investors always want to see ownership of the technology they are funding. Significant monetary losses are possible if somebody else claims ownership of your intellectual property, even if your product is doing well in the marketplace.

This chapter discussed the four categories of intellectual property protection: patents, copyrights, trademarks and trade secrets. In addition, important IP protection mechanisms such as provisional patent applications and non-disclosure agreements are examined.

The next chapter extends our analysis of intellectual property, but specifically examines the impacts of IP theft, piracy, and misappropriations. The next chapter also discusses a variety of different IP strategies that are commonly used during the commercialization process.

CASE: Investing in IP through Equity – How Osage University Partners Accesses and Protects Academic IP

Osage University Partners (OUP) is a venture capital firm that has pioneered a novel approach to acquiring and monetizing university intellectual property by investing in startups that license it.[4] Rather than focusing on direct patent acquisition or licensing negotiations, OUP secures its rights through "participation rights" clauses embedded in university license agreements. These clauses allow OUP to invest in startups on the same terms as other institutional investors when those startups raise priced funding rounds.

Kirsten Leute, a Partner at OUP, leads the firm's university relations efforts. With a background in academic tech transfer (including time at Stanford University), she bridges the gap between research institutions and venture finance. Under her leadership, OUP has formed partnerships with more than 120 academic institutions, enabling the firm to track thousands of university-affiliated startups and selectively invest in the most promising.

This case explores how OUP's model allows it to access protected intellectual property through equity investment, how it evaluates the strength and strategic value of early-stage IP, and how it supports university-born ventures after investment. As this chapter highlights, intellectual property is a core strategic asset. OUP offers a window into how professional investors assess, value, and engage with that asset in the context of commercialization.

A Unique Entry Point: The Participation Rights Clause

In many license agreements between a university and a newly formed startup, there is a participation rights clause. This clause allows the university, or an assignee like OUP, to invest in future-priced rounds of the startup, under the same terms as other institutional investors.

Rather than directly negotiating licensing terms or acquiring patents, OUP partners with over 120 universities to gain access to these participation rights. According to Leute, "We share in the upside of successful IP commercialization without requiring universities to act as venture investors".

This structure gives OUP indirect but meaningful exposure to intellectual property. It doesn't hold patents. Instead, it holds equity in companies built around licensed patents. In doing so, it gains access to high-value university inventions, while relying on the startup structure to handle IP management, protection, and commercialization.

How OUP Evaluates IP-Backed Startups

Because OUP only invests in startups that have licensed university IP, their diligence process begins well after invention disclosure and patent filing. By the time OUP reviews a deal, the startup typically has:
– A founding team,
– An exclusive license to university IP,
– An initial product or technical validation plan,
– And a syndicate of professional venture investors.

Still, not every deal moves forward. OUP screens thousands of startups annually but invests in only 10–12. Their diligence focuses on:
– IP strength and exclusivity: Is the core IP well-protected? Is it foundational to the company's competitive edge?
– Freedom to Operate (FTO): While the startup is responsible for FTO analyses, OUP's technical team, largely comprised of PhDs, reviews whether the IP is likely to be enforceable and defensible.
– Market opportunity and exit potential: Is the IP addressing a meaningful problem in a scalable market? Would future acquirers value the patent position?
– Team capability: Most importantly, does the founding team have relevant expertise to advance the IP into a viable product?

Valuing the IP but through an Equity Lens

Although OUP does not "buy" patents outright, the value of a startup's IP underpins its entire investment thesis. "We back-solve from expected exits", says Leute. "If the current valuation doesn't pencil out based on projected dilution and potential returns, we pass".

This process underscores the role of IP in early-stage valuation. The startup's technology must support venture-scale returns, starting with strong, protectable IP.

Strategic Post-Investment IP Support

OUP's role doesn't end after the check is written. Although they often hold observer seats rather than board positions, the firm:
– Helps startups identify additional IP from university portfolios.
– Guides teams in managing university relationships and license compliance.
– Advises on strategic patenting decisions as startups refine or expand their claims.

In these ways, OUP helps ensure that startups treat IP not as a one-time asset but as a dynamic portfolio that evolves with the business.

Conclusion: Aligning Investment with IP Strategy

This case illustrates a growing trend: acquiring university IP through investment, rather than licensing. OUP doesn't own the IP, but it shares in its value. By structuring access through participation rights clauses, and selecting only the most promising IP-backed startups, the firm gains meaningful exposure to cutting-edge innovation.

In doing so, OUP also reinforces a key point of this chapter: protecting intellectual property is not a static task. It requires strategic judgment, thoughtful timing, and expert navigation of legal and commercial frameworks. When done well, as OUP's model shows, IP becomes a lever for value creation not only for startups, but for universities and investors alike.

Chapter 6
Developing an Intellectual Property Strategy

This Chapter
- Examines the risks of intellectual property (IP) theft, piracy, and infringement in the commercialization process.
- Describes effective strategies for protecting against IP theft and misuse.
- Highlights how leading developers and technology firms use IP strategies to support successful commercialization.

Key Management Tools and Best Practices
- Checklist and best practices to address patent infringement
- Best practices for developing an appropriate IP strategy

! **INSIGHT**

The unauthorized use, if not overt theft, of people's ideas and inventions has been a problem for centuries. Combine this with the rise of modern technology, the increasing importance of intellectual property as the basis for successful technology commercialization, the rapidity with which innovations take place, and the importance of developing a comprehensive IP strategy has never been clearer. This is true whether the technology developer is a small, entrepreneurial entity or a large, global corporation. IP strategy must be considered hand in hand with commercialization strategies. These decisions must be well-thought-out, explicit, and effectively implemented.

Introduction

Intellectual property (IP) lies at the core of technology commercialization. Not only does innovative know-how result in useful technologies, but like any asset, IP must be defended. Losing IP advantages, whether to the unethical behaviors of bad players, or simply because of better innovations being introduced to the market by competitors, seriously impacts the ability to commercialize a technology at its full value.

In the previous chapter we discussed the four basic methods of protecting intellectual property: patents, copyrights, trademarks, and trade secrets. We also discussed the importance of pre-patenting protection, such as the use of provisional patent applications and non-disclosure agreements. In this chapter we discuss in more detail the issues of IP theft and misappropriation and suggest various real-life strategies that are used to manage intellectual property by successful organizations.

By its very nature IP theft is very difficult to detect. If hard assets or physical property are stolen, such as a shipping container or semi-truck full of electronics, the owner of those assets becomes almost immediately aware. Police can be notified,

https://doi.org/10.1515/9783111684420-007

investigations take place, insurance claims can be made, and perhaps the stolen material will be recovered.

This is not the case with intellectual property. Critical know-how can be stolen, and easily incorporated into a competitor's technology, and nobody may even be aware of it. Some studies suggest that less than 20% of IP theft is ever identified. Even if a victim of IP theft or infringement is made aware and takes action, it might be years of expensive legal maneuvering before restitution can be made. By this time, new technologies have probably appeared, perhaps even making the original IP obsolete. In some countries, full legal restitution is almost impossible to obtain if your home country is out of favor with the current government.

The development and protection of intellectual property must always be considered strategically. For example, do we patent our technology in just one country or region, such as the United States or the European Union, or do we want to have a protection that extends to all countries? What are the strategic differences between platform technologies versus technologies with very narrow applications? How do I strategically consider the hazards of intellectual property theft? What are some of the common strategies successful developers are using to manage IP?

The Global Issue of IP Theft

As mentioned in the previous chapter, almost every country in the world has laws that protect intellectual property. Patent, copyright, trademark, and trade secret laws may differ slightly by country, but they all seem very comprehensive on paper. The problem is that some countries are much more effective than others in implementing these laws in real life. Additionally, some countries clearly see IP enforcement, or lack of it, in the context of their broader national interests.

The theft of know-how is quite understandable. Let other technology developers do all the heavy R&D work. Let others incur the costs, time, testing, and frustrations inherent in any early-stage technology. Once something looks promising, or even introduced in the market, then just take that knowledge, sometimes legally and sometimes illegally, and build a clone at a lower price point or add a few new bells and whistles to make it look new.

Not only is this copycat strategy attractive to certain developers, but it also appears to be a national economic strategy from some nations, perhaps even supported by governments in spite of what their IP protection laws say.

Every year the United States Office of Trade Representative publishes the detailed *Special 301 Report.* The stated concerns in the *Special 301 Report* are clear, to identify the "(a) challenges with border and criminal enforcement against counterfeits, including in the online environment; (b) high levels of online and broadcast piracy, including through illicit streaming devices; (c) inadequacies in trade secret protection and enforcement in China, Russia, and elsewhere; (d) troubling "indigenous innovation" and forced or pressured technology transfer policies that may unfairly disadvantage . . . right holders in markets abroad; and (e) other ongoing, systemic issues regarding IP protection and enforcement, as well as market access, in many trading partners around the world".

The *Special 301 Report* receives stakeholder input regarding over 100 countries. The worst of the offender countries are categorized on the "Priority Watch List". The list does not change much from year to year. The worst offending countries seem to stay pretty much the same. The 2025 *Special 301 Report* lists Argentina, Chile, China, India, Indonesia, Russia, and Venezuela as "Priority Watch List" countries.

China, in particular, seems to present a particular problem. Since all the commercial enterprises in China are associated, if not controlled, by the government, acquiring IP has become an important and stated national focus for the Chinese government. The *Special 301 Report* specifically notes problems with China's actions with respect to trade secrets, online piracy, counterfeit products, patent examiner biases in the Chinese patent offices, and particularly the difficulties of bringing patent infringement litigation against Chinese firms.

The impact of IP theft can be enormous. Various studies have reported that the United States alone loses over one trillion dollars per year to Chinese IP theft, with up to $600 billion for just the theft of trade secrets. Other countries with significant original IP development, such as Japan, the European Union, and Israel also report significant IP losses due to theft, piracy, and misappropriation to the countries identified in the *Special 301 Report.*

Corporate Espionage

IP theft and infringement is not just a global issue, where IP is regularly targeted by countries as part of national policy. It also occurs at a much more local level, where developers and companies vie for position in the highly competitive marketplace for technologies. One form of formalized IP theft is corporate espionage, where one company intentionally takes its competitors' intellectual property, trade secrets, and propriety know-how without consent. While much corporate espionage is between companies from other countries as part of their national policies, it also regularly occurs among competitors within the domestic market.

Corporate espionage is when one company intentionally takes their competitors' intellectual property, trade secrets, and propriety know-how without consent.

Corporate espionage generally occurs through one of four methods: 1) a disgruntled employee that is targeted by a competitor, b) computerized hacking and cyber-attacks,

c) through a planted spy, or d) by a misrepresented business partnership that is designed specifically for intelligence gathering and possible IP theft.

Intentional corporate espionage is a crime in most countries, but the stakes are often high, and the penalties can be weak in many parts of the world. Even large and well-known companies such as P&G, Fiat-Chrysler, Uber, and Oracle have been involved in corporate espionage cases in the recent past. Corporate espionage cases can result in hefty monetary damages. In 2022 Appian Corp received a $2 billion verdict after suing Pegasystems, Inc. for stealing trade secrets through corporate espionage. The case is still working through various appeals. These types of awards are rare, however, since most corporate espionage may not even be detected.

Various reports suggest that corporate espionage has increased dramatically in the past decades. A common form of corporate espionage occurs at major research universities and government laboratories, where a purposely planted student research assistant might sneak into the R&D lab, and photocopy the notebooks, designs, prototypes and experimental results, sending these back to either their employer, or selling them on the" black" market.

Patent Infringement

Corporate espionage tends to focus on acquiring trade secrets illegally. Another common type of IP threat is patent infringement. This is a critical issue, since a key component of any technology commercialization process is having ownership or the right to use the know-how and intellectual property embedded in that technology. Patent infringement may be accidental or intentional.

When a patent is published, critical information, designs and claims are immediately available for all to see. But there are millions of patents, and attempting to work around existing patents to create new technologies can be extremely difficult. This is often referred to as "navigating the patent minefield". If a technology is clearly utilizing the know-how established in a prior patent, it is always appropriate to arrange a license to use that intellectual property.

There tends to be a lot of ambiguity when it comes to patent infringement. This is particularly true since technology development companies will purposely "design around" prior patents. In fact, many legal firms and design consultants specialize in working with technology developers on how to design around existing patents to avoid patent infringement. The ability to "design around" patents has encouraged many technology development firms to follow a patent strategy of filing multiple patents to make sure all variations of the technology are protected – even ones they might not use. However, this type of strategy works for larger firms with significant resources but is often too expensive for independent developers and smaller, early-stage entrepreneurial firms.

A patent allows one to exclude others from using the know-how identified in the patent claims without permission. If somebody is suspected of patent infringement, there are some standard steps to follow.

Checklist for Addressing Possible Patent Infringement

Consider the following checklist when addressing patent infringement issues.
1) Carefully analyze the suspected product or process to confirm it falls under the claims of your patent.
2) Send a cease-and-desist letter to the offender. Cease-and-desist letters are typically written by a patent attorney. Less aggressive letters are called "notice letters". The danger of a "cease-and-desist" letter is that it might trigger the recipient to seek a declaratory judgement if they can persuade a judge that there is no infringement and/or the patent is invalid. Timing and cost become an important consideration with sending cease-and-desist letters.
3) If the patent holder is willing to license the technology, this option can be placed in the cease-and-desist letter.
4) Oftentimes several cease-and-desist letters will need to be sent before action is taken.
5) Attempt to negotiate a settlement. The settlement will vary depending on the specific situation.
6) As a last resort, file a patent infringement lawsuit. In the U.S. this is filed in a federal district court. A successful patent infringement lawsuit might involve an injunction to stop the activity and provide for damages.
7) If the patent infringement is in another country, a serious cost-benefit analysis must be done. What is the process for filing a patent infringement lawsuit, and perhaps most importantly, how likely is it that the courts in that particular country will be fair? Many technology developers will not bother to file patent infringement cases in countries that are high on *The Special 301 Report* watch lists. It is simply a waste of time and money.

Patent infringement lawsuits are time consuming and expensive, so the key issues are a cost-benefit analysis and the likelihood of prevailing in court (is it really infringement, is their evidence to prove it or can economic damages be shown?)

Walking the Tightrope of Cease-and-Desist Letters

In the modern world, most technology developers will receive a number of cease-and-desist letters during the commercialization process. This is especially common after the technology is successfully introduced into the marketplace and its specifications and functions become visible to others. When analyzed, oftentimes there does not appear to be significant infringement of a prior patent. Other times cease-and-desist letters may clearly indicate a serious infringement issue.

Watch Out for Patent Trolls

A whole cottage industry has developed where some companies and their patent attorneys send out hundreds of cease-and-desist letters in the hopes of getting payments through intimidation when there is only a small chance of actual patent infringement. These are called "patent trolls". Patent trolls attempt to enforce patents well beyond their actual economic or technological value.

Some patent troll groups, supported by investors, actually buy portfolios of unused patents from other developers specifically for the purpose of threatening and filing lawsuits against other companies, ultimately to obtain a settlement. Patent trolls might be satisfied by only a small payment from smaller developers and entrepreneurs, while others might demand millions if going after a larger, deep-pocketed corporation.

Patent trolls, and their aggressive and abusive patent lawsuits, have become such a problem in some industries, such as renewable energy, that it has reportedly impacted the rate of innovation. Several recent studies report that billions of out-of-pocket dollars have been paid to patent trolls. Unfortunately, some larger corporations will also use questionable cease-and-desist intimidation tactics with smaller firms that cannot afford lengthy lawsuits.

Cease-and-desist letters are technically not legal documents. They do not have the legal authority to enforce the cessation of your use of the technology by themselves. Although not legally binding, cease-and-desist letters must be considered seriously since they can be used as evidence that you are aware of the issues that may lead to legal action. However, a cease-and-desist order issued by a court or government agency is a legally binding document that requires compliance. Our recommendation is to always discuss cease-and-desist letters with a qualified patent attorney to develop a response. The patent attorney might suggest a range of recommendations, depending on how serious the infringement is.

Developing a Comprehensive IP Strategy

Developing an Intellectual property strategy must be considered hand in hand with developing a technology commercialization strategy. At every step in the technology development process, from the early-stage concept and lab validation (TRLs 2 and 3) to the final stages of system demonstration and full market deployment (TRLs 8 and 9), the protection of intellectual property must always be part of the managerial mindset.

Pre-patent protection and subsequent patent decisions are generally issues seen early in a technology's development. Later in the development process as technologies are licensed, sold, or integrated into larger systems, property rights need to be clearly understood, communicated and perhaps even transferred. Both private equity investors and internal corporate management teams probably will not provide the necessary funding to continue development unless progress toward strong IP ownership is obvious. Ultimately, significant future profits might be lost if the bundle of IP that is embedded in a product, particularly patents and trade-secrets, is not protected as competitive products are introduced.

Developing an Intellectual property strategy must be considered hand in hand with developing a technology commercialization strategy.

A comprehensive IP strategy needs to consider a number of issues. These include:
- The nature of the technology, whether it is a "platform" technology or a technology that can only be used in highly specific applications,
- The cost related to obtaining and protecting IP versus the future benefit associated with the commercialization of the technology,
- The resources a developer or entity has to develop and protect IP,
- The threat of competitive products that might infringe on a technology's IP,
- The capability of potential competitors to reverse engineer designs and computer code,
- Whether patents, copyrights, trade secrets, or a combination of these protection approaches are best suited to the technology,
- The countries that the technology will be used or sold into, and the inherent biases in country-specific IP protection,
- Which countries will the product be made in.

Successful IP Strategies

The following sections present various IP strategies that are seen in practice. A successful and comprehensive IP strategy might consider a combination of these different approaches.

IP Strategy: Align IP Investments and Protection with Corporate Goals

It is always important, for companies large and small, to explicitly view the range of intellectual property protection investments in concert with both corporate goals and its approach to commercialization. Technologies that have a six-month shelf life should be viewed differently from technologies that might last 10 years or 20 years in the marketplace.

IP Strategy: Select Key "Choke Points" for IP Investment and Infringement Defenses

Many technologies have a targeted application or customer base. Why spend the money obtaining patents in every country in the world, when perhaps the technology might only be used in a few countries? Key factors to consider when deciding where to focus your IP investment are: a) Does the country have the capabilities to develop, reverse-engineer, and/or utilize your technologies? b) Where could your technology actually be manufactured or produced? and c) Which countries and markets do you plan on selling your technology in to, either directly, by partnerships, or licensing?

IP Strategy: Focus on "Crown Jewel" IP

Technologies are most likely built upon one or two major IP platforms. These are the crown jewels. However, developers will often create other IP that supports, enhances, or facilitates these crown jewel IPs. Companies should emphasize protecting their crown jewel IP, particularly if resources are limited. This is really the foundational platform for a technology's success, and what investors and licensees look for. This is particularly true for smaller entrepreneurial firms with more limited resources. For example, utilize the international PCT filing process and file in all countries for "crown jewel" technologies. For the non-crown jewel IP, perhaps a more targeted strategy using specific country filings would be appropriate.

Strategy: Platform Technologies versus Specific Technologies

Some technologies are "platform technologies" that can be used for a number of specific applications. For example, consider a biology-based technology that can penetrate cell walls and carry another molecule with it into a targeted place in a cell. This technology, informally called an "Escortin", was developed by scientists at the University of North Carolina Wilmington and actually exists. This technology can be considered a platform technology, since a variety of different pharmaceutical uses can be considered depending on which therapeutic molecule is attached to the Escortin.

The therapeutic molecule can be transported through the cell wall and directly to where it is needed inside the cell. Escortins might be used for treating different types of cancers, therapies for addressing other diseases of specific cell-organelles, and even for dermatology purposes. Platform technologies tend to be more valuable and wider IP protection effort makes sense versus technologies that are very narrow and specific.[1]

Strategy: Consider Practical Enforcement Issues

It is well-known that some countries, such as the ones listed on the *Special 301 Report Watch* list, simply do not uniformly enforce their IP laws. For these countries there are significant biases in their national courts. Patent examiners will favor patent applications from local firms and often reject applications from foreign firms. Lawsuits in these countries can be very expensive and long-lasting with uncertain outcomes even in strong IP misappropriation cases. Many technology developers will simply not bother to file patent infringement cases or litigate in these countries since they know it is probably useless and expensive. Many companies will not even bother filing patents in some of these countries.

Strategy: IP Complementarity

In the modern world, this is probably one of the most important IP strategies. Patents are published, and the underlying knowhow is disclosed even though it is theoretically protected. Anybody in the world can see the critical IP with a simple key word search and the press of a button, or the use of AI. It certainly makes sense to patent the critical IP, but keeping critical components and functionalities of the IP as a trade secret is oftentimes the best strategy. A fancy word for this strategy is "IP complementarity", that is, using patents, copyrights, and trade secrets in a synergistic combination. This exists when there are trade secrets behind the technology that allow the developer to more effectively use the technology described by the patent, thus keeping competitors at a disadvantage.

Sometimes patents and trade secrets are viewed as substitutes, but with a strategy of IP complementarity, trade secrets provide the underlying value to using what is covered in patents.

This IP strategy started to become much more evident in the early twentieth century when chemical firms started filing patents for specific compounds while retaining secrecy over the composition of specific dyes. The combination of compounds and dyes made for the most successful products. A fascinating example of the IP complementarity strategy, discussed in the case example to this chapter, led to the QWERTY keyboard design, a format that still dominates after 150 years.

There are a number of more recent examples where developers have patented certain elements of the underlying technology while keeping other aspects secret. Some well-known examples of this strategy include GE's process for making industrial diamonds, Pilkington's float glass technology, various hormone therapies produced by pharmaceutical companies, and even C&F's technology for freezing ingredients for pizza toppings. The IP complementarity strategy can also work with software, where the written binary code is registered with the copyright office, while the critical source code is kept secret. The key to the IP complementarity strategy is to explicitly and strategically explore the optimal patent/secret mix and then make an effect to protect each component in the appropriate manner.

Strategy: Patent Wrapping

Patent wrapping essentially means having primary patents for the critical components of a technology but also recognizing that many competitors will attempt to design around existing patents. Competitors who want to "design around" somebody's patent will always look carefully at the scope of the original patent claims, to see if something has been forgotten, not covered appropriately, or can be improved upon. This is particularly true if new technologies emerge that might not have been covered in the original patent.

As a real-life example, one of the authors worked with a government agency that filed a patent for an automated technology designed to dig deep exploration holes in the ground and then transmit detailed videos of the surrounding walls of the deep hole looking for indications of water or other important elements. However, the original patent defined the lighting mechanism for the system somewhat narrowly. A competitor saw this weakness, subsequently filed and received another patent that emphasized the use of more modern lighting technologies, such as fiber optics. This might have been prevented by patent wrapping (or broader claims). Patent wrapping also means filing patents for different variations of the primary technology, with each secondary patent expanding specific claims.

The idea of this strategy is to create an IP buffer or protective wrap of other patents around the patents that are most important. In many industries this is also called developing a "patent thicket", an analogy to the thorned, dense thicket fences that are very difficult to penetrate. Patent examiners often complain about too many claims in a patent application or when the patent application language tries to capture everything under the sun. This is when patent wrapping can also be used.

Strategy: Patent Blocking

Patent blocking takes patent wrapping one step further. Patent blocking strategies involve filing multiple patents on technologies that you actually do not intend to use.

Suppose your research team comes up with a design, but there are several different ways that the design can be implemented that your team discovered. Patent blocking means not only filing patents to protect the favored approach you plan to take to market, but also filing for patents on all the other approaches even though you don't plan on using them. This approach blocks competitors from perhaps using and developing a successful design with one of these other approaches.

Patent blocking essentially means flooding the IP space with patents. This obviously requires significant resources and effort, since each non-productive patent costs money and does not produce any income. But it does keep potential competitors from using these approaches.

Large-scale patent blocking is usually seen with larger companies. Smaller developers could also perform this strategy on a much smaller scale, with a much-targeted set of intellectual property blocks. With AI systems assisting in the writing of patents, it has sped up the process immensely, and more companies are now using patent blocking strategies. Chinese companies, in particular, perhaps supported by the government, appear to be the most aggressive in flooding the patent process. China now leads the world in international patent filings, with many large Chinese multinational firms having patent filing rates that are double, and even triple, the patent filing rate of similar U.S. and European international firms.

Strategy: Rapid Innovation and Speed to Market

Many technology firms that design and manufacture computer products for both the retail and OEM markets are now focusing on speed to market strategies rather than complex patent strategies. In some industries, it seems like every time an R&D firm develops and commercializes a new, improved version of their core product, it is immediately reverse-engineered, the core IP is then stolen and cloned by the same competitors.

Many companies are simply getting tired seeing generic versions of their technology on store shelves throughout the world within a year's time. This is particularly frustrating since these generic clones are inevitably offered for sale at lower price points, grabbing a significant part of the market. Filing patent infringement lawsuits is useless due to the rapidity of change, the immense cost of filing lawsuits in different countries, and the inherent biases in many of the international patent courts where these products are being cloned in.

Some companies have developed an innovative strategy of simply having a new, improved design ready to go approximately every six months or so. Other than having a few core platform patents, they do not focus on defending patents. Instead, these companies have adopted a strategy focused on rapid innovation and speed to market. Their goal is to outpace competitors by ensuring the time to market is shorter than the time it would take others to reverse-engineer, manufacture, and distribute copycat versions. The instant the clone technology appears in the market, these development firms immediately ship the new, improved version, thus always staying one step ahead of the clone competitors.

The focus of this strategy is then on rapid technological developments and increasing speed to market, while only developing and defending the core platform technologies.

Over time, the emphasis on rapid development and speed to market can become part of the corporate culture. This strategy is now used by a number of major players in the technology marketplace.

Strategy: Constant IP Auditing and Risk Analysis

This strategy should be part of any IP strategy. Given the speed of technological innovation, and the current first-to-file patenting process, which encourages rapid patent filings, all firms working in technology spaces should have an active IP auditing process in place. Current AI programs have been developed to constantly scan patent applications throughout the world, looking not only for both possible infringement of the firms IP but also new technologies that are being introduced. This IP auditing process should be combined with a formal IP risk analysis, where development teams regularly meet and discuss new developments in IP protection, both as possible threats and opportunities.

Concluding Insights

The development of a strong intellectual property strategy is no longer optional. It is a critical element of the technology commercialization process. As this chapter demonstrates, protecting intellectual property requires more than filing patents; it demands constant vigilance, strategic decision-making, and a deep understanding of the legal, technical, and global environments in which technologies are developed and deployed.

Developers must proactively anticipate IP risks, whether through global IP theft, patent infringement, or internal misappropriation. They must then design layered IP protection strategies accordingly. Effective IP strategies consider the nature of the technology, the most likely competitive threats, and the practical realities of international enforcement. The tools and frameworks introduced in this chapter – such as IP complementarity, patent wrapping and blocking, country-specific filing decisions, and speed-to-market strategies, are not one-size-fits-all templates. Instead, they provide a customizable playbook for navigating the complex, high-stakes terrain of technology protection.

Above all, intellectual property strategy must remain dynamic. As markets evolve and new competitors emerge, so too must the approach to safeguarding innovation. The most successful organizations treat IP as both a legal necessity and a strategic asset. An effective IP strategy can create long-term advantage if managed thoughtfully, deliberately, and in close alignment with commercialization goals.

Chapter Example: IP Complementarity – Typewriter Development and QWERTY

The QWERTY keyboard format is one of the most misunderstood inventions in history. QWERTY is often referenced as a classic example of an inferior standard that was adopted and then locked in over time as people got used to it. Some economists and politicians even use QWERTY as proof of why more government intervention is needed for standard setting. In fact, QWERTY is actually a great example of how different IP assets can complement each other.

The Problem

The first successful typewriter was invented by partners Christopher Latham Sholes and James Densmore in the 1870s (see head shot of Sholes in Figure 6.1). By modern standards the early typewriter seems a bit odd. Unlike the "visible" print mechanical typewriters that were sold for most of the twentieth century, the early typing machine was designed with a typebasket hanging below the paper; thus the typist could not clearly see what they typed on the paper. But the early typewriter had another problem. When adjacent typebars in the basket were pushed, jamming would often occur. The inventors needed to find a design where it was unlikely that adjacent bars on the typebasket were struck right after each other.

Figure 6.1: Christopher Latham Sholes.

The Solution

Sholes brilliantly came up with a sequence of letters for the typebasket. Part of this sequence included the letters QAZSXDCFVGBHNJMK. Why was this critical? There are very few words that contain letter pairs associated with this sequence of letters, in either direction (e.g., QA or AQ; JM or MJ, CF, or FC, etc.) – thus Sholes' solution to jamming was based on a principle of "infrequent letter pairs". However, given the mechanics of the early typewriter, where each button on the keyboard pushed a designated typebar in the basket, this particular sequence of letters in the typebasket resulted in the QWERTY keyboard format; thus the QWERTY keyboard implemented the QAZSXDCFVGBHNJMK sequence of letters in the early typebasket (see photo of Sholes and Densmore's typewriting machine in Figure 6.2).

Was this a true solution? Recently economist Neil Kay used Mark Twain's 145,000-word popular book, "Life on the Mississippi" and found there are less than 150 times in the manuscript when words contained letter pairs that were also adjacent on the Sholes type basket. An experiment using the Dvorak keyboard format (patented in 1936, which many people argue is more efficient) results in over 2,300 such pairing events, about 16 times more frequent with much greater jamming potential. Other keyboard designs of the day, such as the ABCDEF keyboard, performed much worse. Sholes was clearly working with the principle of creating a typing system of "infrequent letter pairs".[2]

So why didn't Scholes patent the QWERTY format? It is certainly possible to patent keyboard formats, and many have been patented over the years, including the Dvorak design. This is the key question. Most likely he wanted to keep the logic behind QWERTY,

Figure 6.2: Sholes and Densmore's typewriting machine.

that is the principle of "infrequent letter pairs" a trade secret.[3] The first real example of the QWERTY keyboard design in a legal document was in Sholes and Densmore's patent for his "improvement in typewriting machines" that was eventually published as US patent 207559 on August 27, 1878 (see photo of Sholes and Densmore's patented keyboard design in Figure 6.3). However, this is not a patent of QWERTY. In fact, other than the QWERTY diagram, patent 207559 does not mention QWERTY at all; the claims are all related to typewriter mechanics.

But by showing QWERTY in the patent, the inventors essentially made QWERTY part of the public domain, but did not have to describe the logic behind it. To patent QWERTY would have required publishing the logic behind QWERTY, that is, the principle of "infrequent letter pairs" through patent claims.

Complementarity of Intellectual Property

The complementarity between patent and trade secret protection was critical. Without the patent protection of the typewriter design, imitators could easily reverse- engineer the Scholes and Densmore typewriter and produce their own clone machines. Competitors certainly tried to build other typewriter designs that did not infringe on the Sholes and Densmore patents, but competitor typewriters using QWERTY, or any other layout, without understanding the principle of "infrequent letter pairs" would inevitably create jamming problems for their new design. The intellectual reasoning

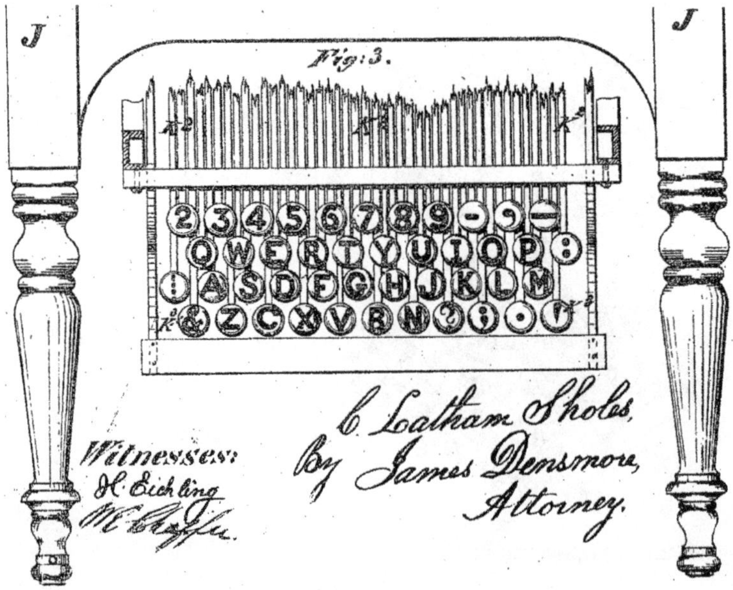

Figure 6.3: Sholes and Densmore's keyboard design.

behind QWERTY (and the QAZSXDCFVGBHNJMK letter sequence) cannot be reverse-engineered, it remained a trade secret.

By 1900, however, typewriters had changed to a "visible" print design, and jamming was less of a problem. And with modern computerized word processing, nobody even thinks of jamming – yet QWERTY endures after 150 years. Was there perhaps another trade secret at play?

Sholes was also a professional typesetter and knew the importance of efficient hand movements. There are a few other combinations of keyboard design that would still maintain the principle of "infrequent letter pairs". But compared to all the other proposed keyboard layouts, QWERTY appears to also maximize alternate hand use when typing the most popular two and three letter combinations (bigrams and trigrams). Alternate hand use has been shown to be most important for achieving both speed and fewer mistakes for all types of people, from two-finger "hunt and peck" typists to trained touch typists. Could Sholes have known this when settling on the QWERTY option to implement the infrequent letter pair principle? We may never know, but it seems likely, and QWERTY remains with us today.

Chapter 7
Performing a Commercialization Study

This Chapter
- Outlines the key steps involved in conducting a formal commercialization study.
- Differentiates between various types of commercialization studies and explains their purpose and structure.
- Emphasizes the value of these studies for identifying promising market verticals.
- Introduces practical tools and frameworks to support the commercialization study process.
- Highlights the growing role of artificial intelligence (AI) in conducting and enhancing commercialization analyses.

Key Management Tools and Best Practices
- Pipeline analysis
- Technology comparison matrix
- Technology interest package (TIP)
- QUAD sheets
- Steps for performing a technology commercialization/feasibility study
- Use of AI in technology commercialization studies

! **INSIGHT**

There are different types of commercialization studies used in practice. The type of commercialization study to be performed is usually tied to both the stage of the technology development and the decisions that need to be made regarding the technology. Some studies are highly detailed, while other studies can be considered "quick look" efforts. Each step in a commercialization study, however, involves proper diligence, extensive research, professional insight, and control of any biases. When performing a commercialization study, it is important to have an established protocol in place. Without a protocol or template, oftentimes important questions and details are overlooked. Finally, artificial intelligence (AI) is being used more and more frequently to assist in commercialization studies.

Introduction

Any technology needs to be assessed at various points in its development. Often, there is a cost-benefit component to any of these decisions. Is it worth the investment to continue the development of this technology? Do I need to pivot my research given competitive technologies or changing markets? Can I speed up development and get the technology to market earlier?

These questions are critical. For example, early technologies in the TRL2 or TRL3 stage might need to be patented. However, patenting is an expensive and time-consuming process. At this point, any organization, whether it is a university technology

https://doi.org/10.1515/9783111684420-008

transfer office (TTO) or the senior management of a corporate R&D lab, needs to have some general insights about the future competitive potential of the technology.

As technologies get closer to being actually commercialized, the focus of decision makers evolves. Now, the interest is more on identifying the best segments or market verticals to enter, who the specific customers might be for the technology, and how to effectively communicate the technology's advantages with these potential customers.

In regulated sectors such as medical devices or diagnostics, commercialization studies must incorporate additional complexity, including clinical validation milestones, regulatory pathway assessments (e.g., FDA 510(k) or De Novo), and health economic evidence. These studies often need to align with the formal documentation, such as the intended use and indications for use, which can influence trial design and reimbursement strategy. This contrasts with commercialization for unregulated technologies where go-to-market validation may focus more on rapid prototyping, customer feedback loops, and agile iteration cycles.

Types of Commercialization Studies

Frequently, technology developers, technology transfer managers, and entrepreneurs will simply do an informal assessment of a technology's potential. Commercialization experts hear this all the time, even from experienced professionals. Many people believe that they have so much experience in technologies, that they can just "feel" the level of potential. However, this attitude often leads to extreme biases and poor decisions. In fact, research has indicated that administrators, entrepreneurs, and managers are not very accurate at informally predicting an early-stage technology's success.

Commercialization studies can generally be classified into five types: A "quick-look" study, a "full-commercialization" study, a "full-commercialization with contacts" study, a "due diligence" study, and an internal "phased-review" study.

Developing a formal process overcomes many of these biases. The degree of formality varies depending on the situation. Formal commercialization studies can generally be classified into five types: a "quick-look" study, a "full-commercialization" study, a "full-commercialization with contacts" study, a "due diligence" study, and an internal "phased-review" study.

Quick-Look Studies

A quick-look study is often used by TTOs for early-stage technologies, or by entrepreneurs and technology developers that are somewhat restricted by resources. A quick-look study primarily focuses on customer research. This approach involves talking to industry experts in the most likely market application for the technology. It also typically involves contacting potential customers/licensees to see what their requirements are for the solution provided by the technology, and to get an indication of interest. A quick-look study might only take a week or so to perform, while other quick-look studies might include a more detailed "voice of the customer" analysis. No matter what, quick-look studies focus on the customer.

Full-Commercialization Studies

A full commercialization study, often referred to as a "technology feasibility study", includes comparing the target technology with competing alternatives at various stages of development. It also involves identifying key customer segments or market verticals, assessing their size and potential, and using market research tools such as focus groups to uncover specific customer requirements.

A full-commercialization study will always incorporate a formal "voice of the customer" component. Ultimately, a full commercialization study is designed to answer several key questions. Can the target technology satisfy customer requirements better than current and future competitive technologies? What are the appropriate markets for the technology? What are the best methods to enter those markets? Where might improvements need to be made to the technology?

A full-commercialization study is commonly performed by consultants and entrepreneurs that are seeking private equity investment, with the results of the study often included in the pitch to angel investors and venture capitalists. A full commercialization study may also be required when a larger enterprise is interested in acquiring an early-stage company built around an important primary technology. A full-commercialization study often takes one to three months to perform and culminates in a formal report.

Full-Commercialization Studies with Contacts

This type of commercialization study is the same as a full-commercialization study but goes one step further. One of the most valuable aspects of a commercialization study is to create an actual list of potential customers or licensees for the technology. This type of study will attempt to specifically identify and classify potential customers or licensees as to their possible interest in the technology and how the technology might satisfy their specific needs.

This approach requires a detailed understanding of not only the requirements of the customer but also a deep understanding of the customers' technologies, if the target technology is to be marketed as a component in an integrated system. These studies often provide specific contacts, such as addresses, emails, and phone numbers for key individuals like R&D managers, product development leads, or technology officers. In addition, they may include recommendations on how best to communicate with these potential customers or licensees, along with suggested strategies for entering and gaining traction in the market. Full-commercialization studies that incorporate contact outreach typically require the most time and effort to complete.

Due Diligence Studies

A due diligence study is often performed when an early-stage company is seeking private equity capital from angel investors and venture capitalists. Generally, the start-up company will develop a business plan and presentation, which inevitably involves discussing the competitive and financial potential of the technology. Not surprisingly, these funding pitch presentations tend to be quite optimistic. Accordingly, the private equity investor needs to undertake their own due diligence process to validate and confirm the statements made during the funding request.

Some private equity groups will perform the due diligence process internally, while other private equity groups will farm out the due diligence study to consultants. Depending on the organization, the amount of the funding request, and how legitimate the original statement appears to be, a due diligence study can be simple or very complicated. Regardless of complexity, a due diligence study will involve: a) validating important statements and data made in the funding request, b) talking with different independent experts about both the viability of the technology and market potential, and c) double checking on the IP claims being made: Have the patents really been issued, or are they still provisional patent applications? How strong and defensible are the patents? Do the patents cover only a minor part of the technology or a key component? How secure are any trade secrets? Typically, investors will expect a "freedom to operate" letter from a qualified IP attorney.

Phased-Review Studies

A phased-review commercialization study is part of an internal process of progressing through the internal technology development process in larger organizations. Phased-review processes (covered in detail later in this book) provide structured checkpoints where a technology's viability is assessed before it can advance from early development to full commercialization. These studies are typically used for internal go/no-go funding and support decisions. Every corporation is different, but generally each major step in this internal approval process involves some type of formal assessment of market potential and technical viability. In a phased-review process, early evaluations focus more on the technology and engineering capabilities, while later evaluations emphasize market characteristics and entry channels.

Steps of a Commercialization Study

The following discussion identifies the steps in a full-commercialization study with contacts. This commercialization protocol was developed by the Center for the Commercialization of Advanced Technologies (CCAT), a Department of Defense-funded technology commercialization and granting agency. This protocol was used as the basis for hundreds of technology commercialization studies and has been adopted in various forms by a variety of consulting firms and technology transfer agencies. This protocol also provides a good framework for instructing how to perform a technology commercialization or feasibility study.

These steps are presented sequentially; however many steps can be completed concurrently, particularly if the commercialization study is a team effort.

Step 1: Talk to the Inventor or Developer

The first step in any commercialization study is to talk to the inventor or development team. The technology developer most certainly has thought a lot about the potential for commercialization. However, always remember that technology developers will be highly optimistic in their opinions. After all, they have spent an enormous amount of time on the technology, they are heavily invested emotionally, and for some, their future careers might be impacted by the success of the technology.

Activity and Deliverables. Get a good and complete description of the technology, its advantages and drawbacks, and the problems solved (minor or significant). Make sure the stage of development is understood (TRLs). Most developers have a professional network. They read journals and go to conferences. They also have a lot of insight about the market potential of their technology, and the various competitive technologies that might be coming out in the same market space.

Probe for the developers' knowledge in these areas. Be sure also to ask the developer about possible experts in the field to talk to (remember, the developer will probably be the best connected in the field, so this is a critical question).

Always use a pre-established check list of questions that cover the above issues, and any other issues that you think the developer might provide. Without a pre-established list, it is easy to forget some critical issues. Make sure this list is complete prior to talking with the technology developer. If appropriate, this list of questions, and the developer's responses, can be included in the final commercialization report.

It is at this time that the team performing the commercialization study needs to acquire a good working knowledge of the technology, including the proper terminology associated with the technology and industry. Most developers are willing to demonstrate the technology but do a little homework first. Having a working knowledge of the technology is critical when doing market research. Without this working knowledge, it is easy to lose legitimacy when talking to other experts and potential customers.

Step 2: Write a Description of the Technology

Write a preliminary, but detailed description of the technology. This write-up should include a description of the technology and the specific market problems it addresses. It should also cover its key advantages, potential drawbacks, whether it solves minor or significant issues, its current stage of development, and the overall value it offers.

This description needs to walk the fine line between being too detailed or technical, and too broad. It needs to be accurate and understandable to a reasonably knowledge-able person.

Activity and Deliverables. Most of this information will come from discussions with the developer. Depending on the technology, additional information can be obtained from prior grant applications, patent filings, TTO license opportunity descriptions, and published or internal reports. Putting the technology description into writing has several purposes. First, it forces the team to clearly understand the technology, so they can describe it to others. It also provides a written document that can be used when talking with potential customers and industry experts, as well as performing a voice of the customer (VoC) analysis. In this description, it is also useful to start identifying the critical performance data, and perhaps how the technology performs on critical dimensions compared with competitive or current technologies.

Step 3: Perform a Technology "Triage"

A "technology triage" refers to investigating the full range of competing technologies that potentially can solve the same problem. These technologies may be at different levels of development. This step includes not only existing technologies in the market-place, but also competitive technologies that are in the pipeline of other developers.

A "technology triage" refers to investigating the full range of competing technologies that potentially can solve the same problem.

This is important since the technology that is being investigated is most often not ready for product launch. It might be months or years before it is ready for launch. Thus, the viability of the technology needs to be compared with other competitive technologies also in the pipeline. This is critical since in many cases a technology being developed is only compared with the existing technologies in the marketplace (which is important), and not technologies that might be introduced to the market at the same time. Without looking at other technologies also in the pipeline, it is impossible to fully understand if our technology is truly competitive.

We call this step a "technology triage" since like a medical "triage", this is a step where hard decisions need to be made. In particular, is there any hope for a technology that would warrant further investigation and investment? Or is the technology essentially "dead on arrival". The technology triage process will provide the commercialization team a sense as to whether the technology under investigation can actually compete in the marketplace. This step is generally a "first-cut" analysis using secondary data sources prior to doing a VoC analysis. However, a preliminary VoC analysis is often conducted alongside this stage to help clarify the key dimensions that customers and users use to evaluate technologies in this market space.

Activity and Deliverables. There are three basic steps in a "technology triage".

Pipeline Analysis. A pipeline analysis typically involves identifying competing technologies at various stages of development. This includes:
–   technologies still in R&D (using patent database searches),
–   technologies nearing commercialization (from product announcements, government grant databases, GitHub repositories, and trade newsletters),
–   technologies already on the market (using targeted keyword web searches).

AI tools can assist significantly in this process. For example, AI-powered patent search engines can quickly surface relevant filings and even highlight overlapping claims. AI can also be used to scan large volumes of online data, including funding databases, technical repositories, and social media platforms that track emerging technologies to identify promising competitors.

After collecting the data, a shortlist of 10–20 technologies should be selected and ranked based on relevance. This list should then be reviewed with the original developer to validate findings and identify any overlooked competitors. Oftentimes you will find that the developer did not even know that many of these competitive technologies were actually in the marketplace or being developed by other innovators. At this point, the developer will recognize that there might actually be better competitor technologies or they might need to pivot their designs to stay relevant.

Technology Comparison Matrix. Create a matrix that compares the technology being evaluated against competitive alternatives in the same space. These alternatives may include technologies that are still in development as well as those already available in the market.

The matrix needs to provide a comparison of the technology's performance along the dimensions that appear important. This matrix will be tweaked later as additional market research from the VoC process is performed to better understand the critical performance dimensions. The more detail the better in this matrix. The matrix can have a ranking score, as shown in Figure 7.1 below, or actually list the performance measures across the different dimensions.

Brand Attributes | Competitive Matrix

ATTRIBUTE / BRAND	Crawler Reach	Price/Value	Security	Support	User Interface	Complete Solution	Speed
Xentari Systems	10	8	7	8	7	10	10
Veltrix Dynamics	5	7	7	8	7	7	7
AetherCore	8	6	4	3	5	5	8
Nexaris Forge	4	3	5	3	7	3	7
Orionex Industries	5	2	6	8	5	4	8

Figure 7.1: Competitive technology comparison matrix.

Technology Evolution Discussion. As mentioned above, technologies undergoing a commercialization study are usually in a development stage, at a lower TRL. It might be months or even years before the targeted technology is ready for the market. Based on the research from the pipeline analysis, the team should discuss how the competitive market for the technology will change from the present to when the target technology is likely to be ready for the market, and beyond. Technologies continually evolve, and it is important to project the pace of these advancements. The real comparison lies in understanding what the market's performance expectations will be by the time your technology is ready for launch.

Step 4: Develop a "Technology Interest Package

Before doing primary market research, such as talking to experts, surveying potential users, or performing focus groups, it is important to put together an effective way of telling people about the technology, its performance, what problems it solves, and the potential markets. The method of communication can take many forms at this point. These are the most common methods:

Technology Interest Package (TIP): A two- or three-page detailed and attractive description of the technology, its performance, what problems it solves, and the potential markets.

QUAD Sheets: A one-page description of the technology divided into four different sections (thus the term "QUAD"). Each of the four sections has a specific purpose. QUADs are often used when communicating a technology within and between government contracting and defense technology organizations. Some government granting organizations also use a QUAD model.

Video Presentation: A short two- or three-minute video presentation that can be sent to people. This method of communication is particularly useful if the technology has a working prototype that can be demonstrated.

Power-Point Presentation: Essentially provide the same information as in a TIP or QUAD, but in the form of a 4–5 slide presentation.

In practice, a combination of the above methods can be developed and used, depending on who, and for what purpose the communication is being used for. But this is an important step prior to Step 6 in the protocol. These methods can also be used to connect with potential customers or licensees later in the process. In later chapters, we discuss these communication methods in much more detail.

An important reminder: always make sure the technical information in the TIP, QUAD or any other communication is approved by the legal team or TTO. This is particularly important if the technology has not been protected or patented. One of the dangers is providing too much detail that can be used by competitors or represents a type of "publication", thus hurting the opportunity to get a patent for the technology. Clearance by the appropriate organization officials is absolutely necessary before sending these communication-related documents out to people.

Step 5: Select the Market Verticals for Further Examination

The developer of a technology may have only one specific market application in mind, but many times, the features of the technology might also be useful in a number of different market verticals. A market vertical refers to a specific industry segment in which businesses serve a common customer base with specialized needs. This step identifies the potential market verticals a technology might compete in and then ranks which market verticals offer the best chance for successful commercialization. It is in these more promising market verticals that further analysis will be carried out.

Activity and Deliverables. There may be many different market verticals to investigate. At this point, the study should start to narrow down the market verticals to investigate in detail. All potential market verticals should be presented, along with a discussion as to why certain market verticals are recommended for further analysis. If there is obviously only one market vertical or application for the technology under investigation, this needs to be stated and supported.

Secondary Research. Part of this step is to perform a preliminary analysis of the potential market verticals. This often involves using secondary source materials to determine the market size of the different verticals as well as any specialized aspects that recommend certain verticals as being of higher potential than others.

Step 6: Analyze in Detail the Selected Market Verticals

This is the time to analyze, in detail, the selected market verticals.

Activity and Deliverables. Investigating the selected market verticals always involves two types of analysis – secondary, economic research and primary research to determine the "voice of the customer".

Background Economic Data on the Chosen Verticals. This step involves identifying and documenting the market size of the different selected verticals, the past and future forecasted growth, and the competitors along with their market shares.

A number of excellent secondary resources are available for this step, including IBIS reports, industry reports from trade associations, articles in trade journals, reports from consulting groups such as Frost and Sullivan, and other secondary resources from the web. Some of this information is free, some can be obtained from local university libraries, some require a small cost or membership in a trade organization, and some reports can be quite expensive, particularly if they are issued by a large consulting firm.

This step is also when artificial intelligence (AI) programs, such as ChatGPT, can be very useful. The results of this analysis should be discussed with appropriate charts and graphs. Each vertical being examined should be analyzed separately.

Voice of the Customer (VoC) and Industry Experts. This is the key primary research step. The market research team conducting this study needs to completely understand the behavior and requirements of the critical channel players. Try to get at who are the demand creators, the potential users, the incentives for use, and what are the key success factors or requirements for successful adoption.

This includes the following:
– Communicating with market vertical and industry experts (journal editors, consultants, authors of articles, and heads of trade organizations).
– Talking with technical experts (other engineers or scientists, to provide an opinion of the viability of the science and technical considerations).

- Talking to potential customers (either individually or in focus groups, depending on the technology). Customers may be individuals, or may be groups. If the customers are "firms" the research team needs to focus on the individuals who have a say about "purchasing or licensing" the technology, like a product engineer or buyer.
- If appropriate, talk with other stakeholders, such as investors.
- Apply the appropriate VoC tools (discussed later in this book).

Understanding the VoC is such a critical step in technology commercialization that a full chapter is devoted to this topic.

However, it is also important to consider that for regulated markets, the VoC often extends beyond end users. Critical stakeholders may include regulators (e.g., FDA), clinicians (who adopt and prescribe the product), and payers (who determine reimbursement). Each of these groups can significantly influence adoption, and their needs and incentives should be considered as part of the VoC research process.

Step 7: Accurately Define the Purchase Attributes for the Key Market Verticals

From the VOC and secondary research, the commercialization study now needs to carefully define the purchase attributes.

Activity and Deliverables. Define the multiple (four to eight) dimensions that customers would typically use to evaluate a new technology such as price, performance, and other functionalities and product attributes. These dimensions should be detailed with specific "engineering" performance parameters. Look at:
- minimum required performance on each dimension
- which dimensions are most important
- where the future will be on the dimensions (1 to 3 years out).

Put together a detailed chart of purchase criteria and how the target technology addresses these requirements. Some information may overlap with data gathered during the technology triage process. This is the time to finalize the technology comparison chart, using well-researched and clearly defined purchase attributes. This information can also be used to update the documents, such as the TIP, QUADS, and Power-Points, which will be used to communicate with potential users and licensees.

In regulated markets, such as medical devices and healthcare technologies, purchase decisions often involve more than just technical performance and price. Developers must also consider regulatory and reimbursement-related factors. These may include the existence of billing codes through the Centers for Medicare & Medicaid Services (CMS), such as CPT or HCPCS codes, or the need to apply for new ones. Additionally, health economic modeling (e.g., cost-effectiveness or outcomes-based analysis compared to the current standard of care) can be essential, particularly for gaining hospital or payer adoption. These reimbursement and economic factors should be treated as core purchase attributes when performing commercialization studies for healthcare and other regulated sectors.

Step 8: Chart the Market Channel and Key Points of Influence

Each market vertical involves distinct channel relationships, some of which may be critical to successful technology adoption or commercialization, even if they are not direct customers or immediately apparent at the outset. This is also the time to define exactly what channel might be the most important for success, and who the major influencers are.

In regulated markets, such as healthcare, the commercialization pathway is shaped less by traditional supply chain dynamics and more by clinical, regulatory, and institutional influences. Key opinion leaders (KOLs), clinical care guidelines, and payer reimbursement policies often determine whether and how a technology is adopted. Even if a hospital has procurement authority, actual adoption may depend on guideline inclusion, physician advocacy, or whether the device is reimbursable under existing codes. For technologies in these markets, mapping the full ecosystem of influence, including regulators (e.g., FDA), clinicians, and economic stakeholders, is essential. These players often exert more impact on purchasing decisions than traditional buyers alone.

Example: Shipping Container Tracking and Warning Systems. To help prevent the theft of shipping containers and their contents, an entrepreneurial start-up funded by a DoD grant developed a sophisticated real-time tracking and warning system that could be discreetly installed in standard shipping containers. The formal commercialization study (contracted by the DoD and performed by the authors), however, discovered that both shipping container manufacturers who would ultimately be the customers of the technology and freight shipping companies were not interested in the technology unless insurance companies would reduce their rates for shipping containers incorporating this technology.

The commercialization study team then interviewed various insurance companies and discovered they needed clear proof that these systems would actually reduce theft before reducing their insurance rates. Based on this feedback, the commercialization study team recommended the need to provide proof of theft reduction through a large-scale study before market introduction.

Activity and Deliverables. Provide a figure or chart showing stages and segments a product moves ultimately through to the final consumer. This information can be presented in a figure. The purpose of this step is to show decision-makers, the technology developers, and users of the technology how the industry actually functions, who are the buyers and sellers in each stage of the industry, and particularly who appear to be the primary influencers, and what steps need to be made, in order to successfully commercialize the technology. It may not always be simply the final users or customers in the supply chain.

Step 9: Use a Commercialization Readiness Scorecard

At this point in the commercialization study, the team should have a good understanding of the technology advantages and disadvantages, the requirements for success in the market, and a sense as to whether the technology might be successful. This is when a scoring system or commercialization readiness scorecard might be used. A commercialization readiness scorecard may have two different objectives at this point. First, it attempts to quantify the probability of successful commercialization. Second, it measures the organization's overall readiness to commercialize the technology, including the support process, adequacy of funding, and knowledge about the market. These scoring systems are used primarily to communicate and summarize the team's final assessments along different dimensions, such as the technical viability, market potential, and ability of the developer team to push the technology forward.

Scoring systems are also used by some angel investment groups and venture capitalists to compare investment opportunities, as well as by government granting organizations to evaluate and compare different grant applications.

While formal scoring systems do not guarantee a technology's success or failure, they do offer decision-makers valuable insights into market readiness, the likelihood of successful commercialization, and areas where additional resources may be needed to improve commercialization prospects. This step is usually an independent analysis by the commercialization team.

Be aware, however, that developers or entrepreneurs might disagree with the team's analysis at this point. For this reason, many commercialization studies do not include the technology readiness scorecards in the final report but rather submit it separately to the decision-makers in order to facilitate further discussions. Technology prediction models and commercialization readiness checklists and scorecards are examined in more detail in Chapter 14 and Chapter 15.

Step 10: Recommendations and Conclusions

This section represents the culmination of the analysis and should address the key issues identified throughout the study. Remember that the objective of the commercialization study will differ by the stage of technology development, the type of commercialization study being performed, and the needs/objectives of the decision-makers, or why you are doing the commercialization study.

This is when the study can make sense of all of the research, data, information, knowledge, and even intuitions that surround the technology, whether it can be successful, and how to best pursue commercialization. This section can also include recommendations such as attending important conferences, calling certain people and influencers, presenting or publishing papers using the technology, and commercial targets for future beta-testing.

This is where the recommendations are made to take the technology to its final launch into the market, however that market is defined.

Step 11: Identify Potential Licensees and/or Customers

Generally, this step is not included in a regular commercialization or technology feasibility study, but many times a client or developer may want this step as part of the study. If so, this step becomes one of the most important sections, and significant time and effort needs to be put into this effort. Government labs and university TTOs typically focus on potential licenses. However, private sector firms may want not only potential licensees or customers to be identified but sometimes ask for joint venture partners and/or potential investors to be identified. Make sure you clearly understand the objectives of the developer, management team, or consulting client. This list should be "qualified" with the name and contact information.

List by type of contact. Also rank the importance of the contacts (prime contacts, second-level contacts, or third-level contacts). This list should be "qualified" with the name and contact information, at least for the prime contacts. It is important that the contact information is the person who is actually responsible for evaluating a possible technology that might be incorporated into their system or making a purchase decision. This might include individuals with the title of product engineer, R&D manager, product development officer, acquisition manager, or VP of product development.

Remember, it is often part of the job descriptions of these individuals to evaluate different technologies that might be useful to their product and technologies. Oftentimes one can get contact information by simply calling the organization, explaining the purpose of needing the contact information, and then asking for an e-mail to send materials for review. Most R&D and technology development managers are generally willing to consider new technologies that might make their systems better.

Step 12: Contact Potential Licensees and/or Customers

Some commercialization studies go one step further and ask the commercialization team to initiate contact with the individuals or organizations identified in Step 11. This contact is not a marketing function, but rather simply to initiate contact by sending one or a combination of communication documents, such as a TIP, QUAD or video presentation. As part of this communication, if the recipient is interested in the technology, then it is recommended that they contact the developer directly. Keep in mind that while a well-executed commercialization study can support effective marketing, it is not a marketing tool in itself. A commercialization study, including data, information, and recommendations, needs to always take an independent and impartial perspective.

Use of Artificial Intelligence in Commercialization Studies

Recently, AI has started to become a powerful tool for performing commercialization studies. Some of the steps in the commercialization study protocol described in this book lend themselves to AI applications, while others really are not currently in the realm of AI. However, AI systems are constantly being updated, some with a specific focus on the commercialization process while others are general AI systems that can be accessed to assist in commercialization studies. Based on the authors' use of AI systems in commercialization studies and interviews with many leading experts from top university TTOs to specialized consulting firms, the following reflects the current state of AI application in this field.

Caveats Regarding AI

First, some caveats regarding the use of AI for commercialization studies:
- Most applications of AI act as powerful search engines. In fact, some programs are regularly sold as "AI", but they really are not. They are just very efficient search and database development systems. These systems are often marketed as AI in order to gain attention and traction. However, these efficient search and database management systems are still valuable resources for some steps of commercialization studies.
- What is new is that AI now incorporates very efficient learning systems.
- At the present time, however, AI still only operates within well-defined parameters, working with data and information that are available. For this reason, AI is still not good at strategic issues, intuition and decision-making.

Where in the Commercialization Process Is AI Currently Being Effectively Used?

While there are some specialized AI systems targeted toward the commercialization profession in various stages of development, most technology commercialization professionals still use generalized AI systems, such as ChatGPT to assist in their analysis. The following is where AI currently has the most application in the commercialization process:

Step 3 in the Protocol. Asking AI to identify potential competitive technologies. This includes searching for product announcements and published information to assist in both a technology pipeline analysis and developing a competitive technology comparison. AI can also analyze patent databases for important and relevant patents based on key words, patent citations, patent licenses, and usage. In this case, AI might assist in determining the strength of the target technology's intellectual property. However, patent strength analysis using AI is not overly effective for very new technologies or technologies that have been patented recently.

Step 4 in the Protocol. Step 4 represents the development of communication methods. Once a model for communication is selected, AI can assist in the effective design of these documents, including how to better word the communication, and the appropriate graphics for the target audience.

Step 5 in the Protocol. AI can assist in identifying potential markets, sectors, and uses for a technology. AI can produce interesting applications that might not have been considered.

Step 6 in the Protocol. Once target market verticals are selected, AI can provide assistance with secondary research, such as size and growth of markets, competitors, market share, and other important aspects of secondary research. AI can also assist in identifying industry experts who you might want to contact.

Step 11 in the Protocol. AI can assist in identifying high-quality contacts (potential customers, partners, and licensees) for the technology. It can also assist in developing a list of critical contacts.

Where in the Commercialization Process Is AI Currently Not Effective?

While becoming increasingly powerful and more available, AI does still have significant limitations. In these areas, humans still need to do research and make decisions with respect to commercialization. These include, but are not limited to, the following:

AI **CANNOT** determine or rank the success of a technology in the marketplace.

AI **CANNOT** tell you the best way to manage the movement of a technology through its development stages.

AI **CANNOT** determine go/no-go technology investment decisions.

AI **CANNOT** tell you the best market verticals to examine in detail or focus on.

AI **CANNOT** perform VoC research activities. This step represents one of the key areas of a successful commercialization study. Humans need to talk to experts, perform focus groups, survey customers, and then apply this information.

AI **CANNOT** tell you the best strategy for launching a technology.

AI **CANNOT** tell you when to pivot to a new design or to a new market segment.

AI **CANNOT** determine the correctness of the data inputted into a pro-forma, nor tell you the fair market value of a technology.

AI **CANNOT** network at conferences and trade shows.

AI **CANNOT** generally make managerial decisions, particularly of a strategic nature.

Concluding Insights

Commercialization studies are a fundamental process of technology commercialization. Commercialization studies provide critical background data and information for the key decisions behind a successful commercialization process. As we have seen, there are different types of commercialization studies, each with its own level of detail and purpose.

An informal analysis of a technology's feasibility rarely works in practice. In spite of some commercialization expert opinions, intuition is simply not sufficient – there are too many biases in this approach, and oftentimes key questions are overlooked.

A formal commercialization study can certainly be complicated and highly detailed, or it can be as simple as a "quick look" analysis. The focus, complexity and detail of any study depends on the stage of a technology's development, the purpose of the study for the organization and decision makers, and the resources that are available to perform the study. Regardless of the type of study, however, it is important to have some type of a formal checklist or protocol appropriate for the situation. This chapter lays out the steps for a complete commercialization study.

AI can certainly assist in many areas of a commercialization study, but most steps and activities still need at least significant human oversight and input. Ultimately, humans need to talk to other humans and make critical managerial decisions.

The following chapters go into much more detail about some of the topics that are raised during a commercialization study.

Chapter Example: Develop a Forward-Thinking Strategy – Preventing Hearing Loss through Photobiomodulation – The Story of RayBalance

The Challenge

Darrel Drinan, a seasoned medical entrepreneur, has spent over 20 years developing solutions for unmet medical needs. His latest venture, *RayBalance*, focuses on addressing a critical gap in healthcare: the prevention of hearing loss.[1] Unlike hearing aids and cochlear implants, which compensate for lost hearing, no existing solutions restore or prevent hearing loss.

Hearing loss affects millions worldwide, with primary causes including age, noise exposure, infections, and ototoxic drugs (e.g., chemotherapy). Notably, 60% of chemotherapy patients experience a 20-decibel reduction in hearing, yet oncologists rarely address this issue because no viable preventative treatment exists. Darrel saw this as a "*white space*", an area with no effective solution. He set out to change that.

The Solution

RayBalance is pioneering a light-based therapy using photobiomodulation, which involves exposing cells to low-energy photonic stimulation to stimulate innate responses to prevent their degradation. The key innovation is the application of light energy to the cochlea's hair cells, which do not regenerate once damaged. The treatment stimulates increased ATP production, reduces inflammation, and helps sustain the viability of these critical auditory sensory cells.

To bring this technology to market, Darrel faced several major challenges:

1. *Defining the Market Entry Point*: Should the product target preventative care (prophylactic use) or treatment of an existing condition?
2. *Navigating FDA Regulations*: With no direct predicate device, approval would require either a 510(k) clearance or a lengthier De Novo pathway.
3. *Securing Investment in an Unproven Market*: Unlike hearing aids, which consumers and investors understand, preventative hearing loss treatment lacks market precedent.
4. *Identifying the Right Customer*: Perform a solid commercialization study. The primary stakeholders, oncologists, audiologists, and oncology nurses, have differing levels of influence in the adoption process.
5. *Identify Promising Paths to the Market*: Different market segments might have different pathways. For each market segment, a good commercialization study should identify the best path to the market including the legal, governmental, and competitive barriers and requirements. Each pathway has its own players and influencers that need to be considered. Some of these key people may not be obvious at first.
6. *Choose the Best Pathway*: Start in a targeted manner. Gain traction before attacking other market segments.

Strategic Market Entry: Targeting Chemotherapy-Induced Hearing Loss

RayBalance's beachhead market is chemotherapy-induced hearing loss, a condition where oncologists currently have no preventative intervention. This decision was strategic for several reasons:

Ethical Considerations: It is unethical to induce hearing loss for clinical trials. However, chemotherapy patients already experience this side effect, making them an ideal test population.

A Defined Patient Pool: The U.S. has 1 million chemotherapy patients annually, creating a high-value, low-volume initial market.

A Controlled Study Design: Clinical trials can compare one treated ear vs. one untreated ear, offering strong statistical validity.

By focusing on a niche, high-value population first, RayBalance can later expand into broader markets such as noise-induced hearing loss in military and industrial workers (22 million affected in the U.S. alone).

Strategic Insights

Solve the Right Problem before Developing a Solution

Darrel emphasizes the importance of starting with an unmet need rather than a technology in search of a problem. His approach involved studying multiple solutions before selecting photobiomodulation as the best fit.

Your Target Customer May Change over Time

At different stages, RayBalance's primary customer shifted:

Early-stage: Investors (securing funding to continue development)
Regulatory phase: FDA and clinical researchers (proving efficacy)
Market entry: Oncologists, audiologists, and oncology nurses (adoption and prescriptions)

Entrepreneurs must tailor their messaging to each audience, understanding that investors care about market potential, while clinicians prioritize clinical efficacy.

Be Strategic about Timing and Disclosure

Unlike consumer tech start-ups that rely on early hype, RayBalance has chosen more of a "stealth mode" to avoid alerting competitors. The company has kept its website minimal and avoids premature publicity until FDA approval is secured, preventing well-funded competitors from fast-tracking a similar product.

Choose the Right Pathway for FDA Approval

With no existing devices for preventing hearing loss, RayBalance must convince the FDA that its technology fits within existing photobiomodulation applications. A 510(k) clearance (based on equivalent devices) is preferable to a De Novo application, which requires full regulatory review.

Align with Existing Healthcare Economics and the Key Players

Hearing loss prevention is not a priority for oncologists because there has never been a solution. However, oncology nurses, who see the effects of chemotherapy firsthand, may be the key influencers in adoption. Additionally, workman's compensation insurers and military health programs could drive adoption in future markets.

Actionable Steps for Entrepreneurs in Medical Technology

Find a white space with no effective solutions, but strong demand. Avoid incremental innovation in crowded markets.

Select a beachhead market that validates the technology and provides a viable path to scaling. High-value, low-volume markets are ideal for initial traction.

Conduct early technical feasibility of treatment to establish efficacy. It is important to find out if it works.

Tailor messaging to different audiences (investors, regulators, clinicians) based on their priorities.

Protect your competitive advantage by balancing secrecy with strategic disclosures. Leverage clinical research and insurance reimbursement strategies to drive adoption.

By aligning technological innovation with a well-defined problem, RayBalance exemplifies how medical entrepreneurs can pioneer new markets, navigate regulatory challenges, and secure investment for breakthrough healthcare solutions.

Chapter 8
Voice of the Customer (VoC) Analysis

This Chapter
- Explains the importance of conducting a Voice of the Customer (VoC) analysis during the technology commercialization process.
- Describes various methods used in VoC analysis for technology-based products.
- Discusses the unique challenges and approaches in VoC analysis when targeting either end users or system integrators.
- Emphasizes the value of effectively communicating VoC findings to internal and external stakeholders.
- Introduces common tools and formats for presenting VoC results in the context of technology development.

Key Management Tools and Best Practices
- Technology Requirements Charts
- Position and Perceptual Maps
- House of Quality
- Checklist for Expert Interviews
- Focus Group Best Practices
- Customer Interview Best Practices

! **INSIGHT**

A well-done VoC analysis is an important step during a technology's development. Organizations developing technologies will need to know the market structure for their technology, the requirements that customers will demand of the technology, how these requirements might change in the future, and how these customer requirements correlate with the design features of the technology. These are all questions that need to be answered by a well-designed VoC analysis, particularly for technologies in the TRL 2–TRL 6 stages of development, before actual beta testing and final commercialization.

Introduction

When conducting a commercialization study, whether it is a comprehensive, detailed analysis or a quick-look assessment, two stages stand out as particularly important. These are the technology triage phase and the voice of the customer (VoC) analysis. A well-done technology triage is critical since, like medical triage in combat zones, it separates those that have the potential to survive versus those without much hope. When an effective technology triage is conducted, many technologies are found to be essentially "dead on arrival". In some cases, better alternatives are already in development, while in others, competing technologies more effectively meet customer or integrator needs

https://doi.org/10.1515/9783111684420-009

at a lower price point. In addition, the cost of adapting or pivoting the technology to market conditions may be too high, or, as discussed in earlier chapters, it may infringe on existing intellectual property. At this point, many technologies are appropriately abandoned.

However, if a technology passes the initial triage, the next step is to identify the most promising market verticals to target. This involves clearly defining customer needs within each vertical, ensuring those needs align with the technology's current capabilities, and determining where further development may be required. Ultimately, this process helps clarify the most effective path to successful commercialization. This is when the VoC process comes into focus. Generally, a VoC analysis occurs when technologies are in the TRL2 to TRL6 stage, that is, from early concept formulation and proof of principle through prototype development and testing in relevant environments.

While the technology triage and VoC analysis is presented sequentially in this book, many commercialization studies perform both aspects concurrently, since potential pivots that might save a technology are often uncovered by the VoC.

Once a technology reaches TRL6, customer requirements should be well-researched and the path to market clearly defined. At this stage, the focus of commercialization shifts toward demonstrations for target customers, beta testing, and preparing for product launch. This stage does not eliminate the need for market research; rather, it shifts the focus toward more targeted insights as the technology approaches final commercialization.

A VoC analysis can be relatively simple, such as talking to a few experts or quite complicated involving focus groups, surveys, and sophisticated VoC modeling. The depth and type of analysis really depends upon the situation. In this chapter we discuss a number of different methods and tools for doing a VoC analysis.

A VoC analysis can be relatively simple, such as talking to a few experts, or quite complicated involving focus groups, surveys, and sophisticated VoC modeling.

All VoC approaches share a common foundation: they rely on primary research methods that involve directly engaging with people, typically through interviews, surveys, or structured conversations. VoC is different from secondary research, which involves library and internet searches to obtain information about market size and competitors. Secondary research can also be facilitated by modern AI programs. Primary research, however, involves significant human contact and face-to-face interactions.

Talking to Experts

Talking to experts is one of the most important steps in any commercialization study, particularly when a technology is in its early stages. Technically, talking to experts is not a VoC, since experts are not customers, but the questions we ask experts often take the perspective of customer requirements.

The first step is to identify experts we want to talk to. The starting point to identify possible contacts will likely be the technology developer or R&D team. Most technology developers are relatively familiar with the industry, and who the major players are. Technology developers go to technical conferences, they read scholarly journal articles and reports, and they talk to other people within their professional network. But the VoC researcher must be careful. Sometimes developers believe they can answer all the key commercialization questions on their own. However, it is important to remember that they are often understandably biased toward their own technological approach, especially if they have invested significant time, resources, and professional reputation in it. Because of this, developers may overlook important aspects of market behavior. They are not the customers; they are creators with a vested interest in the success of their solution.

The type of experts we want to talk to might include the following:
1) Opinion leaders in technology. These might include players on technical blogs programs or social media.
2) Lead authors of the most current articles or reports in the field.
3) Technical editors of the key journals in the field.
4) If there is a professional trade organization in the field, the chairperson or president of the trade organization.
5) If there is a standard setting organization (SSO) for the technology, contacts at the SSO. Be careful about this, however. Most members of SSOs are competitors, but there might be some unbiased and independent people, such as industry consultants who would be useful to talk to. If there is ample time for data gathering, it might make sense to join the SSO to receive information.

The next step is to arrange a discussion with people on the list. From our experience, as long as there is no conflict of interest, most experts in the field are quite willing to talk and provide their opinions.

However, there are some very important warnings prior to talking with anybody on this list.
1) These are experts and, by definition, represent "people skilled in the art". If you plan to send experts any materials describing the technology, such as a technology interest package (TIP), a video, or a PowerPoint presentation, take precautions. Always ensure that this information is reviewed and approved by your IP legal team or technology transfer office before sharing. This is an absolute requirement. You do not want to create a "publication" problem or be accused of putting critical IP into the public domain. Some experts may be willing to sign a non-disclosure agreement (NDA), but generally not. Just make sure that any technological information that is discussed does not rise to the level of "publication" or the release of a "trade secret".

2) Make sure you interview experts with a written list of questions. Without a list, it is easy to forget a critical point. Most of the time you only have one chance to talk to people. Also, make sure you are fluent enough about the technology to carry on a legitimate and intelligent conversation. Experts will not talk with anybody who does not have legitimacy. Depending upon the situation, it might be appropriate to have a member of the technical development team be part of the conversation with industry experts. Discussions of specifications, functionality, and performance can often get deeply technical in these conversations. However, the technical development members probably should not lead these conversations since the key is to uncover information in a somewhat neutral and unbiased manner.

Checklist for Expert Interview Questions

The key questions to cover with these experts include:
1) What are the market segments for this type of technology?
2) What are the key functions and requirements that customers will demand?
3) Where is the future going with these technologies, including possible forecasts on performance and specification requirements?
4) Who are some of the competitors that are playing in the space?
5) What are the requirements for selling into the market, and what steps are necessary to gain traction and success?
6) Then, if possible, allow these experts to give their opinion about your technology (provide them with a TIP or other written material that has been approved by your legal team)
7) Then always ask if there is another expert you should talk with.

Talking to Customers (the Actual VoC)

The techniques of gaining the actual customers' perspectives tend to be different depending upon the technology. Technologies that will be sold into the end-user markets often require a different type of VoC process than intermediate technologies that will be integrated as part of a larger system.

End-user markets are not just retail consumers. End-users are best described as people or organizations that utilize the technology as a final product, and have some say in the purchase decision. Thus, first responders would be the end-users for a new specialized white-powder anthrax testing kit. Shipping container manufacturers would be the end-user for a container tracking technology. Crime scene investigators might be end-users for a new fluid sampling and testing system designed for field use. Performing a VoC analysis for end-use technologies will normally employ traditional market research methods, such as focus groups.

Technologies that will be sold into the end-user markets often require a different
type of VoC process than intermediate technologies that will be
integrated as part of a larger system.

Intermediate users, however, are more like system integrators. Here our early-stage
technology, if successfully developed, will become a "component" in a larger system. A new,
long-lasting nano-battery technology might be sold to various computer and telecommu-
nication companies for integration into their next generation of products. Developing
an innovative, ultralight solar cell technology with high conversion efficiencies would
likely be used by the solar panel industry for integration into future panel designs. The
example of the "Escortin" cellular transport system, discussed earlier, would never be
used by itself but rather adopted perhaps by a dermatology hand-cream developer or
a drug delivery device firm. A VoC analysis of technologies sold to the intermediate
market generally requires more one-on-one discussions with company representatives
or system integrators. In many cases, system developers will have developed standardized specification and requirement sheets for components, but even with this, it is still
useful to have a one-on-one conversation.

Focus Groups

Focus groups are often seen as the go-to method for end-user market research. Focus
groups can be very effective if done correctly. A focus group is essentially bringing
together a small group of individuals within a well-controlled moderated setting. Focus
groups can be face-to-face, or online. Some of the key issues when performing a technology-based focus group are:

1. The optimum size of a focus group for early-stage technologies should be 5 to 10
   individuals.
2. Focus groups generally last about 1–1-½ hours.
3. Focus group members should be from the same target market segment. In some
   cases, if the technology is somewhat sensitive, or if the focus group attendees might
   be competitors, then each focus group conducted might need to be from the same
   organization.
4. You may have to pay or otherwise provide an incentive, such as food, to attend.
5. The moderator should be a good communicator and know how to manage a focus
   group. Focus groups need to be fairly structured, but also allow for discussion, and
   even tangents. But then, get back on track.
6. There are key questions that need to be answered when talking with potential
   users.

- How do you currently operate in the technological space, and what are current problems you encounter?
- What are the required functionalities or attributes of the technology that are key to a purchase decision?
- What weight is placed on these different attributes?
- What are the future price points and use if the technology was commercialized?
- Where do you think the technologies will be in the future, and what function-alities are changing?
- What is critical in order to bring this technology to the market?
- Are there recommended paths to the market?

Clearly, the set of questions will vary depending on the technology, but it is important for the moderator to have a set of questions that need to be answered.

7. If there is preliminary technical data that can be presented, have this ready.
8. It is always best to start the focus group with general questions, and then later become more specific on the technology and the details.
9. Focus groups always work better when early-stage technologies can be demonstrated. The best is a lab- or even early field prototype. If there is no working prototype, then use a dummy prototype, a picture of the technology, or a wire-frame presentation.
10. As always, be aware of IP issues. Some focus group members will sign NDAs but always clear a presentation with the legal team or technology transfer office.

Example: VoC with End User – Oysters

North Carolina farmed oysters are considered some of the tastiest in the U.S. However, they tend to be smaller and more irregular in shape. The highly competitive oyster farming industry tends to work the same way around the world. Young oysters are generally raised in independent hatcheries and then sold to oyster farmers either as eyed larvae or seedlings.

The larger oyster hatcheries are becoming more and more sophisticated each year. Rather than simply working on intuition and tradition, the leading North Carolina hatchery wanted to find out what end users (restaurants owners and oyster consumers) really wanted.[1] This was critical since a combination of components, such as water temperature, salinity, genetic selection, and other environmental factors can dramatically impact both the shape and taste of oysters. Face-to-face interviews were performed with the two major end-use markets throughout the U.S.: restaurateurs who purchased oysters and consumers who order and eat oysters. Both groups are important for commercial success. For example, raw oyster bars typically offer between 4 varieties and 8 varieties each day, and issues related to shape, taste, and branding/location appear highly important in these outlets.

A number of focus groups with oyster consumers were also conducted. In addition to a variety of taste, willingness to pay, and origination preference questions, the VoC research also involved showing consumers a variety of different photos of the *Crassostrea virginca*, or "eastern" oyster with an oyster knife for size reference (see Figure 8.1). Customers then provided a numerical rating for each photo. This part of the research was to uncover an accurate preference scale regarding the physical attributes of an oyster.

Figure 8.1: Visual comparison of *Crassostrea Virgenca* oyster types.

The results of the study indicated a strong preference for uniform shapes of oysters. Preference was also indicated for medium-sized, rather than very large or small oysters. Very large-sized oysters were actually seen by the sample majority as "unappealing". Other physical dimensions deemed important were top proportion, cup shape, color, and a depth/width ratio. In addition, approximately six different taste characteristics were uncovered. An analysis was performed to obtain a sophisticated mathematical model of the optimum look and taste. This attribute model was then adopted into the hatchery's technology and research, thus creating the foundation for a highly competitive and premium future oyster from North Carolina.

Personal Interviews

Direct Interviews are also very effective when doing a VoC analysis for early-stage technologies. Many times focus groups do not make sense or are simply too difficult to arrange. In these cases, direct interviews can work very well. Direct interviews can also be performed in combination with other methods, such as focus groups. As with focus groups, the interviewer needs to go in with a specific set of questions and prototypes if available. The advantage of a face-to-face interview, whether in person or using an online conference system, is that sometimes it is easier to uncover nuances. In addition, focus groups might be subject to "group think" and dominant personalities. However, like focus groups, any information that is being communicated must be approved by the developer's legal team or technology transfer office. Unlike focus groups, however, generally personal, face-to-face interviews tend to be shorter in length.

The optimum time for face-to-face interviews tends to be around 20 minutes. Oftentimes, a VoC analysis for an early-stage technology can be achieved with a relatively small sample of interviews, often 10–40 individuals depending on the technology.

Obtaining interviews with intermediate system integrators is probably one of the most difficult parts of a VoC analysis for component technologies. There are generally six ways to access the right person to talk to at a larger system integrator. Several of these methods are all considered "active" technology transfer methods, where significant effort needs to be taken to obtain connections. A good VoC analysis will combine these different approaches:

1) It is often relatively easy to get interviews with system developers simply by calling the firm to speak to the appropriate person, such as the product engineer or R&D manager. It might also be possible to get a contact e-mail and then send a TIP or PowerPoint presentation to start the discussions. From experience, the key issue here is not to seem like a salesperson, but rather a true cutting-edge technology developer interested in understanding the required functionality and future requirements for a component, or subsystem. Most product engineers and R&D managers are interested in new and improved component technologies, as these can enhance the competitiveness of their final products.

   The largest of the system integrators, developers, and manufacturers, such as Lockheed Martin, SpaceX, and Siemens, will inevitably have portfolios of multiple large future projects in development, each with its own requirements and stage of development. Many of these larger system integrators will also work with other large partners and sub-contractors for different subsystems. Sometimes each subsystem within these large firms will have a designated "system integrator" specifically responsible for managing the seamless integration of future technologies. Each of these systems, subsystems, and system integrator teams will have a contact person for legitimate discussion about future required parameters and functionality of components.

2) Develop a strong network of personal contacts, by attending relevant academic conferences, industry trade meetings, and standard setting organizations. Interviews with successful technology transfer officers and early-stage developers emphasize the importance of networking, networking, and networking.

3) Use a technology linker. Technology linkers are generally consultants who specialize in matching leading-edge technologies with potential users. They already have a strong network, they know the system requirements, and they understand the current technological developments in the field. These consultants tend to be very

industry-specific and may be independent consultants or employees of large consulting organizations.

4) In certain cases, there might be specific consortiums to facilitate technology transfer. For example, the Federal Laboratory Consortium for Technology Transfer assists technologies being developed at U.S. Government R&D laboratories. Individual states might offer assistance in developing contacts if the technology has export potential.

   The North Carolina Department of Commerce offers assistance to "find customers and partners" for technologies being developed within North Carolina. Most states with a high technology profile within the U.S., such as California, Texas, North Carolina, South Carolina, Illinois, Indiana, New York, Florida, and Massachusetts, might be able to provide effective linking assistance with certain technologies.

   Every country with a strong technology development orientation will also have national and regional agencies that might be of assistance in opening doors. South Korea, for example, has the National Research Council of Science & Technology (NST), with a specific mission to "promote technology transfer and commercialization" of home-grown technologies.

5) In many technology sectors, detailed reports are regularly published that forecast future requirements. For example, a search of future requirements for solar panel technology will uncover various reports that forecast the categories of the likely dominant technological approaches, such as perovskite cells, the expected future conversion rates, cost per kilowatt hour, environmental standards, durability standards, and other functionality requirements.

   These can be short-term forecasts, such as likely trends within a year's period, or longer-term forecasts with a five- to ten-year horizon. It is relatively easy to match a forecast with the expected date of commercialization for your early-stage technology. These types of forecasting reports are regularly published by top universities, academic journals, industry trade associations, consulting firms, and "white papers" from government agencies. Not only is the information useful, but the authors of these reports are often open to more detailed conversations as part of the VoC analysis.

   In addition, governments also publish many reports, often called "technology roadmaps" for large-scale government-related projects, such as space exploration. These can be quite detailed regarding future system and subsystem requirements and timing. Finally, formal grant announcements, such as Small Business Innovation Research (SBIR) and Broad Agency Announcements (BAA) in the U.S. can provide contacts.

6) Primary contractors, and their subcontractors, for large-scale systems like NASA's Mars Exploration Program may have already defined and even published specific system, subsystem, and component requirements for future bids and procurements. These large system developers will also hold regular Q&A sessions that might provide excellent information and contacts regarding future requirements.

Surveys and Telephone Interviews

Surveys and telephone interviews are common market research methods. However, remember that the VoC analysis at this point serves several purposes. It is generally used to uncover key functionality requirements identified by potential users. It also helps assess demand characteristics, understand the nature of competing developments, and identify the best path to market. This is particularly important for technologies still in relatively early stages of development, typically TRL2 to TRL6. VoC analysis almost always requires a back-and-forth process of feedback and discussions of functionality/specifications. In addition, a good VoC might also involve the possible demonstration of an early-stage prototype and other aspects of the technology that are difficult to obtain from paper surveys and telephone interviews.

There might be some cases, such as showing a wire-frame presentation for a new potential telephone app that will be sold into the mass market, where more traditional survey and telephone market research techniques might be appropriate.

Example: Telephone VoC with Intermediate Users – Facial Recognition Technology

Facial recognition technology is highly sophisticated and complex. In essence, facial recognition technology involves developing an algorithm for analyzing various features and points on a face (see Figure 8.2). However, to obtain an accurate algorithm, hundreds of thousands of different full frontal face images need to be analyzed using various databases, such as the well-known MORPH facial recognition longitudinal image database. The resulting algorithms can be licensed by facial recognition development companies, who then incorporate these algorithms into their systems. Many companies would rather license just the image databases and then develop their own facial recognition algorithms.

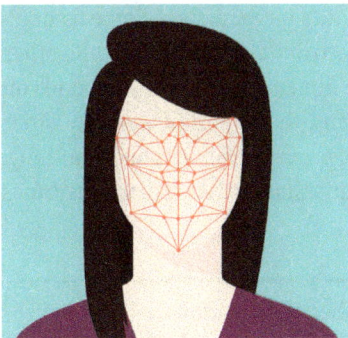

Figure 8.2: Facial recognition programming.

Facial recognition is used extensively for security reasons. However, a major problem is that most of the time people are not looking directly at the cameras in public places, such as in airports, malls, or banks. The camera often sees only partial or side views. In addition, the current algorithms are generated from almost expressionless or simple smiling facial images, when most people in reality are showing a variety of emotions, such as laughing, frowning, or talking, all which alter facial features.

A leading algorithm and facial recognition database developer needed to know what new features were going to be demanded by facial recognition system developers in the future.[2]

Telephone interviews with over 30 major international facial recognition system developers, both small entrepreneurial firms and many larger corporations, uncovered the need for developing a large-scale, full 3D image databases with six of the most common expressions, such as smiling, frowning, laughing, etc. Much more accurate algorithms can then be created to capture views from various facial positioning and normal expressions. This information provided the database developer with a clear target, including the most important facial expression functionality for future database development and commercialization.

Understanding Key Technology Requirements

One of the most important steps in any technology commercialization process is to clearly and accurately understand the dimensions that users, customers, and in some cases, influencers, use to evaluate competitive technologies. That is a key purpose of the VoC process.

Any technology or product may have multiple attributes that people can look at. However, psychological studies have shown that most customers use only a limited number of dimensions or attributes when they evaluate a product and then make their purchase decision depending on how a customer perceives a technology and how it scores on these dimensions or attributes. This is true of consumer technologies, end-user technologies, or components that are integrated into a larger system. Some technologies are evaluated on perhaps only a few important attribute dimensions, while other technologies might be evaluated on up to 10 attribute dimensions. It really depends on the technological space, but after these key dimensions, the importance of any other product attribute or dimension in the decision-making process drops to almost nothing. The VoC analysis should be designed to accurately understand what critical attributes and dimensions are being used by customers.

Most customers use only a limited number of dimensions
or attributes when they evaluate a product.

The VoC is critical in this effort, since the technology developers will often focus on only a few of the critical attributes and often not clearly understand the full range of evaluative attributes, or what is most important in the minds of the customers. The example below explains the technology requirements from a real-life VoC analysis from one of the technologies discussed throughout this book.

Example: System Components (Oscillating Quartz Crystals)

Component technologies also have a set of critical evaluative dimensions. For example, consider the component technology of oscillating quartz crystals. When electricity is applied, these quartz crystals change shape and oscillate at a very fast but predictable rate. This is known as the piezoelectric effect. When oscillating, it changes the voltage. Integrated circuits can then recognize this change in voltage and use it for accurate timing. This technology has a wide set of applications, such as regulating time in electronic watches and other instruments that require accurate timing, providing a stable clock signal for digital integrated circuits, and stabilizing frequencies for various communication systems. Applications include automotive and aircraft engine control, GPS systems, electronic warfare systems, navigation, and communication.

Quartz crystal engineers and inventors are always working on improvements to the technology. A VoC analysis completed for a quartz crystal development company indicated five basic attributes that different quartz technologies are evaluated on:[3]

- exactness of mean oscillation
- deviation of oscillation
- cost per unit
- failure rate over time
- resistance to shock events, and
- sensitivity to heat

There are certainly other product dimensions, but these were simply not as important. Since there are multiple applications for quartz crystal technologies, each application might have different requirements along the different attribute dimensions. For the key requirements, system developers will typically incorporate these within their bid procedures and contractual specifications. However, oftentimes important purchase attributes are not specified requirements, but still looked at seriously by system integrators. Within each dimension space, innovators can develop different and new approaches to the technology (either crystal-based, or using another technology that achieves the same, or perhaps better performance), as long as these requirements along the attribute dimensions are satisfied.

Each technology will have a different number of key dimensions. Most technologies are probably evaluated by customers on 10 or fewer key attributes. Of course, highly complex systems with major failure risks, such as aircraft control systems or rocket launch systems, may have many more requirements than the average technology. But a key part of a solid VoC analysis is to define these dimensions and the requirements within each dimension for different customer groups or system applications.

Presenting the Findings

The findings from the VoC analysis should always be organized and presented in a formal manner. There are a number of different, and often sophisticated, tools and models that might be used to present the information from a VoC analysis. In this chapter, we discuss three common approaches: technology requirements charts, position maps, and House of Quality tools.

Technology Requirements Charts/Table

The simplest and most common type of VoC presentation can be described as a "technology requirements chart or table" (see Figure 8.3 for an example of a technology requirements table). This is essentially a chart or table that identifies the important parameters, including the functionality, price, and design requirements that have been uncovered in the VoC analyses. Generally, a technology requirements chart/table will indicate the various parameters examined on the left column and sometimes, a future time frame on the top row, such as "current", 1 year out, 3 years out, etc. The matrix is then filled with the detailed information uncovered from the VoC analysis.

Technology Requirements Table					
Portable Weaponized Vapor Detection Detection Systems: Sarin (GB)					
Parameter	IDLH mg/m³	DH ppb	Current year 2026 Response Time	Forecast year 2029 Response Time	Forecast year 2032 Response Time
Sensitivity (Sarin)	0.1	15	<1 minute	<15 seconds	<3 seconds
False Positives			<5.0%	<1.0%	<0.1%
Detection Limits			3.0ppb	1.0ppb	0.5ppb

DH - Damage to Humans, ppb=parts per billion
IDLH immediately dangerous to life and health
Note: Modern portable vapor detection systems can detect many different dangerous chemicals.
Each chemical would have a separate requirements table to fully understand the full product requirements

Figure 8.3: Technology requirements table.

Position and Perceptual Maps

Position maps, or perceptual maps, are excellent tools to present findings when the attributes of a product or service being evaluated by the user include perceptual decisions. Position maps are generally employed for retail, consumer products, and when there are different groups of consumers, each with a particular preference for a product. Position maps can be used to understand the market dynamics of any type of product or service, including technologies. A comprehensive position or perceptual map can also identify unfulfilled needs in the market – that is, finding the "white spaces".

Although position maps are generally used when user perceptions are important, position maps are also useful in technology-driven products when there are multiple functionality dimensions, and a number of products are in the market using different combinations of these functionality requirements.

Steps in Position Map

There are three basic steps in developing a position map:

Step 1: Determine the Critical Purchase Dimensions That Customers Use to Analyze a Particular Product or Service. A product, such as an automobile, can literally have hundreds of attributes that might describe the product. Step 1 attempts to find the most critical dimensions, or "attributes" that users or customers view as important when analyzing products that lead to a purchase decision. For example, research has shown that customers tend to use four or five basic dimensions when analyzing mobile phones. These dimensions are often labeled the technology's screen size, color/aesthetics, apps and usability, cost, and handset features.[4]

The key at this stage is to identify the most critical factors influencing the customer's purchase decision from among the many possible product attributes. For technologies, this process can also assist in writing a "value proposition" for the technology, since a value proposition needs to focus on the key dimensions.

Step 2: Find the Preferences of Different Customer Segments. Markets for technologies, whether end user or system integrators, will tend to have different market segments. The requirements for quartz crystal oscillators that need to provide highly accurate timing for high-end, expensive wrist watches will be different from the market for quartz crystal oscillators that might end up in children's toys. Each of these market segments will place different levels of importance on the key dimensions from Step 2 – they will have preferences that will vary between customer groups or segments. These preferences are sometimes called "ideal or optimum points" for each of the market segments.

As an example, a small R&D laboratory developed an innovative through-wall motion detection system under contract with the Department of Defense (see figure 8.4). This system could be placed against a wall's exterior where the waves could penetrate through the wall. Once the waves penetrated the wall, the system could identify motion from living organisms inside the next room and then get that information back through the wall to the motion detection unit.

The unit, still in a laboratory prototype (TRL5) stage when the VoC was performed was not only highly accurate, but tunable where shorter penetration distances would have even higher sensitivity. A full VoC analysis was performed to determine potential markets and requirements.

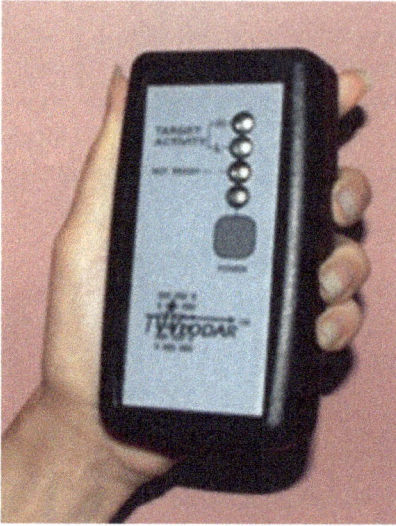

Figure 8.4: Laboratory prototype: Through-wall motion detection system.

Two important civilian target markets were uncovered through interviews and focus groups.[5] The most obvious included the SWAT market where police might be interested in locating a hiding suspect in a room. However, the VoC research uncovered another important market segment not originally considered, the pest control market, where the targets were mice or even insects moving within a wall. The results of the VoC analysis were effectively presented in a position map (the positioning map in Figure 8.5 is simplified, with sensitivities, distances, and other information removed for confidentiality reasons).

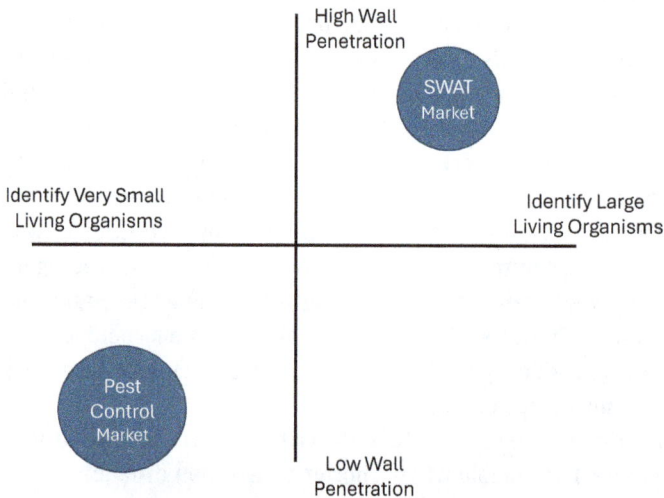

Figure 8.5: Position map: Through-wall motion sensor technology.

Unfortunately, Step 2 is often skipped in a position map analysis. However, Step 2 is essential for understanding the requirements of key market segments – and determining whether a single, generic technology can meet the needs of diverse users, or if multiple models, brands, or technological approaches are necessary to serve distinct submarkets. This is a key question during the development phase of any technology or product.

Step 3: Determine the Perception That Customers Have Regarding Different Products, Brands, or Technologies In this step, for retail goods, consumers are asked their perceptions as to how different brands rank on the critical purchase dimensions. For more intermediate technology products or components, actual specifications for the different technologies can be assessed on the critical dimensions.

This third step is usually completed when there are actual brand names or products on the market. The two-dimension perceptual maps often shown in textbooks are simple examples. Actual perceptual mapping is almost always multi-dimensional, which can be presented in different ways. The Figure 8.6 below shows one approach for presenting step 3 along multi-dimensions[6]:

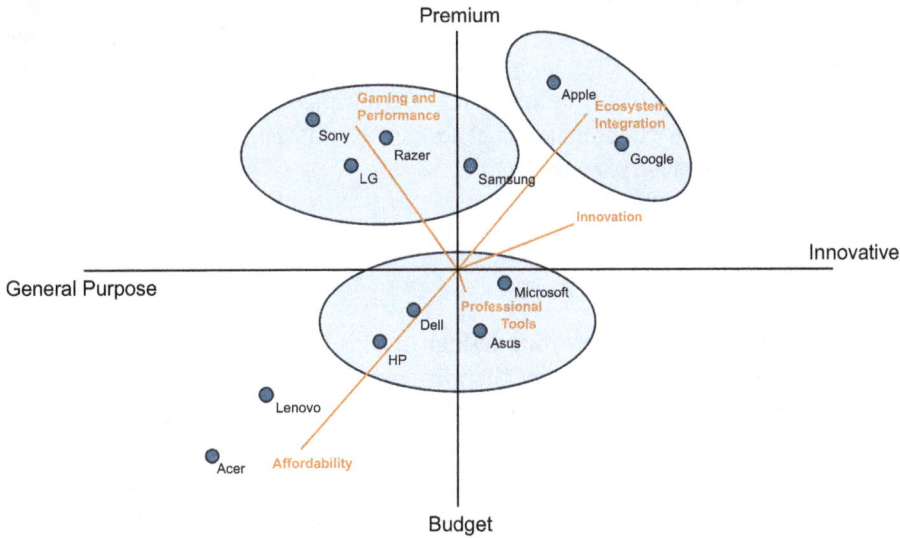

Figure 8.6: Example of a multi-dimensional perceptual map.

Market researchers will oftentimes only perform Step 1 and Step 3 resulting in a map of brand positioning, as shown in the above shampoo map. However, much greater insight can be obtained by combining all three steps on the same map. When customer segment preferences (Step 2) are shown on the same map with the perception of different products or brands (Step 3), it will then indicate which products or brands satisfy the preferences on certain markets, and perhaps where there are opportunities and gaps in the market for a new product. This is particularly helpful when developing new technologies or products for the segmented market, whether these markets are end-users or system developers. Finding gaps or "white spaces" in the market is always considered one of the key issues for successful technology commercialization. This can also assist in developing the "value statement" for a new technology when pitching to investors or stakeholders.

Summary of Basic Position Maps

Position maps are powerful tools, particularly for communicating the results of a VoC analysis or market research. While position maps are most commonly used to analyze brand positioning in retail markets with consumer products, their utility extends beyond that. These tools can be easily adapted to technology-based products and services. This is especially helpful when a technology developer is trying to identify gaps and opportunities within an existing market.

Properly determining the actual underlying dimensions or critical attribute bundles in Step 1 is where most errors are created in perceptual mapping. There are several different approaches to asking the right questions during a VoC analysis in order to create an effective position map, depending on what positional mapping tool is being used. The analysis can also be highly technical, utilizing advanced statistical techniques such as factor analysis and multi-dimensional scaling. Specialized position map programs can easily be downloaded from the web.

Weighted Perceptual Maps

Perhaps the major criticism regarding position maps is that all the attribute dimensions are presented as equally important. There is no weighting regarding how important one attribute, such as cost or a functional aspect of the technology, is against all the other attributes that a customer uses to evaluate a technology or product. As such, a number of variations have been proposed attempting to overcome this limitation. The simplest is a "weighted perceptual map". The advantage of showing dimensions can be significant, since importance weights are used to reflect the relative significance of different attributes in shaping the customers' perception, and by incorporating these weights, the perceptual map becomes much more nuanced.

Using a perceptual map with importance weights can assist in identifying gaps in the current marketplace as well as tailoring the communication of your technology's advantages to potential customers.

Since perceptual mapping is a visual presentation, the relative importance and the weightings are also visual in nature. The most common method to show the importance of particular dimensions to the consumer is either by color or by the width of the dimension arrow line.

Other more advanced techniques, such as the Kano method, have also been developed to incorporate attribute importance. These tools and techniques are often covered in advanced marketing classes.

House of Quality

The House of Quality is a presentation tool that combines both customer requirements and design/engineering standards. Position mapping, for example, focuses only on understanding the market. However, every technology or product also needs to match its design to the market requirements. The House of Quality is one important tool that combines these two issues.

The House of Quality is a presentation tool that combines both customer requirements and design/engineering standards.

The House of Quality and its variations are often taught in advanced design management courses, as tools of "quality function deployment", or QFD. QFD methods and tools are used to transform user demands into design quality. QFD is regularly taught in training and certification programs such as Lean Six Sigma. The House of Quality is an effective QFD tool, particularly for technologies still in development phases, or even in the market, where there is still an opportunity to improve certain design elements.

Steps for a House of Quality Analysis

The House of Quality analysis has six basic steps:

Step 1: Similar to Step 1 in position maps, we need to research and understand the requirements of users or customers and rank the importance of these requirements to the purchase decision. This information is usually placed on the left side of the "House".

Step 2: We then determine the elements or features in the product or technology design, such as weight, size, and functionality performance, which correspond with the different purchase requirements. This information is placed on the top of the house.

Step 3: We compare how our product or technology performs on each of these product design or engineering components. This information is analyzed within the house matrix.

Step 4: We then map how competitor products or technologies perform on each of these design or engineering components. This is often called "competitive benchmarking" and is often placed on the right side of the house.

Step 5: Interactions between design features are determined. These interactions are shown on the roof.

Step 6: We can then determine where improvements are most needed in our design in order to increase our market success. This is shown on the lower level or foundation of the house.

The House of Quality attempts to visually combine these steps into one diagram. The diagram represents a house with sides and roofs, thus the name "House of Quality". There are different formats of the House of Quality, and slightly different approaches will use different symbols and rating systems.

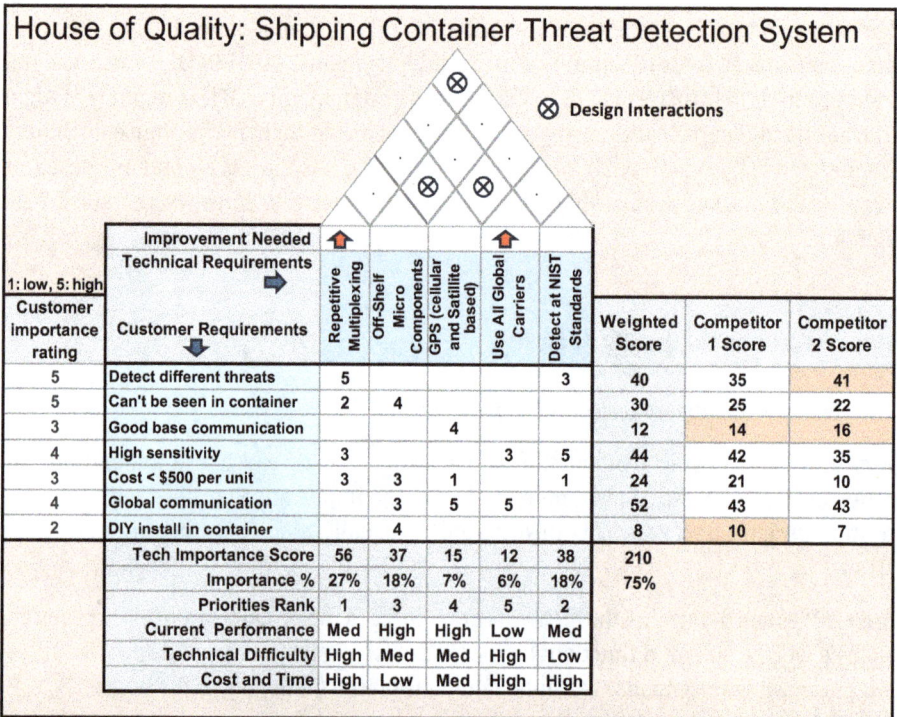

House of Quality: Shipping Container Threat Detection System

⊗ Design Interactions

Customer importance rating 1: low, 5: high	Customer Requirements	Repetitive Multiplexing	Off-Shelf Micro Components	GPS (cellular and Satilite based)	Use All Global Carriers	Detect at NIST Standards	Weighted Score	Competitor 1 Score	Competitor 2 Score
5	Detect different threats	5				3	40	35	41
5	Can't be seen in container	2	4				30	25	22
3	Good base communication			4			12	14	16
4	High sensitivity	3			3	5	44	42	35
3	Cost < $500 per unit	3	3	1		1	24	21	10
4	Global communication		3	5	5		52	43	43
2	DIY install in container		4				8	10	7
	Tech Importance Score	56	37	15	12	38	210		
	Importance %	27%	18%	7%	6%	18%	75%		
	Priorities Rank	1	3	4	5	2			
	Current Performance	Med	High	High	Low	Med			
	Technical Difficulty	High	Med	Med	High	Low			
	Cost and Time	High	Low	Med	High	High			

Figure 8.7: Example of a House of Quality.

A comprehensive House of Quality analysis combines a VoC analysis with the design and engineering team. It is considered one of the most effective presentation tools to assess a technology's design and identify potential areas for design improvement.

Figure 8.7 utilizes an actual example from a shipping container threat detection system. House of Quality designs all have the same elements, but can be presented in a simple or complex manner.

Concluding Insights

A voice of the customer (VoC) analysis is one of the most important steps in any technology commercialization process. A VoC can be relatively simple, as in a quick-look" early-stage commercialization assessment, or it can be highly detailed and time consuming. In general, the more detailed the VoC analysis, the better the results will be. But an actual VoC analysis depends on the nature of the technology, whether the technology is being sold into the end-user market or as a component within a larger system, the technology's stage of development, and the resources available to perform the VoC analysis.

Gut intuition does not work well when it comes to understanding technological markets. Intuition, while part of human nature, is often biased and highly incomplete when assessing technology commercialization. Some intuition might be helpful, but the more we can talk to and understand the customers' voices, the better decisions we will make regarding the best designs for commercialization.

A VoC analysis might show there is little hope for successful commercialization, in which case the technology may need to be abandoned. In many cases, a VoC analysis will identify potential opportunities, and whether a pivot is needed to target the appropriate set of customers, whether these customers are end users or system integrators. In addition, a VoC analysis will assist in identifying what functionalities are required to meet customers' demands and where we need to place our design efforts. A VoC analysis will also help design a communication strategy for the technology.

Presenting a VoC analysis, whether by a simple technology requirements table or something more complex such as a position map or House of Quality, is also critical. A well-done VoC presentation not only allows management, investors, and the design team to understand the critical issues, but the effort of putting together a VoC presentation will also likely bring the major commercialization issues into better focus.

This chapter only touched upon the major presentation tools. There are a number of other sophisticated statistical and presentation tools, such as Kano models, conjoint analysis, stated choice methodologies, and other decision-based design and quality function deployment tools that can be employed, depending on the nature of both the technology and market.

Chapter Example: VoC and Understanding Customer Requirements – Rapid Response Biological Toxin Testing Kits

Problem

On September 18, 2001, only one week after the 9/11 World Trade Tower attack, another attack against civilians occurred. Letters containing weaponized anthrax were mailed to a number of people, including two U.S. Senators. Five people died, and many more were hospitalized. This attack immediately raised concerns about future bio-terrorism events.

There are a number of biological toxins that can be used by terrorists. Toxins generally attack the nervous systems of mammals and can lead to death. Toxins are biological in nature, unlike chemical weapons such as the nerve gases and blistering mustard agents used in WW1. Chemical agents are still present in everyday life. A pepper spray is a chemical irritant, and many insect repellents function by targeting nervous system pathways, similar to low-grade nerve agents. Weaponized toxins are generally more sophisticated and deadly, since they do not dissipate easily in air.

Anthrax is a naturally occurring bacterium, but to make it deadly enough to constitute a weapon, anthrax needs to be "weaponized" into a highly concentrated "white powder". This is a difficult process. Once weaponized, anthrax is extremely deadly, particularly if it comes into skin contact or inhaled. However, there are other potential biological threats, such as ricin, staphylococcal enterotoxin B, botulinum toxins, abrin, and T-2 toxins.[7] All of these have been used in various terrorist attacks in the past several decades and are part of the portfolio of biological warfare agents developed by programs in various countries and by terrorists. Most of these agents are also delivered in powder form. Millions of government dollars continue to be allocated to develop rapid, first-responder white powder detection systems, since weaponized biological toxins look like many other daily use white powder products.

After the anthrax attacks in 2001, anytime somebody noticed white powder in a public place they would immediately call the emergency numbers. A fully suited HazMat, first-responder team would show up, collect the sample, and shut down the building for 24–48 hours while an outside lab ran complicated tests to determine the nature of the white powder. Almost always, it turned out to be sugar, baking powder, baby powder/talc, or flour.

But the economic damage was done, including shutting down schools, libraries, corporate and government offices, and factories for long periods of time. Even the Los Angeles Airport was closed for hours due to a white powder scare that turned out to be dairy creamer. While the public fear has died down a little in the last several years, white powder seen in envelopes, government buildings, or any place where it seems out of place still generates an immediate response. In fact, white powder alerts are still the number one mail threat seen by the U.S. Post Office with thousands of white powder incidents per year.[8] Thousands more per year are still reported in buildings, where first responders need to respond.

Due to the immense amount of concern, a large number of R&D groups in universities, corporations, and government laboratories have worked on the problem of detecting biological threats. At one point, the authors of this book were asked by a Department of Defense agency to conduct a commercialization study on various toxin testing systems. The goal was to determine which technological approach had the highest potential for future success. Congress was demanding that the agency focus its funding more strategically. There are many highly sophisticated approaches to the problem. These included traditional molecule markers, micro-pore methods, wavelength bending techniques, electrical conductivity techniques, and chemical techniques to name a few. All of these approaches were based on excellent, advanced science, and all could reasonably detect tiny amounts of biological agents with minimal false negatives (saying it is safe, when not).

What Did the Market Actually Want?

The detailed VoC analysis was performed with first responders and found there were actually many other technology characteristics that needed to be considered in addition to low false negatives and sensitivity to microscopic amounts of the agents.[9] The VoC uncovered several additional dimensions that mattered to users. These included low false positives, so buildings would not be shut down unnecessarily. Portability was also important, as the equipment needed to be easy to transport on-site. Durability was critical because first responders often drop or rough-handle gear. Other key attributes were multiplexing or the ability to detect multiple types of biological agents, ease of use, and quick response speed. Finally, cost was a major factor. Users did not want to spend $1,000 every time the device was triggered, especially if the substance turned out to be something harmless like baby powder (see Figure 8.8).

All these dimensions were important to the first responder customers, with some such as sensitivity and false negatives being most important. About 20 early-stage competitive detection technologies were then assessed on these dimensions, with different technological solutions scoring differently on different dimensions,

The vast majority of the highly sophisticated technologies did not score high on many of the other key requirement dimensions. Ultimately chemical approaches became the recommended solution for quick, first-responder white-powder identification. The market had spoken.

Lesson

Good science or an elegant solution is never sufficient for commercial success. The market will often determine the dominant product design based upon a number of customer-based criteria. That is the purpose of a good commercialization study and VoC analysis. Oftentimes the market-based criteria may result in a dominant product design that is not the most advanced or technically elegant but best satisfies customer requirements.

Solution

Building upon these multiple customer requirements, currently one of the most commonly used solutions for first-responder testing for a white powder threat is the BioCheck 20/20 powder screening kit. This solution identifies 99% of the white powders as non-threatening. If the screening markers turn red, however, then call HazMat and let the lab do the final testing.

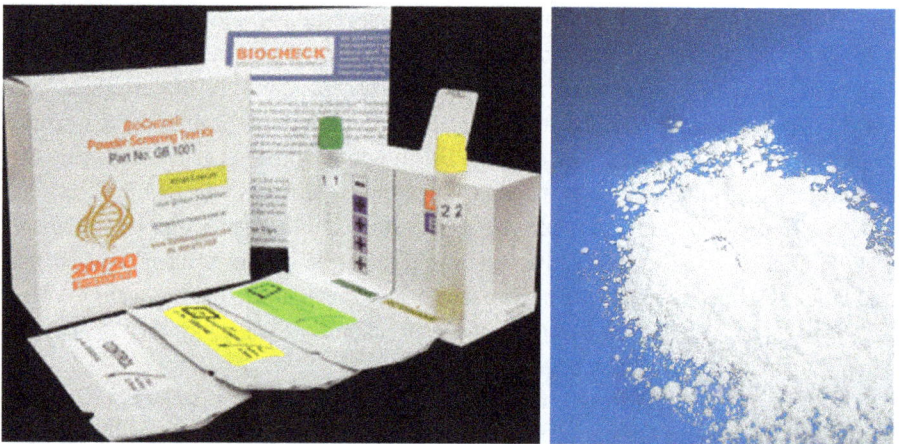

Figure 8.8: Baby powder or terrorism?

Chapter 9
Phased-Review and R&D Portfolio Management

This Chapter

- Examines the challenges faced by large organizations managing a diverse and evolving portfolio of R&D and technology development projects.
- Introduces the phased-review process, a widely used managerial tool in large technology-focused firms.
- Explains the role of gate scorecards in evaluating progress within the phased-review process.
- Highlights the importance of managing R&D initiatives as a portfolio and presents tools such as the Technology Project Portfolio Map (TPPM) to support strategic decision-making.

Key Management Tools Discussed

- Phase-review methods
- PhaseGate scorecards
- Technology project portfolio maps (TPPMs)

❗ INSIGHT

While most start-up entrepreneurial firms are built around only one or two innovations, larger corporations typically have dozens, if not hundreds, of R&D programs and technologies being developed, all at the same time.

This creates unique managerial problems for these larger organizations. What technologies should I support when I have only limited resources? What is the process for evaluating and reviewing technologies as they move toward commercialization? What criteria should I use for these decisions?

These questions required a formal evaluation process. Formal phased-review processes have become almost standard in larger, technology-driven firms.

Introduction

The popular press often argues that small businesses are responsible for the bulk of technological innovation. After all, the entrepreneurial spirit, combined with non-bureaucratic, nimble decision-making and focused research efforts, should, it is believed, encourage the most, and best, innovation. The actual truth is a little more complicated.

https://doi.org/10.1515/9783111684420-010

The U.S. Small Business Administration (SBA) reports that the largest corporations engaging in R&D actually have more patents issued per employee than small R&D businesses under 500 employees. But the rate of innovation for business is actually very curvilinear. The smallest U.S. R&D firms, under 20 employees, patent far more than all other firms, small or large. When it comes to patent applications, micro firms with fewer than four employees have the highest rate of patent filings. Unfortunately, the success rate is not very high with these smallest of firms.

Recent data also suggests that larger corporations are now innovating with a higher success rate than they were 20 years ago. Almost 50% of the U.S. patents are filed by the largest 2% of U.S. companies. Larger firms are even more dominant in other regions throughout the world, such as Asia and Europe, which do not have the same entrepreneurial culture as in the U.S. Innovation dynamics also vary across industries. In some sectors, smaller firms drive much of the innovation, while in others, larger firms tend to dominate the technology commercialization process.

Not surprisingly, over the past two decades, larger firms have become much more strategic in the way they approach all aspects of innovation, technological development, and commercialization. Perhaps the rise of new, now commercially viable technologies, such as AI, nanotechnology, space exploration, and biotechnology, is forcing the issue. Perhaps there is simply more global competition from large players in rapidly developing countries such as China, India, and South Korea. Regardless of the reasons, larger firms are now much more serious in implementing basic technology management principles than ever before. To be successful in the modern world, even large organizations must now be agile and fluid, or to paraphrase the title of an early best-selling book by James Belasco, "Elephants can be taught to Dance".[1]

While prior chapters are relevant to all technology-driven organizations, large or small, this chapter focuses primarily on the key commercialization processes typically used by medium- and large-sized organizations.

Keys to Creating an Innovative Culture

Much has been written about the keys to successful innovation in larger organizations. Courses are now offered at many universities that specialize in technology management and innovation. Even the term "corporate entrepreneurship" has taken on new meaning.

Successful management of technology and innovation can generally be summarized by six critical points (see Figure 9.1).

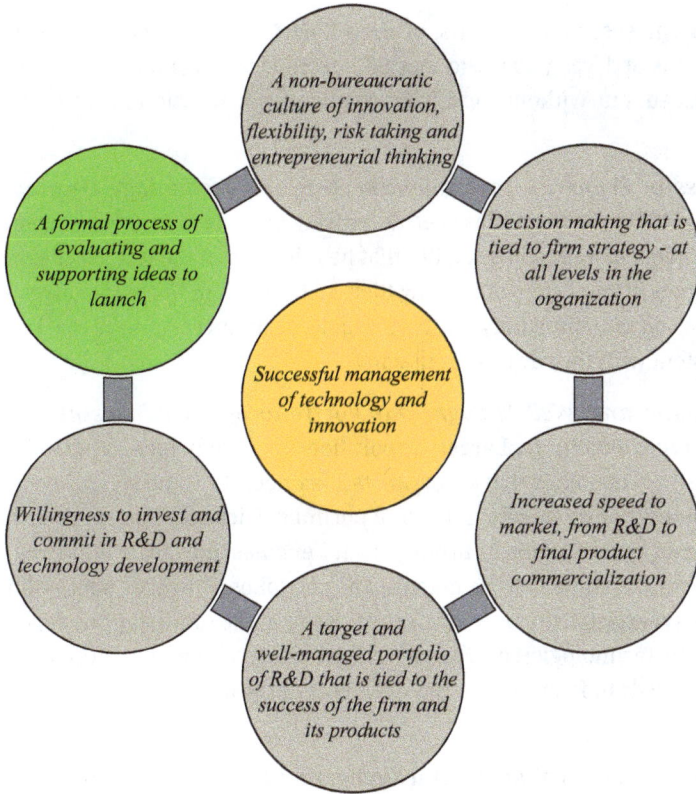

Figure 9.1: Six critical points of successful management of technology.

Point 1: A Non-Bureaucratic Culture of Innovation, Flexibility, Risk Taking and Entrepreneurial Thinking. Innovative organizations, particularly larger entities, need to purposely develop a culture that is conducive to innovation. This always requires aggressively reducing corporate bureaucracy, making the organization flatter, and rewarding entrepreneurial thinking at all levels.

Point 2: Decision-Making That Is Strategic at All Levels in the Organization. Old organizations are often stuck in formal planning systems that can take years to implement key decisions. There is simply no opportunity for real-time decision-making and pivoting. Modern technology-driven organizations need to think and respond immediately as new innovations are discovered, competitive products appear in the marketplace, and regulations change. Few of these events fit into an annual formal planning cycle.

Point 3: Increased Speed to Market, from R&D to Final Product Commercialization. Speed to market is key in the modern business world. Decades ago, radical product innovations might occur every 5 or 6 years, or even longer. Now, product life cycles might be only 6 months or 1 year. Speed to market – from idea to commercialization – needs to be shortened, but without sacrificing good strategic decision-making and quality.

Point 4: Willingness to Prioritize Investment in R&D and Technology Develop-ment. Over the years, R&D investment has been decreasing in many industries, as companies became more bloated and top heavy. But that has changed in the last decade, as successful firms are now dramatically increasing their R&D spending. Corporate investments need to refocus on one thing only – activities that create success in the marketplace that are consistent with the corporate mission.

Point 5: A Synergistic and Well-Thought-Out Portfolio of R&D Investments, Technologies, and Final Products. Larger corporations inevitably have a portfolio of products. Successful technology-driven organizations need to think about every step in their internal technology development as a portfolio. Each step in the process, R&D programs, patents, technologies in prototype and engineering stage, and products actually in the market, all need to be managed as portfolios. However, successful portfolios need to be synergistic, not only with other efforts at the same stage of development, but also with technologies in different stages of development. Ultimately, however, everything needs to focus on the requirements of the customers in creating value.

Point 6: A Formal Process of Evaluating and Supporting Technologies, from Idea to Commercialization. Moving technologies through the various development phases and making sure all the requirements are met, such as improving time to market, identifying synergistic relationships, increasing the likelihood of commercial success, efficiently allocating scarce resources among multiple projects, and analyzing product fit with the organizational strategies and mission, is not easy. It requires a formal process of evaluation and decisions.

While all six points are critical for any organization operating in technology markets, the last two points are the focus of this chapter. Developing a process of evaluating and supporting technologies, from idea to commercialization, is critical for any organization, regardless of size. In larger organizations, this process needs to be formal while considering the complexity of managing a portfolio of different R&D and technology projects.

Most small entrepreneurial start-up firms are built around one core technology. By nature, these entrepreneurs will think about nothing else. Most likely, however, much of this focus will be informal in nature – after all, everything for these small firms, from people to resources, is focused on just that one technology. It is almost like a birthing process.

Larger organizations are different. There are always multiple R&D and development programs, each competing with others in seeking internal support and funding. It is likely, however, that only a small fraction of the early-stage technologies being developed in a corporation's R&D labs will make it to the final market. In these situations, there needs to be a formal process that evaluates potential and then decides on what technologies to support into the future. Difficult go/no-go decisions need to be made. For any large organization, each technology project, regardless of the stage of development, is simply one part in a larger portfolio of products. Some technologies might be absolutely critical to the future success of the organization. Other technologies might take more of a supporting role and many technologies might simply be pushed off to the side.

This problem is common among all types of large organizations involved with product development, whether they are relatively new, fast-growing high-tech enterprises or more traditional consumer product firms, like Proctor & Gamble, Unilever, or Whirlpool Corp. They all need to make tough decisions about what innovations to support, and what to let die.

Review, Evaluation, and Support: A Phased-Review Process

One of the earliest leaders in thinking about how to develop a formal process for reviewing, evaluating, and supporting new products as they move from idea to commercialization was Dr. Robert Cooper, a research fellow at Penn State University's Smeal College of Business.[2] Early in his career, he saw that while many large corporations had informal methods for evaluating product development, there needed to be a formal, standardized process. He subsequently designed the StageGate® process that formalized the review process from "Idea to Launch".

The Original StageGate®

The idea behind the StageGate® process, while cleverly named, is fairly simple. There are Stages where activities are performed in the organization, such as R&D effort to move a technology through the patenting process or to get a lab prototype working. Then there are Gates, or review and approval steps where a technology or product must get through in order to move to the next stage. StageGate® formalized this phased-review process.

Figure 9.2 shows an example map of a simple 5-gate StageGate® or phased review process.

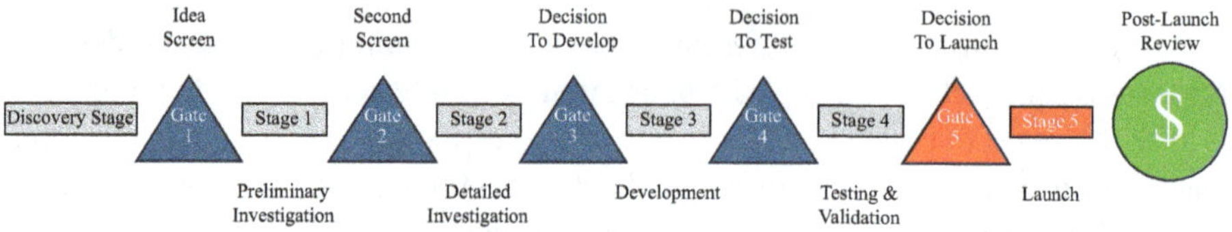

Figure 9.2: Simple map of the StageGate® process.

The StageGate® tool was originally designed for new product development in more traditional, retail-oriented market spaces, such as household goods and appliances. In a technology-based firm, however, the stages might be better defined as activities involved in moving a technology through different TRL levels, while the gates would be an approval process when a technology gets to a particular TRL phase and needs support to move forward to the next TRL. Figure 9.3 shows a simple example of what a StageGate® process might look like when applied in a technology-based context.

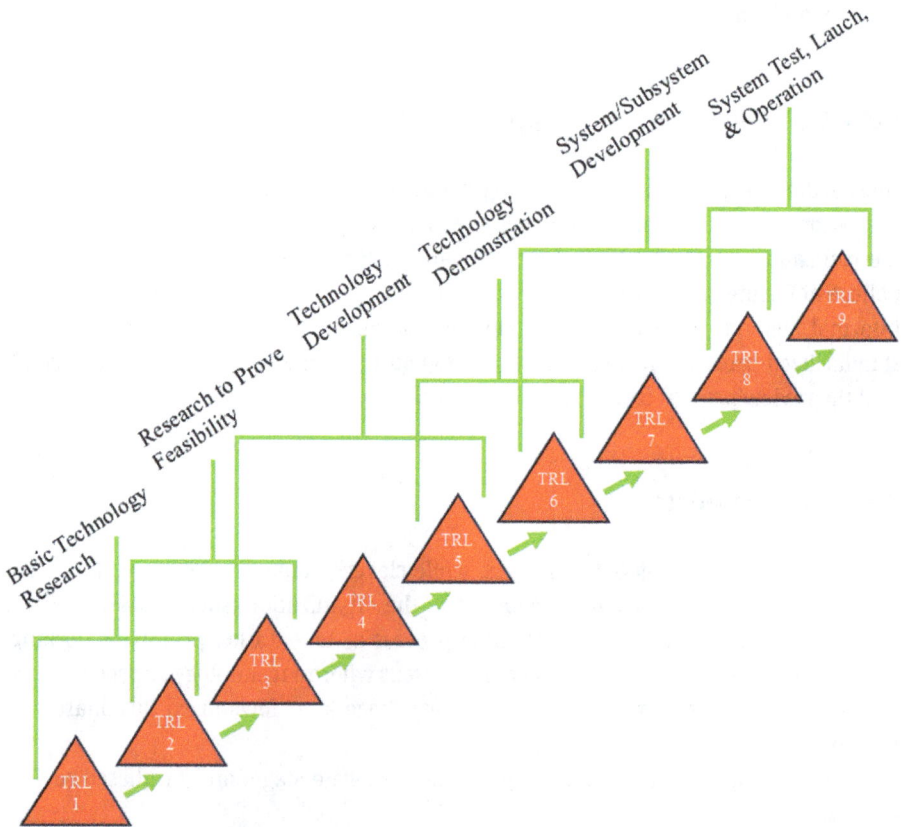

Figure 9.3: Example of a technology-based StageGate® process.

For a pharmaceutical company, the stages might be defined more along the lines of R&D, in vitro drug development, animal testing, and the 3-phased human testing process in order to obtain governmental drug approval, rather than TRLs.

Regardless of how the activities or stages are defined, the "gates" represent a formal review process that follows a carefully crafted format. In this process, there can certainly be other, more frequent review steps during each stage, such as monthly or weekly progress reports and discussions, but major support decisions need to get through these highly formalized gates. While a number of different phased-review formats have been created for larger corporations, the major contribution of the original StageGate® probably lies in how the gates, or review steps should be organized.

In general, each gate in a "best-practice" phased-review process has certain requirements.

1) The gate is where resource allocation and prioritization takes place. Go or No-Go decisions are made at the gates.
2) The gate is where key issues for each product or technology are evaluated. The critical issues will be different for each gate as a product or technology progresses through its development cycle. Corporate management needs to carefully structure when the gates occur and what specific issues need to be evaluated at each gate.
3) The gate should use a scorecard to examine each of the important issues at that particular gate. These scorecards can provide a numerical score that might allow a product or technology to pass through the gate, be rejected, or sent back for more work.
4) The gate needs to employ interdisciplinary teams for the review. The make-up of the teams will vary, depending on the gate. An early gate might have more technical reviewers, a mid-cycle gate will have more engineering and manufacturing reviewers, and a later gate will probably have more marketing and distribution reviewers.

Example of a Gate Scorecard in a Phased-Review Process

An example of a gate scorecard based on many of the topics discussed in this book is shown in Figure 9.4. We have adapted this scorecard to reflect a technology-oriented product. This specific example might be typical for a gate when moving a technology out of the R&D lab (e.g., TRL3/TRL4) and into the prototype development phase (TRL5). This gate scorecard incorporates both "Go/No-Go" requirements, and a scoring process based on items under each category. Actual gate scorecards would be specifically designed for the needs of each organization, and the topics/weights would change for each gate along the development cycle. The issues to be evaluated and rated on each gate's scorecard should be carefully considered and agreed upon by senior management.

Gate Scorecard: Advancement to Prototype Development	Yes Go	No No Go	Weight Importance	Scoring 1=not known/not positive, 10=known/very positive										Weighted Score
				1	2	3	4	5	6	7	8	9	10	
Commercialization Study Completed? X														
Expert Opinions			5.00%	1	2	3	4	5	6	X	8	9	10	0.35
VoC Customer Requirements Known			10.00%	1	2	3	4	5	6	7	X	9	10	0.8
Market Verticals Established			5.00%	1	2	3	4	5	X	7	8	9	10	0.3
Path to Market Known			10.00%	1	2	3	4	5	6	7	X	9	10	0.8
Technology Triage Completed? X														
Strength of IP			10.00%	1	2	3	4	5	6	7	8	X	10	0.9
Ability to Generate Future IP			5.00%	1	2	3	4	5	6	7	8	9	X	0.5
Ability of Team to Develop			5.00%	1	2	3	4	5	6	7	8	9	X	0.5
Technical Feasibility			5.00%	1	2	3	4	5	6	7	8	9	X	0.5
Financial Analysis Completed? X														
Pro-Forma Developed			5.00%	1	2	3	X	5	6	7	8	9	10	0.2
Initial Valuation Positive			5.00%	1	2	X	4	5	6	7	8	9	10	0.15
Return on Investment			5.00%	1	2	X	4	5	6	7	8	9	10	0.15
Risk Analysis Completed			5.00%	1	2	3	4	5	X	7	8	9	10	0.3
Strategic Fit? X														
Presented to Senior Management			5.00%	1	2	3	4	5	6	7	8	9	X	0.5
Synergistic with Other Technologies			5.00%	1	2	3	4	5	6	7	X	9	10	0.4
Consisted with Strategic Plan			10.00%	1	2	3	4	5	6	7	8	9	X	1
Project Team Established			5.00%	1	2	3	4	5	6	X	8	9	10	0.35
Total			100.00%											7.7000 times 10
Support>70, No Support<40, Revaluate 40 to 70														77

Figure 9.4: Example of a gate scorecard.

In this example, all the initial Go/No-Go criteria are met – a commercialization study, technology triage, and financial analysis have all been completed. Additionally, the technology fits within the overall corporate strategy and mission. Once these "go/no-go" criteria are met, then the review team can score the different items. In this case, with a 77 score, the technology passes to the next stage, with support. It is also obvious from the scorecard results, however, that a stronger financial analysis needs to be done, and this might be an additional request by the review team.

Proper Use of Gate Scorecards

Gate scorecards must be used properly and judiciously.

1) The development team typically presents their technology or product to the review team as a formal process, almost like an entrepreneur might present to an angel investor group.
2) The review team should be interdisciplinary, with members from different functions within the corporation. The make-up of the team will vary, depending on the gate. For the example above, a review team might include mostly engineers and manufacturing people, with a couple of marketing and finance folks.
3) After the presentation, the review team should try to gain a consensus about the scores.
4) While scorecards can provide Go and No-Go decisions based upon high and low scores, respectively, technologies with middle scores are often asked to do more research on the low-scoring items and then repeat their presentation at a later date.

Gate Scorecards versus Technology Readiness and Commercialization Success Scorecards

There is somewhat of an overlap with the idea of the Technology Readiness and Commercialization Success prediction models discussed in a later chapter, and the gate scorecards discussed in this chapter. While there are similarities, the objective is somewhat different.

Technology Readiness and Commercialization Success prediction models are primarily designed to predict how successful a technology might be in commercialization, and whether the technology is developed enough to even think about commercialization. These are most often used by interested external reviewers, such as grant reviewers, consultants, and private equity investors.

Gate scorecards are internal review tools used to move technologies through the various stages of the development cycles within larger, more integrated organizations. They are essentially tools used for internal funding and support. Gate scorecards should also be different for each gate, with an emphasis on the critical issues for that particular gate.

Thoughts on Phased-Review Processes

Phased-review processes, such as StageGate®, are a very clean way of organizing the internal review and support process as R&D programs, technologies, and products move from early-stage ideas to final market commercialization.

The vast majority of larger corporations, and many medium-sized firms, now use some type of a phased-review process.

The vast majority of larger corporations, and many medium-sized firms, now use some type of a phased-review process. This process might have different names in different organizations, such as "PhaseGate", "Phase-Review", "TollGate", "Decision Gates" "Waterfall Process" "Go/No-Go Reviews", or StageGate®. Some corporations have extremely sophisticated procedures, while others might be less formal. But they all have a common idea of technology or product development, followed by a review process, to gain support for the next phase of future development. All of this is done with the goal of identifying and supporting the technologies or products with the highest potential for successful commercialization.

A formal internal phased-review process can also help reduce infighting among different technology development programs. Larger technology development companies are well-known for different R&D teams aggressively lobbying for their share of scarce resources – an understandable problem, given that the careers of scientists, software developers, and design engineers are often at risk, if involved in out-of-favor projects.

Artificial Intelligence is now starting to be used in certain internal phased-review processes. A full review of the possibilities of using a phase-based process of internal technology development review, whether calling it StageGate® or something else, can readily be found online, and in various articles and books.

Analytical Tools for Phased-Based Management

The most sophisticated phased-based processes can also employ a variety of statistical and analytical techniques and tools (see Figure 9.5 for an example of a statistics and quality tool that can be used in innovative environments). Some of these statistical and analytical tools are most appropriate for early stages of development, while others are useful for later stages.

In previous chapters, we discussed some of the tools available when presenting a Voice of the Customer analysis. These included technology requirement tables, position maps, and House of Quality. However, many other statistical and analytical tools are also available. Some are quite sophisticated, while others are relatively simple. Some of these tools are used for project management, since almost all technology commercialization involves project teams. Other tools are used as part of quality development, design thinking, or market research. These tools include conjoint analysis, regression analysis, risk management tools, design thinking tools, simulations, technology

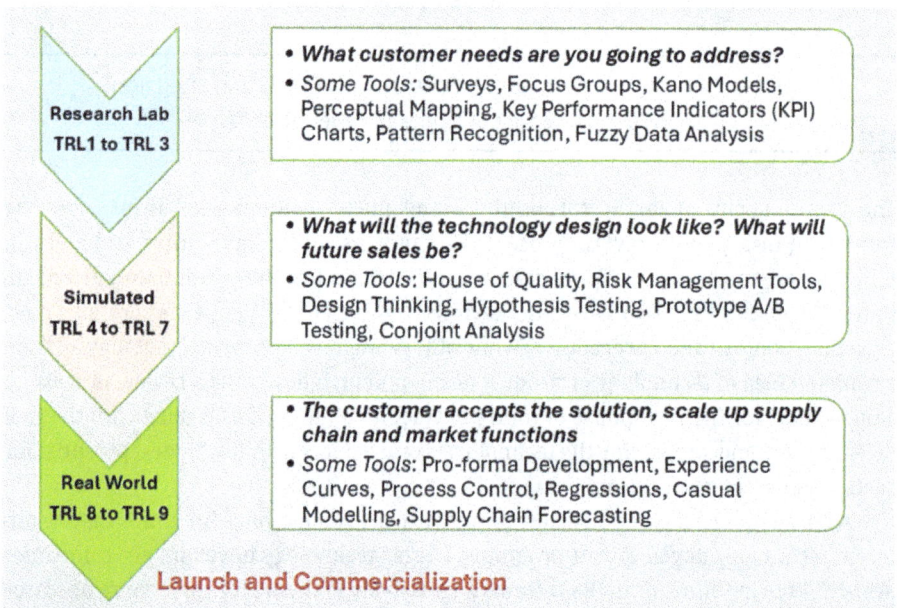

Research Lab TRL1 to TRL 3

- **What customer needs are you going to address?**
- *Some Tools:* Surveys, Focus Groups, Kano Models, Perceptual Mapping, Key Performance Indicators (KPI) Charts, Pattern Recognition, Fuzzy Data Analysis

Simulated TRL 4 to TRL 7

- **What will the technology design look like? What will future sales be?**
- *Some Tools:* House of Quality, Risk Management Tools, Design Thinking, Hypothesis Testing, Prototype A/B Testing, Conjoint Analysis

Real World TRL 8 to TRL 9

- **The customer accepts the solution, scale up supply chain and market functions**
- *Some Tools:* Pro-forma Development, Experience Curves, Process Control, Regressions, Casual Modelling, Supply Chain Forecasting

Launch and Commercialization

Figure 9.5: Statistics and quality tools in innovation.

forecasting, technology roadmaps, neural networks, and fuzzy data analysis. A detailed description of these many tools is beyond this chapter, but they are all focused on ultimately creating value for the customer.

These tools are used not only by large corporations in their phased-review processes but are also used by technology commercialization consulting firms when working with a client's particular technology.

R&D and Technology Project Portfolio Management

Major technology and pharmaceutical corporations can literally have hundreds of R&D projects operating at the same time, all in different phases of development. The largest firms regularly file hundreds, and some firms file thousands of patents in a single year. Even medium-sized firms might have dozens of concurrent technology projects in the works. For these firms, not only is a phased-review process crucial, but technology commercialization must also be considered a type of portfolio management.

In finance, portfolio management is a commonly taught topic. A portfolio of stocks, bonds, and other investments needs to be properly managed in order to maximize the risk-return profile of clients. A portfolio of R&D projects and technology development programs is actually more complicated. Technology portfolios are dynamic in nature; they change as development takes place through the different phases. The portfolio's risk-return structure is not only related to the other projects in the same development phase, but also dynamically with technologies in both earlier and later phases. In addition, technologies in development are not isolated entities. Synergies between projects can be very high, where new ideas discovered on one project can be shared with other projects, perhaps in very different target markets.

For firms with multiple technology development programs, not only is a phased-review process crucial, but technology commercialization must also be considered a type of portfolio management.

Finally, the risk profile of a technology project portfolio is harder to understand since there is much more uncertainly related to the arrival of competitors' technologies that might better satisfy the customer's requirements. A best practices technology portfolio management process must consider six major issues.

Objective 1: Profit maximization, combined with risk reduction

Objective 2: Strategic alignment with corporate objectives

Objective 3: Synergistic balance, within and between, development stages

Objective 4: Designed to achieve the greatest flexibility and speed to market

Objective 5: Work within the existing phased-review process at the corporation

Objective 6: Track overall corporate resource capability, individual project resource demand, and possible cost overruns in real time

At the present time, specialized programs such as Planview®, which are designed to assist technology program portfolio management, offer a combination of visual presentation tools, portfolio tools, and project management tools.[3] These R&D and technology program portfolio systems provide a number of benefits. These include automating the phase-review development process, capturing the Voice of the Customer into presentation tools, matching the corporation's resource capacity with technology development pipeline demands, tracking cost overruns and time to market, and providing an estimated return on investment.

Technology Project (Program) Portfolio Map (TPPM)

One of the most valuable tools of a portfolio analysis, whether performed by hand or with one of the specialized programs, is a presentation as to how different technology programs or products fit into the corporate strategy. TPPMs are spin-offs of earlier strategic diversification maps, such as the well-known market attractiveness-competitive strength charts, or the Boston Consulting Group matrix, used by many firms in their strategic planning.

A TPPM visually plots the different R&D and technology development projects or programs by four critical dimensions.

Dimension 1: The Stage of Development for Their Different R&D and Technology Projects. These stages can be described in terms of development phases, such as pre-patent R&D, prototyping, or final production engineering, or defined using TRL classifications, or a combination of both. With a drug development or pharmaceutical company, the stages might be more appropriately defined as early-stage R&D, in vitro drug testing, pre-clinical animal testing, and the 3-phased human testing process, in order to obtain governmental drug approval.

Dimension 2. The Administration Department/Strategic Business Unit That Houses the Different Programs. Most individual R&D efforts and technology development programs will be housed in different administrative departments or strategic business units (SBUs). For example, a computer storage device company might have different administrative departments/SBUs for different markets, such as internal hard drives, external hard drives, and solid-state drives.

Dimension 3. A Financial Measure. The financial measure needs to be a risk-adjusted measure of either the present value of future income that is expected for technology or a fair market valuation figure for technology. The financial return measure must be risk adjusted, since early-stage R&D projects have much more uncertainty in forecasting future income than products near final commercialization. The chapter of financial analysis and valuation discusses this in more detail.

Dimension 4. A Fitness Measure. Most often, the fitness measure is calculated from the gate scorecards used in a phased-review process. The fitness measure can be based on the total gate scorecard score, or subset of the gate scorecard items, depending on managerial preferences. Using the gate scorecards from periodic phased-reviews will then update the TPPM on a regular basis. However, in cases where a phased-review process is not in place, a TPPM can also be created as a single presentation, like a snapshot. In this case, the fitness measure can be calculated from a modified technology success or readiness scale, such as the CloverLeaf™ model, discussed in a later chapter.

TPPM Example

Figure 9.6 shows a typical TPPM. This example might highlight the need to place special attention on understanding Department B's current R&D programs. Department D might need their funding reduced, or perhaps a recommended pivot to a different technological platform. Similarly, Department C's projects in the technology demonstration phase might need to be stopped due to a combination of low risk-adjusted forecasted returns and overall lack of fit with the overall corporate strategy. Department A's projects look very promising and need full support to move it into the final commercialization stage.

Concluding Insights

Technology commercialization, whether in a micro-entrepreneurial start-up or a large corporation, often involves several common elements: securing and protecting intellectual property, conducting a feasibility or commercialization study, performing a technology triage to evaluate viability against competing solutions, and completing a risk-adjusted cash flow or valuation analysis.

However, larger corporations tend to have several additional areas of concern. Many larger corporations will have dozens, and sometimes hundreds, of different technology projects scattered among various departments, units, or subsidiaries. Some of these technologies might still be in basic R&D research, while others might be on the verge of commercialization. Other technologies will be in various middle ranges of development.

Unfortunately, the majority of early-stage R&D programs will never see the light of a successful commercial launch. Corporations must screen these early-stage technologies, and allocate their limited financial, organizational, and human resources to the technologies most likely to succeed.

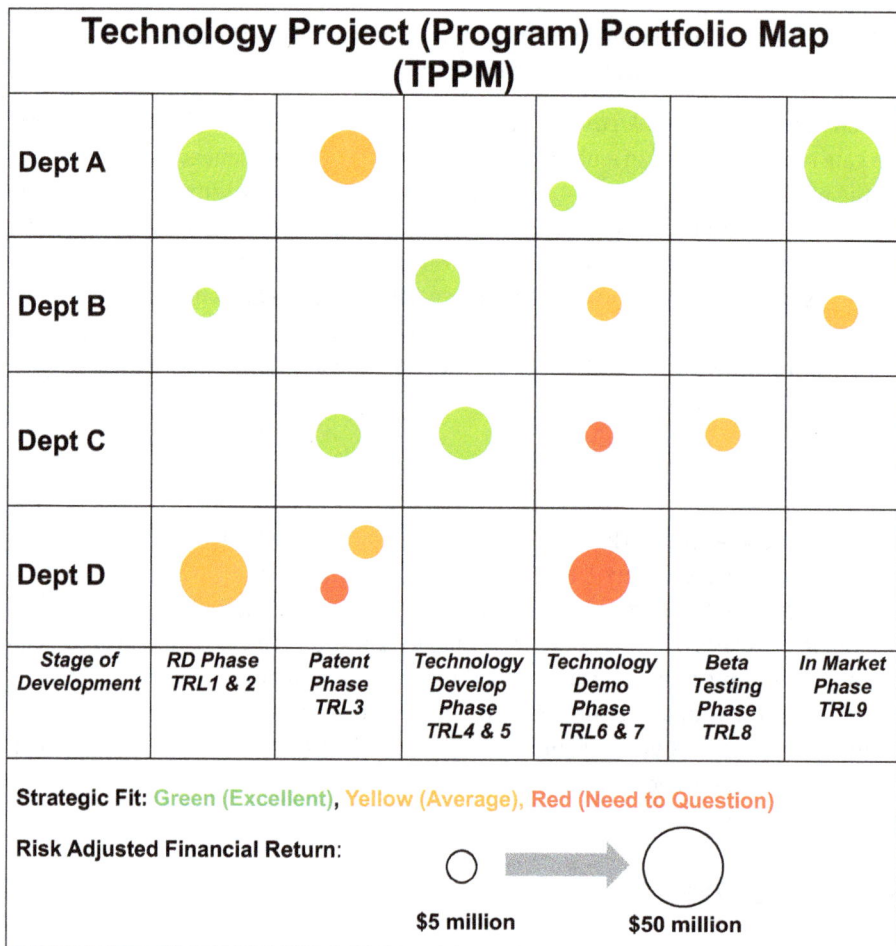

Technology Project (Program) Portfolio Map (TPPM)

Stage of Development	RD Phase TRL1 & 2	Patent Phase TRL3	Technology Develop Phase TRL4 & 5	Technology Demo Phase TRL6 & 7	Beta Testing Phase TRL8	In Market Phase TRL9

Strategic Fit: Green (Excellent), Yellow (Average), Red (Need to Question)

Risk Adjusted Financial Return:

$5 million $50 million

Figure 9.6: Technology project portfolio map.

This chapter discussed two of the most important aspects of the management of technology commercialization in large organizations. One important concept is the idea of phased-review, where technologies need to pass through gates in order to receive the necessary support for the next stage of development. The second critical component is to always understand that multiple internal technology programs are a type of portfolio. As a portfolio of projects and programs, they need to be managed as such. While there are a number of tools that might assist in the process, the use of a Technology Project or Program Portfolio Map is an effective tool to visualize how the different programs and technologies play out within the overall corporate strategy and mission.

Chapter 10
Pro Forma Development

This Chapter

- Emphasizes the importance of assessing the financial condition of early-stage technologies.
- Describes how to develop high-quality financial projections – or "pro formas" – to support commercialization planning.
- Outlines best practices for preparing accurate and credible financial forecasts.
- Differentiates between risk-adjusted and non-risk-adjusted financial projections.
- Highlights the role of financial projections and pro forma in the broader process of technology valuation.

Key Management Tools and Best Practices

- Best practices of pro forma development
- Methods of predicting revenues in financial projections
- Risk and non-risk adjusted pro formas

INSIGHT

One of the most important questions asked when commercializing a technology is "what will the future look like"? Ultimately organizations, particularly in the private sector, invest in R&D efforts and technology development for the primary purpose of generating future revenues and cash flow. Almost every step of the commercialization process, from pre-patent decisions to the final launch into the marketplace will always be evaluated by its financial implications – what is the current cost, and what are the future financial benefits? Internal reviewers at each gate in a phase-review process will ask this question in deciding whether to support future R&D and technology development. The financial component is always the primary interest of external investors who ultimately want a return on their funding commitments. Yet, understanding the future financial impact of early-stage technologies is one the most difficult and speculative aspects of technology management.

Introduction

The underlying purpose of most technology commercialization efforts is to generate positive cash flows sometime in the future, either as a standalone product or integrated into a complex system that will in turn be sold into the market. Understanding the financial potential of any productive business effort, including technology commercialization, requires working through the drivers that create value.

The financial potential of any technology will be evaluated many times during its path from early R&D stages to its final launch to the market, and then afterwards as it

https://doi.org/10.1515/9783111684420-011

hopefully grows in market acceptance. Financial projections are ultimately required at various points in any technology's development. For example:

1) Corporate phased-review gates often require financial projections in combination with scorecards to obtain future support. Financial projections increase in importance as technologies enter engineering, production, and demonstration stages as costs begin to increase dramatically. These projections become even more critical at the last gate, when deciding to enter beta-testing and ultimately the marketplace.

2) Early-stage entrepreneurial efforts always include financial forecasts during fund-raising. Private equity investors will want to understand the potential of the firm's underlying technologies. This is particularly true if the business, like many entrepreneurial start-ups, is founded on a single technological platform. Investment banks will also want to review pro formas before taking on a firm considering an initial public offering (IPO) or shopping for an acquisition partner.

3) Top scientists, engineers, and senior managers are often offered stock options and other equity perks to join an early-stage firm. They may want to see the financial projections in order to determine what these perks might be really worth.

4) Large government granting or partner agencies may want to review the financial projections of a technology, particularly if the technology requires a significant amount of governmental support.

5) For smaller firms, banks and other lending institutions may want to review the final projections before offering a business loan or credit line.

Most organizations do not really expect detailed pro formas to be created for technologies in the earliest stages of development. For pre-patent technologies, typically in the TRL2–TRL3 levels, only broad assumptions about market segments, technology penetration rates, final product pricing, and competitive environments are possible. With these earliest technologies, there might be discussions about future financial numbers, but only in the broadest sense. An exception commonly seen is when a prototype or large-scale demonstration system is already envisioned. In these cases, a financial projection of the projected cost of building the prototype or system might be expected. In general, however, the importance of pro formas and financial projections grows almost exponentially as the technology matures over its development cycle.

Developing a Pro Forma: The Key to Understanding Technology Value

Developing a financial projection is the most important part of understanding the future financial condition of a developing technology. Essentially a pro forma takes what people are talking about and puts numbers to their words. This is true whether the technology is at the early prototyping stages or moving toward final commercialization.

The importance of pro formas and financial projections grows almost
exponentially as the technology matures over its development cycle.

Technologies that are not yet commercialized are often called "pre-revenue" technologies. Pre-revenue technologies are still in the development stages and have not yet been sold into the market. For pre-revenue technologies, financial forecasts are required to understand how the current investments in R&D and development will be reflected in future financial benefits. Even a technology that has already entered the market will still need a financial projection of future revenues and cash flows as the technology expands its acceptance in the market.

Generating a financial forecast is normally called a pro forma. Pro forma is actually a Latin term meaning "as a matter of form", which originally meant not giving something much attention. However, in modern finance terminology, a pro forma represents a detailed projection of revenues, associated expenses, and net income or cash flows. In the vast majority of cases, creating a pro forma is the starting point for the financial analysis of technology at any stage of development, particularly after the intellectual property has been established and somebody has made a commitment to bring the technology to the market.

In practice, pro formas for technologies typically employ a time frame of 3–5 years after commercialization. Start-up entrepreneurial firms also use the same 3–5-year time frame for their projections. Revenue and earnings projections beyond 3–5 years are often considered too speculative by most people and largely ignored. In the fast-moving world of technological development, many pro formas use monthly calculations rather than annual buckets.

To understand the different types of pro formas, and best practices when developing pro formas for technologies, we illustrate two simple examples. In both cases, the technology is still being developed in the first and second years and then expected to be commercialized in the third year. The pro forma ends in the third year after commercialization, or a 5-year overall projection. Clearly, these are simple examples, and a real-life pro forma would be much more detailed.

Profit-Loss versus Cash Flow. Pro formas can be created as either "profit-loss" statements or "cash flow" statements. Profit-loss statements include various accounting measures, such as depreciation and interest expenses from loans. Profit-loss statements are generally used for a total business entity, such as a start-up firm seeking private equity funding, or a self-contained business unit that might be presenting its forecasted financial situation within a broader corporate planning cycle.

Alternatively, "cash flow" statements attempt to measure the direct flow of funds used in activities related to the technology and then generated from the technology after commercialization. Cash flow looks at the movement of funds, in and out. Run out of cash, and the firm has a serious problem.

The "burn-rate" measures the speed you are using up your cash reserves.

One important term heard in the entrepreneurship world is a firm's "burn-rate". An early-stage firm's "burn-rate" is defined as the average dollar rate (usually per month) that a firm or technology project uses of its available funds prior to generating revenues. The burn-rate measures the speed that you are using up your cash reserves. Burn-rates are generally applied to a firm's use of external support funding, such as private equity but are equally important to internal technology development projects. While the notion of a burn-rate is important, pro formas are a more sophisticated method of looking at the future financial picture. Pro formas certainly incorporate burn-rates, but a burn-rate is still an important financial metric that is used in conversations and presentations.

Unlike corporate pro formas, technology-specific pro formas tend to be more cash flow-oriented in nature. One of the major differences between a profit-loss and cash flow statement for a technology is how lab equipment and other R&D expenses are recorded. In a cash flow statement, for example, the full amount of funds "used" to purchase the expensive lab equipment is recorded. In profit-loss statements, however, only the depreciation of the equipment might be recorded as an expense. Profit-loss statements are heavily impacted by various tax and accounting rules, whereas cash flow statements simply look at funds flowing in and out of the operation.

However, profit-loss and cash flow" statements are closely related, and may be the same under certain circumstances, particularly when examining a specific technology. For this reason, we use the terms earnings, profit, and cash flow somewhat interchangeably when discussing technologies, when, in fact, there are subtle differences.

In reality, entrepreneurial firms and large-scale technology programs within a corporate business unit might present both a profit-loss pro forma and a cash flow pro forma, along with a statement of "assets and liabilities". This is really when the accounting team needs to be involved with developing a pro forma.

Pro Forma Example: Technology Licensing: The first example represents a licensing agreement (see Figure 10.1). Typical licenses are structured as a percentage of the revenue generated from customer products that incorporate the licensed technology. Depending on the negotiations and how critical the technology is within the licensee's product can vary. In this example, assume a 7% license deal, which means that our firm receives 7% of the overall revenue generated by the customer who licenses our technology.

Typically, licensing revenue forecasts will rely upon the customers' forecast of base revenues, since it is their product, which is being sold in the market, not the component. However, sometimes we might forecast our component's penetration into an existing product as a replacement for older components that are being used. This penetration rate could be based upon several types of information, including the results of our VoC analysis, a formal technology substitution forecast, and our strategy for approaching the current system developers.

Our license revenues are then estimated by multiplying the end-product revenues by our license percentage. This is a simple example since many license contracts will differ as to how the license payments are calculated over time.

In this example, our technology does not start generating revenues from license payments until year 3, when it will be finally incorporated into our partner's final product. For the first two years we are still perfecting our technology and forecast to have significant technology development costs.

Over the whole cycle, we still have various administrative costs such as accounting, legal, and insurance expenses. Generally, however, in licensed technologies, these future administrative costs are relatively low. That is one of the major advantages of licensing a technology – do not have a lot of administrative costs and other internal headaches.

For this example, we forecast a negative cash flow in years 1 and 2 as we continue to invest in our technology's development and prototype engineering but then start generating a small profit in year 3 (the first year in the market) as the partner product that incorporates our technology enters the market, and we start receiving our 7% license fee. The pro forma then forecasts significant earnings from license fees in year 4 (in market year 2) and year 5 (in market year 3) as the end-product gains more traction among customers. As mentioned before, the pro forma simply puts numbers to our words and beliefs. Note that in this example, we are assuming $20,000,000 end-product revenues the first year it is commercialized growing to $300,000,000 by the third year, so this is a pretty optimistic forecast from our licensee partner. We get 7% of this as our license fee.

Example 1: Licensing Pro-Forma Example					
	Development Year 1	Development Year 2	In Market Year 1	In Market Year 2	In Market Year 3
Customer's Total Revenues	$0	$0	$20,000,000	$100,000,000	$300,000,000
Our License Agreement (7%)			7.00%	7.00%	7.00%
Revenues from Licensed Technology	$0	$0	$1,400,000	$7,000,000	$21,000,000
Expenses					
Development	$1,000,000	$0	$0	$0	$0
Final Prototype Engineering	$0	$500,000	$0	$0	$0
Marketing & Distribution	$0	$100,000	$0	$0	$0
Administration and Other	$1,000,000	$500,000	$500,000	$500,000	$500,000
Total Expenses	$2,000,000	$1,100,000	$500,000	$500,000	$500,000
Net Earnings (Before Tax)	($2,000,000)	($1,100,000)	$900,000	$6,500,000	$20,500,000

Figure 10.1: Licensing pro forma example.

Pro Forma Example: End-User Commercialization: The second example illustrates a possible end-user commercialization strategy (see Figure 10.2). In this example, we not only develop the technology, but then engineer, manufacture, and ultimately launch the technology as a final product into the end-user market. In this example, we are assuming a 60% "cost of goods and labor", which would include the material and direct labor costs used to manufacture the product.

Since we are commercializing the product ourselves, we are also likely to have additional engineering expenses for the five-year period since improvements and tweaks to the product will constantly be needed. Since we are also selling the product ourselves, there are continuous marketing, distribution, and administration costs. After all, these expenses need to be deducted in order to obtain net earnings or cash flow projects. In addition, although not shown in this simple example, we would likely also have equipment purchases (with depreciation), aftermarket service expenses, inventory requirements, and a variety of other expenses directly associated with the business. For this example, we assume the same revenue forecast as in Example 1.

In the pre-commercialization period, we show negative net earnings or cash flows for the first two years of development. After commercialization we start to generate some positive cash flows, and by the second and third year after commercialization, both revenues and earnings are predicted to expand greatly as our technology is adopted by more customers. Again, for illustrative purposes, perhaps a pretty optimistic forecast.

Example 2: End Product/User Pro-Forma Example					
	Development Year 1	Development Year 2	In Market Year 1	In Market Year 2	In Market Year 3
Revenues from Product Sales	$0	$0	$20,000,000	$100,000,000	$300,000,000
Cost of Goods			60.00%	60.00%	60.00%
Gross Profit	$0	$0	$8,000,000	$40,000,000	$120,000,000
Expenses					
Development	$1,000,000	$0	$0	$0	$0
Engineering	$3,000,000	$3,000,000	$1,000,000	$1,000,000	$1,000,000
Set-up & Manufacturing	$1,000,000	$1,000,000	$2,000,000	$10,000,000	$30,000,000
Marketing & Administration	$1,000,000	$1,000,000	$3,000,000	$15,000,000	$45,000,000
Total Expenses	$6,000,000	$5,000,000	$6,000,000	$26,000,000	$76,000,000
Net Earnings (Before Tax)	($6,000,000)	($5,000,000)	$2,000,000	$14,000,000	$44,000,000

Figure 10.2: End-product pro forma user example.

Revenue Forecasts for Pro Formas

Projecting revenues after commercialization is considered the most difficult and speculative components of a pro forma. While various expenses can be reasonably estimated, how our technology will do in the market after commercialization is really open to debate. Projected revenue is the part of the pro forma that will be most closely scrutinized and challenged the most by internal reviewers, lending institutions, and external investors.

Projecting revenues is considered the most difficult and speculative component of a pro forma.

Revenues for pro formas are typically forecasted using one of four methods:

Forecasting Revenues: Market Share Method. The "market share method" of revenue forecasting determines the total size of the market and then applies the percentage of the market that we anticipate obtaining at various points after commercialization. The market share method is commonly used for technologies launched into an end-user market. For example, the total marine battery trickle charge technology market is about $500 million dollars per year. The customers for marine battery trickle charge systems are boat owners who want to continuously keep their batteries charged when docked at the marina. Suppose we have developed a smaller and more effective trickle charge system, but it costs a little more than the existing systems. We believe that we can get 5% of the market next year with our new technology and then capture another 5% of the market for each of the next couple of years as our prices come down. This would result in a 5%, 10%, 15%,... share of the market in future years. In this approach, the total market size is generally obtained from industry research, while the market share obtained might be estimated from our voice of the customer (VoC) study, industry expert opinions, and perhaps past experiences or examples of similar technologies introduced earlier.

Forecasting Revenues: Substitution Rate Method. The "substitution rate method" is similar to the market share method. When our technology is a new component in an existing system already in the market, we need to forecast the rate of substitution our new technology will have for the older technology currently being used in systems and final products. This is somewhat the same as the market share method, but focuses on how system integrators will adopt our technology as a replacement for an existing component. The substitution rate will be determined again from a detailed VoC analysis with system integrators, perhaps combined with applying technology forecasting methods such as the Fisher-Pry technology substitution model. We can also use an "S" shaped diffusion model, such as the logistic curve or Gompertz curve, if we already have some sales data.

Forecasting Revenues: Direct Sales Method. The "direct sales method" projects the numbers of units we believe we can sell for each of the models or versions, and price we expect to sell these different units for. Multiplying volume times unit price provides our projected revenues. This method is commonly used when our technology is somewhat unique and might create a whole new market. It can also be used in combination with the market share and substitution rate methods but provides more detail since the focus is on different models, their prices, and projected volume rather than a simple percentage of the total market. The projection of both units sold and expected price is estimated from the results of our focus groups, market research, VoC data, and industry expert opinions.

Forecasting Revenues: Comparable Product Method. The final method is the "comparable product method". Often, we may be aware of a similar product that has already entered the market along with its performance over time. This data might come from prior products in our own organization or from information we have gathered from our connections in the industry. We then apply the same revenue growth model to our pro forma.

Regardless of which method we use for calculating and projecting revenues, it must be carefully grounded by the results of our commercialization study, particularly the feedback from industry expert opinion, focus groups, industry analysis, and our VoC analysis. We cannot just make up revenue projections.

Risk-Adjusted versus Non-Risk Adjusted Pro Formas

In our examples, we are using what can be described as a "non-risk-adjusted" pro forma. A non-risk-adjusted pro forma uses our best estimates of forecasted revenues and projected cash flows assuming we are successful in the market. This is what we really believe will happen based upon our knowledge and research. Non-risk-adjusted pro formas and projections are the most common approach in practice. There is certainly a lot of risk involved in achieving these projections, but the issue of risk is accounted for later in the discount rate if we are using the pro forma to place a value on the technology.

Many companies and consultants, however, use a "risk-adjusted" forecast, where the pro forma estimates are adjusted or multiplied by a "probability" of success figure as a final step. In Example 2, we projected revenues for the first year after commercialization as $20,000,000. For a risk-adjusted pro forma we would then perform one additional step and adjust this by a probability figure. For example, we might be only 50% confident of our forecast. In certain industries there might be good estimates about the probability of commercial success at different stages of development. Perhaps our research, for example, indicates that only 50% of technologies at our particular stage of development are actually commercially successful.

Many companies and consultants use a "risk-adjusted" forecast, where the
pro-forma estimates are adjusted or multiplied by a
"probability" of success figure.

In a risk-adjusted pro-forma we would then multiple our revenue figures by this
50%. Thus our $20,000,000 revenue projection would become only a $10,000,000
revenue projection in a risk-adjusted pro forma. Risk-adjusted pro formas are very
common in the pharmaceutical industry, since there are well-known success figures
for drugs in different stages of development and human testing. Some corporations
might require a "risk-adjusted" pro forma for their phase-review gate process. One
can also complicate it and do a weighted average risk adjusted revenues, when three
or four different revenues forecast are created, each with its own probability. The
probability weightings might be obtained from internal discussions. The weighted
average revenue would then be the different revenue projects multiplied by its specific probability.

Either approach is fine, but it does impact both the pro forma results and the
calculation of the appropriate discount rate when determining the value of the technology. It is important, however, to make sure everybody knows which method is
being used.

Pro Forma "Best Practice"

Pro formas are immensely complicated, but absolutely necessary. The following are
best practices when developing pro forma and financial projections:

Best Practice 1: Be Detailed and Use Subsidiary Spreadsheets. Each entry on
the base pro forma, whether for revenues or expenses, probably should have a
hidden or subsidiary spreadsheet that details how that particular number was
determined. There can be dozens of hidden spreadsheets. The revenue line might
have a subsidiary spreadsheet for each model we plan to sell, the number of units
forecasted to be sold, and the price per unit. Each expense item might have a separate subsidiary spreadsheet to calculate the details. For example, a labor spreadsheet might show each person working on the technology, their expected hours
spent on the technology, and their salary and benefit costs. A good technology pro
forma will have dozens of detailed subsidiary spreadsheets. This is important since
it is almost certain that reviewers, whether internal or external, will ask how a
particular number was calculated. It is much easier to open up the subsidiary sheet
than fumble from memory.

Activity/Materials	Quantity	Units	Cost	Cost
Subsidiary Spreadsheet For Component A, System "Far Reach"				
Prototype Demonstration Model Development - Total Cost for Component A				**$839,802**
Direct Personal Total				**$290,160**
Principal Investigator - Project (Dr. G)	620	Hours	$230.00	$142,600
Engineering (Mr. R)	620	Hours	$145.00	$89,900
Total Direct Personal				$232,500
Direct Benefits	24.80%			$57,660
Internal Consultants (Component and System Integration) Total				**$239,616**
Dr. F, Principal Investigator - Technical	480	Hours	$200.00	$96,000
Mr. M, Chief Engineer	480	Hours	$200.00	$96,000
Total Internal Consultants				$192,000
Corporate G&A/Benefits	24.80%			$47,616
Equipment and Material Total				**$131,355**
Mechanical Systems (Heat Exchangers)	1	LS	$28,000	$28,000
Recirculation Pumps	8	EA	$1,200	$9,600
CO2 Scrubber	1	EA	$40,000	$40,000
Water Removal System	1	EA	$45,000	$45,000
Consumables				
Chemical A	500	lbs	$5	$2,500
Total Equipment and Materials				$125,100
Materials Overhead	5.00%			$6,255
Travel Total				**$10,000**
1st Demostration of Unit	1		$10,000	$10,000
External Subcontracts Total				**$28,704**
Mechanical Assembly Support	100	Hours	$230.00	$23,000
G&A	24.80%		$23,000	$5,704
Subtotal				**$699,835**
Contingency	20%		$699,835	**$139,967**
Total for Component A				**$839,802**

Figure 10.3: Subsidiary spreadsheet for pro forma.

The example in Figure 10.3 (names and identifying information have been deleted) shows a real-life subsidiary spreadsheet for the first-year development costs for the prototype demonstration phase of a component within a larger system (internally labeled "far research"). The analysis indicates a development cost of $839,802 for this phase of component A.

Not only are direct costs estimated, but also internal consulting expenses, materials, travel, and the corporate overhead associated with these activities. In addition, this particular project uses a 20% contingency fee for likely project overruns or additional needs. As a component in a larger system, this spreadsheet is then linked to other component spreadsheet, and ultimately to the appropriate "development expense" cell in the pro forma for the whole "far reach" system development.

Best Practice 2: Reference and Support Every Line Item. Pro formas are often accused of being just crazy speculation or, at best, simple educated guessing. While there might be some truth to this in some cases, the reviewers' suspicions can be significantly reduced by referencing, citing, and supporting every line item in the pro forma. How did you find the insurance costs? How were the engineering and design costs determined? Who are the people behind the labor costs? And how did somebody come up with the revenue projections? Addressing these issues will also make the pro forma much more accurate.

Best Practice 3: Don't Mismatch What You Say versus the Pro Forma. Make sure any oral presentations are consistent with the pro forma. Don't tell people that the product is going world-wide in the second year, when the pro forma does not reflect increased revenues until the fourth year. Don't argue that development costs will stay stable for the first two years while the pro forma shows a doubling of development expenses in the second year. Remember, the pro forma essentially puts numbers to what you say and believe.

Best Practice 4: Don't Forget Line Items. Forgetting an expense item is embarrassing. It can also be disastrous during an important presentation. Did you forget to put in a "product-liability insurance" expense? What about "lab equipment rentals"? Should you have a "contingency" item? Having a reviewer point out a missing item seriously hurts the legitimacy of the whole pro forma.

Best Practice 5: No Mistakes!! Perhaps the only thing worse than forgetting a line item is to find a mathematical or "linking" mistake in the spreadsheets. Spreadsheets, particularly with multiple subsidiary spreadsheets, can be extremely complex. Mistakes will often creep-in. One of the authors is regularly contracted by a large U.S. government agency to double check contractor or grant applicant pro formas – 50% of the time simple math or linking mistakes are found. Not good.

Best Practice 6: Don't Be Too Optimistic – Be Reasonable. R&D personnel, developers, engineers, entrepreneurs, and sales teams all tend to be very optimistic. After all, this technology or product is their "baby". Pro formas however, need to be as accurate as possible. When forecasting revenues, be honest in analyzing the results of the VoC, technology triage, and market research. Be honest about cost overruns, delays in engineering, time to market, ability to capture market share, or possible quality control issues.

Best Practice 6: Be Careful about Showing Different Scenarios. People are often taught in college business classes to present pro formas representing "best-case scenario", "worst-case scenario", and "most-likely" scenario. The natural tendency of reviewers, whether internal at a phased-review gate or external reviewers, such as potential investors, is to be cautious. When presented with different scenarios, reviewers will always focus on the "worst-case" scenario and ignore the others. Be careful about showing different scenarios. Focus on the scenario that you honestly think is the most accurate. As a note, different scenarios, with associated probabilities, might be a useful exercise, but then incorporate this information into one final pro forma.

Best Practice 7: Regularly Update the Pro Formas. As technologies move through the different development phases, more and more information will become available about the marketplace, competitive technologies, customer requirements, and cost development structures. In later development phases, this information will also be more accurate. Pro formas should be updated regularly as new information becomes more available.

Best Practice 8: Pro Formas Need to Be a Team Effort. Many people become emotionally distressed when developing pro formas. It often seems much easier to simply pass it off to the accountants. Accountants, indeed, might feel more comfortable with profit and cash flow calculations, but all the numbers, relationships, assumptions, and support in a pro forma need to come from the full development team. R&D, engineering, production, distribution, and marketing personnel all need to be involved with occasional input from the finance and accounting people to make sure all the final numbers look right and link together properly.

Best Practice 9: Have a "Revenue Model" Well-Supported. A good pro forma needs a good "revenue model". The pro forma needs to align revenue projections with your sales strategy. How are you going to generate these revenues? When forecasting revenues, it is not enough to simply present numbers. Reviewers will want to see how those numbers are supported by a realistic sales strategy – the revenue model. This includes clearly describing how you plan to reach customers –whether through direct sales, distribution partners, online platforms, or some combination – and how your team is structured to execute that plan. If your pro forma shows $5 million in revenue by Year 2, but you only have one part-time salesperson, credibility will suffer. For consumer technologies in particular, be sure to explain the size and structure of your sales force, the number of leads you expect to generate, and your anticipated conversion rates. Grounding your revenue projections in a concrete, well-supported go-to-market strategy strengthens your case and builds trust with stakeholders.

Use of AI in Pro Forma Development

There are a number of sophisticated AI programs in the market that are specifically designed to generate pro formas. These AI programs ask essentially the same questions as discussed in this chapter. The AI programs create prompts to include questions addressing the different categories of products or services being offered, the expected revenues and expenses associated with the different product categories, overhead costs, and the duration of the projections. Using AI, some of the programs can then tap into global knowledge about industry financial ratios and other market information. Then, literally by pressing a button, these programs will generate an attractive set of projected financial statements, such as profit-loss statements, cash flow statements, and balance sheets.

There are several caveats associated with specialized AI pro forma programs. First, while these AI programs appear very powerful, they are primarily focused on the business or firm level thus often missing the nuances of generating pro formas for individual technologies. Second, input into these programs still require the developer or entrepreneur to personally estimate the projected revenues, development costs, and other organizational expenses, and how these might change over the future time periods. Making projections is by far the most difficult process of generating pro formas, not the generation of an attractive financial statement. Third, these AI programs simply cannot create the detail required in subsidiary spreadsheets – and this is really where the accuracy of pro formas is made or lost. Fourth, generating a pro forma from bottom up will always raise questions during the process. Is that expense category correct? Am I missing something? Why am I generating a negative cash flow? How much funding do I need to cover my future financial burn-rate? Creating a pro forma always challenges your basic assumptions simply by the act of developing it. Creating a clean pro forma financial statement is a give-and-take learning experience, oftentimes uncovering problems with the technology's financials that were previously overlooked.

Concluding Insights

Understanding the financial aspects of early-stage technologies as they move toward commercialization is critical. Part of the underlying motivation of any technology commercialization process is to generate financial benefit above the cost of development. In a modern economy, financial benefit is highly correlated with social benefit. If a technology can satisfy the requirements of users and customers more effectively than competitive technologies, it will most likely generate positive revenues and cash flows. It will also advance society, whether the technology is in the healthcare sector, transportation sector, or computing sector. Sometimes the societal contribution will be enormous; with most technologies it will be incremental, but still positive. That is always part of the value statement of any technology – value to advancing society and financial value to the inventors and innovators.

But the ability to predict the financial benefit of early-stage technologies is difficult. Public and private entities constantly spend funds on development with the hope of generating revenues and cash flows sometime in the future, after successful commercialization. But few technologies ever reach the point where they are profitable, while others might be incredibly successful.

This chapter focused on the financial aspects of early-stage technologies. This question is constantly on the mind of both internal decision-makers that need to fund future development of technologies, as well as external investors who financially partner with early-stage technology-oriented entrepreneurial firms. Creating financial projections or pro formas are critical to this process. Pro formas essentially put numbers to people's words and beliefs. This chapter discussed many of the best-practice principles of creating pro formas for early-stage technologies.

Chapter 11
Valuation of Early-Stage Technologies

This Chapter

- Introduces three foundational methods for determining the fair market value of early-stage technologies, along with common challenges associated with each approach.
- Explains the role of risk and discount rates in valuation and outlines how to calculate a preliminary discount rate tailored to a given technology.
- Provides examples and models to help estimate fair market value in real-world technology commercialization scenarios.

Key Management Tools and Best Practices

- Comparable transaction method of technology valuations
- Income methods of technology valuation
- Technology Development Discount Rate Model (TDDR)
- Technology Industry Discount Rate Adjustments
- Discount rates for pharmaceutical development
- Cost methods of technology valuation

! INSIGHT

One of the most important questions asked when commercializing a technology is what the technology is "worth". Technology commercialization generally happens in order to generate some future value, typically measured by financial metrics, such as revenues and cashflow. Almost every step of the commercialization process from pre-patent decisions to the final move into the marketplace will always be evaluated by its financial implications – what is the current cost, and what is the future financial benefit. Internal reviewers at each gate in a phase-review process will ask this question in deciding whether to support future R&D and technology development. The financial component is always the primary interest of external investors who ultimately want a quick return on their funding commitments. Yet, understanding the financial aspects, and valuation of early-stage technologies, is one of the most difficult and speculative aspects of technology management

Introduction

Creating "value" is fundamental to any business activity. In fact, the creation of value is the key to all aspects of business success, economic development, and societal advancement. While creating "value" is a nice philosophical concept, defining and measuring value becomes much more problematic.

What is something worth? In the world of technology commercialization, this is the "million-dollar question". Acquiring, developing, and ultimately commercializing a technology as either a stand-alone product or component within a larger, highly integrated

https://doi.org/10.1515/9783111684420-012

system involves multiple steps. In each of these steps, decision makers are either informally, or more often, formally assessing the value of the technology.

There are five common situations or scenarios when formal technology valuations are typically required. The first is during the phased-review process at larger corporations. In order to proceed through a phased-review gate and receive support for the next development phase, a formal assessment of the technology's value may be required. The degree of formality and detail might vary from gate to gate, and from company to company, but generally as a technology gets closer to the final commercialization decision, the requirements for a clear understanding of the technology's value increase.

The second scenario is when a representative of an early-stage entrepreneurial venture is pitching to private equity investors. The Angel Capital Associations reports that 77% of "pre-seed" funding and 41% of "seed" funding go to pre-revenue technology firms, with the vast majority of this funding targeted toward a combination of technology development and prototyping.[1] Inevitably, angel investors and early-stage venture capitalists who fund pre-revenue entrepreneurial efforts need to have serious discussions of valuation related to both underlying technologies, and the ability of the entrepreneurial team to pull it off. Agreeing on a valuation figure determines how much equity is received for the required investment.

The third scenario is during a merger or acquisition process. A larger, technology-based corporation acquiring a smaller firm will need to value the smaller firm. For most of these deals, the primary asset of the smaller firm is found in its IP and technologies.

The fourth scenario is litigation. Unfortunately, in the modern world, almost every technology-based entity, large or small, will find themselves in some form of litigation involving their technology. Patent infringement, theft of trade secrets, and breach of contract cases all require a valuation to determine damages. Even divorce, where one or both of the parties have significant ownership in a small technology-based enterprise, or its underlying IP, requires valuations for determining the appropriate distribution of marital assets.

The fifth scenario involves licensing or joint venture negotiations. When organizations engage in technology licensing or form joint ventures, a formal valuation is often needed to inform the structure of the agreement. This includes establishing fair royalty rates, equity splits, or upfront payments based on the value of the technology being contributed. Technology valuations also play a central role in licensing discussions between university or government technology transfer offices and potential licensees. In these cases, valuations help justify licensing terms and support negotiations with startups or established companies interested in commercializing publicly funded research.

While these five scenarios represent the most common situations requiring a formal technology valuation, others do exist. For example, regulatory or financial reporting compliances such as GAAP or IFRS standards may require companies to assign fair market value to certain intangible assets. Additional scenarios may include internal portfolio prioritization, intellectual property audits, or obtaining insurance coverage for high-value technologies.

What Is Something Worth? Three Methods of Valuation

Valuation theory typically centers around three fundamental methods for determining value.

Method 1: Income Methods. An asset, such as a business or technology, can generate income. Income methods attempt to understand the future income, or cashflow, from that particular asset, and then discount that future income to a present value. But future income is always uncertain. The risk associated with obtaining the projected future income of the asset always needs to be considered. If the future income is relatively stable, and the asset relatively common, this valuation process can be straightforward. For example, when valuing an office building, the commercial real estate appraiser will predict the future rents, subtract off likely expenses and possible vacancy, and then discount this future net income stream to a present value using a discount rate that is appropriate for that type of property.

There are three fundamental methods for determining value: income methods, market or comparable transaction methods, and cost or asset methods

---

Method 2: Market or Comparable Transaction Methods. This method determines what similar assets are selling for in the market. If a person is selling a used car, of a certain model, mileage, and condition, they can easily look up similar prices on the web. Residential real estate appraisers will examine nearby homes that have recently sold and apply the price per square foot along with other objective measures, such as the number of bedrooms or distance to beaches, to the target property. This is exactly what real estate apps do. An appraiser, however, might also visit the house and then adjust for the unique characteristics of the property, such as yard condition, needed repairs, and possibly its historical value.

Method 3: Cost or Asset Methods. Cost methods are often used in valuing assets. The definition of costs might vary depending on the asset being examined. But generally, cost refers to the prior expenses and investments used to create that asset in the first place. Another approach might be to figure out the cost it would take right now to recreate the asset. In business valuation, this approach is sometimes called a liquidation method. The liquidation method might be to figure out what could be obtained when the equipment and inventory of a bankrupt business are sold at auction. In general, the liquidation value, which is often associated with the cost method, is the minimum value of something.

Challenges of Applying Traditional Methods When Valuing a New Technology. The valuation of early-stage technologies follows these same three methods. However, each of these three methods becomes immensely more complicated when examining technologies still in development stages. Why is this?

First, for income methods, technologies in development stages by definition are almost always "pre-revenue" assets. They are probably not yet generating income or cashflow, or if technology is generating some revenues, it is still in very early stages of adoption. Future years might look very different from the present. With early-stage technologies, almost everything is probably still on the "expense side" of the ledger, creating a negative cashflow situation at the present time. Development requires investment. In order to perform the income method, future earnings or cashflows need to be forecasted based on unproven demand, regulatory approvals, or technical milestones. Accordingly, projections can be highly uncertain and risky. This level of uncertainty changes dramatically as a technology moves through its development cycle toward final commercialization. Forecasting future earnings, and calculating the risks associated with a new technology, makes the income method of valuation extremely difficult.

Second, when applied to early-stage technologies, the market method involves identifying comparable technologies that have been recently licensed, sold, or acquired. There simply may not be similar technologies that have been sold. In fact, the lack of similar technologies may be exactly why our target technology is being developed in the first place. Finding true comparable technologies can be difficult due to the uniqueness of most innovations, limited public data, and the variability in deal structures. Even if a similar technology has been sold, the prices are both hard to find and put into a multiple that can be applied to our technology.

Third, the cost approach is not even relevant in most cases of technology development. Unlike the hard assets of most businesses, such as machinery, office equipment, and inventory, the major asset behind a technology is intellectual nature. In some cases, we might be able to approximate the intellectual asset by adding up the various R&D costs and development investments that have been made over time to create the intellectual asset. But this approach doesn't account for radical innovations, break-through technologies, or even market acceptance. These challenges make the asset or cost approach very difficult in the world of technology valuation.

The Standard of Value

There are many definitions of value. "Intrinsic" value represents something with special meaning. A family heirloom may hold great personal value but would likely fetch only a fraction of its "intrinsic" value at auction. "Investment" value considers a particular situation. Somebody in a certain tax bracket, at a certain age in life, with no family members, and with other investments might value a particular asset very differently than people in different situations.

For business valuation, including the valuation of technologies, the term "fair market value" is typically used. The term "fair market value" is defined as follows:

> The price at which the property would change hands between a willing buyer and a willing seller, neither being under compulsion to buy or sell, and both having reasonable knowledge of relevant facts.

Definitions of fair market value used by various valuation and appraisal professionals all have these common characteristics, (a) the buyer and seller are typically motivated but are not being forced into an exchange, (b) both parties are well informed and acting in their best interests, (c) a reasonable time is allowed on the market, and (d) the market has other characteristics of market efficiency. Our examination of financial analysis and valuation for technologies will generally assume a "fair market value" definition.

Technology versus Business Valuation

Calculating the value of an early-stage technology is the key question for many. It is also one of the hardest questions. Many serious mistakes are made at this point. Technology valuation is very similar to business valuation, but there are also important differences.

Business Valuation

A business valuation examines the value of the whole business entity, such as a corporation or limited liability company. For a publicly traded corporation, the valuation is fairly straightforward – simply add up the market value of all the outstanding, publicly traded stock. In finance, this is often called the "capitalization", or "equity value" of a business. It certainly can become more complicated with the various classes of stock, such as common stock and preferred stock, but the general rule is that for publicly traded firms, the "fair market" equity value is the sum of all the outstanding stock.

Various analysts might certainly argue that a stock is undervalued or overvalued based upon their understanding of the firm's potential and problems. People arguing about this exact point is what creates the huge and highly profitable industry of stock analysts, investment advisors, and active stock traders. But the fair market value of a publicly traded company is probably pretty close to what the stock market says it is at any point in time.

The term "fair market value" is defined as the price at which the property would change hands between a willing buyer and a willing seller, neither being under compulsion to buy or sell, and both having reasonable knowledge of relevant facts.

Equity v. Enterprise Business Value. When discussing business valuation, it is important to understand that there are actually two different measures of business value, an "enterprise" value and an "equity" value. It is important not to confuse these two definitions. "Enterprise" value is essentially the value of something without assuming debt or other significant business obligations. For example, if a real estate appraiser concludes a house is worth $500,000 based on a comparison of nearby sales, somebody might be willing to pay $500,000 for it. But when paying $500,000, the buyer would certainly want the title free and clear from any debt or obligations. In most cases, part of this $500,000 would be used by the seller to pay off any outstanding mortgages and taxes. This is normally part of the sales contract. The seller would then receive the net proceeds. This initial $500,000 would be similar to the "enterprise" value of a business.

But let's say there is a $300,000 mortgage against that house. The "equity" value in the house is only $200,000. In this case, a buyer of that house could possibly pay the owner only $200,000 and then assume the existing $300,000 mortgage, assuming the mortgage holder would agree.

Knowing the difference between enterprise and equity value is important when valuing a business. In the case of publicly traded companies, the stock price represents an equity value since the stock price represents what the market thinks the business is worth, including the business servicing the debt and other obligations. One can approximate an "enterprise" value for publicly traded firms by adding the debt and other business obligations to the "equity" value.[2]

The case of "closely held" enterprises is different. Closely held or private firms are not publicly traded on a stock exchange, but they are often sold. There are various subscription databases, such as *DealStats* and *Bizcomps*, that collect and report transaction data for smaller, closely held firms. However, like the residential housing market databases, the sales of most closely held firms do not include the assumption of any debt. That is, if I buy a closely held business for a certain price, the expectation is that the previous owner pays off the major debt and other business obligations with those proceeds. Thus, the sales prices reported in these private firm transaction databases are more like "enterprise" values, and not "equity" value.

The difference between publicly traded stock or "equity" value and the "enterprise" values from comparable transaction databases is important to understand, particularly if attempting to use comparable data to value a business or technology.

Technology Valuation v. Business Valuation

Business valuation is different from technology valuation in another important manner. A business valuation represents the value of the whole business. This includes not only the technology and IP it might own, but also its equipment, machinery, vehicles, designs, inventory, contracts, obligations and debt, and administrative structure. An ongoing business might also have developed significant "goodwill". A technology valuation represents the value of the IP, and in later stages of development, the actual technology designs (prototypes, etc.) or the rights to the commercially ready finished product.

Finally, a larger corporation might have many, if not hundreds of technologies. In technology valuation, the focus should be on a specific technology and its long-term potential to generate income or cash flow – either through direct sales or licensing revenue, or by enhancing the performance and economics of a larger integrated system, such as improving efficiency or reducing costs.

Oftentimes, a smaller, early-stage entrepreneurial enterprise will be built on a single technological platform. In this case, the value of the entrepreneurial firm is really the value of the underlying technology, with an adjustment perhaps for the managerial skill required to actually commercialize the technology. It is often said that a top technology will bring itself to the market, but mediocre technologies can still be immensely successful if the entrepreneurs have the passion, insight, skills and knowledge to make it happen.

Technology Valuation: Income Methods

The most common method of valuing a technology during its development cycle is the income method. The income method is typically what is required as part of the gate scorecards in a phase-review process. Many of the more sophisticated private equity investors will use an income method when they look at technology-driven entrepreneurial enterprises. Finally, if there is litigation about the technology for any reason, the courts will often use the income method to determine value.

For valuation purposes, most pro-formas for pre-revenue technologies will only look out 3 to 5 years after expected commercialization.

The starting point for any income valuation method is the pro-forma discussed in the prior chapter. The pro-forma, if properly done, will provide the best forecast of the future earnings or cashflow associated with the technology. As mentioned previously, most pro-formas for pre-revenue technologies will only look out 3 to 5 years after expected commercialization.

The second part of the income method is to "discount" these future projected earnings or cashflows to the present. Present value essentially means determining what somebody is willing to pay today to obtain these future cashflows, given the risk involved with obtaining these future cashflows. By definition, a present value analysis considers "risk". Risk is incorporated into the discount rate that is used to calculate a present value.

Present value analysis, also called "discounted earnings", is taught in every basic finance course around the globe. We often call the analysis a "Net Present Value" or NPV, if we also include the net cashflow (positive or negative) associated with a technology. If the pro-forma is already a risk-adjusted projection (discussed in previous chapter), the net present value is often represented by a small "r" before the NPV, that is, "rNPV".

Figure 11.1 below illustrates the formula for a net present value analysis:

$$NPV = CF_0 + \frac{CF_1}{(1+k)^1} + \frac{CF_2}{(1+k)^2} + \ldots + \frac{CF_n}{(1+k)^n}$$

Figure 11.1: The formula for a net present value analysis.

where CF represents the negative or positive cashflow for the different time periods. This, of course, comes from the pro-forma. K represents the discount rate. The discount rate is what incorporates the risk associated with the projected cashflows. With technology valuation, the discount rate can be as difficult to calculate as the future cashflows.

Calculating the Discount Rate for Technologies

Calculating the discount rate associated with early-stage technologies is somewhat different from the discount rates for a business valuation, where a business might have been generating revenues and profits, perhaps from a portfolio of products, for decades.[3] In determining the appropriate discount rates for technologies, the focus is squarely on a particular technology, and its stage of development – this is where the majority of the risk lies. Technologies in earlier stages of development are much riskier than technologies in later stages. Pre-revenue technologies are far riskier than technologies in the marketplace producing revenues.

The discount rates used for technologies in different stages of development are often kept secret by consulting groups, larger corporations, and large venture capital firms for good reason. We offer two models in this chapter. The first discount rate model is based upon the experience of the authors in working with hundreds of technologies in all stages of development, from patent decisions to final commercialization. The second discount rate model used published data from a study of pharmaceutical products.

The Technology Development Discount Rate (TDDR) Model

The Technology Development Discount Rate (TDDR) Model is developed by the authors and has been used in a number of technology valuations. The TDDR is a type of "build-up" model, combining the current "risk-free" rate (yield rate on a 20-year government T-bond), the stage of technology development premium, an industry risk adjustment, and then a final adjustment for specific characteristics of the technology. The calculated discount rate is then applied to the non-risk-adjusted forecasts in the pro-forma. Each company, consulting group, or investor group might have their own discount rate model, so the TDDR presented in this chapter, although based on extensive experience and research, should only be considered instructive in nature.

Technology Discount Rate = Risk Free Rate + Stage of Development Premium
× (Industry Premium) + Specific Adjustments.

Stage of Technology Development Premium. The stage of a technology's development drives the majority of the risk associated with an early-stage technology valuation. Many financial analysts and college instructors familiar with discounted cashflow techniques used in analyzing normal business projects, financial investments, or well-established stable enterprises might find these premiums very high. However, that is the nature of the risk associated with R&D and technology development.

This risk is certainly understood by private equity investors that invest in small, pre-revenue technology development firms. A commonly heard rule of thumb by these early-stage investors is to target a return of "10 times their investment within 5 years". Why so high? – they need this return target since only a small fraction of their investments will actually pay back anything. This often-cited target of 10 times investment in 5 years results in a discount rate of around 60%, fairly consistent with our calculations, considering that most early-stage investors fund entrepreneurial firms developing technologies in the TR4 to TRL6 ranges.[4]

The stage of a technology's development drives the majority of the risk
associated with an early-stage technology valuation.

Figure 11.2 represents a typical average premium that might be applied in the TDDR model in order to calculate the appropriate discount rate associated with the projections presented in the pro-forma. This premium would be added to the risk-free yield rate. The two stages where the risk decreases significantly, reflected by a lower discount rate, are: a) when development actually starts on a technology after the IP protection is fully established and b) with a successful beta test.

Technology Development Discount Rate Premium (TDDR)

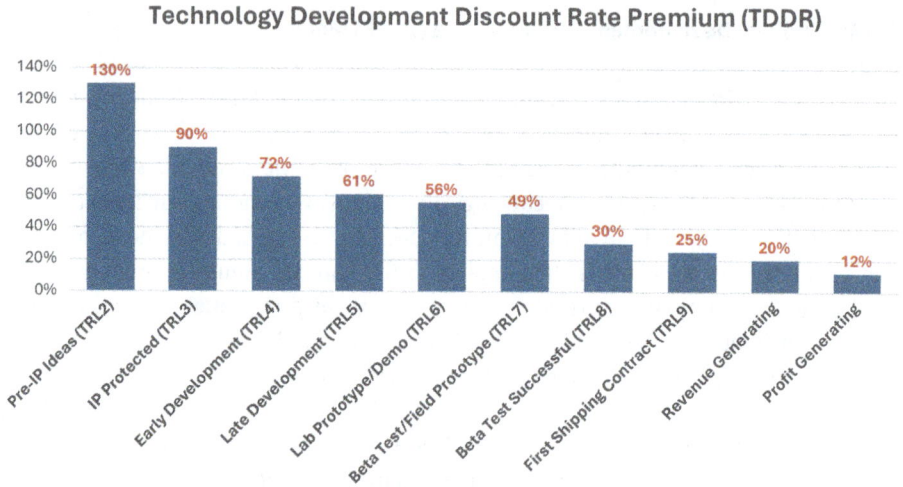

Figure 11.2: Technology development discount premium.

Technology Industry Discount Rate Adjustment. Some industries are just riskier than other industries when commercializing technologies. For example, at the present time, developing a new software system or phone app is generally considered more difficult to commercialize than new, improved technologies for households or healthcare. The Technology Industry Adjustment is calculated from a combination of different sources, including surveys on success rates in different industries, and the published risk "betas" associated with the stock prices of publicly traded firms in different industries.[5] Figure 11.3 illustrates the Technology Industry Adjustment for various technology industry sectors. The industry risk will vary over time as one industry expands faster than other industries. The Stage of Development Premium is multiplied by the Technology Industry Adjustment.

Technology Industry Adjustment	
(Multiply Industry Adjustment by Development Stage)	
Industry	**Premium**
Computer Services	0.92
Computer Hardware	1.02
Consumer Electronics	1.05
General Electronics	0.92
Healthcare Products	0.94
Household Products	0.90
Software Internet	1.11
Sotware Systems and Apps	1.08
Software Entertainment	1.13
Telecom Equipment	0.99

Figure 11.3: Technology industry adjustment.

Technology-Specific Adjustment. The final component looks at the specific technology and then makes a "subjective" adjustments to the model. The three main components of a technology-specific adjustment are the evaluation of the strength of the intellectual property, the ability of the development team, and any regional or international risk.

In calculating the specific premium, it is important to remember that a strong position reduces the discount rate, while a weak position increases the discount rate.

The TDDR model is derived primarily from U.S. data. In general, economically developed regions such as Canada, Western Europe, Japan, and Australia have similar risk profiles due to strong capital market institutions and protection of IP. However, many parts of the world do not have these protections, and commercializing a technology in these markets incurs more risk.

International risk premiums have been studied extensively for the stock markets, but not for early-stage technology commercialization. As a reference, however, one could possibly add an additional country risk premium to the TDDR from these stock market studies. This premium would range from a "0%" premium (developed countries), 2% for India, to 3% to 5% for Eastern European Countries and most South American countries. Some struggling countries with weak institutions, such as in Africa, Latin America, or the Middle East, would be above 6%.[6]

As an example, suppose that we believe that our IP is very strong on a number of dimensions. In this case we would have a reduction in our specific premium related to IP. But let's also consider that our development team might not have a lot of commitment, perhaps since they are working on different projects. In this case, we might increase the discount rate to reflect these problems. Let's also assume that we will only be commercializing our technology in countries with strong IP protection, such as the U.S. or Europe. In this example, the combination of IP and development team issues decreases the overall discount rate of the technology, resulting in less risk than the average technology in the same stage of development. Figure 11.4 illustrates possible adjustments based on a technology specific premium.

There are a couple of important points about technology-specific premiums. First, the scoring is subjective. Hence, the adjustment probably should probably not account for more than a 20% adjustment of the discount rate in either direction. Second, it is important that the scoring on the technology-specific premium does not reflect issues taken into account when generating the pro-forma. For example, a weak IP position or many competitive products already in the market are certainly serious risks. However, if these weak positions were taken into account in developing the pro-forma, it should not be included in the technology-specific adjustment since that would result in a double counting of risk.

Technology Specific Premium (Added to Risk Calculation)	
Intellectual Property	**Adjustment**
Defensibility of IP Rights	–5.00%
Possibility of Disputes	–1.00%
Remaining Length of IP Rights	–2.00%
Narrowness/Breadth of Rights	–3.00%
Sub-Total	–11.00%
Development Team	**Adjustment**
Ability of Development Team	0.00%
Commitment of Development Team	3.00%
Speed of Development	1.00%
Development Team Resources	0.00%
Sub-Total	4.00%
International or Regional	**Adjustment**
International Risk Adjustment	0.00%
Total Specific Premium	**–7.00%**

Figure 11.4: Technology-specific premium.

The calculation of discount rates discussed above assumes a "non-risk-adjusted" forecast of future revenues and earnings. As mentioned in the previous chapter, some companies and consultants, particularly in the pharmaceutical industry, use a "risk-adjusted" pro-forma where the forecasted post-commercialization revenues and earnings are adjusted by a "probability" figure. Calculating a risk-adjusted forecast is perfectly fine; however, if using a "risk-adjusted" pro-forma, it would be inappropriate to use the discount rates discussed above, since this would "double-count" much of the risk. The discount rates used on "risk-adjusted" pro-formas to obtain a net present value are significantly lower.

Case Example of Net Present Value Calculation. As an example, let's suppose that we are developing a net present value calculation for a phase-review gate that would move a technology from having a demonstration prototype (around TRL6) to final development of a field prototype (around TRL7). This is still pretty far from beta testing and generating revenues, so riskier. We would probably use the demonstration prototype stage discount rate, since that is the TRL phase we are currently in – we may not get to TRL7. This would result in a base development stage risk premium around 56% (TRL6). Our technology is targeted toward the consumer electronics market, so the 56% would then be adjusted by 1.05, resulting in a 58.8% industry adjusted development stage premium. Let's assume, as above, that we have a strong IP, but a somewhat problematic development team, for a –7.0% technology-specific adjustment. Finally, the current risk-free rate is 3% (yield rate of the 20-year government T-bond). All together, this would result in a total 54.8% discount rate (see Figure 11.5).

Technology Development Discount Rate (Example)	
TRL6 (from TDDR Premimum)	56.0%
Consumer Electronics Industry Adjustment	1.05
Industry Adjusted TDDR	58.8%
Specific Technology Adjustment	–7.0%
Specific Technology Adjusted TDDR	51.8%
Add Risk Free Rate	3.0%
Total TDDR for Technology	**54.8%**

Figure 11.5: Technology development discount rate example.

To complete the net present value analysis, we then need to apply this 54.8% discount rate to the net cashflow or earnings from our "non-risk-adjusted" pro-forma. In real life, this analysis is all done on spreadsheets, such as using Excel's NPV function. Oftentimes when using a pro-forma to determine an income approach to valuation, there is a calculation of "terminal" value in the end year. The terminal value attempts to calculate the value of all the years afterward. This is normally computed by taking the earnings of the last year in the pro-forma and then dividing this figure by the discount rate. This is often called a "capitalization of earnings" process to obtain a terminal value. Some corporations use a terminal value, while others do not use a terminal value in their calculations since a terminal value assumes the income will continue in the long term.

Using the pro-forma in Figure 10.2 from the previous chapter, this results in a total NPV (incorporating the early development expenses plus the positive cashflow projections after commercialization) of $47,933,476. This is the typical analysis that looks at both negative and positive cashflows from the present time.

Some corporations in their phased-review might use just the earnings after commercialization and not include the pre-commercialization development expenses. In this example, the post-commercialization present value is calculated at $131,151,180 (see Figure 11.6). However, this certainly overestimates the true net present value. As you can see, there are many different ways that people can calculate this; just make sure that the method you are using is made clear and, if appropriate, follows the corporate guidelines.

Anything that reduces risk in the technology development process and thus reduces the appropriate discount rate in that stage of development will increase the value of the technology.

Net Present Value Early-Stage Technology						
		(Example)				
	Development Year 1	Development Year 2	In Market Year 1	In Market Year 2	In Market Year 3	Terminal Value Year 3/DR
Net Earnings/Cashflow	($6,000,000)	($7,000,000)	$14,000,000	$104,000,000	$134,000,000	$244,525,547
Discount Rate	54.8%					
NPV (All Cashflows)	$47,933,476					
NPV (Post-Commercialization)	$131,151,180					

Figure 11.6: Early-stage net present value example.

As a final comment, the discounting of early-stage technologies can be quite dramatic. In addition, present value calculations are highly sensitive to discount rates, so careful attention needs to be given to these calculations. However, this exercise always brings a better understanding of the impact of risk into technologies still in early development stages. This analysis can assist senior management in targeting their strategic efforts in reducing risk, even for early-stage technologies. Anything that reduces risk in the technology development process, and thus reduces the appropriate discount rate in that stage of development, will increase the value of the technology.

Discount Rates for Pharmaceutical Products

As previously discussed, the development cycle for pharmaceutical drugs is fundamentally different than most technologies due to the nature of the different stages in drug development, such as pre-clinical activities, animal testing, the different phases of human testing and ultimately obtaining governmental approvals. For pharmaceutical products, the descriptive labels of the stages reflect this process. For example, a study by *Avance* of 242 drug companies, investors, and consultants indicated the following discount rates used in different stages of drug development[7] (see Figure 11.7).

The discount rates reported in the above table would be applied to the earnings projections from the pro-forma. Like the TDDR model, as a technology gets closer to commercialization, the discount rate decreases dramatically.

Discount Rates for Net Present Value Analysis (Pharmaceutical Products)		
Stage of Drug Development	*Discount Rates for "Non-Risk Adjusted" Projections (NPV)*	*Discount Rates for "Risk Adjusted" Projections (rNPV)*
Early-Stage (Pre-clinical/ Phase 1)	40.1%	18.6%
Mid-Stage (Phase 2 Human Testing)	26.7%	16.0%
Late-Stage (Phase 3 Human Testing)	19.5%	13.5%
Source: Avance		

Figure 11.7: Discount rates for a pharma net present value analysis.

This table shows the discount rates for both "non-risk-adjusted" projections and "risk-adjusted" projections since "risk-adjusted" forecasts are much more common in the pharmaceutical industry. Although not reported in the above table, the expectation is that even earlier stages of drug development, such as patenting phases, in-vitro testing, and laboratory work would have much higher discount rates, perhaps similar to the TDDR model. Of course, each company might use their own, established discount rates for internal purposes.

Present value calculations are highly sensitive to discount rates, so careful attention needs to be given to these calculations.

Technology Valuation: Market Method

Like any appraisal or valuation process, the second approach is a market method. The market method involves finding a similar technology that was acquired by another corporation and then applying the same multiples to our technology. While simple in theory, there are several difficulties with this approach.
1) Most technologies are different, so we need to be very careful as to how comparable these other sold technologies really are.
2) Most acquisitions of technologies by larger corporations are private deals, with the specifics of the deal carefully guarded.

3) Technologies are purchased or acquired at different stages. It is very difficult, or impossible, to determine an appropriate "multiple" when a technology has no revenues or earnings.

4) Some corporations acquire whole entrepreneurial firms in order to acquire their IP or technologies, while other corporations might just acquire the IP. It is easier to find the multiples when a whole firm is acquired, since this is often publicly announced or available on many of the merger and acquisition databases.

5) A final method of finding data from a comparable firm is when a technology firm performs an initial public offering (IPO). This will immediately place a fair market value on the equity of the company. It might be possible, if the firm going through the IPO is working with a similar technology for a similar market, to use the IPO results.

Common Application of the Market Method

Market methods of valuation are often presented to, or used by, private equity investors, such as angel groups and early-stage venture capitalists. When used by the private equity community, it is generally placed within the context of a future, or anticipated exit or liquidity event where the technology (or entrepreneurial firm formed around a technology) is expected to be sold sometime in the future. This is important since private equity investors generally only receive a return on their investments during an "exit" or "liquidity" event, such as a future acquisition or IPO. They don't expect dividends or any share of the firm's annual profits; rather they want all profits, if any, to be reinvested in order to scale the operation up to its maximum future value. Most private equity investors want this "liquidity" event to occur within a three-to-five-year target period. The value of the technology, or business, is then determined by "back solving" (in other words, determining the present value) from the future exit value to the present time.

Market methods of valuation are often presented to, or used by, private equity investors, such as angel groups and early-stage venture capitalists.

While commonly used by the private equity community, market methods can be used by anybody, not just for purposes of an "exit". Larger firms, for example, can also value technologies in the same manner, but more on a hypothetical basis and not with the actual expectation of "exiting" the technology. In this respect, a firm may use a combination of the income method and the market method to obtain a better understanding of the technology's fair market value.

Revenue multiples are more common in this type of analysis, since many early-stage technology firms may still not be making a profit when they are acquired, but they may have some revenues. Revenue multiples can also be obtained from initial public offering (IPO) events.

Obviously, the closer the "exit" or liquidity event is to the present time, the higher the present value of the exit event assuming the same revenues. But revenues do grow over time, so it is really a tradeoff. As mentioned above, the major drawback of the market approach is making sure that the technologies and/or target market of the comparable M&A or IPO firms are truly comparable.

Using Merger and Acquisition Data

There are a number of databases that provide merger and acquisition data. However, most of these are subscription databases. The key in using merger and acquisition data is to determine some type of multiple that can be used to assess our technology. The most common multiples are revenue multiples and earnings multiples, such as earnings before interest, taxes, depreciation, and amortization (EBITDA). Multiples from merger and acquisition data are regularly published and are industry specific. Figure 11.8 illustrates the most recent average multiples from published mergers and acquisitions data.[8]

Average M&A Multiples by Technology Sector		
Industry	Average Revenue Multiple	Average EBITDA Multiple
AdTech	2.36	9.06
AgTech	2.63	10.00
B2B Software (SaaS)	2.90	10.86
Cybersecurity	2.80	11.00
Fintech	2.90	11.36
Hosting	1.93	9.33
Managed Services	2.50	9.60
Software (SaaS)	2.80	10.80
Semiconductors	3.16	11.20
Software Development	2.62	10.13

Figure 11.8: Average M&A multiples by technology sector.

Figure 11.8 shows the average M&A multiples across all sized companies. In every case, however, larger revenue or profit generating firms have higher M&A multiples, while smaller firms tend to have lower M&A multiples.

How can these multiples be used to value a pre-revenue, early-stage technology? The most common comparable method is to go back to the pro-forma analysis. In this process, a "realized" value in the future is calculated, such as when we might actually consider "selling" our technology or business. We then calculate an appropriate discount rate, depending on what stage of development our technology is in, and then compute a net present value.

For example, suppose we are developing a technology for the agricultural market, and our pro-forma predicts revenues of $100,000,000 three years after commercialization (see Figure 11.9). Our management team is thinking about possibly selling the technology (or business) at the end of this 3-year period after commercialization or five years from now since we still have two years of development time before commercializing our product. What is the current value of this technology?

The current average M&A revenue multiple for the AgTech average is 2.63. Assuming no debt, this results in a $263,000,000 "realized" value five years from now in our pro-forma, or our third year after commercialization. To obtain commercialization, we need to spend $5million in development cost for each of the first two years. Let's assume we calculate the appropriate discount rate for a technology at our stage of development to be 45%. This would then result in a net present value for our technology at this present time of $35,204,946.

Comparable Market Approach in Valuation of an Early-Stage Technology (Example)					
	Development	Development	Year 1	Year 2	Year 3
Net Revenues			$30,000,000	$50,000,000	$100,000,000
Revenue Multiple (AgTech)					2.63
Realized Value	($5,000,000)	($5,000,000)	$0	$0	$263,000,000
Discount Rate	45%				
Present Value	$35,204,946				

Figure 11.9: Comparable market approach in valuation of an early-stage technology.

We could perform the same analysis type of analysis using the EBITDA ratios, and an EBITDA projection on the pro-forma.

Caution in Using M&A and Private Equity Deal Data

Many technologies, and technology-based small firms, are sold well before generating any revenues or profit. Likewise, most "seed" private equity investments are for small firms, and their technologies, that are in early development stages before commercialization and revenue generation. Ideally, this information would be very useful in the determination of value, since it is much more comparable to the stage of development our technology might be in. But there are several problems.

Sometimes we know the acquisition price or funding for these types of pre-revenue technologies or businesses, but most often they are kept private. The published data might provide the deal price, but not the financial conditions of the private firm, so it is hard to calculate multiples. But for pre-revenue technologies or firms, even if the investor funding amount or acquisition price is known, we cannot use a revenue or profit multiple as described above – there are no revenues. In these cases, it is difficult to calculate a useful ratio that we can apply to our technology or business. Sometimes we can calculate a price per employee ratio that might be useful, but most people just subjectively apply their personal knowledge of these deals.

Technology Valuation: Cost Approaches

The cost approach is probably the least useful approach to value a technology. The reason is simple – the success of a technology is not highly correlated with the cost to develop a technology. Companies constantly pour millions of dollars into developing technologies, only to have most of them fail to reach the market.

The cost approach is often used to value IP in a variety of legal situations, such as patent infringement cases, or when small slices of IP are being examined, such as developing a specific piece of software and databases, developing technical libraries, creating food recipes or chemical formulations, or even determining the value of a trained technical workforce. Valuing these types of IP is difficult since there really is no external market for them, and the cost approach may be the only reasonable method to consider.

The cost approach is also used when selling a patent, well before any reasonable forecast can be made about its future cashflow potential.

The cost approach is often used to value IP in a variety of legal situations, such as patent infringement cases, or when small slices of IP are being examined

---

While there are several approaches to the cost approach in valuing early-stage technologies, the most common is to simply add up all the expenses that was required to get the technology to this point. These are assets that are "used up" to create the IP. The difficulty is documenting all these costs, expenses, and investments. This would include:

1) The labor, wages, and benefits paid to all the scientists, engineers, developers, and product designers who worked on the technology in the past.
2) Out of pocket expenses for patent filing fees, maintenance fees, patent attorney fees, trips to conferences, etc.
3) The cost of the lab equipment and materials required to bring the technology to the present point of development.
4) Any direct overhead and support/management staff expenses. This might include a fair market charge for the lab space, insurance, accountants, and management time.
5) Payments to acquire other IP that might have been used in the development of the current technology. This would include any direct cost for external IP, but also any internal IP that was developed earlier in the corporation that was foundational to the development of the current IP. If the prior foundational IP was internal, then the cost approach would require determining a fair market "license" or contribution equivalent for this foundational IP.
6) The value of any external development grants that were obtained, such as early SBIR phase 1 grants or other developmental contracts.

Adding all of these together results in a cost method of valuation. The idea is that all of these inputs would be required to obtain the current level of technology development. The accuracy of the cost method as a true indicator of a technology's fair market value decreases dramatically as a technology gets closer to market commercialization. The accuracy of predicting commercialization success, and its associated cashflows, increases dramatically in later stages of development. But for very early technologies in the pre-patent or early post-patent stages, the cost method might provide a somewhat reasonable valuation since it is much harder to predict market success at these stages.

Concluding Insights

Valuing early-stage technologies is one of the most challenging yet critical aspects of the technology commercialization process. Whether a technology is being pitched to investors, advanced through a phase-review process, involved in licensing negotiations, or part of a merger, acquisition, or legal dispute, a clear and defensible valuation is essential. As this chapter illustrates, each scenario presents a unique context in which valuation plays a central role in decision-making and resource allocation.

This chapter explored the three foundational valuation approaches – income, market, and cost – and examined how each becomes more complex when applied to emerging technologies. The income approach, while commonly preferred, is complicated by the uncertainty of future earnings and the difficulty of determining appropriate discount rates. The market approach relies on identifying truly comparable transactions, which are rare for early-stage technologies and often lack transparency. The cost approach, although the least used in practice, can be useful in early development or litigation settings where market or income-based projections are not yet feasible.

A critical takeaway is the distinction between technology valuation and business valuation. While business valuation includes all tangible and intangible assets – like equipment, staff, contracts, obligations, and "goodwill" – technology valuation focuses specifically on a single asset or platform and its potential to generate future value, either directly or as part of a larger system.

Finally, the chapter introduced methods for calculating discount rates tailored to the risk profiles of technologies in various stages of development. These models emphasize how deeply uncertainty, market readiness, and the capabilities of the development team influence value. The importance of selecting the right valuation method, and applying it with transparency and discipline, cannot be overstated – particularly when decisions about funding, partnerships, or commercialization hang in the balance.

Chapter Example: Translating Research into Revenue? How Tech Transfer Professionals Assess Value at the Earliest Stages of Development and Commercialization

Valuation of early-stage technologies is notoriously difficult – especially when technologies are still pre-revenue, pre-prototype, pre-product, and even pre-patent. Yet, university tech transfer officers (TTO) must make judgment calls every day about whether to invest in protecting intellectual property, what licensing terms are appropriate, and whether a faculty member's startup plan is credible.

This case draws on interviews with seven experienced university commercialization leaders from diverse research institutions. We sought to explore how valuation is embedded in their daily work with the earliest stages of technology development.[9] While a few might use formal financial models at the initial stages, all must assess potential value through a mix of technical, market, and relational signals.

The First Valuation Gate: Is This Technology Worth Protecting?

When a faculty member discloses a potential invention, the first major decision is whether the university should invest in IP protection, and in how many countries. This is often the first time a technology is really assessed as to its commercialization potential. At this point, the decision maker is deciding whether or not to support moving a technology from the TRL2 stage, pre-patent stage into the TRL3, or possibly a TRL4 stage of development. This support might include the cost of patenting the technology and, in some cases, a follow-up commitment to support developing an early-stage prototype or demonstration system. At these early stages, it is almost impossible to develop a sophisticated pro-forma or detailed valuation analysis. The questions are often therefore framed as an informal valuation decision: is this asset likely to generate enough future value to justify the up-front costs?

What is interesting is the diverse approaches that these professionals take during these earliest stages of technology development. The different approaches are, in part, determined by the number of disclosures the university TTOs receive per year. Some large, flagship universities will generate hundreds of disclosures per year. For example, in 2024 Purdue University's Office of Technology Commercialization received 466 technology disclosures, all with varying degrees of commercial potential. Not surprisingly, the technology transfer offices of these large research universities need to operate in a very efficient manner, even with a larger staff. For example, the TTO at one large research university takes a broad and fast approach, filing provisional patent applications on roughly 75% of the disclosures made to its office and letting future market feedback during the normal 1-year life of the provisional patent application guide subsequent IP protection steps on an individual basis. A TTO from another large research university applies a somewhat more selective strategic lens, using structured internal team reviews to assess market potential, patentability, and strategic alignment before filing for a patent – this university has a large staff, with diverse skills to internally review the potential of different technology disclosures.

Smaller- and mid-sized research universities with fewer Ph.D. programs will receive significantly fewer disclosures, often under 30 per year. They have to approach the problem differently – fewer disclosures with smaller TTO staffs. For these smaller research universities, we find a more externally focused voice of the customer commercialization approach from the very beginning. For example, two different universities with smaller portfolios of technologies use small "proof-of-concept" funds to filter disclosures. These proof-of-concept funds allow graduate student teams to perform actual "quick-look" commercialization studies on the different disclosures that appear to initially have some potential. For these TTOs, however, finding potential from a quick-look commercialization study is generally not enough. These smaller TTOs also look for a deep commitment from the faculty inventors to carry the technology forward, and work with any potential license partners. Only then is an investment made in the patenting process.

For example, in addition to a quick-look VoC analysis one of the smaller TTOs surveyed also requires a preliminary pro-forma to be developed for any technology that will require a prototype or demonstration model. Using this strategy, this particular TTO has been able to achieve a top ten ranking in the U.S. on both start-ups formed and licenses signed when the metrics are normalized for university R&D expenditures, basically a "bang for the buck" measure of technology transfer success.[10] For promising technologies, this university has a commitment to not only cover patent costs but also support initial prototyping and further technology development if necessary. This support for technology commercialization goes all the way to the Chancellor, who was originally an executive VP of a successful pharmaceutical development firm. In this case, the TTO, working with the faculty inventor, will create a preliminary calculation of the future projected cost structure required to develop a demonstration prototype or experimental data sufficient enough to properly interest potential licensees.

Despite these differences, all seven professionals are doing an early-stage technology triage – evaluating novelty, feasibility, and relevance to assess which inventions warrant further investment. Their choices reflect different disclosure volumes, resource levels, organizational structures, and commercialization philosophies. What is interesting, however, is that the vast majority of the actual license or royalty income that any university receives, whether the university is large or small, generally comes from only a small handful of successful technologies; the vast majority of license deals simply do not pay much, or anything, in the long run. In spite of some famous case examples, data show that approximately 60% of university licenses in the U.S. do not generate any revenue, while less than 1% of academic licenses result in over $1million of royalties over the lifetime of the license.[11] It is a tough business, but proper commercialization strategies, even at these very early stages, can increase the chances of success.

Pricing the Opportunity: Valuation in Licensing

Once IP is protected, valuation takes a new form: informed licensing negotiations. Whether licensing to an external firm or a faculty-led startup, the TTO must develop a view of what the technology is worth.

Some offices draw on internal benchmarks and deal history. Larger TTOs, for example, tend to emphasize milestone-based deals, comparable deals, and internal controls. These larger TTOs have done hundreds of license deals, and they can readily draw upon their internal experiences and data. However, TTOs from the smaller research universities tend to use simplified marketing tools (e.g., pitch decks or tech summaries) to generate external interest and then calibrate pricing based on signals from prospective licensees. We also find that the license deals from smaller universities tend to be more advantageous to the licensee, essentially reflecting a "get the deal done" attitude.

Another difference is the importance of networking. Larger universities can draw from a much larger network consisting of alumni, prior start-ups entrepreneurs, the local VC community, and government granting organizations. Not surprisingly, these larger TTOs rely more on relational capital such as personal networks, domain expertise, and iterative conversations, to arrive at terms that balance market potential with development risk. One larger TTO, for example, has an agreement with a large private equity firm to assist with preliminary valuation before the university negotiates its deals.

Across all seven interviews, valuation is a blend of pattern recognition, partner feedback, and institutional experience. At these early stages of technology development, most TTOs do not use formal spreadsheets or cash flow models. The methods explored in Chapter 11 – income, market, and cost – are present in spirit, if not always in form. Deal value is assessed through risk, relevance, and readiness. The exception, as noted above, is the one TTO that does create preliminary pro-formas for technologies that need future university investment for developing prototypes or demonstration systems to shop around.

When the Inventor Is the Entrepreneur

A particularly complex valuation challenge arises when the potential licensee is also the faculty inventor. In these cases, the university must evaluate not only the value of the technology but also the viability of the team, the business plan, and the pathway to success if the faculty inventor wants to "spin out" a start-up firm around the technology. This start-up would then license the inventor's own technology since the university officially owns the IP. Many large research universities have recently made the faculty inventor-entrepreneur combination part of their academic culture. Financial success stories do breed interest, even among die-hard academic researchers.

Here again, the seven professionals take divergent approaches. Mid-sized TTOs often require validation steps (such as accelerators or SBIR grants) to demonstrate founder commitment. The largest TTOs, however, often have significant resources to support faculty driven startups through mentoring and business development, while perhaps deferring licensing until the venture is de-risked. These large universities also offer special deals on licensing arrangements to faculty inventors that may want to try their hand at entrepreneurship. Not surprising, many of these largest research universities have a number of institutional support mechanisms and centers to assist faculty turned novice entrepreneurs. The smaller research universities, however, tend to license selectively to their faculty, often structuring deals to balance affordability with accountability. For these smaller universities, the culture of faculty members becoming entrepreneurs is still in its infancy, although much of the smaller TTO's time is personally spent on educating faculty inventors about the potential of taking their technology further toward the market.

Valuation in these scenarios becomes a holistic judgment. The team, the timeline, the funding model, and the use of university resources all factor into the deal. Faculty passion alone is not enough. TTOs seek signs that the startup is viable, fundable, and aligned with university interests.

Conclusion: Valuation as Strategic Judgment

These different TTO professionals illustrate how valuation in tech transfer of the earliest stage technologies is less about discounting future cash flows and more about informed judgment. This is not surprising, given these TTOs are often looking at technologies in the TRL2 and TRL3, earliest stages of development. The three formal approaches outlined in this chapter, income, market, and cost, may underpin high-stakes decisions or later stages of technology development, but day-to-day, tech transfer professionals for these very early-stage technologies often rely on a different toolkit:

- Inventor interviews to assess commitment and goals
- Market scouting to identify interest or competition
- Accelerator partnerships to test viability
- Templates, pitch decks, and early-stage metrics to screen for potential commercial viability and obtain feedback from potential licensees
- Possible preliminary expense side pro-forma development for technologies that might require additional support or prototyping prior to licensing.
- Quick look commercialization studies to frame the technologies with high potential
- Networking with alumni and the surrounding support community for feedback and possibly even investment interest

Each university adapts its valuation practices to fit its mission, scale, and strategy. But in every case, valuation is central. Whether deciding to file a patent, setting licensing terms, or working with a faculty entrepreneur, tech transfer professionals are making constant assessments of risk, potential, and value. Their judgments shape not just individual deals – but the future of innovation, investment, and impact.

Chapter 12
Managing Technology Projects: Planning Tools and Risk Management

This Chapter

- Outlines the five basic phases of project management and how they apply to technology development efforts.
- Introduces essential project management tools, including Gantt charts, used throughout the commercialization process.
- Highlights the importance of risk management in both technology development and commercialization.
- Explains the distinction between pure risk and speculative risk, and why it matters for tech ventures.
- Discusses the role of insurance and identifies common insurance gaps faced by technology companies.
- Presents key tools of risk management, including risk checklists, risk registries, and risk repositories.

Key Management Tools and Best Practices

- Five Phases of Project Management
- The Project Plan
- Subsidiary Plans
- Activity Cost Estimates
- Assumption and Change Logs
- Gantt Charts
- Project Risk Management
- Risk Checklists
- Risk Register and Repository

❗ INSIGHT

Technology development, and ultimately bringing a new product to the market, is always a team effort. Every stage in the technology development life cycle from R&D to market introduction involves people working together to move the technology to the next stage. One important key to the process is implementing effective project management techniques. Proper project management needs to consider five different phases of any project: initiation, planning, execution, performance & control, and project conclusion. The planning phase impacts the success of any technology development project. There are a number of tools, including Gantt Charts and risk management procedures that can significantly increase the probability of successful technology commercialization.

Introduction

Every step in the technology development process, from the earliest R&D effort through prototype development to final launch, involves teams of people working together

https://doi.org/10.1515/9783111684420-013

toward a common objective – successful commercialization. But teams need to be properly managed – that is the role of "project management". Project management and technology development go hand in hand.

Project management and technology development go hand in hand

---

In the fast-paced world of technological development, managing the steps along the way is both complicated and highly dynamic. In a corporate phase-review process, each step of technology development might have different members on the team. The R&D phase, for example, will likely be made up of scientists and design engineers. The prototyping phase will need people with more product engineering and manufacturing backgrounds. Marketing and distribution skills will be required during the beta testing and final commercialization phases. Each of these phases represents a somewhat self-contained project – pull together a team to quickly advance the technology to the next phase of development. In addition, there is also the overarching, grand process of managing the technology through all of the development stages over time, that is, perhaps getting a TRL3 technology to the final TRL9 phase of commercial introduction.

This complexity is true whether the entity is a large corporation with multiple, overlapping technology projects or a small, entrepreneurial effort built on a single, foundational technology. This is also what makes project management within the field of technology development unique. Most projects, such as constructing a high-rise office building, have clearly defined endpoints resulting in delivering a finished product. Once construction starts, it is likely to be completed. In the world of technology development, however, every step involves uncertainty and perhaps even a significant loss of support. Unlike most business-related projects, technologies in early stages of development will often never make it to final product launch. Only the best technologies, combined with the best management effort, survive to the point of market launch.

Even in the face of constant uncertainty, applying proper project management techniques and tools will make the technology development and commercialization process run as smoothly as possible. Each development stage can then hopefully be completed within the required time constraints, resource limits, and development targets while still allowing for rapid change and quick pivots.

Whole books have been written about project management. In this chapter, we review some of the basic concepts and tools of modern project management that appear to be most applicable to the technology development and commercialization processes.

Project Management Overview

There are five basic phases of any project: initiation, planning, execution, performance and control, and project close (see Figure 12.1).

1	2	3	4	5
Conception & Initiation	Definition & Planning	Launch & Execution	Performance & Control	Close & Review
Project need/problem	Resource requirements	Resource allocation	Monitor progress	Project handing
Recommend solution	Task identification	Deliverables met	Track KPIs	Contract termination
Feasibility study	Project Plan	Team meetings	Corrective actions	Project Analysis
Project manager appointed	Timeframes	Project pivots	Modifications	Improvement reports for future projects
Project started	Budget planning	Risk & quality management	Status reports	
	Risk & quality management			

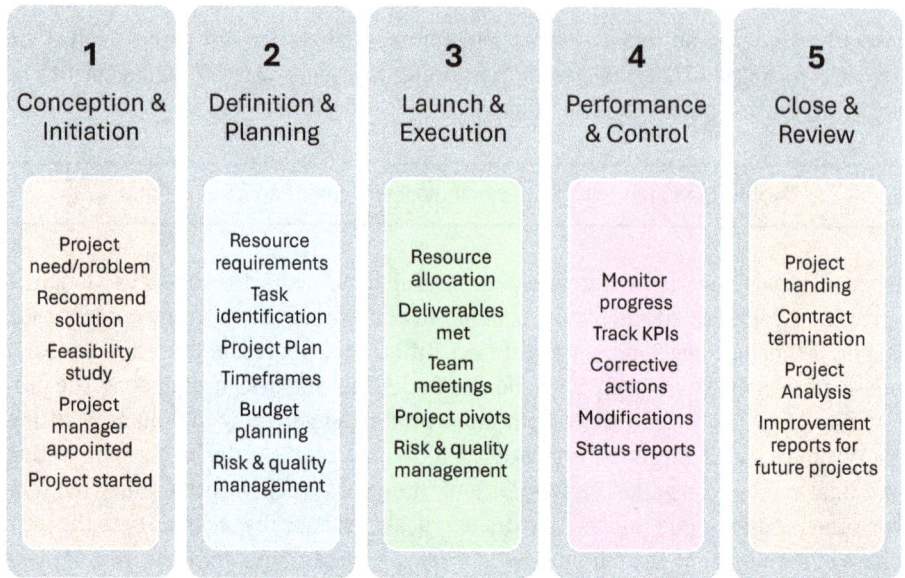

Figure 12.1: Five phases of project management.

While all five phases within a project management effort are important, the focus of this chapter is primarily on the second, or Planning Phase. The Planning Phase is when the project really comes together in technology development.

At the highest level of analysis, moving a technology through its different development phases, from early R&D efforts to final market entry should be considered a project in itself. In organizations with multiple R&D efforts and technologies in different stages of development, almost always each technology has a designated project team. Individual members in these project teams may be dedicated to that one technology or perhaps shared among a number of different technology programs. At this overarching level, the Planning Phase outlines the key tasks and activities required to move a technology through its various development stages and ultimately to market. In a phase-review process, project tasks are defined for each development stage, including the reviews and decision points associated with all the gates.

However, each of the technology development stages is also a well-defined project, with its own set of tasks, activities, human team efforts, resources requirements, time constraints, and objectives. Some of the project team members may also be different for each stage of development, creating a constant flux of behaviors, personalities, and skills. It is important that each of these individual technology development stages must also be properly planned and managed. The Planning Phase involves creating a detailed work plan to accomplish the task, regardless of whether it applies broadly across the project or to a specific stage of technology development.

The Project Plan is the written output of the Planning Phase. The resulting Project Plan is the work plan, with all its details. The Project Plan is not the actual work. Rather, the Project Plan identifies and designs the work in terms of the human, material, and resources needed to accomplish the project objectives.

Each of the technology development stages is also a well-defined project, with its own set of tasks, activities, human team efforts, resources requirements, time constraints, and objectives.

But technology commercialization is also a risky effort. Most early-stage technologies are never commercialized. Not only will there be the normal delays in contracts and cost overruns, but technologies are constantly threatened by intellectual property infringement, new competitive products entering the market, the overall ability of our technology's functionality to satisfy the key requirements of customers, and possibly the reduction of support as other in-house technologies may rapidly become more important to senior management. An important part of the Planning Phase must therefore address how to identify and manage risk.

While this chapter focuses on Planning Phase tools, it is the Execution Phase when the actual work is performed on the technology. The Execution Phase is when day-to-day management and leadership skills come into focus. The Execution Phase involves regular team meetings, making sure the specified deliverables are met in a timely manner, and ultimately incentivizing the talent within the project team. In corporations that use a phase-review process, key deliverables are designed to advance the technology to the next stage and successfully pass through the next review gate. The final stage, of course, is customer delivery of a high-quality product. Even entities that may not have a formal phase-review process, such as small entrepreneurial efforts, these support decisions still need to be made based upon measurable performance criteria.

Useful Tools for the Planning Phase

The Planning Phase is where the success or failure of projects starts. Poor planning will result in poor outcomes. Good project planning requires a degree of formality. Project Plans, however, can be very complicated. The best Project Plans generally have Subsidiary Plans that examine specific issues.

Subsidiary Planning

For technology development projects, the Project Plan should contain a number of interrelated subsidiary plans. At a minimum, there should be consideration of twelve subsidiary plans (See Figure 12.2). Not every organization will use all twelve subsidiary plans as formal documents, but they should be considered as part of the overall strategy. For technology firms formalizing the project management process, each of these subsidiary plans should be separate but linked. Using formal subsidiary plans reduces the chance of overlooking important issues that might threaten the project's completion. Developing subsidiary plans also provides much of the detailed financial data for the pro-forma discussed earlier in this book.

The subsidiary plans do not necessarily need to be long or complicated. It depends on the technology and the organization. For many technologies in development, a subsidiary plan might only be one page in length. For very complicated systems or larger-scale technologies, the subsidiary plans might be highly detailed. The key issue of subsidiary planning is to consider the full range of issues that might arise during a project, and to adjust the length and detail of the subsidiary plans to the particular technology program.

Primary Subsidiary Plans

Communication Management Plan	Cost Management Plan	Human Resource Plan	Project Improvement Plan
Procurement Management Plan	Quality Management Plan	Requirements Management Plan	Risk Management Plan
Schedule Management Plan	Scope Management Plan	Stakeholder Management Plan	Change Management Plan

Figure 12.2: Twelve areas for possible subsidiary project planning.

Planning Documents

The Project Planning phase will also require a number of documents. Some of these documents might be at the top level, while other documents might be within each of the subsidiary plans. We classify ten different types of documents that might be useful (See Figure 12.3).

A good project management leader will make sure that all of the required documents are complete. For larger R&D and technology-oriented corporations with dozens or even hundreds of technologies in different stages of development, these documents may be required as part of corporate policy. These firms will likely use specialized project management programs to organize, record, index, and manage these documents.

In smaller, entrepreneurial organizations some of these documents, such as assumption and change logs, may be less important, while other planning documents such as Gantt charts, activity cost estimates, and contracts are more critical.

Some of these documents, such as activity cost estimates, contracts, and proposals, are somewhat self-explanatory. Some of the other documents appear a little less obvious.

For example, an "Assumption Log" records any of the important assumptions made during the project planning process. An assumption during the prototype development phase plan might be, "there is adequate capacity in the design lab to produce a sufficient number of prototypes for the technology". Who made this assumption? What action is required to validate this assumption? Perhaps the chief design engineer, Dr. Frank, made this assumption, and the corresponding action would be for "Dr. Frank to meet with the operations manager on January 20th to discuss capacity requirements". The assumption, who made it, and the required action to validate the assumption would all be recorded in the assumption log. This allows for both documentation and assignment of responsibility.

The "Change Log" is another interesting document. In technology development as unexpected challenges and new opportunities arise, incremental adjustments and sometimes even large-scale pivots from the original plan are common. A change log records all changes made during the project. Change logs are typically seen more in larger projects.

Gantt Chart	Activity Cost Estimates	Assumption Log	Change Log
Contracts	Performance Reports	Proposals	Quality Checklists
	Resource Calendars	Teaming Agreements	

Figure 12.3: Ten different types of project planning documents.

Gantt Charts, however, are probably the most important of the project planning documents.

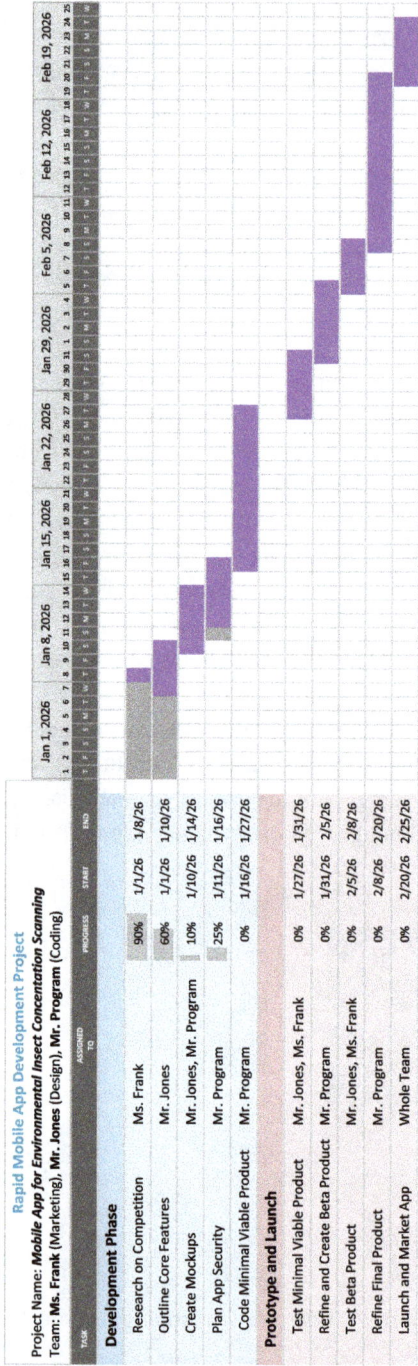

Figure 12.4: Sample Gantt Chart for a mobile app development project.

Gantt Charts

Gantt Charts should be part of any technology development and commercialization process. Gantt Charts were invented by Henry Gantt (1861–1919), one of the early pioneers in scientific management. Gantt Charts, and its variations, remain the most commonly used project planning tool in the modern world.

Gantt Charts, and its variations, remain the most commonly used
project planning tool in the modern world.

A Gantt Chart defines the required activities or tasks to accomplish the overall project, who is responsible for each activity or task, and the time frame for each activity or task (see a sample Gantt Chart in Figure 12.4). On the left of the chart is a list of the activities, and along the top is a suitable time scale. Each activity is represented by a bar; the position and length of the bar reflect the start date, duration, and end date of the activity.

Gantt Charts visually outline the whole project. Gantt Charts can also be adapted to finding the critical paths through the activities. A critical path represents the sequence of activities that define how long a project will take. Other less critical path activities can be delayed without impacting the overall project, but activities or tasks on the critical path need to be completed in a timely manner.

Gantt Chart spreadsheets are easily downloaded from the internet. Gantt Charts are also a critical part of any Project Management software package.

Risk Management

It is clear that technology development and commercialization, by its very nature, is a risky endeavor. But what is risk? In simple terms, risk can be defined as the "chance or possibility of a loss". Accordingly, the effective identification and management of project risk is one of the most important subsidiary planning steps.

The concept of risk is often discussed under two types, "pure risk" and "speculative risk". "Pure risk" refers to situations where the only possible outcome is a loss. Examples include a tornado damaging your house, a car accident, or a family member suffering a broken arm. These events offer no potential for gain – only the possibility of harm or expense.

The concept of risk is often discussed under two types,
"pure risk" and "speculative risk".

"Pure risk" is the focus of the insurance industry. House, car, and health insurance protect people in "pure risk" situations. There are certainly many situations when businesses should protect themselves against "pure risk" events – a customer slips on a wet floor, you suffer a cyberattack, your product injuries somebody, or a natural disaster disrupts your firm's ability to generate income for a period of time.

The other type of risk is called "speculative risk". "Speculative risk" is when there is a possibility of both gains and losses. Investing in the stock market involves "speculative risk". Insurance does not protect against "speculative risk".

"Speculative risk", however, is a key aspect of developing and commercializing technologies. Huge profits can be made, but there is also a significant chance of failure.

Protecting against Pure Risk: Insurance

Commercial insurance is a huge industry. Any business wants to protect their buildings and property. There are certainly standardized property and personal liability insurance policies designed for most businesses. These are called "Commercial Package Policies" (CPPs). CPPs tend to be menu driven – check what you want, what coverage limits, and how much are you willing to pay.

Most businesses tend to be under-insured, or sometimes even over-insured paying more money than they need to. Insurance trade groups report that 50% of small business owners don't even read their insurance policies until something happens, but then it is often too late. Larger corporations, however, generally have a specialized department responsible for obtaining proper insurance coverage. Technology oriented firms, however, often have a number of unique issues not commonly seen in other types of industries. The following represents commonly seen insurance gaps, particularly in technology firms. These are areas where technology firms may want to consider insurance programs.

Insurance policies only address situations of "pure risk".

Any company, of course, can "self-insure" against these perils, and many smaller firms do "self-insure". But it is wise to at least consider the cost-benefit of purchasing external insurance. Most obvious, however, is the dedicated effort of any company to reduce exposure to these serious perils by proper risk-reducing behaviors.

Employment Practices Insurance. This includes the three areas of sexual harassment, discrimination, and wrongful termination. Other claims might be related to lack of promotion issues, a common theme one hears in technology companies. 60% of small businesses will be sued by an employee, with approximately 40% being sued just in the last year.[1] Almost 100% of large firms will face employment lawsuits. There is some evidence that technology-oriented, fast-growing small firms tend to suffer a higher rate of employment practice claims than other types of industries and businesses. This is often due to the larger differentials in pay being paid to some of the most critical technical workers, an attention which might anger other workers not on a fast-career path. Another trending area of employment lawsuits is worker classification issues filed by employees in the "gig economy".[2]

Product Liability Insurance. Product liability insurance can help cover legal expenses if someone claims that a product sold, made, or distributed caused an injury or property damage. This type of insurance covers if the product damages someone's property, causes a bodily injury, makes someone sick, or causes wrongful death. In technology industries, such claims are especially common with pharmaceutical and other tech-based products, particularly in the medical and healthcare sectors where there is a risk of customer injury. Product liability issues should be addressed in the earliest stages of a technology's development, both in product design and managerial policy.

Intellectual Property Insurance. 50% of technology firms report losses related to intellectual property. These losses often arise when a former employee leaves the company for a competitor or starts their own business. As discussed in prior chapters, IP and trade secret theft is a serious problem in technology-oriented companies. Intellectual property insurance can also protect against patent infringement issues. This is not a common policy but is available from specialized insurers. Major issues in this type of insurance are what is covered (are trade secrets covered?), the definition of IP, and the valuation method that will be used. Unlike other assets, as we discussed in our valuation chapter it is hard to place a value on IP loss. There is always a valuation method described in these types of policies.

Cyber Liability Insurance. Cyber liability insurance can cover a number of issues. These include, 1) Data Breach Liability and claims for failure to protect private information, 2) Data Breach Expense, which covers notification letters to victims, public relations, forensics and credit monitoring expenses due to an unauthorized exposure of private information, 3) Website Liability, such as claims for libel, slander, right of privacy, plagiarism, misappropriation of ideas, and infringement of copyright and trademark arising from the organization's website activity, 4) Identity Theft, including credit monitoring and other personal expenses incurred by board members, owners or partners in resolving Identity Theft, and 5) Cyber Extortion Threat Expense. These coverages can include extortion payments, cost to hire negotiators and rewards to catch extorters. Cyber liability insurance has become much more expensive in recent years due to the increase in cyber-attacks worldwide.

Errors and Omissions (E&O) Insurance. Errors and Omissions is a type of liability insurance designed to cover providers of services or products. In some industries this is called "Professional Liability Insurance". E&O and professional liability insurance protects against making mistakes, miscalculations or errors in your services that impact somebody, generally a customer. Specialized "Technology E&O policies" are designed for technology firms, such as IT contractors, software developers including mobile and web developers, businesses that manufacture electronic hardware, technology startups, e-commerce businesses, and technology consultants. Technology E&O policies can cover exposures to both liability and property loss.

Key "Person" Insurance. This represents life insurance on key members of the organization, to replace the cost of that person dying. In smaller firms, it is often used by partners to insure each other in order to purchase the deceased ownership percentage. Key person insurance is often used in technology firms, large and small, to insure key scientists and engineers and provide funds to pay short-term technical consultants and search for a new technical employee if a key technical person dies.

Business Interruption Insurance. This type of insurance protects when something, like a flood, interrupts your business activity. Business interruption insurance can cover lost profit, utilities, and rent. Business interruption insurance might also cover the wages of certain technical employees while the firm is "down". Covering the wages of critical engineers and scientists is often important, since when the company is down, you don't want your best people quitting and running to a competitor firm in order to not lose their monthly salary. The advice is to always check what is covered, what perils are included, and the limits to the coverage. Business interruption insurance became an important issue during the Covid-19 shutdowns, when most insurance companies excluded coverage since the shutdowns were technically due to government action versus a natural disaster. For pre-revenue technologies, business interruption insurance could possibly be used to cover the cost of interrupted R&D and design activities.

Protecting against Speculative Risk: Project Risk Management

While insurance is designed to protect against situations of "pure risk", a good risk management program addresses both types of risk, pure and speculative. Technology firms can never eliminate speculative risk, but good project risk management can reduce risk. Project risk management starts as one of the subsidiary planning processes in the Planning Phase.

There are generally five components in any project risk management process.
1) Risk Identification
2) Risk Evaluation
3) Risk Mitigation and Contingency Planning
4) Risk Monitoring and Control

5) Risk Measurement

Large technology-oriented firms typically require different templates and tools to assist in this process. These tools include:

Risk Checklists. Risk checklists are used to identify the risks involved in each phase of technology's development as it progresses toward market introduction. Risk checklists are one of the most valuable tools for risk management. The risk checklist will vary depending on the stage and between organizations. For example, a risk checklist for an early R&D project will be different than a risk checklist for a technology in beta test. Well-designed risk checklists will typically have a number of components. These could include

---

Good risk management programs address situations of both
"speculative risk" and "pure risk".

---

a. Risk category, such as materials, contracts, or personnel.
b. A statement of the risk. These are sometimes defined as "if-then" statements, such as, "if we don't receive a 'mass spectrometer' that was ordered by the delivery date, then the R&D completion period will be extended by 2 weeks". Risk statements identify the important risk associated with a project. Managing risks ultimately revolves around the risk statements, so they need to be broad-ranging, complete, and honest.
c. The probability that an event will happen. This is often on a 1 to 5 rating.
d. The impact of the risk. This is also a rating, such as 1 to 5.
e. A risk severity score. Oftentimes computed by multiplying the probability score by the impact score. Risk severity scores can also be obtained directly, without the need for probability and impact discussions.
f. Mitigation/Response plan. A statement as to the actions to be taken to either prevent the event from occurring or if it does occur, what will be done. Greater emphasis needs to be placed on risk statements that present higher levels of risks. This step can result in immediate responses or the development of contingency plans in case a particular identified risk actually happens.
g. Ownership of managing the risk. Identifying an individual who is responsible for the tracking and, if necessary, managing the risk. Identifying risks, and particularly their solutions, needs to have ownership. Without assigning formal responsibility, the risk will likely be ignored.
h. A status statement regarding risk. Did it happen or not. If the risk event happened, what is the current status of the mitigation? When will it be addressed?
i. Comments or notes regarding the overall success of the mitigation. This will be useful if future project managers want to see how previous projects identified and managed similar risk.

Project Risk Register: Drug Delivery Wafer Design Prototype

Risk Category	Description of Risk	Probability Occurring 1 to 5	Impact on Project 1 to 10	Risk Score	Description of Severity Score	Risk Trigger	Response Plan (full plan #)	Owner
Ingredients	If ingredients (binding, active, filler) don't arrive, delays in prototype development.	2	6	16	Had on time deliveries on other projects	Delays in supply chain, improper ordering schedules.	No current issues (File 23.1).	Joe Dehone (Supply chain manager
Equipment	If JDY 1.5W punch tablet pill press equipment breaks down, we can't produce prototypes.	1	9	9	Pill press is in good condition	Component breaks during early prototype production runs.	Have repair person on standby. Have backup components in house (Files 23.4, 23.7)	Mary Phillips (Production manager)
Packaging	If package printing firm doesn't deliver, we can't ship prototypes, lose beta test contracts.	3	10	30	Package printer appears over committed; delays might be likely	Notification from package printer that they can't meet delivery schedule.	Have second source printer already contacted. If deadline missed, will cancel primary printer contract (Files 23.14-15).	Devon Samual (Marketing assistant)

Figure 12.5: Example of an advanced project risk register.

Risk checklists need to be updated regularly. Trigger point for updating the risk check-lists is when a potential event actually occurs, the responsible party is contacted and mitigation strategies implemented.

Many firms, particularly smaller entrepreneurial efforts, do not use a full risk checklist, but will at least focus on formally identifying the most important risks and then develop actions and contingency plans to mitigate these risks.

Risk Register. Larger technology firms might use a "risk register". A risk register is designed to collect and catalog the various risks identified, and their proposed miti-gation strategies, for a particular project (see Figure 12.5). Essentially, the risk register merges the various risk checklists of a complex project into a single, searchable data-base. The senior project manager will regularly access the risk register when needed. Risk registers are used for more complicated projects that might have a number of sub-groups working with different risk scorecards.

Risk Repository. The risk repository is a risk management documentation tool that acts as a library for how previous project teams addressed the risks and whether their mitigation strategies were successful or not (see Figure 12.6). This provides an historical collection of events and mitigation strategies. This risk repository can then be accessed and searched by current project team members. The risk repository essentially allows a project team to identify risk and possible solutions quicker, using the experience of prior projects. This is particularly useful in large corporations with a history of hun-dreds of past technology projects.

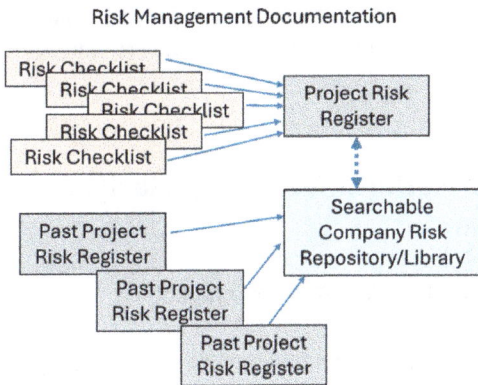

Figure 12.6: Risk management documentation.

Concluding Insights

A well-structured project management process is essential for successful technology development and commercialization. While it cannot eliminate all risks, strong project management significantly increases the chances of meeting timelines, budgets, and performance expectations. It provides a critical framework for navigating the complexity and uncertainty that often define technology environments, whether in a large corporation or a small entrepreneurial venture.

This chapter focused on practical tools and techniques most relevant to managing technology-driven projects. Among the five core phases of project management, the Planning Phase is especially vital. It involves designing a detailed work plan, building subsidiary plans, and applying formal documentation tools such as the Gantt charts. These elements not only guide project execution but also inform key financial planning tools such as pro-formas.

The chapter also emphasized the importance of risk management in technology projects. From situations involving "pure risks" like product liability or cyber-attacks, which can often be managed by a well-thought-out insurance strategy, to "speculative risks" such as market failure or deadline delays, it is critical that management accurately identify and then properly managing these threats. This chapter offered a number of different tools to consider, such as insurance programs that might be highly relevant to technology firms. In addition, risk management tools such as risk checklists, risk registers, and risk repositories help teams respond proactively and build a culture of informed decision-making.

Not all firms will use the complete list of tools discussed in this chapter. Some of the tools, such as Gantt Charts and modified risk assessments/response planning, tend to be more commonly employed than other tools. However, all the tools in this chapter are used in various forms by technology firms. Ultimately, however, effective project management is about structured flexibility. With the right systems in place, teams can adapt to unexpected challenges, maintain forward momentum, and move technologies closer to successful market entry.

Chapter Example: The EpiPen – a Platform Technology Navigates Risk, Pivot, and Project Execution

Project Background: From Military Innovation to Commercial Opportunity

In the early 1950s, Dr. Stanley Sarnoff, a cardiologist and inventor, developed a spring-loaded auto-injector system designed to administer lifesaving drugs quickly in emergency situations. Originally created for potential use with heart attack patients, the device delivered medication without requiring clinical training.[3]

The U.S. military soon identified a more urgent application: rapid delivery of antidotes to nerve agent exposure on the battlefield. Dr. Sarnoff adapted the auto-injector for self-administration in combat conditions, and it was quickly adopted by the Department of Defense. Even NASA began to stock the device on its space missions. These government contracts helped validate the platform, but they were not sufficient to scale a viable commercial enterprise.

To expand beyond government use, Sarnoff founded Survival Technology Incorporated (STI). Recognizing the need for business expertise, he recruited Brian Dovey, a medical products executive, to serve as President. STI initially refocused the auto-injector toward a civilian use case for heart attack treatment, but the application faced insurmountable technical and regulatory challenges. At this point, STI's leadership confronted a major strategic inflection: either find a commercially viable market or risk the technology never reaching the broader public.

Planning the Pivot: Market Exploration and Risk Assessment

Dovey led STI into a new planning phase. He assembled an interdisciplinary team, including Napoleon Monroe (sales and business development) and Michael Mesa (engineering and product development), to explore alternative markets for the auto-injector platform. Their internal project team treated this as a high-stakes market discovery initiative, a formal evaluation of where STI's platform could create real value and gain adoption.

One early hypothesis centered on the agricultural industry. Farmers and field workers, often exposed to toxic pesticides, might benefit from portable emergency treatment tools. The case of use mirrored the military need, and the core injector technology could be easily repurposed for this context.

– **Execution**: Monroe led exploratory outreach to assess market demand; Mesa evaluated technical modifications for field conditions.
– **Outcome**: While viable in principle, the agricultural use case proved too small to be profitable. The market lacked scale and a reliable path to adoption.

This process highlighted the importance of structured assumption testing, risk checklists, and the evaluation of technical feasibility alongside market fit – core elements of the project planning tools emphasized in this chapter.

Breakthrough: A Signal from the Market

In 1980, STI received a signal that would reshape the company's direction. Dr. Steven Lockey, an allergist, published an article in the *Journal of Asthma Research* suggesting that STI's auto-injector could be used to administer epinephrine to treat life-threatening allergic reactions (anaphylaxis).[4] The article gained traction in the allergy community and sparked internal discussion within STI.

This was the market signal the team needed. Recognizing the unmet need for simple, reliable, needle-based epinephrine delivery, STI launched a full internal project around this new opportunity. The team moved into an intensive execution phase, applying many project management best practices:

– Mesa and the engineering team redesigned the device to be compact, consistent in dosage, and easy for laypeople to operate.

- Monroe led efforts to gain regulatory approval, working with physicians and key advocacy groups to build adoption pathways.
- Dovey ensured strategic alignment across functions and secured funding for scale-up and commercialization.

The result was the EpiPen – a repurposed auto-injector that became the dominant product for emergency allergy treatment for the next four decades.

Figure 12.7: Photo of early EpiPen prototypes. Courtesy of Napoleon Monroe.

Execution, Risk Management, and Scaling Success

The transition from military origins to allergy treatment illustrates how effective execution – coupled with a bit of luck, not just invention – determines success. As Napoleon Monroe put it, "Luck is somewhat made when management and the entire environment encourages and rewards collaborative eyes". STI's internal coordination, from risk management and planning to production and stakeholder engagement, created a repeatable model of applied project management for the different applications and pivots:

- The team adapted the core technology across contexts, tailoring the design to market-specific needs.
- They listened to influencers, responding quickly to external feedback (Lockey's article) and validating assumptions with key stakeholders.
- For each potential application, a project team was created with a specific focus.
- STI identified the right market sweet spot, using structured exploration and iterative planning.

- Most importantly, they executed with a shared sense of urgency, with aligned leadership and accountability across functions.

Lifecycle Extension and Decline: The Next Disruption

Following its commercial success, STI was eventually acquired, and the EpiPen changed ownership through companies such as Mylan and Viatris. Despite changes in control, the product retained its basic design and continued to dominate the market.

However, in 2024, the FDA approved a needle-free epinephrine nasal spray – Neffy, developed by ARS Pharmaceuticals. This new product which involves a unique technology which "loosens the spaces between the nasal cells to help epinephrine be absorbed into the body"[5] introduced a fundamentally different delivery mechanism for the same emergency treatment – no needle. This marks a potential disruption event for the traditional EpiPen technology. With Neffy offering a less intimidating and easier-to-administer form factor, the EpiPen may now be entering the late maturity or early decline phase of its lifecycle.

For technology leaders, this raises key project management questions:
- Can the auto-injector platform be adapted to new use cases?
- Is it time to invest in platform reinvention or next-gen technology?
- How can firms manage the risk of obsolescence even after decades of dominance?

Lessons for Technology Commercialization Projects

The EpiPen case underscores that successful commercialization depends as much on project execution as on the underlying invention. It also illustrates the power of:
- Pivot planning: Systematic evaluation of use cases and markets, not random guessing.
- Team alignment and accountability: Clearly defined ownership of engineering, regulatory, and business roles.
- Risk management tools: Market, regulatory, and technical risks must be anticipated and addressed in planning.
- Structured adaptability: Teams must be ready to shift strategy as external feedback and market dynamics evolve.

Finally, the case shows that even a dominant product is never safe from disruption. Ongoing risk management – for both pure and speculative risks – is essential across the technology lifecycle.

Chapter 13
Communicating Technology: Approaching the Market

This Chapter

- Explores the differences between passive and active communication strategies for promoting new technologies.
- Identifies key components for optimizing keyword searches on technology websites.
- Compares Technology Interest Packages (TIPs) and Quad Charts as structured formats for communicating innovation.
- Describes the essential elements of a compelling elevator pitch for technology ventures.
- Offers guidance on crafting effective formal presentations, including tips on content, structure, and delivery style.
- Highlights the role of both academic and trade publications in technology communication.
- Discusses effective strategies for communicating and marketing technology products to consumer audiences.

Key Management Tools and Best Practices

- Passive vs. active communication strategies
- Best practices for keyword and AI-enhanced search visibility
- Technology Interest Packages (TIPs) and Quad Charts
- High-impact technical presentations and pitch preparation
- Use of short, targeted videos for technology communication
- Strategic networking for building interest and partnerships
- Leveraging academic and professional publications for credibility
- The Reach, Act, Convert, and Engage (RACE) media model for consumer technologies

! INSIGHT

Communicating the benefits and specifications of a technology is a constant challenge during the technology development process. From the earliest stages of innovation, through the protection of intellectual property, to prototyping, and ultimately for final commercialization, technologies must be communicated. Sometimes the communication is for marketing purposes, and sometimes it is for support reasons. Sometimes the communication may come in short 30-second bursts, while other times communicating might be during a formal presentation. Communication can be passive in nature, or active in effort. This chapter explores different ways of communicating technology for different situations, different objectives, and with different media. But regardless of the format, it is important that the technology manager is well prepared and uses the most appropriate method when communicating the functionality and benefits of their technology to stakeholders.

https://doi.org/10.1515/9783111684420-014

Introduction

Communicating the advantages of a technology is a constant, ongoing effort. Communication starts from the earliest stage of development, when ideas are just being bantered about in the R&D lab, to the final launch of the technology into the marketplace. Communication can be informal, such as chatting with colleagues at a conference luncheon, or highly formal such as a thirty-minute pitch presentation to an investor group.

Regardless of the form or method of communication, it must always be effective. Effective communication may account for a large part of a technology's success. This chapter focuses on the formal aspects of communication and provides guidance on commonly used formats for presenting the features and benefits of a developing technology. Rather than offering a comprehensive overview of marketing strategies, especially for consumer-facing technologies, the focus here is on illustrating key communication methods commonly used throughout the technology development and commercialization process.

Technology Communication Is Not "Fake It, 'Till to You Make It'"

Communication of technology, however, should not be confused with the "hype" or "fake it, till you make it" mentality one often hears, unfortunately, in some prominent entrepreneurship programs, popular business books, and student business plan competitions. The "hype" mentality might work with less sophisticated information consumers and investors, but most consumers of the type of technology communication discussed in this chapter tend to be fairly sophisticated and knowledgeable. There are always exceptions to this technology communication "hype" rule, however. One of the most dramatic exceptions was seen by Elizabeth Holmes' ability to convince engineers, employees, scientists, investors, and large institutional customers that the blood testing technology of her company, Theranos, actually worked when it was all just fake. Other monumental tech start-up failures largely built on "hype" strategies were Jawbone's wearable fitness tracker and the solar panel company, Solyndra, promoted by the President Obama's administration. All of these enterprises ultimately lost billions of investor dollars while destroying the careers of many highly qualified engineers and scientists. Although these extreme examples of "hype" communication make for great headlines, hopefully they are rare.

Technology communication needs to be honest but targeted toward the needs of the recipient. There is definitely a fine line between using common promotional words in communication, such as describing the technology as "powerful", "innovative", or "novel" in order to gain attention in a highly competitive world versus statements that push the communication into the realm of untruths, serious exaggeration, and possibly even fraud. Real scalability is, of course, a positive component of technology development and commercialization, but "hyped" fake scalability generally will not gain traction with sophisticated recipients of communication,

Passive Technology Communication

Technology communication is often classified as being "active" versus "passive". Passive communication simply means that the emphasis is on interested parties needing to seek out your technology and initiate contact. With this approach, passive communication is just the starting point, and often the "first contact". After initial contact, and the level of interest determined, communication with stakeholders can always become much more interactive and richer.

The best example of passive communication is when a university technology transfer office puts information about a particular technology on their website. Every research university has a technology transfer office, typically with a dedicated webpage where interested parties can browse technologies developed at the university that are available for licensing. If somebody is interested in the technology, then additional information can be requested.

Many universities and other technology developers across the globe also use AUTM's searchable listing of technologies. Previously known as the Association of University Technology Managers, AUTM has become the world leader in facilitating technology licensing. AUTM's "Innovation Marketplace" now has over 30,000 technologies available for licensing. This platform, however, is a passive form of technology communication since interested parties must still perform "key word" searches in order to find what they may be looking for.

In addition to the hundreds of university technology transfer office webpages, there are a number of other sources where interested parties can search through lists of technologies that are available for licensing. For example, individual government R&D and development laboratories all have technology transfer programs. In the U.S., these include large R&D operations, such as NASA's Technology Transfer Program with hundreds of technologies listed in their portfolio, ranging from aerospace to manufacturing and medicine. The U.S. Department of Defense has over 70 government-owned and government-operated (GOGO) laboratories and centers, all working on advanced technologies that might be useful for the commercial market.

In addition, many governments operate R&D programs jointly with other entities, such as universities or the private sector. In the U.S. these are called Federally Funded Research and Development Centers (FFRDCs). A total of twelve different U.S. agencies currently operate almost fifty different FFRDCs. The most well-known FFRDCs in the U.S. are the Lawarence Livermore National Laboratory, the Los Alamos National

Laboratory, and various centers through the U.S. operated by the RAND Corporation. All of these have their own individual technology transfer office webpages, or work with contractors, such as Montana State University's "TechLink" program. In fact, TechLink has managed over 60% of all the technologies that have been licensed by U.S. Department of Defense R&D labs.

The volume and range of technologies available through these sources are astounding. However, these online sites are all considered "passive" forms of technology communication. They require interested parties to do the key word searches, sort through the available technologies, ask for additional information, and then follow up on contacts. Passive communication methods, however, do have some advantages.

Advantages of Passive Communication

1) Minimal Cost. There is little expense involved with placing information about a technology on a website.
2) Full Coverage. It is impossible to know all the potential entities that might be interested in your technology. These entities might include large system developers looking for a particular component technology to potential entrepreneurs looking to start a business by licensing an innovative technology. Interested parties might be truly global, people who we simply have no familiarity with or knowledge about. Obtaining the highest level of exposure on such sites will increase the chances of somebody finding your technology and then ask for more information. This is particularly true since potential licensees or users throughout the world have access to these online platforms.
3) With the increase of AI generated searches, there may be a greater likelihood that interested entities might find a broader range of potential technologies. Before AI, websites needed to be individually searched by keywords. But AI generated searches can quickly find technologies on many websites via a single AI search prompt. More and more entrepreneurs and system developers are regularly using AI prompt searches to find and track relevant technologies. Given enhanced AI capabilities, it is important that websites that list available technologies are created to maximize both key word and AI searches.

Disadvantages of Passive Communication

1) Potential users may not use the same keyword or technological information when searching for potential technologies. Developers may describe their innovations

with technical or specialized language, while users might search using broader or different terms. This disconnect can prevent strong matches from appearing in search results, thus reducing visibility and limiting opportunities for engagement.

2) Potential users will simply forego keyword searches and rely only on known providers of a technology. In many industries, decision-makers prefer to engage with familiar or trusted sources rather than browse online listings. This reliance on existing networks means that even if a listed technology is highly relevant, it may be overlooked because the potential user never performs a search in the first place. As a result, promising innovations can remain undiscovered simply due to the user's preference for established relationships over exploratory searches. This fact often creates a bias against new, innovative, and possibility revolutionary technologies from being discovered by potential users.

Passive communication of technologies is common not only among early-stage technology developers, such as universities, but also within large organizations, especially during government-supported system development projects. For example, many government laboratories, research centers, and institutions in developing countries tend to focus on specific stages of technology development as part of their stated mission. A key question has always been how to move technologies from one government-related R&D lab to the next stage of development being operated by a different entity, but perhaps within the same government. Historically, this has also been a somewhat passive process where the system developer often has to search for useful technologies from both internal and external providers, thus lengthening the time it takes to produce a final fielded system.

Communication via Websites, Key Word Searches, and AI

As discussed above, the most common method of communicating early-stage technologies is through a webpage. While this is generally considered a passive form of communication (i.e., posting information online and hoping someone finds it via a keyword search), it doesn't have to be entirely passive. In fact, several proactive steps can be taken to significantly increase the likelihood that a technology will be discovered by potential users or licensees.

There is a growing literature outlining best practices for improving the visibility of technologies through strategic webpage design and content. Unfortunately, many technology developers simply upload a basic description and perhaps a downloadable document, such as a patent or technical summary. But in today's competitive and search-driven environment, it is critical that developers treat their online listings as a strategic communication tool. This is especially important when multiple competing technologies may surface during a user's search process.

By applying a few key best practices such as optimizing keyword placement, improving content structure, and aligning with how target users are likely to search, developers can actively improve their chances of being discovered and contacted.

Best practices for maximizing keyword searches in website content include:

A) Determine the most relevant keywords. Don't just use the technical description but also expand the number of relevant keywords on the webpage for maximum coverage.

B) Look at competitive technologies, and make sure that you use similar keywords.

C) Strategically place the keywords in high visibility areas on the site including placement in the title of the technology, in headings, and in the content.

D) Use meta-descriptions. A meta-description is a short summary under the title of the technology.

E) Use "long-tailed keywords". A long-tailed key word is more of a description, rather than a single one- or two-word keyword. Long-tailed keywords tend to be targeted toward a market niche or application. Long-tailed keywords for technology might include an envisioned application, such as "best LCD analog display for high-end wrist watches". Long-tailed key words can be product-specific, information seeking, comparative (using words such as "best" or "most"). A webpage can include multiple long-tailed key words, each targeted toward a specific market. This approach helps distinguish your technology from others based on application and performance.

F) Use AI to generate appropriate keywords based on selected audiences.

G) Search engines generally cannot read image files, so make sure you have a description for any technology image on the webpage.

Maximizing AI Searches for Technologies. More and more searches are being performed through artificial intelligence prompts. Asking ChatGPT to identify relevant component technologies that could be integrated into a larger system with specific requirements can generate a list of promising early-stage technologies. This type of an AI search can then be refined by additional prompts and questions.

An AI search not only uses key words but also attempts to understand both the meaning and context behind the prompt. So, while key word searches will tend to focus on the exact keyword match, an AI search will expand the criteria based upon its understanding of the context. Best practices for maximizing technology webpages for AI searches include:

A) Ensure your technology webpage is accessible to AI crawlers. Your site should be publicly available and not restricted by login barriers. Use clean HTML formatting, include descriptive meta tags, and avoid content that relies heavily on JavaScript.

B) Make sure your technology webpage is mentioned or connected to other sites and channels on the web.
C) AI searches are looking for fast load-ups, so make sure your webpage is efficient.
D) Place a much greater emphasis on discussing the technology, including its range, application, and future potential rather than just listing the technology's name and specifications.
E) Implement schema markups. Schema markups are specialized code added to your technology webpage to assist AI searches understand the content.

Semi-Active Communication: Technology Linkers and Intermediaries

To overcome the problems of passive technology communication, and the fact that much of the technological advances being made in the laboratories were not being translated into field systems, some large government entities, such as the U.S. Department of Defense, started using formal "technology linkers".[1] The primary function of technology linkers was to understand the future needs of their user base, and then match developing technologies with these needs. In many industries, a form of technology linking still exists. In modern terminology, technology linkers are often referred to as "technology intermediaries" or "knowledge brokers". Technology linkers, intermediaries, or knowledge brokers are often consultants who are hired to stay abreast of new technological developments and pass this information on to their clients. Technology linkers, intermediaries, or knowledge brokers need to keep current on all relevant technologies and will regularly perform web searches for relevant new technologies. They regularly attend conferences, read journal articles, and develop significant informational networks in order to stay constantly abreast of both emerging technologies and customer requirements. In some industries, such as drug development, these consultants also need to stay current with the ever-changing regulatory landscape. Technology linking is sometimes referred to as a "semi-active" mode of communication. If formal technology linkers, intermediaries, or knowledge brokers tend to operate in your industry, make sure you know who they are, and develop a relationship with these individuals or groups.

Active Technology Communication

While passive communication will always remain an important part of technology communication, the remaining part of this chapter focuses on "active" communication. However, given the capabilities of modern internet and AI searches, many of the templates and models provided in this chapter can also be used within a more passive model of communication.

Active communication is when the technology developer takes the initiative to contact and communicate with stakeholders, such as potential partners, licensees, customers, users, investors, and, if necessary, even regulatory agencies. In general, active communication is thought to be the most effective in developing relationships and ultimately commercializing a technology. Active communication has two key objectives. First, it involves searching out and then initiating communication. This is important since many stakeholders simply may not know much, or anything at all, about your technology. Second, active communication involves an educational component. It needs to effectively increase the knowledge of the interested party about your technology, not only in description but also its applications and potential benefits.

Technology Interest Packages (TIPs)

Inevitably, active communication is a multi-step process. The first step is to create interest, or "open the doors". Once somebody is interested in a technology, then further steps will be involved to communicate, find a match, and ultimately "close the deal".

One of the most common tools to start the conversation is through a Technology Interested Package. The term "Technology Interested Package" or TIP was initially coined by the Center for Commercialization of Advanced Technology (CCAT), but any organization that is involved with communicating technologies will likely have a similar tool. Essentially, a TIP is a 2-to-3-page document that describes the technology in an attractive format. The key parts to a TIP are a) identifying the problem that the technology solves, b) how the technology solves the problem, c) the advantages the technology has over competitive technologies, d) its development status, and e) any data or functionality that can be provided.

TIPs are a generalized communication tool and can be sent to potential customers, licensees, and investors via e-mail. TIPs can also be printed and distributed during conferences and trade shows. TIPS can also be linked to webpages, as part of an overall communication strategy. TIPs are generally used in concert with other communication processes and tools discussed in this chapter.

Figure 13.1 is an actual TIP that was developed by an early-stage biotechnology firm, O.TM Biotech, in partnership with the University of North Carolina Wilmington. The technology being developed was a molecule that might be used for treating cancers. The method of communication was to send this TIP via e-mail to targeted science directors at large pharmaceutical firms to initiate further discussion regarding partnerships. Several important conversations were initiated as a result of sending out this particular TIP.

Technology Interest Package UNIVERSITY *of* NORTH CAROLINA WILMINGTON

Breakthrough Molecule for the Treatment of Conceivably all Cancers

GOAL
To validate the universal target across 30 cancer cell lines and hence define a broad spectrum treatment against cancer.

BACKGROUND
On Target Molecules Biotech, Inc. (O.TM Biotech) in partnership with the University of North Carolina Wilmington (UNCW) seeks to accelerate its new biotechnology platform towards clinical trials. Building on its successes, O.TM Biotech is poised to take on the remaining phases in its fight against cancer at scale and speed. Currently three variable sequences leading to eight therapeutically significant and viable drug products are in the pipeline. O.TM has developed a strategic alliance with UNCW to enable research and development of the anticancer biologic via its core facilities and faculty.

PROBLEM
A multifaceted picture has emerged for cancer with metastatic escape and resistance phenomena.

SOLUTION
O.TM Biotech has achieved a therapeutic solution for the treatment of cancer by the use of three technologies.

1] The use of existing technology for targeting cancer tissues by-passing non-cancerous tissues.

Image: Apoptosis & Autophagy in treated cancer cell lines

2] The use of existing technology about the genetically engineered adenovirus vector for transcription of the O.TM fusion protein under a CMV promoter.

3] O.TM Technology - By targeting a universal cancer biomarker, cell death has been achieved; multiple actions include diminished autophagy and Caspase 3 initiated tumor apoptosis followed by cell lysis with stimulation of antiviral and antitumor immune responses.

KEY ADVANTAGES
A broad spectrum anticancer biologic drug against perhaps all cancers.

DEVELOPMENT STATUS
The company is commencing detailed preclinical studies, including IND-enabling studies, to develop, obtain regulatory approval for, and commercialize many variations of its sequenced and patented monoclonal antibodies against all indications of cancer.

University of North Carolina Wilmington
Office of Innovation & Commercialization
803-G South College Road
Wilmington, NC 28403

Phone: 910.962.2886
Email: oic@uncw.edu
www.uncw.edu/oic

OIC

Figure 13.1: Technology Interest Package: O.TM Biotech.

Technology Interest Package

UNIVERSITY *of*
NORTH CAROLINA
WILMINGTON

RESEARCH & DEVELOPMENT STAGE

O.TM Biotech has achieved exceptional milestones if its development of a universal cancer therapy. The company has filed an International preliminary IP for three VR regions of three monoclonal antibodies. It has 44 clones in the freezer for future R&D studies. 10 VR regions have been sequenced from 10 of 92 clones produced by hybridoma technology. In vivo experiments reveal apoptosis in mouse xenografts for one breast tumor and one melanoma up-to 75% in 7 days with 2 doses. The Scfv-hc fusion protein causes apoptosis in 24 cancer cell lines tested thus far in-vitro.

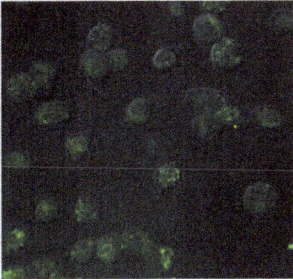

O.TM Biotech has established the therapeutic dose. The Scfv-hc fusion protein enters a cancer cell and is sequestered by lysosomes in less than 15 seconds, the initial step to diminished autophagy. Tests show no apoptosis observed in human hepatocytes in the first 48 hours on drug application and no apoptosis observed in MCF10A normal breast cells on drug application at the same therapeutic dose.

Image: O.TM Fusion protein green tag enters prostate cancer PC3 cells and sequestered in lysosomes in less than 15 seconds.

In zebra fish embryos toxicity tests were conducted over 14 days. Embryos were injected with the fusion protein at twice the concentration of the therapeutic dose on day 1, day 3, day 7, and day 10. Observations were recorded for acute toxicity, hepatoxicity, ototoxicity and cardiotoxicity. Behavioral assays were conducted. In zebra fish embryos, *no toxicity* was observed over a 14day investigation.

Comparison Table

O.TM ENGINEERED PROTEIN	ANTIBODY COMPETITORS
Uniquely constructed protein	Conventional style constructs
Antibody does not bind tissues outside tumor in two models of mouse with implanted human xenografts – breast & melanoma	Off targets bind tissues outside tumors
24 cancer cell lines undergo an average of 75% apoptosis with 2 doses over 7 days	Predominantly work on one or two or three cell lines
No drug conjugation required	Drug conjugation to Ab additional problems for QC and side effects
Endosome-Lysosome path targeted with near 100% efficiency	Lysosome path targeted with near 3% -10% efficiency in leading brands
Broad spectrum attack on several (50 to 100) targets having a consensus biomarker	Single point target on a single point biomarker
Probably will work on all cancers	No such claim world over
Metabolomics depict very low disturbance of cellular lipids and proteins on antibody treatment	Very little data on metabolomics
Hepatocytes do not undergo apoptosis at the concentration that cause apoptosis in cancer cell lines	Hepatotoxicity a huge problem Necrosis
Strong IP – Composition, Method, Surprising utility across cancers – perhaps a cure	History will compare the final outcomes
Low cost	High cost

University of North Carolina Wilmington
Office of Innovation & Commercialization
803-G South College Road
Wilmington, NC 28403

Phone: 910.962.2886
Email: oic@uncw.edu
www.uncw.edu/oic

OIC

Figure 13.1 (continued)

Technology Interest Package

UNIVERSITY *of* NORTH CAROLINA WILMINGTON

PROPOSAL

Funding is required for one year for preclinical and IND filing procedures. Operations could commence in mid-2017. Capital will be used for biomarker validation across 30 cancer cell lines as well as animal toxicity and efficacy models toward an IND file. These processes will be done as a strategic alliance with the University of North Carolina Wilmington.

CONCLUSION

The creative innovation herein lies in diminished autophagy and increased apoptosis observed experimentally across several cancers. Crossing the cell membrane with ease and sequestering of the fusion protein in lysosomes via the endosomal-lysosomal path in a few seconds is a remarkable breakthrough.

SUMMARY OF THE FUSION PROTEIN

A] Apoptosis observed in 24 cancer cell lines of 25 tested *in-vitro*

50% to 80% in 7 days 2 doses of fusion protein

Two Exceptions – 7 days 2 doses of fusion protein

1. Pancreatic cell line showed resistance to the fusion protein with zero cell death
2. Glioblastoma cell line showed resistance to the fusion protein with 20% cell death

1. MCF7	BREAST	
2. ZR-75-1	BREAST	
3. MDA-MB-231	BREAST Triple Negative Cell line	
4. SUM159	BREAST	
5. EFM19	BREAST	
6. BT474	BREAST DUCTAL	

MCF10A NORMAL BREAST   No cell death

7. A549	LUNG CARCINOMA	
8. DMS53	SMALL CELL LUNG CARCINOMA	
9. JVM13	B CELL LEUKEMIA	
10. DU145	PROSTATE CARCINOMA	
11. A375	MELANOMA	
12. HS294T	MELANOMA	
13. A101D	MELANOMA	
14. 5637	BLADDER	90% apoptosis in 7 days two doses fusion protein
15. SW948	COLON	
16. CFPAC-1	PANCREAS	The only cancer cell line which resists apoptosis
17. U-138MG	GLIOBLASTOMA	
18. SNU-423	LIVER	
19. BPH-1	PROSTATE	
20. C-4 II	CERVIX	100% apoptosis in 7 days two doses fusion protein
21. CaOV3	OVARY	
22. DETROIT562	HEAD &NECK	
23. HTB9	BLADDER	
24. PC3	PROSTATE	

For more information regarding the technology, please use the contact information below:

University of North Carolina Wilmington
Office of Innovation & Commercialization
803-G South College Road
Wilmington, NC 28403

Phone: 910.962.2886
Email: oic@uncw.edu
www.uncw.edu/oic

OIC

Figure 13.1 (continued)

A survey of technology commercialization experts indicates that the most effective TIPs, or similar written communications, are those that contain data and tables about specific functionality and performance. Functionality and performance measures are often the key issues that recipients of such communications, such as product engineers and R&D directors, look at.

Quad Charts

The purpose of a Quad chart is similar to a TIP. Quad Charts, often shortened to simply "Quad", are one-page, one-sided documents that are divided into four sections or quadrants (thus the term Quad). Quads were initially used internally to communicate technologies within the U.S. Department of Defense systems development programs.

Recently, however, Quads are beginning to be more popular as a form of communicating technologies in a well-defined, compact, and easy-to-read package. Quads are often required by granting agencies. Not only can Quads be used to describe technologies, but Quads are now being used to succinctly describe a variety of topics, such as the status of an overall program and to summarize a strategic planning process within organizations.

A Quad is like an abstract for the technology. Quads provide a concise format for describing the technology. Quads often use bullet points and pictures. In a Quad, the upper left quadrant is where the technology is described, perhaps with a picture of the technology. The upper right quadrant often shows a short problem statement and then the proposed solution including the operational performance capabilities of the technology. The lower loft quadrant discusses the stage of development and the future needs to develop the technology. The lower right quadrant discusses the problem, target customer segment, market opportunity, and contact information. Different organizations might use slightly different definitions of the quadrants.

Figure 13.2 represents a typical Quad using the same information as in the TIP described earlier. While a TIP might provide more information, Quads are useful when the reader might only want a short, 1-page description, or if a short description of the technology is the required format for communication, such as in Broad Agency Announcements (BAAs) grant programs within the U.S.

Technology: Breakthrough Molecule for the Treatment of Conceivably all Cancers

Image: Apoptosis & Autophagy in treated cancer cell lines

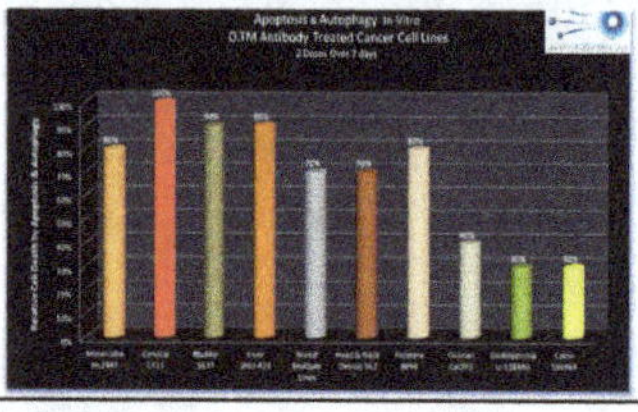

Research & Development Stage

O.TM Biotech has achieved exceptional milestones if its development of a universal cancer therapy. The company has filed an international preliminary IP for three VR regions of three monoclonal antibodies. It has 44 clones in the freezer for future R&D studies. 10 VR regions have been sequenced from 10 of 92 clones produced by hybridoma technology. In vivo experiments reveal apoptosis in mouse xenografts for one breast tumor and one melanoma up-to 75% in 7 days with 2 doses. The Scfv-hc fusion protein causes apoptosis in 24 cancer cell lines tested thus far in-vitro.

O.TM Biotech has established the therapeutic dose. The Scfv-hc fusion protein enters a cancer cell and is sequestered by lysosomes in less than 15 seconds, the initial step to diminished autophagy. Tests show no apoptosis observed in human hepatocytes in the first 48 hours on drug application and no apoptosis observed in MCF10A normal breast cells on drug application at the same therapeutic dose.

Problem:
A multifaceted picture has emerged for cancer with metastatic escape and resistance phenomena.

Background:
On Target Molecules Biotech, Inc. (O.TM Biotech) in partnership with the UNCW seeks to accelerate its new biotechnology platform towards clinical trials. Currently three variable sequences leading to eight therapeutically significant and viable drug products are in the pipeline. O.TM has developed a strategic alliance to enable research and development of the anticancer biologic via its core facilities and faculty.

Goal:
To validate the universal target across 30 cancer cell lines and hence define a broad-spectrum treatment against cancer.

Solution:
O.TM Biotech has achieved a therapeutic solution for the treatment of cancer by the use of three technologies.
1] The use of existing technology for targeting cancer tissues by-passing non-cancerous tissues
2] The use of existing technology of genetically engineered adenovirus vector for transcription of the O.TM fusion protein under a CMV promoter.
3] O.TM Technology - By targeting a universal cancer biomarker, cell death has been achieved; multiple actions include diminished autophagy and Caspase 3 initiated tumor apoptosis followed by cell lysis with stimulation of antiviral and antitumor immune responses.

Proposal:
Funding is required for one year for preclinical and IND filing procedures. Operations could commence in mid-2017. Capital will be used for biomarker validation across 30 cancer cell lines as well as animal toxicity and efficacy models toward an IND file. These processes will be done as a strategic alliance with the University of North Carolina Wilmington.

Conclusion:
The creative innovation herein lies in diminished autophagy and increased apoptosis observed experimentally across several cancers. Crossing the cell membrane with ease and sequestering of the fusion protein in lysosomes via the endosomal-lysosomal path in a few seconds is a remarkable breakthrough.

Corporate Information:

O.TM Biotech

For more information regarding the technology, please use the contact information below:

Project Coordinator   Project Director

Figure 13.2: Quad Chart: O.TM Biotech.

Formal Technical Presentations

Formal presentations of technology are almost certain to occur during the development and commercialization process. Companies with a formal phased-review process will inevitably require the development team to present their technology in order to receive further support. Entrepreneurial firms will need to pitch their technology to investors. Some granting organizations require formal presentations. A formal presentation of the technology may be required to create interest among potential customers.

Much has been written about effective presentation techniques. In this section, we focus specifically on what recent research has uncovered about effective presentations when advanced technologies are the topic of interest.

Technical presentations do differ from a normal business presentation in many different ways. First, advanced scientific and technical information must be effectively communicated. Second, while some audience members might be highly fluent in technical matters, other audience members are likely to come from more financial and business backgrounds. The key to an effective technical presentation is to target both types of people at the same time. Third, the presenters are often scientists and engineers that might not have a lot of experience in business presentations.

Any type of technical presentation, whether to investors or a phase-review team, needs to be persuasive in nature. The effectiveness of technical presentations can be considered as having four critical dimensions: presentation form, presentation style, presentation passion, and presentation preparedness.[2]

Presentation Form. Two dimensions of presentation form appear to influence how a technical presentation is perceived. These are presentation "attractiveness" and the use of "visuals". "Attractiveness" refers to how professional the presentation appears to be. Do the slides used in the presentation use colors, and are the fonts large enough to be read? In addition, a single slide should not stay up for too long (perhaps no more than 2 minutes). Slides should have pictures, charts, or graphs (perhaps > 50% of slides). Presentation attractiveness, however, also refers to the presenters themselves, their dress and demeanor. Dress and demeanor signals respect to the audience. Dress, however, should match the target audience. An audience of lab scientists might expect a different dress than an audience of bankers and accountants. An additional component of presentation form is the use of props or prototype demonstrations of the technology.

Presentation Style. It is surprising how little, and perhaps even silly, things can severely impact an audience's perception. These factors are often called "kinesics-proxemics" factors. For example, the importance of presenter movement (movement and standing closer to the audience is better), the number of hand gestures (above the waist), vocal pitch (variation in voice), and speed of talking (medium to fast, > 120 words per minute). While seemingly trivial, these stylistic components all create a more positive perception of technical presentations. This often means practicing or even purposely selecting presenters who have these stylistic characteristics.

Presentation Passion. Many research studies have indicated that entrepreneurial passion is one of the key factors in obtaining funding from investors. This is also true with technical presentations. We know passion when we see it, but passion is hard to really define. Studies have shown that passion can be broken down into different components. These include 1) Intensity – do the presenters appear intense in their feelings toward the technology? 2) Positiveness – presenter passion is always perceived as a positive viewpoint. 3) Absorption and dedication – do the presenters appear to be dedicated to their technology, and are they really absorbed in its benefits? Passion is often reflected in presentation style.

Presenter Preparedness. Of course, presenters need to be prepared. But presenter preparedness is a perception, not necessarily a fact. How can presenters appear to be "well-prepared". Demonstrating preparedness involves responding to questions confidently, anticipating likely inquiries during the presentation, having supporting data readily available, and maintaining composure, even when faced with difficult questions.

An Example of Presentation Failure. A stunning, but unfortunately all too common, presentation failure was witnessed by one of the authors of this book who for years was an active member of an angel investment network. For this network, there are monthly presentations by invited technology entrepreneurs seeking funding. On one recent occasion, what appeared on paper to be a very promising medical technology was being presented by an entrepreneurial team seeking early-stage funding. The presenters made several critical mistakes. First, their pro-forma was incorrect, with obvious errors. Second, they were not clear as to the strength of their IP. But perhaps most importantly, the presenters forgot that many physicians, who often have significant assets, were members of this particular angel investment group. The presenters spent much of their presentation stating how poorly physicians did their job. This obviously did not go over well. Throughout the presentation, it was becoming more and more obvious that many of the potential investors were getting quite upset at these insensitive comments. The funding request, not surprisingly, was quickly voted down even though the technology seemed excellent. Lessons learned: presentation style and form do matter.

Videos

Short videos can represent a very effective communication media for technologies. Video presentations of technologies were initially popularized by crowd funding platforms, such as Kickstarter and Indiegogo. Now videos are almost a standard method to communicate technology, particularly when the technology can be demonstrated as a prototype. Technology videos can be linked on webpages; they can be presented at trade shows and then can be sent, along with TIPs or QUADs, through e-mail to potential licensees or users.

There has been significant research on what makes for an effective technology pitch video on crowdfunding sites. Much of these insights are also applicable to technology-based videos. Some best practices for preparing an effective communication video include:

1) Present the necessary technical information for the user or licensee.
2) The length of the video should probably be no more than 3 to 5 minutes.
3) The quality of video does matter, like any presentation, using the proper format and style holds attention. Key issues are:
   a. Demonstrate the technology.
   b. The video should be professionally made and be of high quality.
   c. Tell the story of the technology, and why it is superior to competitors.
   d. Remember, however, not to make the video too "flashy" or "emotional". Cute and emotional videos are common for crowdfunding, but the most common viewers of technology videos will be advanced system developers, technology

application users, and potential licensees. These viewers will likely be professional, highly educated and technology oriented. This is not the normal audience for crowdfunding videos. Keep the target audience in mind.

Elevator Pitch

An elevator pitch is a quick, 30 to 60 second summary of a technology. The analogy is how much a person can communicate in a short elevator ride. Elevator pitches are common presentation devices taught in entrepreneurship classes, but they also apply to technology communication among professionals. For example, at a trade show, you might only have a minute to communicate with somebody who shows interest at your booth. When networking at a conference, while attending a technology standard setting meeting, or simply among colleagues, perhaps only a minute or so might be available to communicate your technology and create interest. Networking requires fast, efficient, and on-target communication. Elevator pitches are often called the "pure" form of communication – to the point.

The key to having a successful elevator pitch is to practice. Before attending conferences, or networking, know what you want to say. Write down the key elements of your technology, its functionality, and what problem it solves. It is important to always ask if you can follow-up with more information, such as sending a TIP or video. Practice keeping your pitch within 30 to 60 seconds without hesitation. A technology developer never knows when they might be given the opportunity to communicate and pitch the technology in short bursts of enthusiasm.

Academic and Professional Articles

Academic Publications

Academic publications in scholarly journals are generally considered blind peer reviewed. This means that multiple knowledgeable peer reviewers from the field evaluate the merits of a paper without knowing who the authors are. Blind peer review is a standard in all academic fields. To many, a technology being published in an academic journal represents a degree of quality control and a form of due diligence that the technology works to a particular standard.

Many technologies have found traction with potential users through academic publications. In fact, in some fields, it is almost required that an early-stage technology has been published in scholarly journals in order to be commercialized. This is particularly true in drug development and other related fields where scholarly journals regularly report the results and outcomes from experiments using the technology. Once intellectual property is sufficiently protected, it is possible to submit positive findings from early experiments for publication. This is a common strategy in many scientific fields.

In other situations, developers can strategically place a technology as part of a scientific study or experiment to create interest. For example, researchers at the U.S. Naval Undersea Warfare Center (NUWC) developed a sophisticated statistical program called the Bayesian data reduction algorithm (BDRA). Originally designed as a way of detecting patterns among fuzzy, complicated and uncertain data in order to assist submarines identify objects under water, the developers realized it could also have commercial potential in other fields, such as insurance and finance. Working with a group of economic researchers, the BDRA was used as a statistical technique in several published studies attempting to define different management behaviors. The use of the BDRA in these published studies led to a number of contacts with potential licensees.

There are, however, two important caveats when publishing a technology in an academic forum. First, as previously discussed in this book, it is important that protection of the intellectual property is well established prior to publication, or what is published in the academic paper does not rise to the level of providing sufficient information to defeat IP protection. Second, if the published study is specifically designed to show the positive aspects of the technology, it must clearly be noted who funded the study in order to identify any conflicts of interest. The same issues apply to academic conference papers.

Professional Publications

Another valuable publication strategy is through professional outlets, both written and online. Every field of technology has professional outlets. These are normally not blind, peer reviewed like academic publications but rather written by contributing professional authors and reviewed by editors. Professional publications are often associated with trade organizations, large consulting firms, or for general popular readership targeted toward the general population interested in science and technology. These types of publications are hungry for content and look for material to write about. A very good communication strategy is to reach out to editors and correspondents of these more popular technology-oriented outlets.

Many examples of successful technology commercialization, such as the EpiPen, found their major market success when other product managers and engineers read about the technology in these professional and popular forums, and realized the opportunity the technology might have in their particular market or system application.

Another advantage of publications, whether scholarly or professional, is that both key word searches and AI prompt searches can easily access this material once it is placed on the web. In addition, recent AI-driven search engines are being developed to find relevant topics in podcasts and other social media sites.

Podcasting and Social Media

More and more technology developers are reaching out to podcasters, bloggers and other social media influencers. Similar to professional journals and magazines, there are a number of podcasts and social media sites that specialize in discussing new and upcoming technologies. Some of these technology-oriented podcasters and bloggers have a significant following. Oftentimes podcasts are associated with formal technology development organizations. For example, the podcast "Talk Innovation" is operated by the European Patent Office (EPO), with guest presenters including technology experts, entrepreneurs and patent examiners. Identifying these ever-changing social media outlets, then actively reaching out for interviews and coverage can be an effective communication strategy for many early-stage technology developers.

Networking

We have kept perhaps the most important part of technology communication to the end of this chapter. Interviews with hundreds of technology developers, and examining how successful technology communication takes place, constantly point to the importance of networking. Successful technology commercialization requires asking other people to review your technology. Networking is the foundation for an active approach to technology communication. While sending out TIPS and having a technology posted on a webpage might create leads and interest, networking is critical to the process.

Networking is often called an "art" rather than a science. Research on the "art" of successful technology networking points to some common themes

1) Reach out to people, rather than expect people to come to you. Take an active approach to technology communication, rather than a pure passive approach.
2) Develop a comfort level when talking and socializing with people. Oftentimes technology developers aren't comfortable with networking. Successful technology commercialization requires networking, so either individuals need to develop some level of networking skills or firms need to strategically identify networkers as part of the development team.
3) Join and attend the relevant organizations for your technology. Participate in networking events, both formal and informal. Most professional and trade organizations have networking functions.
4) Formally schedule networking time. This seems trivial, but technology developers often become pre-occupied with the technology and not communication.
5) Leverage technology for networking. Modern networking also involves online communities, such as LinkedIn. In addition, there are specialized networking programs and AI systems.
6) Identify the key influencers that are important in your technology space. Make a special effort to network with these technology influencers.

7) Networking sometimes means giving information as much as taking, but be careful again about giving too much information regarding an IP or technology that is not yet fully protected.
8) Always be ready with an elevator pitch if the opportunity arises.

Marketing Technology Products to Consumer Markets

For most firms, technology commercialization occurs when their innovation is successfully integrated into a larger system. The central focus of this book is understanding how to manage the complex process of advancing a technology through its various readiness levels and ultimately toward commercialization. For some technologies, however, the end point of the development and commercialization process occurs when the product is introduced to the final, retail, or consumer markets.

This is when the focus shifts to consumer marketing and branding. Consumer marketing for technology products is a whole different issue, and somewhat beyond the scope of this present book. Consumer-based technology products can range from mobile apps and games, which are primarily downloaded from the web, to more durable products such as computers, phones, and tools which can be sold in outlets ranging from online operations to brick-and-mortar retail stores.

Selling to the retail and consumer markets is fundamentally different from most technology development and commercialization problems. To reach specific consumer segments, advertising, distribution, branding, and packaging become much more important. While many of these issues have been discussed in this book, consumer marketing for technology products is a whole different field in itself.

While this section is not meant to be a full marketing discussion, there are important insights that have been uncovered with respect to the marketing of technology-based consumer products. Some of the most important insights and best practices are:
1) Consumers are becoming more technology savvy and appear to know more about the technological foundations of their products.
2) Influencers, particularly through social media, are becoming more important to the purchase decision. However, some research on consumer markets indicates that for technology-oriented products, friends are still the primary source of information for somebody considering a consumer technology.[3]
3) Marketing and advertising for technology products has become more target market specific, thus requiring more market research and knowledge about the buying behaviors of better-defined consumer markets.
4) Marketing for consumer technology products is becoming more data driven. AI is becoming more important in defining how to target specific submarkets and cultural generations.

5) While brand loyalty is still important, there is evidence that technology-based product consumers are becoming more aware of competitive products, and willing to change brands based on their perception of functionality and performance.

6) Marketers are becoming more aware of how consumer's buying behavior quickly changes over the technology life cycle discussed in the first few chapters of this book. Early adopters of consumer technologies will look for very different attributes than later purchasers of the technology.

7) Some large consumer product companies now have a professional with the title "Technology Product Marketing Manager" due to the changing nature of marketing and selling consumer technology products.

8) Many smaller firms developing technologies for the retail or consumer markets will often subcontract this final commercialization process to other specialized firms due to the different nature of these markets, and the complexity of marketing to these segments.

9) The importance of different types of media varies by the stage of the consumer's knowledge and involvement with a technology-based product.

There are a number of different marketing mix models, all with interesting titles such as AIDA (Attention, Interest, Desire, Action), DRIP (Differential, Reinforce, Inform, Persuade), STP (Segmentation, Targeting, Positioning), and TOFU, MOFU, and BOFU (top, middle, and bottom of the funnel), that have been proposed for marketing consumer-based technology products. Each of these has a slightly different focus, but the same objective – maximizing the sales of the technology or product. As an example, one model that succinctly describes how marketing a technology, and the impact of different types of media, changes over time uses a "Reach, Act, Convert, and Engage" (RACE) framework. [4]

The model suggests there are four distinct stages of media involvement with individual consumers of a technology-based product.

Reach Phase: The first stage is the "reach" stage. This is when the potential consumer is becoming aware of the product. The purpose of media is to influence the knowledge that the potential customer has of a technology and bring that customer to an "intention to purchase" level. The intention to purchase means that at the first opportunity, such as saving enough money, the consumer will act on the purchase intention.

The media strategy during this phase starts out as primarily "paid media", followed by "owned media", such as a company's own webpage.

Act Phase: The second phase is the purchase "act". This is when customers act on their purchase intentions and make their 1st purchase of the product. They order from the web or walk into a store to purchase a product. Since the intention to purchase has already been established, the importance of media changes. The "act" phase often involves seeking out a specific webpage to purchase online. This requires attention to how the webpage is designed to respond to searches. This is similar to our discussion of technology communication in a prior chapter. Experience becomes important during this phase. Classic merchandizing strategies become critical, particularly for the brick-and-mortar outlets.

Convert Phase: The third phase is the "convert" phase. After the 1st purchase, the consumer experiences the technology. They might love it. On the other hand, some consumers might not be happy with the experience. Much of the focus on marketing technology-based consumer products is on the "repurchase" decision, that is, creating repeat customers. This is to create brand loyalty and goodwill. Much of the media focus at this time will be to reaffirm the positive experiences that consumers have with the product.

Engage Phase: Generating brand loyalty is important, since many large consumer technology companies offer a variety of different products and creating brand loyalty with one product influences purchase behavior with another product. This is called "same brand loyalty". Apple leads the way with approximately 50% of owners purchasing other Apple products. Samsung is second with over 20% owning multiple Samsung products. Even for companies with a single product offering, cultivating customer loyalty is essential as new versions of technology-based products, including consumer goods and mobile applications, are continuously being offered.

Building brand loyalty also builds "brand advocacy", where friends influence other friends. Research also shows that brand-loyal customers tend to stay loyal when making new purchases, and they tend to spend more money on technology-based products, such as smartphones, than other consumers.[5] And of course, brand loyalty also leads to more subscription service revenues. It is becoming recognized that creating a brand-loyal ecosystem is critically important in technology-based consumer markets. The automotive industry has the highest loyalty rate of all products, well over 50%, but some technology markets are coming close.

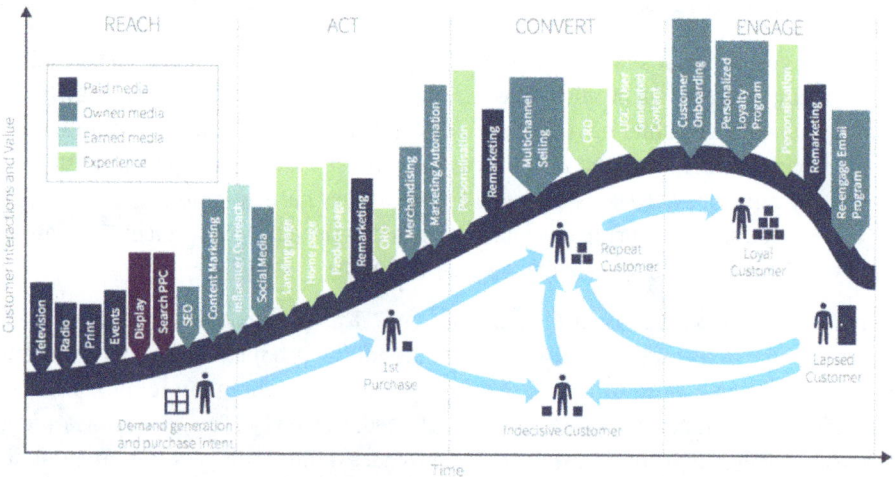

Figure 13.3: Strategies for building brand loyalty.

It is important to note that the RACE model shows the behavior, and media impacts, over time for customers at the same stage of buying behavior. But as we discussed early in the book, consumer adoption involves different consumers entering the market at different points. Early adopters purchase before the late majority. This means that a technology firm selling into the consumer market will have individual consumers in all four RACE phases. Early adopters might be at the convert or engage phase, while late majority consumers might still be at the reach phase. This means that a successful market strategy needs to develop marketing and media strategies for all RACE phases simultaneously to have a best practices marketing effort.

Marketing technology-oriented consumer products is a specialized topic. However, it must be remembered that most of these consumer products oftentimes have literally hundreds of component technologies within the system that have been successfully commercialized into this final system.

Concluding Insights

Effective communication is a critical component of successful technology development and commercialization. From informal conversations at conferences to structured pitch presentations and strategic online listings, communication plays a central role in securing interest, funding, partnerships, and ultimately market success.

This chapter distinguishes between passive and active communication strategies. While passive tools like technology transfer websites and searchable databases help increase visibility with minimal effort, they must be carefully crafted with keywords, AI compatibility, and clear messaging to maximize discoverability. Active communication, however (through tools like Technology Interest Packages (TIPs), Quad Charts, technical presentations, and networking), is often essential for building relationships and advancing opportunities.

The chapter also emphasized the growing importance of digital tools, such as keyword optimization, AI-enhanced search strategies, and high-quality video content. In today's environment, communication is no longer limited to one format or audience. It requires tailoring messages to technical experts, decision-makers, potential partners, and even consumers, often all at once.

Finally, communication is not a one-time activity but a continuous process that evolves as the technology advances. Whether it's crafting an elevator pitch for a chance encounter or preparing detailed documentation for a phased-review gate, being strategic, clear, and well-prepared at every step is essential. Good communication doesn't just describe a technology. Rather, it demonstrates its value and creates the momentum needed to move it forward.

Chapter Example: Omitron Sensors – From Automotive to Energy – Communicating Innovation

The Challenge: Creating a Market-Ready Breakthrough in Sensor Technology

Eric Aguilar founded Omitron Sensors in 2019 with a clear mission: to overcome the critical limitations of Lidar (Light Detection and Ranging) systems in autonomous vehicles and robotics.[6] While Lidar promised accurate environmental sensing for self-driving cars and robots, Aguilar, as a former product manager overseeing Lidar-equipped fleets, saw the technology's painful weaknesses firsthand. Mechanical reliability failures, high costs, and frequent recalibrations were major bottlenecks preventing widespread adoption of autonomous systems.

Together with Dr. Trent Huang, a MEMS (microelectromechanical systems) expert with over 40 patents and experience working on Google's quantum computing initiatives, Aguilar set out to fundamentally redesign the MEMS mirror at the heart of Lidar systems. Their breakthrough was a new MEMS-based mirror that delivered:
– 10x the performance over existing MEMS mirrors,
– Much higher reliability through silicon-based construction (eliminating mechanical wear points),
– And lower manufacturing costs using standard semiconductor processes.

This innovation wasn't just theoretical. Within eighteen months, Omitron had built functional prototypes, demonstrating a denser, more efficient MEMS device that dramatically outperformed traditional solutions. However, solving the technical challenge was only the beginning. To successfully commercialize their breakthrough, Aguilar and his team needed to build market visibility, establish credibility, and engage with potential customers – all before even generating revenue.

Expanding Applications through Strategic Communication

Initially, Omitron targeted the automotive Lidar market, focusing on self-driving car manufacturers where Aguilar already had strong industry relationships. But the automotive sector is notorious for long development and qualification cycles – often stretching five to seven years before large-scale revenue could be realized. With venture capital backing and investor expectations to manage, Omitron needs earlier wins to sustain momentum.

Without abandoning their core automotive focus, the company began experimenting with more proactive communication strategies. They hired a PR firm to raise visibility through targeted media exposure, resulting in features across engineering, tech, and investment publications. Their strategy prioritized high-quality technical coverage – targeting engineers, product developers, and executives likely to be actively searching for next-generation MEMS technologies.

This strategic communication effort seems to be paying off. Companies from other sectors – including energy (for methane detection), space exploration, and data center communications – discovered Omitron through online searches and media coverage. These inbound inquiries opened doors to new market opportunities, particularly in industries where regulatory cycles are faster and product adoption timelines are shorter than in automotive.

Communication Is Everything

As Eric Aguilar notes, "Success in our industry isn't just about having the best technology. It's about building relationships, earning credibility, and making sure people know you exist. Communication is everything". By actively communicating their capabilities through publishing, networking, and conference presentations, Omitron accelerated its market discovery beyond its original automotive target.

Strategic Market Expansion

Critically, Omitron did not "pivot" away from automotive. Instead, they expanded their market opportunities without abandoning their long-term core strategy. Their MEMS technology could be used in methane monitoring, space communications, and data centers without major redesigns – allowing selective diversification without stretching the company's limited resources.

By maintaining technical focus while being open to adjacent markets, Omitron is striking a delicate but powerful balance: build credibility early with faster-to-market applications, while staying committed to the high-volume automotive vision that originally inspired the company.

Key Communication Takeaways

- Early-stage deep-tech companies must be proactive in building visibility and credibility.
- Technical communication – through targeted media, conference talks, and thought leadership articles – can attract unexpected opportunities.
- Market awareness and trust must be developed in parallel with technical development, especially in industries with long adoption cycles.
- Selective market expansion can create near-term revenue pathways without losing long-term strategic focus.

Chapter 14
Commercialization Success Scales and Prediction Scoring Systems

This Chapter

- Discusses the importance of performing formal commercialization success assessments as part of a commercialization or feasibility study.
- Presents three well-tested technology assessment scoring or prediction tools, the CCAT Assessment Scale, the SBIR Impact Scale, and the Cloverleaf Model.
- Emphasizes that technology success and prediction tools provide only a partial indication of future success.
- Underscores that technology success prediction and scoring tools should be used in combination with formal commercialization and VoC studies to obtain the best assessment of future success.

Key Management Tools and Best Practices

- CCAT Technology Assessment Scale
- SBIR Impact Scale
- Cloverleaf Model of Technology Readiness

! **INSIGHT**

At times, prediction models can be quite powerful. Weather forecasting, for example, has been perfected into a science. We can now predict future temperatures, wind, and precipitation very accurately, perhaps even weeks out. But certain types of weather forecasting remain extremely difficult. It is very difficult to predict the formation of tornados, and then the exact location of touchdown and movement, until they are actually in the process of forming. These are "fuzzy data" events. Predicting future commercialization success is a major interest for technology transfer offices, investors, granting agencies, corporate executives, entrepreneurs, and technology developers. Although progress has been made, predicting the future commercialization success of early-stage technologies is more like predicting tornadoes than anything.

Introduction

The final, long-term objective of any technology development effort is the successful introduction of the technology into the marketplace, whether directly to the end-user or integrated into a larger system. There will certainly be various steps, modifications, pivots, and investments that need to be made, but all these efforts are generally made under the assumption that the end technology will be commercially successful. If a technology program is thought to have little future chance in marketplace, then support and resources will quickly dry up.

https://doi.org/10.1515/9783111684420-015

As previously discussed, the record for successful technology commercialization is somewhat discouraging. Most research points to fairly low commercialization rates. However, it is hard to compare studies since the definition of commercialization success differs dramatically depending on the focus. A university technology transfer office, for example, might consider a technology "successfully commercialized" when it is licensed to somebody else, regardless of whether or not that technology ultimately ends up in the market at a later date. In fact, most TTOs officially report the rate of licensing deals as their primary measure of productivity. Others might consider commercialization success being defined by actually generating revenues.

There is no doubt that the probability of success increases as technologies progress along the development scale. A technology that has made it to the prototype phase, TRL5 or TRL6, has a much greater chance of successful commercialization than an early, TRL2 technology that is just being reviewed for a patent application. This is why the discount rate associated with the valuation of technologies decreases dramatically as technologies progress through its technology development levels – the risk of failure decreases.

Several studies, for example, have found that less than 5% of patents ever make money.[1] However, once a technology has progressed to a TRL5 or TRL6 stage, the probability of earning some income from the technology increases dramatically to about 30%, although the chances of being a big hit still remain fairly low.[2] But even at these later stages of development, although the rate of commercialization is a bit higher, there still remains a lot of uncertainty about the future.

Can we predict the commercialization of early-stage technologies? That is the million-dollar question at all stages of a technology's development process. This chapter will examine the issue of technology assessment rating scales that are used in practice and the whole issue of predicting commercialization success.

What Is a Commercialization Assessment Scale?

A commercialization assessment or success rating scale involves a set of questions with a numerical rating. Reviewers then score each question. The numerical scores, either individually or combined, attempt to predict, or at least better understand, the potential of a technology's future success in the market.

These assessment tools range from a fairly simple set of 4 or 5 questions to complex dimensional scales of 30 or more questions. Technology readiness or commercialization rating scales are considered "subjective" measures tools, that is, they are filled out by humans reviewing the technology, the market, and the development team.

These types of scales are used in a number of situations. Approximately 40% of angel investment groups report using some type of a formal rating scale when making funding decisions.[3] Almost all granting agencies will use a rating system to score grant applications. Technology assessment scales are often an important part of formal commercialization studies. They are also used extensively by technology commercialization consultants and technology valuation experts.

The Purpose of Commercialization Assessment Scales

Interviews with many technology transfer officers, R&D managers, and even investors reveal that many don't use formal scales when making decisions. A common theme heard in interviews is they only use their "intuition". Yet, research has shown that administrators, technology transfer officers, project managers, and consultants as a group generally do not have much luck in predicting commercialization success. Interestingly, individuals currently working in the technical field, such as bench scientists, software developers, and practicing engineers, appear to actually have a slightly better sense of predicting future success on the average.[4]

The purpose of technology assessment scales is much more complex than simply trying to predict success. They actually have several very important purposes in the commercialization process.

1) Completing a technology assessment scale, if done properly, may, in fact, provide some indication of future commercial success.

2) More importantly, completing a technology assessment scale will often identify what areas the technology development program directors need to concentrate on in order to increase the chance of future success. In this respect, the scale becomes more "formulative" in nature, rather than "predictive". They help in formulating a future strategy.

3) Completing a technology assessment scales should be done in conjunction with a commercialization study, most often at the end of the formal commercialization study when the best information is available to reviewers. A commercialization study provides important information regarding how competitive the target technology versus competitive technologies; it identifies the best market verticals to initially enter and offers critical insights about the future functionality requirements from both independent experts and the Voice of Customer analysis. This information should lead to a much better subjective assessment when filling out formal commercialization scale.

A Cautionary Note

There have been a number of published studies that attempt to identify the key dimensions underlying technology commercialization success. However, the vast majority of these research studies are *post-hoc* in nature. *Post-hoc* studies examine successful versus non-successful technologies and then, after the fact, use statistical methods to identify important dimensions. It is relatively easy to identify the important dimensions of technology success in a *post-hoc*, after the fact study.

However, while *post-hoc* studies might identify important dimensions to consider, they do not offer truly predictive models of technology commercialization. A true predictive scale is when people actually assess and score an early-stage technology at a particular point in time not knowing about the future, and then we see how well the tool actually predicts commercialization perhaps years later.

To develop a predictive model of technology commercialization, we need to search for *ex-ante* studies. *Ex-ante* means "before" the event. *Ex-ante* research is what provides a true prediction model. We will discuss some of the more proven scales.

A Simple Approach: The CCAT Assessment Scale

Most organizations that use technology assessment tools keep them fairly simple, with only a few broad, multi-dimensional questions. The question becomes, then, are these assessment tools effective in practice? The Center of Commercialization of Advanced Technology (CCAT) was a Consortium funded by the U.S. Congress and managed by the Department of Defense. Founded in 2001, CCAT's mission was to encourage the commercialization of dual use technologies into the general market. CCAT was unique at that time since it not only offered significant grant funds but was the first government related office that also required a formal commercialization study to be completed as part of the grant funding. The combination of grants funding and a commercialization study significantly increased the rate of actual commercialization.

CCAT needed to develop a process to score these applicant technologies. The first step was to have developers (mostly small technology developers and entrepreneurs) submit a detailed application, with all the components of a business plan that might be submitted to angel investor group. This was then reviewed by an interdisciplinary review team. The applicants with the highest scores were then invited to do a face-to-face presentation. As a starting point, CCAT needed to develop a simple numerical scale for the first step. The scale needed to be consistent, valid, and stay the same for the decades that CCAT was in existence.

Starting with a broader set of questions, after reliability and validity testing, it was discovered that four key dimensions were critical: technical merit, market or commercial potential, whether the development team could pull it off, and if the technology could sustain a competitive advantage in the marketplace. A simple six-question scale was agreed upon, with four questions addressing the key dimensions of technology success, and two questions addressing the mission of the agency. What is unique is that the CCAT Scale stayed the same over the decades, and over 750 highly advanced technologies were ultimately reviewed using this scale with over 2,500 total evaluations. The questions used to evaluate technologies are as follows:

1) Technical Merit, Ability of Technology to Satisfy Market Needs (0 to 10 scale)
2) Commercial Potential (0 to 10 scale)
3) Ability to Sustain Competitive Advantage (0 to 10 scale)
4) Ability of Project Team to Execute the Plan (0 to 10 scale)
5) Reasonableness of Request
6) Relevance to Mission of the Agency

Each question was scored on an 11-point scale, 0 being the lowest and 10 being the highest. The review teams were interdisciplinary and ranged between 3 and 8 individuals. For the CCAT Scale, the reviewers read and scored each technology independently in order to reduce bias and group think. Most of the technologies were in the TRL4 to TRL6 stage of development.

CCAT tracked the technologies over time and found that the combined scores on the first four questions of the CCAT Scale were positively correlated to several measures of actual future success, including receiving future grant funding and whether the technology had achieved actual income with a 3-year period. In addition, it appears that reviewers with a strong technical background, such as practicing engineers and bench scientists, had much better prediction capabilities than technology transfer officers, administrators, consultants and even venture capitalists.

Additional analysis indicated possible cut-points. For the first four questions, the combined score could range between "0" and "40", with "40" being the highest. The average combined score of over 2,500 reviews for 750 technologies was "24". Technologies with scores over 25 had a five times better chance of being commercialized within a three-year period than technologies with scores less than 18.

Another Simple Approach: The SBIR "Impact" Scale

Similar simple scales are used for many internal stage-gate review process, some angel groups, and for SBIR award scoring. For example, the SBIR grant review scales and process have changed over time and vary from agency. The current National Health Institute (NIH) uses a scale for early-stage technologies (SBIR 1 awards). This scale is typically filled out by a review team of three individuals in the field. Although the dimensions are similar, unlike the CCAT approach where the scale is filled out by independent reviewers, the Impact Scale is the result of discussions between the reviewers. For the NIH, there are five basic dimensions to be scored
1) Significance of technology
2) Ability of investigators
3) Innovation potential
4) Reasonableness of approach
5) Impact on the environment/market.[5]

Each dimension is scored on a 9-point "backwards" scale, with "1" being the highest and "9" being the lowest. A score of "1" indicates no weakness, while a mid-score of "5" represents a "strong technology with a least one moderate weakness". A "9" represents very few strengths.

An "impact" score is calculated by taking the average score, then multiplying by 10, and resulting in "impact" scores between 10 and 90. In general, Impact Scores lower than 30 or 35 are viewed favorably, although there are exceptions. Other SBIR programs might use a different review process; however, the formal review process is similar. Unlike the CCAT Scale, there is not a lot of information as to how accurate the Impact Score is in predicting future commercialization

In conclusion, a simple scale, such as the CCAT and SBIR Impact Scales, can be very useful. If used properly (with individuals who are familiar with the technology, having technical reviewers on the team, seriously reviewing the technology and plan) these short scales do have significant prediction power about future commercialization success. Most likely the predictive power of such scales (used in the TRL4 to TRL6 stage technologies) is somewhat in the 20% to 30% accuracy range[6] – better than nothing and certainly better than "intuition". Surprisingly, the research also shows that using the scales in combination of both the business plan and hearing a formal presentation of the technology developers only slightly increases the predictive power.

However, used in conjunction with a formal commercialization study, it is likely that the predictive power of the scales increases. In addition, the scales can also be formulative in nature, by identifying areas for improvement

A More Complex Approach: The Cloverleaf Model

The "Cloverleaf Model" was developed and published in 2001 by Louise Heslop, Eileen McGregor, and May Griffith in the Journal of Technology Transfer. Using extensive commercialization data from Canada, this is probably the most valid and reliable technology readiness scoring system developed. It is primarily designed for technologies more in the TRL3 to TRL4 development stage, typical of technologies being reviewed by a technology transfer office at both government and private sector research labs. But clearly, the Cloverleaf Model could be adapted for technologies in later stages of development. The authors started with a large number of questions, and through a rigorous scale development process developed their final model of 30 questions organized into four dimensions, market readiness, technology readiness, commercial readiness, and management readiness (see Figure 14.1). What is unique about the Cloverleaf Model is that each question is rated on a combination of whether the condition is met and the level of confidence in rating the questions. This results in a weighted score.

Examining the success of various technologies, the authors suggest that a score greater than 180 would indicate a reasonable score for continuing with technology development, while a score less than 150 might suggest abandoning the technology. As with any scoring system, the Cloverleaf Model should be used in combination with a formal commercialization study and can underline areas where additional investment might be made to increase a technology's readiness for the commercialization.

Cloverleaf Model™, Modified for General Use

Instructions: For each of the criteria conditions below, enter a score for extent to which condition is met where 1 = not met, 2 = partially met, 3 = fully met. Enter a score from 1 to 3 for level of confidence in the rating where 1 = low confidence and 3 = high confidence. Multiply the two scores for each and enter the product as the weighted score. Finally, sum the weighted scores for a total score.

	Extent to Which Condition is Met		Level of Confidence		Weighted Score
Market Readiness					
The technology offers significant identifiable and quantifiable benefits	3	x	2	=	6
The technology has distinct advantages over competing products	2	x	3	=	6
The technology has future uses	3	x	3	=	9
There is a definable marketable technology	2	x	2	=	4
A defined or target market is accessible	1	x	2	=	2
The target market is a large one	2	x	3	=	6
The target market is a growing one	2	x	1	=	2
The technology has immediate market uses	2	x	2	=	4
The technology will be first-to-market	1	x	3	=	3
Manufacturing and delivery is determined to be feasible	3	x	3	=	9
Total Market Readiness Score (Max. 90)				Subtotal	51
Technology Readiness					
IP has been obtained		x		=	
The technology is a new, non-obvious innovation		x		=	
The patent and literature search are complete and clear		x		=	
There are no other dominant patents		x		=	
The technology is state-of-the-art or major breakthrough		x		=	
The technology is a core or platform technology		x		=	
Total Technology Readiness Score (Max. 54)				Subtotal	
Commercial Readiness					
Prospective licensees/customers are identified		x		=	
Inventors have industry contacts		x		=	
Licensee/Customer financial support is available for further development		x		=	
There is access to sufficient capital and support		x		=	
A positive return on investment is expected		x		=	
Future income expected to provide positive net present value		x		=	
Low marketing costs		x		=	
Government support/grants are available for additional development		x		=	
Total Commercial Readiness Score (Max. 72)				Subtotal	
Management Readiness					
The inventor/developer will champion as a team player		x		=	
The inventor/developer has realistic expectations for success		x		=	
The inventor/developer is recognized and established in the field		x		=	
Good communication skills are available		x		=	
Good management capabilities are available		x		=	
Total Management Readiness Score		x		=	
Total Management Readiness Score (Max. 54)				Subtotal	

>180, reasonable good chance of commercialization at this time   Grand Total Score _____
<150, relatively low chance of commercialization at this time

Heslop et al (2001), Development of a Technology Readiness Assessment Tool: The Cloverleaf Model, *Journal of Technology Transfer*, 25(4), 369-384

Figure 14.1: The Cloverleaf Model™ for scoring a technology.

Other Technology Assessment and Prediction Approaches

The CCAT Scale discussed earlier is an *ex-ante* model – the questions were certainly originally developed from *ex-post* research on successful technology commercialization success, but then thoroughly tested in an *ex-ante* method to determine the ability to predict success. The development of the more complex Cloverleaf Model can also be considered a partial *ex-ante* model, but the advantage of the Cloverleaf Model is its rigorous development of the appropriate questions to ask, and the weighted probability measure. It is difficult to find other true *ex-ante* predictive model models that are based upon subjective scoring.

There are a number of large consulting firms that work with technology commercialization clients. Some of these large consulting firms are known to have developed their own predictive models of technology success. Recently, these proprietary models have started to also use AI approaches. However, consulting firm and in-house predictive models of technology commercialization are clearly considered "trade-secrets", and it is extremely difficult to identify either the specifics of the models, or how successful they are in actually predicting technology readiness or future success.

In addition, certain government organizations have also developed predictive models of commercialization success. In particular, China, Japan, and Korea are known to have developed predictive models of future technology success, but the details of these models tend to also be highly propriety in nature.

Models of Predicting Technology Success Based on Objective Measures

The CCAT Assessment Scale, the SBIR Impact model, and the Cloverleaf Model are all considered subjective scoring tools. Important dimensions are provided, but then reviewers have to subjectively score the technology being reviewed along these dimensions after reviewing the technology, a business plan, or the results of a commercialization study. Being subjective scoring systems, they are naturally influenced by reviewer biases, reviewer knowledge and background, and other human characteristics that sometimes plague subjective assessments. However, these models have been tested against success.

However, after the fact, or *ex-post* studies of technology success can be useful if they are based upon objective measures rather than on dimensions that require subjective scoring. Objective measures that have been linked to future technology commercialization success in published research have included dimensions, such as:

a) the number of times the underlying patent has been cited,
b) the underlying patent connections with other patents,
c) whether the technology has received a prior grant or funding (which implies a prior formal review),
d) the stage of technology development reflected by its TRL score, with later TRL stages having higher commercialization success,
e) whether the development team has a Ph.D. educated member,
f) the amount of prior R&D spent on the technology,
g) the size of parent organization reflected by number of employees,
h) whether a demonstrable prototype exists, and

i)   whether are other technologies being developed by the parent firm.

These are all objective measures. Research has indicated that all of the above objective measures are, in fact, correlated with different measures of future commercialization success and could be used as a predictive model.

For example, using the CCAT data previously discussed, having a Ph.D. trained member on the team is positively correlated with obtaining future grants (a measure of commercialization success), while having a prototype that can be demonstrated is positively correlated with future licensing (another measure of commercialization success). In addition, obtaining either prior grant funding or private equity funding is most significantly correlated with future commercialization success, such as obtaining future investments (grant or private equity) and achieving future revenues from a technology within a 3-year period. This is not surprising since both of these not only imply resources, but also prior independent review.

Concluding Insights

Attempting to predict the future commercial success of an early-stage technology is natural. Before any time of investment and effort is made, people and organizations would like to have a better understanding of a technology's future success. Why throw money into a losing cause?

A number of technology assessment scoring tools have been offered in the literature to assist in these decisions. We know what broad dimensions are important when examining a technology – the merits of the technology, the nature of the target market, the ability of the development team, and the competitive environment that impacts the long-term sustainability of the technology. This has been well studied.

However, only a few of these scoring tools have actually been validated, that is, they can actually predict future technology commercialization to some extent. We have discussed several tools that have some degree of validation. These include relatively simple models, such as the CCAT Assessment Scale and the SBIR Impact Scale, as well as the much more complex, Cloverleaf Model.

William of Ockham, a fourteenth-century philosopher and theologian, offered a rule that later became known as Ockham's Razor. Ockham's Razor states that the best problem-solving principle is one with the smallest number of elements, that is, the simplest solution is probably the best. Ockham's Razor has been shown to be true more often than not. For example, economic research has shown that more complex models do not necessarily result in better economic forecasts.[7] The CCAT assessment scale, with only four key questions, might be an example of Ockham's Razor when it comes to predicting future commercialization success. While the predictive ability of these scoring tools is somewhat limited, perhaps predicting only 20% to 30% of a technology's future success, it is still much better than nothing. And perhaps most importantly, technologies that score very low on these tools are probably not likely to succeed, while those scoring very high are much more likely to have successful commercialization. It is the middle score range that creates the most uncertainty.

However, more complex tools, such as the Cloverleaf Model, can have a very important role beyond forecasting success. By delving into the more detailed components of the critical dimensions, it might uncover specific areas where the technology developer needs to focus future effort, or additional insight might be required from market research. In this respect, predictive tools also have a "formulative" purpose of pointing out areas for improvement.

Most important, however, is that any use of a prediction tool, with simple or complex, should be in conjunction with a commercialization study, whether the study is a quick-look study or a more complex, detailed study.

Chapter 15
Managing Technology: Organizational Readiness Models

This Chapter
- Emphasizes the value of taking a comprehensive, holistic approach to managing technology development and commercialization.
- Introduces different frameworks for thinking about integrative technology management.
- Presents several widely used "readiness" tools that support effective decision-making in technology development.

Key Management Tools and Best Practices
- Business Readiness Levels (BRLs)
- Innovation Readiness Levels (IRLs)
- Commercialization Readiness Levels (CRLs)
- Commercialization Adoption Readiness Assessment Tool (CARAT)
- The Technology Progress Matrix (TPM)

! **INSIGHT**

Technologies don't grow in a vacuum. They need nourishment from the whole organization. This chapter examines how some technology driven organizations attempt to understand and depict the key relationships between the development of various organizational dimensions and the target technology. Matching organizational readiness with the development of technologies is a critical but often overlooked managerial function. The models presented in this chapter are useful at several different levels. First, they remind senior management about the key connections between technological development and the key organizational dimensions. Second, the models help identify those areas in the organization that might need additional effort in order to facilitate successful technology commercialization. Third, the models are excellent vehicles for communicating these relationships, both internally and externally.

Introduction

Every basic management textbook has a definition of the term "management". While the wording might be somewhat different between textbooks, inevitably management involves the process of organizing, administering, and controlling the organization's resources to achieve its objectives. In many cases, particularly within small, entrepreneurial ventures, the entire organization is built around a single technology. Every decision, from hiring and fundraising to marketing and operations, revolves around one goal: to successfully develop and commercialize that core innovation.

https://doi.org/10.1515/9783111684420-016

In other cases, the technology is being developed within a much larger entity. For large technology-oriented multinational corporations, a particular technology is likely part of a much larger portfolio of technologies. But even in these cases, the project team assigned to each technology will still need to concentrate its efforts and properly manage the development of that particular technology through its different phases.

Commercialization certainly represents a progression from idea to market adoption. At its core, technology development, as often defined by TRLs, is what drives everything forward. It is primarily fueled by scientific and engineering effort. If the technical team fails to advance the technology to its next stage, progress stalls, and the opportunity may be lost entirely.

However, from a managerial perspective, success requires more than just technical progress. Other parts of the organization must be aligned with the specific needs of each development stage. While many books explore the broader field of technology management, this chapter takes a more focused approach. We concentrate specifically on tools that help clarify the complex managerial challenges involved in guiding technologies through their various development phases.

Four different models of "readiness" are examined. The first is the "Business Readiness Level" model, or BRL. The second is the "Innovation Readiness Level" model, developed by KTH, the state-owned innovation agency in Sweden. The third is the RCNDE's "Commercialization Readiness Level (CRL)" model. Fourth, we present a modified version of the U.S. Department of Energy's "Commercial Adoption Readiness Assessment Tool (CARAT) and the Technology Progress Matrix Chart (TPM)". All of these tools and models take a more holistic or comprehensive look at the management of technology readiness than TRLs. These tools are also used extensively in practice by various private, governmental, and consulting organizations.

Each of these tools is similar in many respects. They are also related to the commercialization scoring model discussed in the previous chapter, since these scoring models are also inevitably multi-dimension in nature. Most importantly, they all recognize one basic principle – successfully bringing a technology to market is not just about the technology, but also about the organization's ability to make it happen. Each of the tools in this chapter, however, offers a different perspective on how to assess and present an organization's readiness to bring their technologies to the market. These are multi-purpose tools.

Successfully bringing a technology to market is not just about the technology, but also about the organization's ability to make it happen.

While these tools can certainly be used for internal management purposes, they are also excellent presentation tools. They offer a very effective way to visualize how technologies are progressing, along with the necessary aspects of organizational support, toward the end point of commercialization.

Although these tools and models discuss "organization", they really refer specifically to the organization and situations directly involved with a particular technology. This might be the entrepreneurial firm focusing on a single technological platform, or the project team for a specific technology being developed by a larger corporation.

Business Readiness Levels (BRLs)

Organizations need to consider commercialization readiness from a broader perspective, not just from the perspective of the technologies. "Business Readiness Levels" or BRLs look at the whole organizational readiness for commercializing a technology. BRLs are numerical assignments, again on a typical 9-point scale.

BRLs are also often used to analyze smaller, more entrepreneurial organizations by technology funding agencies, such as the European Innovation Council. In addition, BRLs are used by several consulting firms. BRLs attempt to categorize the whole organization's readiness, with a primary focus on the business model for development and commercialization. BRLs are designed to assess the ability of the organization to actually develop and commercialize a technology as well as identifying possible missing skills and resources required to bring a technology to the next level.

BRLs are used in combination with TRLs, and many times with the other readiness level models discussed in this chapter (see Figure 15.1). The goal is to ensure that the organization has reached a point of sufficient business sophistication to support the current development stage of its technology and then move it to the next stage of development. Ideally, the business model should be slightly ahead of the technology's readiness level to enable smoother commercialization. Figure 15.1 shows the relationship between TRLs and BRLs. Since BRLs are used in combination with TRLs, they are technology project specific and can be used to assess the maturity of the business model for each technology in a multi-product firm.

Commercialization and Adoption Readiness Models

Similar to BRLs, the idea of technology commercialization or Adoption Readiness Levels (sometimes referred to as ARLs), is to provide a more managerial model of linking various dimensions of the organization, resource availability, market conditions, and potential environmental barriers, to the stage of technology development. It is then possible to see, from a management perspective, if other dimensions of the organization are properly aligned with the stage of a technology development.

Adoption Readiness Levels (ARLs), however, tend to be both broader and more detailed than BRL tools. In fact, some ARLs incorporate BRLs within their model. We discuss three of these broader ARL models – the KTH "Innovation Readiness Level™" model, the RCNDE "Commercialization Readiness Level" model, and the "Commercial

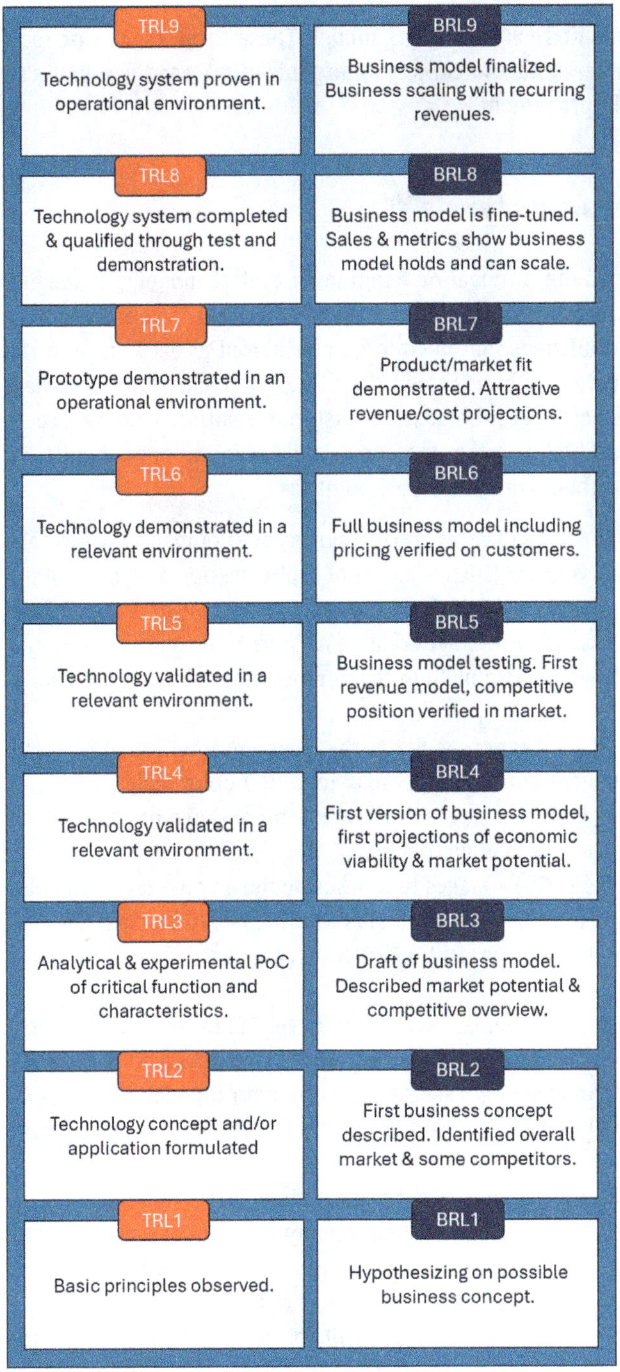

TRL9	BRL9
Technology system proven in operational environment.	Business model finalized. Business scaling with recurring revenues.
TRL8	BRL8
Technology system completed & qualified through test and demonstration.	Business model is fine-tuned. Sales & metrics show business model holds and can scale.
TRL7	BRL7
Prototype demonstrated in an operational environment.	Product/market fit demonstrated. Attractive revenue/cost projections.
TRL6	BRL6
Technology demonstrated in a relevant environment.	Full business model including pricing verified on customers.
TRL5	BRL5
Technology validated in a relevant environment.	Business model testing. First revenue model, competitive position verified in market.
TRL4	BRL4
Technology validated in a relevant environment.	First version of business model, first projections of economic viability & market potential.
TRL3	BRL3
Analytical & experimental PoC of critical function and characteristics.	Draft of business model. Described market potential & competitive overview.
TRL2	BRL2
Technology concept and/or application formulated	First business concept described. Identified overall market & some competitors.
TRL1	BRL1
Basic principles observed.	Hypothesizing on possible business concept.

Figure 15.1: Business Readiness Levels. Source: https://www.acceler8.today/insights/business-readiness-levels/.

Adoption Readiness Assessment Tool", or CARAT model. These three models or tools are designed not only to understand and classify an organization's readiness but also identify problem areas for improvement.

KTH's "Innovation Readiness Levels™"

KTH of Sweden has developed the "Innovation Readiness Level™" model of managing technology development.[1] The Innovation Readiness Level™ provides a comprehensive way of viewing the managerial steps that need to be considered at each stage in the technology development process. It builds upon the notion of Technology Readiness Levels but also considers five other key dimensions: customer readiness, funding readiness, team readiness, intellectual property readiness, and business model readiness. Each of the six dimensions is then scored along a 9-point scale.

> **Technology Readiness Level (TRL)** – stages of technology development, 9-point scale.
> **Business Model Readiness Level (BRL)** – stages of sophistication and detail of the business concept, including revenue projects and feasibility analysis, 9-point scale.
> **Customer Readiness Level (CRL)** – stages related to confirming end-user requirements and interest. This would also include consideration of competing technologies, 9-point scale.
> **IP Readiness Level (IPRL)** – stages that clarify the legal and intellectual property strength and protection, including the ability to defend IP, 9-point scale.
> **Team Readiness Level (TMRL)** – stages that define the organization's ability to secure the right competencies and align the team, 9-point scale.
> **Funding Readiness Level (FRL)** – stages that describe the acquisition of the necessary funding to take the idea to the market. This would apply to both small enterprises, or projects within larger organizations, 9-point scale.

The first two dimensions, the Technology Readiness Level (TRL) and the Business Readiness Level (BRL), have already been discussed. These two dimensions are commonly used by various companies and governments throughout the globe. The "Innovation Readiness Level™, however, adds descriptive stages or levels to the other four dimensions.

Once a technology, and its organization, is scored on each of the six dimensions using a 9-point scale, the results are analyzed. However, unlike many tools, rather than adding up the scores and then predicting the probability of a technology's commercialization success, the KTH "Innovation Readiness Level™" plots the results on a "radar chart" (see Figure 15.2).

Radar charts are useful when presenting the results of multi-dimensional scoring The purpose of this plot is to provide management a better understanding of the balance between the six dimensions. A technology's Innovation Readiness Level for an entity is therefore the core area within all six dimensions.

Technology Readiness Radar Plot

──Technology A   ──Technology B

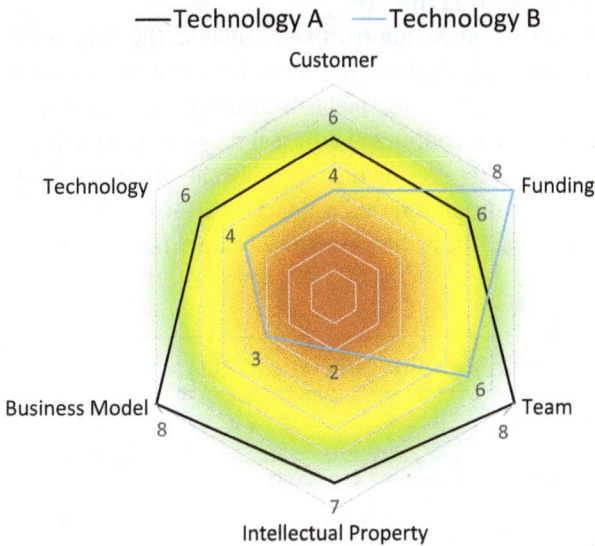

Figure 15.2: The Technology Readiness Radar Plot.

In the above example, the radar plot shows of a balanced picture of Technology A's innovation readiness, where all the dimensions are ranked 6 or above. This might suggest to management that the development process is being well managed, with consideration for developing all the necessary dimensions as an integrated effort.

An unbalanced radar chart, such as Technology B, might indicate that one or more dimensions are lagging behind, particularly if the Technology Readiness Level (TRL) is outpacing the other support dimensions. From a management perspective, this signals a potential bottleneck in commercialization. If supporting areas such as market understanding, regulatory planning, or IP protection are underdeveloped, the technology may stall despite strong technical progress. Addressing these gaps early helps avoid costly delays, misaligned investments, or missed opportunities during scale-up.

Commercialization Readiness Levels and the Technology Progress Matrix (TPM)

While the six dimensions of the KTH's Innovation Readiness Levels™ appear relatively comprehensive as a way of evaluating, scoring, and presenting a technology program's progress toward commercialization, the radar map can be confusing to interpret. A number of different approaches have been developed to simplify the presentation of overall progress. All of these models recognize that Technology Readiness Levels (TRLs) are simply not sufficient alone to capture a more comprehensive view of commercialization management. A broader perspective is needed.

For example, the Research Center for Nondestructive Evaluation (RCNDE), a collaboration between several universities in England and Scotland, uses a Commercialization Readiness Level.[2] Similar to TRLs, the "CRL" tool (see fugure 15.3) uses a 9-level analysis to capture the organization's full readiness at different stages of a technology's development. Much of the information for scoring the CRL will come from the different commercialization studies and financial projections that are performed at various times during the development process. This is then used to develop a Technology Progress Matrix, or TPM.

Commercialization Readiness Levels (CRLs)		
CRL	**Level Description**	**Team Focus**
9	Full Launch and First Revenues	Commercialization
8	Market Introduction and Pre-Revenue Sales Development. Social Media and Influencer Development	Real World Interfacing
7	Initial Marketing, Lead Development and Financial Model Validation. Validated Marketing and Delivery Plan	
6	Technology/Solution Optimization. Detailed Customer Facing Discussions	Proof of Need and Technology Alignment
5	Market Alignment. Define Product and Market Requirements.	
4	Value Proposition. Business Model Development	
3	Technology Application. Validate Problem and Solution Relationship	Knowledge Development
2	Market Awareness and Problem Discovery	
1	Basic Hypothesis and Understanding	

Figure 15.3: RCNDE Commercialization Readiness Level.

Technology Progress Matrix (TPM)

The key managerial issue is to understand and present the relationship between technology development and organization readiness, since they need to develop somewhat simultaneously. While KTH's radar map discussed earlier is one method of presenting this information, many organizations prefer to use a simpler two-dimensional matrix, or Technology Progress Matrix (TPM) which shows two dimensions, the TRL and the CRL (see Figure 15.4).

With the Technology Progress Matrix (TPM), progress can be plotted over time. In a Technology Progress Matrix (TPM), the left dimension is the standard Technology Readiness Level (TRL) scale, while the bottom, CRL dimension can be measured in many different ways. One option is to use the scores from the KTH's five dimensions KTH's

(Business Model Readiness Level, Customer Readiness Level, IP Readiness Level, Team Readiness Level, and Funding Readiness Level) as a CRL measure. Since the KTH dimensions are each measured on a 9-point scale, the average will also result in a 9-point measure of overall "Commercialization Readiness"

Another option is to use the dimensions from either the CCAT Assessment Scale or the Cloverleaf Readiness model discussed in the prior chapter. For example, using the simple CCAT Assessment Scale we develop a typical "Technology Progress Matrix" (TPM), as depicted in Figure 15.4. This is a key advantage of the TPM management tool. It can show whether the technology is progressing according to plan (the green section in the combined chart) or whether there is deviation from the expected path, indicated by movement into the red/purple (danger) or yellow (caution) squares. For this simple example, we have adopted the four dimensions of the CCAT Assessment Scale. Note that we use the CCAT question of "Technology Merit" as a dimension of CRL since it is a different concept than TRLs, which measures the stage of development.

Question 1: Does the Technology have Merit?

1="we believe in general terms that the technology has value, and solves a problem" to 9="we know for certain that the technology/functionality solves a real and significant problem in the market"

Question 2: Has Commercial Potential Been Determined?

1="only in very general terms" to 9="full requirements of customer segments are known"

Question 3: Does the Organization Have the Ability to Sustain Competitive Advantage?

1="sufficient only to support early technology development" to 9="complete support and known ability to successfully launch technology"

Question 4: Does the Project Team have the Ability to Execute the Plan?

1="technology development team is in place" to 9="whole organization, technology, production, marketing, distribution, committed and geared for commercialization"

From this simple CRL measure, we add the four sub-scores together; the full CRL score could then range from "4" to "36". To convert to a 9-point CRL scale, simply divide the total score by 4.

All organizations should develop their own measure of Commercial Readiness Levels appropriate for their organizations. It can either be a very sophisticated CRL model, taking a multi-dimensional approach or a single dimension CRL measure. Regardless, developing a "Technology Progress Matrix" (TPM) is an excellent managerial exercise to understand the complexities of organization support over time, to present how a technology project is actually progressing, and to underline possible areas where additional information or support is required.

Technology Progress Matrix (TPM)

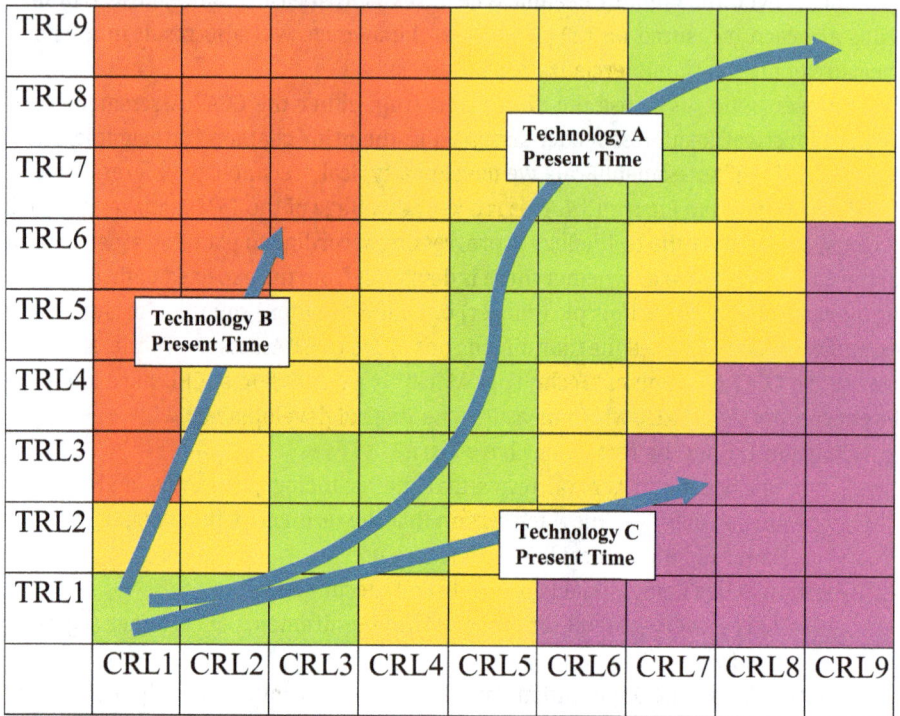

Figure 15.4: Technology Progress Matrix.

Consider a case where our organization is internally developing three different technologies. The TPM is a powerful management tool to present the progress of our efforts and possibly identify upcoming problems. In this example, the combined CRM indicates that Technology A is progressing as planned toward final commercialization. The Technology Readiness Level and the corresponding organization's Commercial Readiness Level are in sync and appear on target for a successful future commercialization.

However, Technology B appears to be somewhat off-course. While Technology B's technical development is progressing nicely, the organization's commercial readiness is lagging. Perhaps we need to spend more effort on identifying the target market or developing financial projections at this point.

Technology C has the opposite problem. Here we have done most of the readiness homework, but our technology is not developing fast enough. Both Technology B and C will not be ready for a timely commercialization event unless changes are made. For example, imagine Technology B is a new diagnostic sensor for hospital settings. The engineering team has a functional prototype, but the business team hasn't yet defined which customer segment (hospital labs, outpatient clinics, or emergency departments) offers the best fit. In contrast, Technology C might be a mobile health app with detailed market research, investor interest, and a launch plan, yet key software features are still unstable, and the product isn't ready for testing. In both cases, the TPM highlights mismatches that must be addressed to avoid delay or failure at launch.

Adoption Readiness Levels (ARL) and the Modified CARAT Tool

The Commercial Adoption Readiness Assessment Tool, or CARAT, was developed by a group of researchers at the U.S. Department of Energy's Office of Technology Transitions. The CARAT model provides a readiness "snapshot" of a technology but presents the results in a manner that is useful for managerial decisions. A number of other government laboratories, such as Sandia National Laboratories and Los Alamos National Laboratory, and global corporations, including ExxonMobil and Siemens Corporation, have adopted the CARAT tool within their "Adoption Readiness Level" (ARL) framework to examine a broader, more managerial perspective of a technology's potential for commercialization.

The CARAT model involves assessing the "risk" of a technology using 17 dimensions spanning four "core risk areas".[3] Each of these 17 dimensions is scored on a 3-point scale – "low, medium, or high".

Originally, the CARAT model was developed to analyze large-scale energy related systems. For our discussion, however, we have modified the CARAT model to be more applicable to a broader set of technologies than just the licensing of energy technologies. The core areas and the associated modified questions and their scoring are below.

Risk 1 – Value Proposition. Assesses the ability for a new technology to meet the functionality required by the market at a price point that customers are willing to pay, to meet the market demand. Under value proposition, there are three questions:

- VP Question 1: Delivered Costs – What are the risks associated with the delivered costs to customers (3-point scale, 1=low risk since proposed technology is more cost effective)
- VP Question 2. Functional Performance – What are the risks associated with meeting or exceeding the functional performance of competitive technologies, (3-point scale, 1=low risk since proposed technology provides more sustained performance)
- VP Question 3. Ease of Use – What are the risks associated with customers' use of the technology (3-point scale, 1= low risk since the technology is easier to use than competitive technologies)

Risk 2 – Market Acceptance. Captures the target market(s) demand characteristics and risks posed by existing players -- including competitors, customers, and other value chain players. Under market acceptance, there are three questions:

- MA Question 1: Market Openness – What are the risks associated with demand uncertainty (3-point scale, 1=low risk since there is a clear pathway to the market)
- MA Question 2. Market Size – What are the risks associated with the overall size of market (3-point scale, 1=low risk since market is both evident and large)
- MA Question 3. Downstream Value Chain – What are the risks associated with downstream players such as licensees, partners, and customers use of the technology (3-point scale, 1= low risk since the technology is easier to use than competitive technologies)

Risk 3 – Resource Maturity. Determines risks standing in the way of inputs that are needed to produce the technology solution. This includes the entity's infrastructure to support the technology development and the risks associated with manufacturing and supply chain. Under resource maturing, there are six questions:

- RM Question 1: Capital Flow – What are the risks associated with availability of capital to move a technology from its current stage to more advanced stages of technology development (3-point scale, 1=low risk since there is either sufficient internal or external funding available to support further development)
- RM Question 2. Project Development, Integration and Management – What are the risks associated with the organization's ability to execute the project (3-point scale, 1=low risk since the project management process being implemented is appropriate to the technology)
- RM Question 3. Infrastructure – What are the risks associated with physical systems in place to support the technology development (3-point scale, 1=low risk since the technology can be developed with the existing systems and resources our organization has in place)
- RM Question 4: Manufacturing and Supply Chain – What are the risks associated with the entities that will produce and market the end product (3-point scale, 1=low risk since technology can be deployed without extensive and new manufacturing or delivery systems)
- RM Question 5: Material Sourcing – What are the risks associated with the availability of critical materials (such as rare earth minerals, etc.) (3-point scale, 1=low risk since required input materials are readily available)
- RM Question 6: Workforce – What are the risks associated with the human capital required to develop the technology (3-point scale, 1=low risk since the existing team has the necessary skills to develop the technology to the required next phases)

Risk 4 – License to Operate. Identifies the societal (national, state, and local), non-economic risks that can hinder the deployment of technology. This dimension might be more relevant for large scale systems or developments, such as a building a new dam or solar power station, but still is worth considering for other types of technology. Under license to operate, there are four questions:

- LO Question 1: Regulatory and Standards Environment – What are the risks associated with availability of local, state, and federal regulations. This also includes existing technology standards (3-point scale, 1=low risk since the technology can be deployed without much interference or within existing/established design standards)
- LO Question 2. Policy Environment. What are the risks associated with future actions by local, state, and federal regulations, or changing standards within the industry (3-point scale, 1=low risk since regulations and standards are likely to stay the same)
- LO Question 3. Permitting – What are the risks associated with actually obtaining approvals for the use of the technology (3-point scale, 1=low risk since technology requires little or no permitting, or if permitting is required it is easy to obtain)
- LO Question 4: Environmental and Safety – What are the risks associated with potential hazardous side-effects (3-point scale, 1=low risk since technology has little inherent environmental or safety risk, or the risk can be easily mitigated)
- LO Question 5: Community Perception – What are the general perception that communities might have about our technology (3-point scale, 1=low risk since technology has little impact, or will be accepted by general society with strong support)

CARAT Model and Adoption Readiness Levels (ARL)

Using the modified CARAT model (see Figure 15.5), a scoring of 1 means low risk, while a 3 means high risk. The scoring instructions for the CARAT model are: Out of the 17 questions, total the number that are labelled high risk (with a score of "3") and total the number of dimensions that have a medium risk (with a score of "2"). Then look up the location on the following "Adoption Readiness Table" to obtain an "Adoption Readiness Level (ARL).

For example, suppose we are scoring a large scale, experimental offshore wind farm operation that we are considering in a particular location. We score each of the 17 questions related to this operation. From this scoring process, 2 of the questions scored "high risk", while 3 of the questions scored "medium risk". The remaining 12 questions scored a 'low risk". Based upon the CARAT model, this would rank a "5" ARL on the matrix, or a "medium readiness". This might suggest issues still need to be addressed by the management team or the technology, depending on the questions that did not score a "low risk".

No. of High Risk Dimensions

No. of Medium Risk Dimensions	0	1	2	3	4	5	6	7	8+
0	9	8	7	5	3	1	1	1	1
1	8	7	6	4	2	1	1	1	1
2	8	7	6	4	2	1	1	1	1
3	7	6	5	3	1	1	1	1	1
4	7	6	5	3	1	1	1	1	1
5	6	5	4	2	1	1	1	1	1
6	5	4	3	1	1	1	1	1	1
7	3	2	1	1	1	1	1	1	1
8+	1	1	1	1	1	1	1	1	1

1-3 = Low Readiness

4-6 = Medium Readiness

7-9 = High Readiness

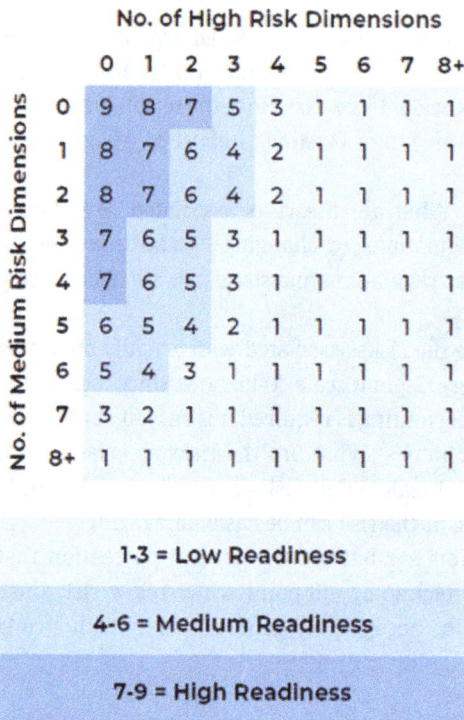

Figure 15.5: A modified CARAT model for scoring Adoption Readiness Levels.

The modified CARAT model provides not only an assessment of technology adoption readiness for a technology but also identifies the dimensions where additional managerial effort needs to take place (the dimensions with high-risk scores).

CARAT Model and Technology Portfolios

Like the Technology Progress Matrix (TPM), the CARAT model's adoption readiness table can also be used in a technology portfolio assessment, when entities might have multiple technologies being developed at the same time, and there is a desire to visualize the progression of these technologies toward deployment. In this portfolio plot, a technology's TRL is plotted against the technology adoption readiness level (ARL).

This matrix can also be used as a portfolio management tool, allowing teams to visualize the position of multiple technologies relative to both technical and adoption readiness. In this format, each technology is represented as a "bubble", with the size of the bubble reflecting either the investment made or the expected financial return from that program. When displayed together, the matrix can help leaders identify which technologies are progressing appropriately, which are lagging in either technical development or market readiness, and where additional resources or strategic adjustments may be needed. For example, if a technology appears high on the TRL axis but low on the ARL axis, it may signal that more effort is needed on market validation, user engagement, or regulatory planning before launch. In response, management might delay further investment in engineering and reallocate resources toward building out the commercialization strategy.

Concluding Insights

The models and tools discussed in this chapter offer structured ways to assess and manage the commercialization readiness of technologies and systems. All of the tools discussed in this chapter are being used extensively by various laboratories, private sector corporations, and government agencies to evaluate the broader pictures of an

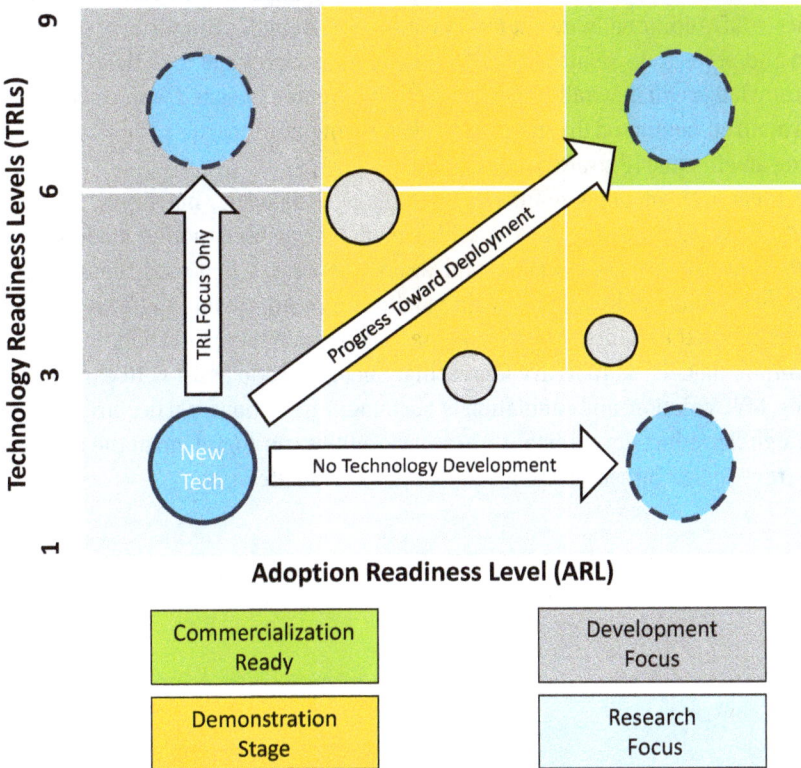

Figure 15.6: CARAT model used for technology portfolio assessment.

organization's readiness to develop and ultimately commercialize technologies in a timely manner.

Whether using BRLs, KTH's Innovation Readiness Levels, various models of Commercialization Readiness Levels (CRLs), the CARAT model, or the Technology Progression Matrix (TPM), each tool provides a structured way to assess organizational and technical development. These frameworks help evaluate progress and identify gaps that may hinder successful market entry.

They are also excellent presentation tools for both internal management and external stakeholders. They provide a succinct method to visualize a technology's progress toward development or commercialization. These tools summarize the technology development progress, identify if things are following the planned trajectory, or suggest if certain remedial actions need to be taken.

These readiness tools also work hand in hand with the information obtained from many of the topics discussed earlier in this book. Much of the scoring in these broader readiness models draws on a wide range of strategic inputs. These include knowledge about competitive technologies and customer or user preferences. They also encompass insights into market size, the likelihood of product acceptance, and the functionality of the product itself. Additionally, evaluators consider the strength of intellectual property protection and projections related to future financial resources and cash flow.

This knowledge will inevitably come from the elements associated with performing both a formalized commercialization study, developing appropriate pro-formas, and establishing an effective IP strategy.

These tools are not one-size-fits-all. Technology developers, managers, support teams, and consultants should consider which model, or combination of models, best aligns with their specific needs and organizational context. When used thoughtfully, these frameworks can guide decision-making, allocate resources more effectively, and ultimately improve the chances of successful technology commercialization.

In addition, modern AI tools are increasingly being used to assist with early-stage prototyping, MVP creation, and simulation of customer interactions, particularly in software and digital product development. These capabilities can complement the broader readiness frameworks by accelerating early validation and iteration.

Chapter 16
Managing Technology: Lean Approaches, Design Thinking, and System Failures

This Chapter
- Introduces two widely used models for managing technology development: Lean Technology Development and Design Thinking.
- Highlights specific tools and best practices associated with both the lean and design approaches.
- Covers the fundamentals of system failure analysis and its relevance to technology development.

Management Tools Covered in This Chapter
- Business Model Canvas
- Minimal Viable Product design
- Split Prototype Testing
- Discovery and Pivoting Team Exercise Tools
- Design Thinking tools, such as empathy maps
- Design Sprints
- System Failure Tools, such as the "5 Whys" and "Cause and Effect Maps"

! **INSIGHT**

A number of different managerial approaches have been developed to assist the technology development and commercialization process. These approaches take a more holistic and integrative view of the problem.

These concepts – lean entrepreneurship, design thinking, and systems-based management – represent important approaches to guiding technology development and commercialization. Each offers a distinct perspective, grounded in both theory and practice. Together, they have generated a substantial body of literature that can inform strategic planning and day-to-day decision-making. They are often taught as separate classes in engineering, architecture, and business. There are numerous training and certification programs in each of these three areas. And there are consultants who specialize in these three areas.

Introduction

This is the second chapter where we examine technology development and commercialization from a more holistic and integrative management perspective. The first of these two chapters considered the idea of integrative adoption and commercial readiness models and how to analyze and present a number of organizational dimensions that all need to align in order to have a successful technology project.

https://doi.org/10.1515/9783111684420-017

The present chapter focuses on three important and widely used management-oriented models related to technology development. First, we discuss the idea of lean technology development, which has its roots in the well-established lean start-up approaches often taught in modern entrepreneurship classes. The second approach is known as "design thinking". Design thinking represents a holistic approach to developing and commercializing technologies, particularly for the end-user or consumer markets. Design thinking includes a wide range of managerial tools that support each step of the process. The final section reviews some of the basic concepts of failure analysis. Complex systems regularly fail, whether the system is a technology, an organization, or a society. Systems analysis, and its component parts of system failure analysis, is a huge field of study. We only touch on some of the most relevant issues related to our topic. Systems and failure analysis is regularly taught in both engineering programs and technology management classes offered in business schools.

Lean Technology Development

A popular managerial approach in entrepreneurship is the notion of "lean startups". The importance of thinking about developing technologies and entrepreneurial efforts in a highly efficient or "lean" manner was originally uncovered in several empirical studies of entrepreneurial behavior during the 1980s and 1990s. These empirical studies found that many successful start-up enterprises were using lean approaches when developing and commercializing their technologies. This is not surprising since many technology start-ups have very limited resources and need to allocate their efforts to only the most important issues. One of its core principles, the Build-Measure-Learn feedback loop, emphasizes rapid prototyping, early testing of assumptions, and iterative learning. While TRLs and readiness models provide a strategic overview of technical and organizational progress, the Build-Measure-Learn cycle helps teams quickly validate market assumptions and adjust before significant resources are committed. Used together, these approaches provide a more responsive and well-informed path to commercialization

Although many technology-oriented entrepreneurial firms had been applying lean principles for decades, the concept was refined and brought into the mainstream by Eric Ries in his 2011 best-selling book, *The Lean Startup*.[1] Around the same time, Alex Osterwalder and Yves Pigneur introduced two other influential works – *Business Model Generation*[2] and *Value Proposition Design*[3] – which provided additional structure to lean thinking by offering practical tools for business model development and customer engagement. Together, these books introduced a number of widely adopted tools and concepts that have become foundational in modern technology development and commercialization. The most critical contributions include: (1) the Business Model and Value Proposition Canvas, (2) the concept of the Minimum Viable Product (MVP), (3) split testing, (4) purposeful pivoting, and (5) engaging with customers as early as possible. Each of these concepts is further explored in this chapter in the context of technology development and commercialization.

Lean Technology Development: Business Model Canvas (MBC). Variations of the business model canvas quickly emerged as it became clear that traditional business plans developed by entrepreneurial start-ups were often too lengthy and limited in practical application. Since this time, particularly after publication of Osterwalder and Pigneur's books, business canvas applications have gained a number of advocates and are now taught extensively in entrepreneurship classes throughout the world.

The idea behind the business model canvas is relatively simple – provide a 1-page visualization of the key dimensions that go into developing a successful business model for success (see Figure 16.1). The key dimensions in the business model canvas are:

1) Customer Segments
2) Value Proposition
3) Customer Relationships
4) Channels
5) Revenue Streams
6) Key Activities
7) Key Partners
8) Resource Requirements
9) Cost Structure

Each of these nine dimensions is represented in a box format in the canvas. Management can use the business model canvas as a tool any time during the technology development process, particularly when key resources and strategic decisions need to be made.

There are a number of business canvas models available. Many can be downloaded from the web, with prompts and questions. Some variations sub-divide the canvas boxes. Other variations focus on industry-specific definitions and terminology. However, all of the canvas models have the same objective – to visualize the key components for decision-making.

For technology development purposes, it is helpful to incorporate three types of posts or comments into the canvas. First, identify assumptions. These should always be questioned and supported with evidence. Second, identify data, such as information on market size, growth trends, and specific technology requirements. Finally, identify decisions that have been made, including resource allocations, the need for additional research, or the possibility of pivoting to new markets.

A business model canvas exercise for technology development is generally performed by a small, interdisciplinary team at different stages in the technology development process. Much of the data and information in a business model canvas will be obtained by the firm's commercialization and VoC studies. However, unlike the

Key Partners	Key Activities		Customer Relationships	Customer Segments
Who are the key partners and suppliers?	**Key Activities** What key activities do our value propositions require?	**Value Propositions** What value do we offer? What problems do we solve for our customers?	**Customer Relationships** How do we maximize our key relationships?	**Customer Segments** What are the potential niches and their needs?
	Key Resources What physical, human, financial and IP resources do we need?		**Channels** What are the key channels? How do we effectively reach them?	
Cost Structure Have we identified all costs? What are the key cost drivers, and can we approach things in a lean manner?			**Revenue Streams** What are the key purchase attributes? Do we have a well-defined revenue model?	

Figure 16.1: The Business Model Canvas. Source: Osterwalder and Pigneur 2010.

commercialization and VoC studies, the idea of the business model canvas is to visually and concisely present the critical information for purposes of decision making.

Lean Technology Development: Minimum Viable Product (MVP). The idea of a minimum viable product, or MVP, has become one of the keys to a lean approach to technology development. Essentially, the MVP strategy is to produce a bare early-stage field prototype, with just enough features that potential customers can provide feedback. With this feedback, the final technology can be developed with a focus on the customer requirements.

Developing MVPs saves time and resources, so that the design effort is only on key functionality requirements of the technology from the perspective of the customers. Ultimately, the aim of the MVP is to obtain early customer feedback during the technology development process.

In fact, customers feedback is the whole purpose behind the MVP concept. Within the TRL framework, the MVP is a type of early-stage field prototype (after a lab-prototype), but with a minimal set of required features. The focus on functionality is centered around the customer's core requirements, rather than attempting to address every possible need. Putting an MVP into the hands of a very few select customers, or internal users, might also be considered a form of "alpha testing", prior to a full-blown beta-test. MVPs are typically not designed as a final beta-test product.

Lean Technology Development Principle: Engaging with Customers as Early as Possible. Another key concept of lean approaches to technology development is to engage with customers as early as possible. This is actually an important part of the quick-look feasibility or commercialization study discussed earlier in the book.

Customer and user feedback throughout the full technology development process is always considered a best practices policy. This is true whether the customer is a system developer that will use your technology as a component within a larger system, or whether your technology is being commercialized as a product to the end-use market.

Customer and user feedback throughout the full technology development process is always considered a best practices strategy.

Lean Technology Development Principle: Split Testing. Split testing, also sometimes called A/B testing, is part of validating the learning process in a lean environment. Technology development inevitably involves developing different generations of prototypes. These prototypes can be dummy prototypes, lab prototypes, minimum viable product prototypes, or later field prototypes. Best practices in technology development indicate the need to constantly obtain feedback from potential customers during the technology development cycle by using these prototypes in focus groups and other forms of market research.

However, there might be a bias in only showing one prototype model, regardless of its stage of development. The idea of split testing is to create two different versions of a prototype. These versions can vary on any appropriate dimension that you think is important, such as shape of the technology, possible tradeoffs in functionality along different performance dimensions, etc. The differences need to be based on the critical dimension or functionality you want to test and obtain customer feedback on. Split testing can be used at any stage of prototype development to obtain feedback. Split testing is regularly used for physical products, but can also be effectively used for mobile apps and software technologies.

Split testing normally involves segmenting the customer sample, having two different focus groups or customer samples, one for each version. However, sometimes the two models can be shown to the same customer group. Feedback is then obtained, verbally in interviews, through questionnaires, or by tracking the actual use of the technology.

Split testing is particularly useful when developing a technology for the end-user market, although occasionally it can be used when developing a component technology for larger system developers when there are tradeoffs between performance dimensions.

Lean Technology Development Principle: Purposeful Pivoting. Successful technology commercialization often requires pivoting. In fact, in the modern world of quick innovation and fast technological change, pivoting has become a foundational concept of technology development and commercialization. Eric Reis, in his Lean Start-up book, aptly uses the analogy of a steering wheel, with a pivot as a "sharp turn" to change directions.

The need to pivot can be grounded in various issues, such as the desire to identify new markets for the technology, or the need to radically change the functionality of the technology due to competitive products or changing needs of the marketplace. In fact, we have provided a whole chapter discussing pivots and offered many examples where pivots become the key to successful commercialization.

Pivoting is not easy however. There are two major barriers to pivoting. The first barrier is psychological in nature. Organizations, and people, after investing significant time, effort, and resources in a technology tend to be emotionally tied to the technology which has its roots in the past. People and organizations simply become entrenched in their ways. This appears particularly true with engineers and design experts that have possibly committed their careers to a particular technological approach or market. However, the past always represents a sunk cost. In technology development, the key is to think of the future, but this is often difficult, given the powerful reality of sunk costs that encourage people to wear blinders.

The second barrier to pivoting is simply not knowing what to pivot to. Identifying new markets for an existing technology in development or redefining the functionality of a non-competitive technology already in the market requires research, knowledge, and data. Identifying the need to pivot, and in what direction, is, in fact, part of the purpose behind a commercialization or feasibility study.

However, within the Lean Technology Development process there are various tools that might help in thinking about the need to pivot. These might include:

1) **Pivot Tool – Continuous updating of the underlying commercialization study**. Updating commercialization plans should generally be performed by independent reviewers since they do not have a biased perspective toward a particular solution.
2) **Pivot Tool – Use AI**. Asking AI appropriate questions about competitors, functionality, or new markets might encourage thinking about the need to potentially pivot.
3) **Pivot Tool – Use of well-established management tools in order to stimulate innovation and creativity in decision-making**. These tools are typically used in 2-to-4-hour training sessions with the project team. By design, these innovation and creativity decision tools can help to break people from their established gestalt or thinking paradigm. Some of the most effective innovation tools for technology pivot identification are:
   a) Formalized Brainstorming – Everybody offers ideas without comments, support, or criticisms – moderator puts all ideas on table for future discussion.
   b) Six Thinking Hats – moderator uses colored hats (or some other colored device if hats seem too "corny") to restrict discussion to only certain types of comments. Moderator will manage these comments and place them on a board. A typical exercise might be.

      White Hat – focus on information and data
      Red Hat – put forth feelings and intuitions without justification

Black Hat – critical judgment
Yellow Hat – positive statements and benefits, nothing negative
Green Hat – creative brainstorming, possible pivots
Blue Hat – summaries and overviews

Six hat thinking, or similar, exercises have been successfully used to identify successful pivots in a number of real-life cases. Identifying possible pivots typically begins with "green hat" brainstorming to generate new ideas, followed by "yellow hat" thinking to explore the potential benefits of those ideas. This is then supported by "white hat" contributions, which focus strictly on facts, existing data, or information that still needs to be gathered.

c) Filament or Tree Branch Thinking. In this approach, the moderator begins by recording a single idea – often generated through brainstorming – and then guides the group in expanding only that idea. Additional thoughts are built out as branches stemming from the original concept, creating a series of sub-ideas. Once discussion on one branch is exhausted, the moderator introduces a new core idea and repeats the process. The result is a visual map resembling a tree, with multiple branches and sub-branches illustrating the evolution of each idea.

Design Thinking

Design thinking has its roots in early systems analysis dating back decades. Design thinking, in its most basic form, represents an interactive, systematic approach to identifying value and then integrates these values into the design. Its purpose is to specifically understand the key requirements of your customers using a formal set of specific tools, challenge assumptions, redefine problems, and then create innovative solutions or prototypes that can be tested. The overall intention of design thinking is to identify alternative, innovative, and entrepreneurial types of strategies and solutions that are not readily available with an initial understanding of the situation. For this reason, design thinking can also be used to identify possible new markets or pivots.

It is sometimes argued that design thinking has its foundation in the idea of "Wicked Problems". The term "Wicked Problems" was coined in the 1960s with the rise of new forces that were creating major social problems, such as the civil rights movement, rising homelessness, rapidly increasing income inequalities, the introduction of new technologies, and the ongoing problems of Vietnam and the cold war. A "Wicked Problem" can be defined as a complex problem that is difficult or near impossible to solve due to its complex, interconnected, evolving, and seemingly contradictory nature.

By the 1970s design thinking as a formal concept with its evolving set of tools started to emerge. Originally design thinking was used in large-scale systems design, particularly in the architectural fields. In 1992 Richard Buchanan published an often-cited article titled "Wicked Problems in Design Thinking".[4] After this, people started to see design thinking as an important concept for the overall problem of technology development and commercialization. By the 2000s design thinking was taught in many universities throughout the world. In fact, some university entrepreneurship programs were founded on the idea of design thinking and still teach technology entrepreneurship from this perspective.

One might consider understanding the need to "pivot" to a new idea, market, or technology as a "Wicked Problem". Perhaps even the larger process of developing a technology, and then successfully commercializing the technology has elements of a "Wicked Problem" – it is highly complex with many unknown and interconnected sub-problems.

Design thinking is built around a five-stage process: empathize, define the problem, ideate, prototype, and test (see Figure 16.2). While this sequence closely aligns with many of the technology development and commercialization practices discussed throughout this book, what sets design thinking apart is its structured use of specific tools tailored to support each stage of the process.

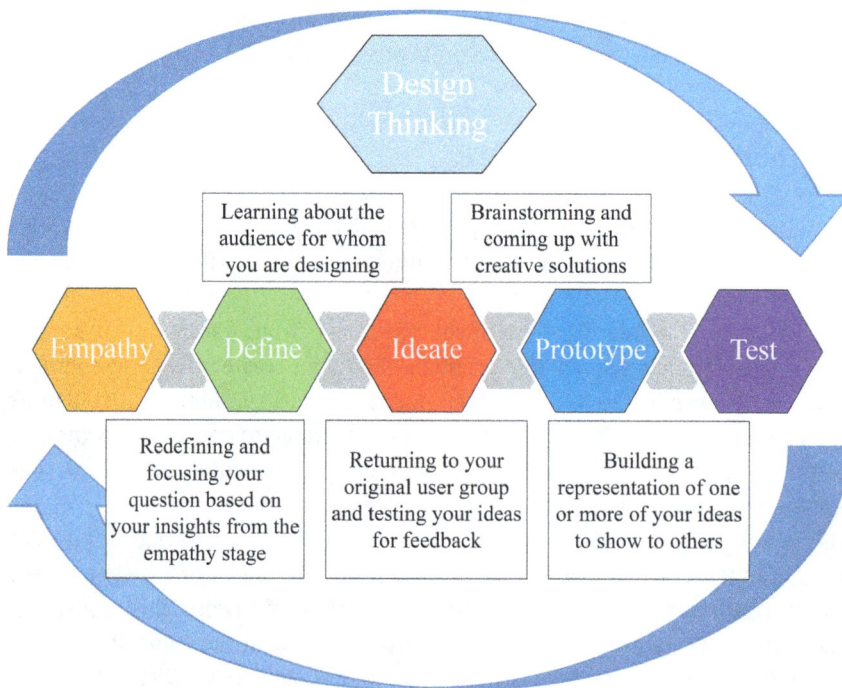

Figure 16.2: The five-stage Design Thinking process.

Design thinking ultimately starts with the customers' needs and requirements and then works backward from this analysis. Given the emphasis and tools used in design thinking, the design thinking model is generally considered most appropriate to developing technologies sold into the consumer or end user market where the markets can be highly fragmented, and the needs, desire, and requirements of different customers are hard to determine. It can also be effectively used when developing a larger technology system, or its critical components, that interfaces with humans. This is why design thinking originally became very popular in the architectural fields.

Design thinking in its purest form is very tool oriented. We will discuss only a few of the tools in this chapter.

Stage 1: Empathize

Empathizing is the first stage in the design thinking process. Because this stage focuses on deeply understanding user needs and experiences, design thinking tends to be especially well-suited for end-user or consumer product markets. It is less commonly applied in contexts where the product requirements are already well-defined by a system developer, such as in large, established systems. However, if the component involves more human interface with the large system, design thinking tools might be very effective. An example of humans interfacing within a large system is how electric car drivers use and access the in-car computer screens, or how to best design the layout or ergonomics of kitchen utensils.

Tool: Empathy Maps. Empathy mapping starts with the idea that in order to develop a technology, or any product or service, the starting point must be "empathy". Empathy essentially means to see the world through "other people's eyes". Empathy requires you to learn about the difficulties people face and then uncover their latent (hidden) views and desires that explain their behaviors. The common tool used in this first step of design thinking is the "empathy map" (see Figure 16.3).

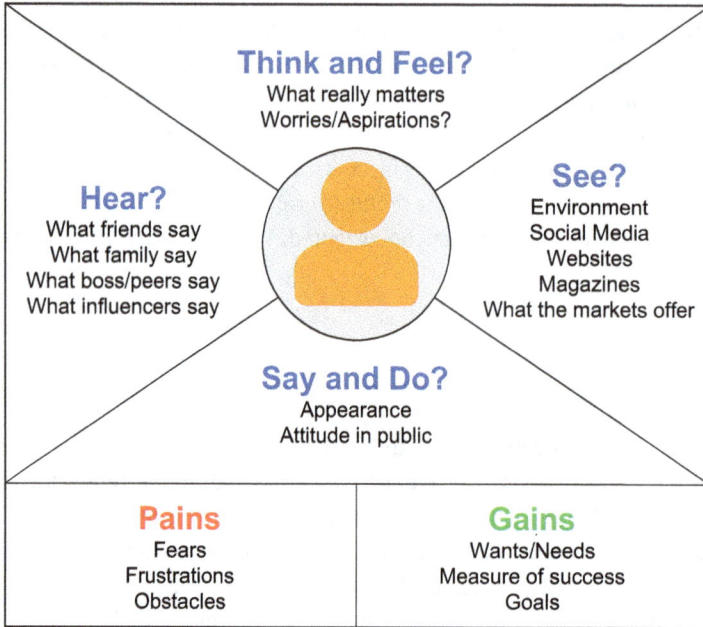

Think and Feel?
What really matters
Worries/Aspirations?

See?
Environment
Social Media
Websites
Magazines
What the markets offer

Hear?
What friends say
What family say
What boss/peers say
What influencers say

Say and Do?
Appearance
Attitude in public

Pains
Fears
Frustrations
Obstacles

Gains
Wants/Needs
Measure of success
Goals

Figure 16.3: The Design Thinking Empathy Map.

Developing an empathy map for customers is much more than simple market research or focus groups. Empathy maps attempt to uncover the hidden dimensions of needs using different techniques. Many of the modern design thinking tools have their origin in work by the Stanford d.school, established in the 1980s. Establishing an empathy map results from a combination of "observe, engage, and immerse", or OEI.

Observe: Shadowing potential customers as they go about the process of solving problems is a common tool for observing,

Engage: The engagement component comes from interacting with, and interviewing, potential customers. Empathy interviews are typically 20-minute, one-on-one interviews with open-ended questions.

Immerse: This involves attempting to solve a customer's problem yourself. Essentially it means putting yourself into the customers "shoes". This is different from shadowing. Immersion means using the technology, or current alternatives, yourself.

An example of an empathy map for a 3D printer is seen in Figure 16.4.

Scenario: Buying a New 3-D Printer
Interview: Oliver Galbraith, IV

Think and Feel

Feels like current 3D printer is too slow

Feels overwhelmed by the 3D printer choices available

"I hope I make the right choice"

Hear

Friend says, *"I chose my 3D printer because it's fast"*

School says, *"We chose our 3D printers because they are easy to use"*

Reviews say, *"Bamboo Labs 3D printers are best for hobbyists"*

See

See advertisements for newer and faster 3D printers

See 3D printed creations online that exceed current capabilities

See videos online of 3D printer reviews

Say and Do

"It needs to be affordable"

"It needs to be better than my current 3D printer"

Timelessly searches customer and product reviews

Pains

3D Printer is too slow

Need a new 3D printer to complete large projects

Gains

Wants a 3D printer with little setup

Will pay more for a 3D printer if proofed

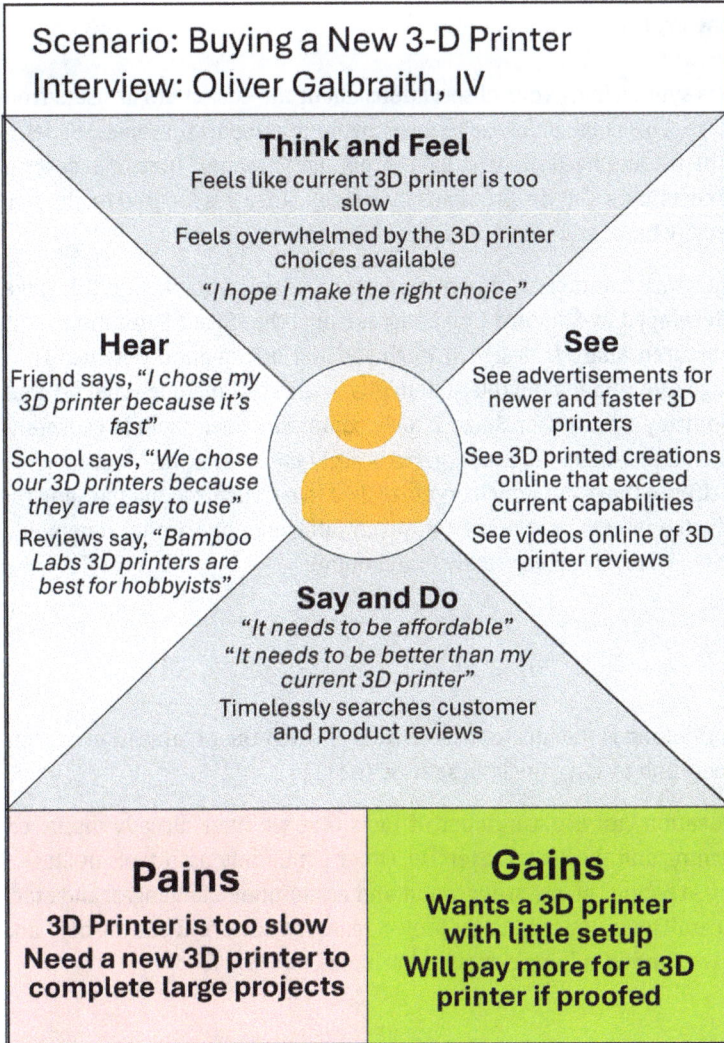

Figure 16.4: Sample Design Thinking empathy map.

Stage 2: Define the Problem

This stage involves synthesizing your observations about the customers or users from the Empathize stage. This stage involves: a) focusing on the important issues, b) defining the "real" problems that need solving, and c) creating "Personas" (personal descriptions of different customers and the problems they face). Stage 2 is focused on the four "whys" – who, what, where, and why.

Stage 2 Tools. There are a number of design management tools available for this stage. One of the tools developed by Stanford University is called the "Space Saturation Tool". This tool is a structured analysis designed to cluster the information obtained from the empathize stage into understandable statements. It also can include timeline analysis and a user journey map. Other Stage 2 tools commonly used include cause and effect tools (such as a fish-bone diagram), various "root cause analysis" tools such as the 5WHYS tool, Affinity Diagrams which organize data in a structured manner, and the SCAMPER tool which analyzes problems from seven different opportunity statements. These and other Stage 2 tools can be readily found online.

Stage 3: Ideate

Stage 3 in design thinking is the ideation stage. This is when the organization concentrates on idea generation to solve the issues raised in Stage 2.

Stage 3 Tools. Ideation can use a number of tools that we have already discussed, such as brainstorming and the six hat exercise. Other commonly used tools in Stage 3 of design thinking are mind maps, provocation and assumption challenges, and story boarding. These are all tools designed to get project teams to think "outside the box" and establish innovative ways of solving customer problems.

Stage 4: Prototyping

The prototype or develop phase of technology development has been discussed extensively in this book. Prototyping is a fundamental step in any technology development process. Design thinking places an emphasis on "rapid prototyping". Similar to the idea of a "minimum viable product", in design thinking stage 4 is to create prototypes based on the outcome of stage 3, ideation. Design thinking relies heavily on feedback loops. Prototypes are quickly tested with customer groups in a process similar to alpha testing, followed by feedback, iteration, and retesting of new versions.

Stage 4 Tools. As with all the steps in design thinking, a number of tools have been developed to assist in this process. Design thinking makes extensive use of 3-D printing technology and clay prototypes in order to develop what we refer to as "dummy prototypes" in this book. These prototypes are also commonly called "low fidelity" prototypes in the design thinking community. Another low fidelity prototype includes wireframing (paper or digital drawing, or pictures such as mobile app development) and mockups. "High fidelity", however, are prototypes that have certain lab or field functionalities where actual requirements can be tested and assessed.

Stage 5: Test and Feedback

The final stage in the design thinking process is testing. This stage involves a variety of methods, such as focus groups to test both low-fidelity prototypes and high-fidelity prototypes, early-stage field testing (alpha testing), as well as quick beta-testing.

The key to understanding the design thinking process is that Stage 4 and Stage 5 are highly linked, where prototypes are rapidly developed and immediately tested, and then feedback is provided to enhance and improve the prototypes for another round of testing. In essence, design thinking is designed to be nonlinear in that it represents a continuous process of feedback between all five stages of the process.

Design Thinking: Some Thoughts

Design thinking appears to be a powerful method to identify problems and develop solutions. There are numerous examples where technologies have been developed and successfully commercialized using design thinking.

However, design thinking has perhaps lost some of its luster in the minds of some due to its heavy reliance on a number of complex tools and the formality by which design thinking is often implemented. Lean concepts and tools, such as the business canvas model; and the idea of a minimum viable product, are often seen as competitive tools to design thinking.

However, some design thinking tools are still highly relevant to technology development and commercialization. Organizations are still using many of the design thinking tools, but not necessarily following the structured five steps in detail.

The real contribution of design thinking in modern technology development is perhaps in two areas. The first contribution of design thinking to modern technology development is the use of empathy tools. Gaining a deeper understanding of the challenges faced by potential customers and users, including uncovering hidden or latent issues, can be a powerful step in the development process. The second contribution of design thinking is perhaps the notion of multiple and rapid prototyping with continuous feedback loops.

As time to market becomes more and more important in the modern world of technology, rapid prototyping is now almost a requirement. This is when a Design Sprint might be appropriate.

Design Sprints

When rapid prototyping is required, perhaps one of the most useful recent design thinking concepts is the idea of "Design Sprints". Design Sprints are intensive 3-to-5-day exercises designed to quickly implement all five stages of design thinking in a short period of time. While using many of the design thinking tools described above, the Design Sprint will accelerate the process. For example, the final testing stage might involve only a few customers, or perhaps other employees of the organization. A typical 4-day Design Sprint is shown below in Figure 16.5.

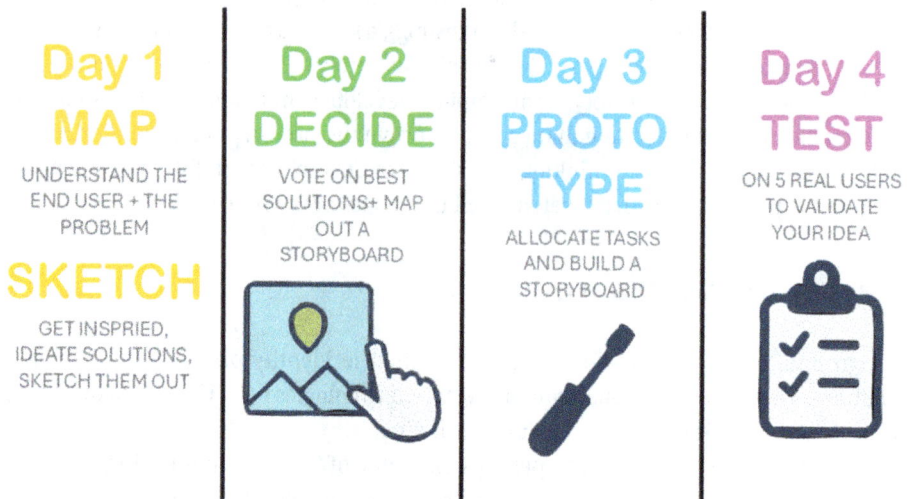

| Day 1 | Day 2 | Day 3 | Day 4 |
| MAP | DECIDE | PROTO TYPE | TEST |

Figure 16.5: Design Sprint process for rapid prototyping.

Design Sprints can be highly effective, but there are some requirements. First, it involves a dedicated chunk of time where the development team focuses entirely on the process. Second, it needs to be properly managed by the team leader. Oftentimes an external Design Sprint expert or consultant will be contracted to manage the Design Sprint. Third, the design team must be willing to participate fully. Some of the design thinking tools might seem a little silly at times, but in order for the Design Sprint to work, everybody needs to be engaged. Remote Design Sprints can also be done, but a probably not as effective as face-to-face Design Sprint experiences.

Design thinking cannot solve all problems, or even most technology design issues. However, when a technology is aimed at the end-user or consumer market or involves significant human interaction, design thinking tools can offer valuable managerial insights and applications.

Programs to Encourage and Manage Technology Entrepreneurship

While the basic business canvas model and design thinking process have strong followings, a number of other programs have been designed to guide technology entrepreneurs through the process of designing, developing and launching products and technologies. Most of these programs represent variations or combinations of major components disused in this book – utilizing some variation of the business canvas model, following the basic tenets of design thinking, that is, specifically designing a technology for customers' needs, a strong focus on applying Voice of the Customer tools to identify these often hidden needs, working with a philosophy of agile and lean design and engineering to reduce time to market, and a continuous focus on finding opportunity even if that requires pivoting.

Some of these models offer an effective way of formalizing thinking at the individual level, or for instructional purposes, while others represent packaged, intense, collaborative and immersive training programs for technology-based start-ups that may last several months. In this section we discuss several different models as examples. The IDEATE approach, for example, represents more of a formalized approach to developing an entrepreneurial way of thinking, while the "I-Corps™" program represents a series of training modules designed to assist "Deep" technology developers to bring their technology closer to commercialization. Accelerators are formal, high immersive and networked programs that focus on getting selected technology start-ups to the point of pitching investors and product launch. These are just a few examples of many different approaches that have been developed by government entities, academics researchers, popular writers, and consultants, to assist in this exciting, but difficult process.

IDEATE: A Model for Entrepreneurial Thinking

IDEATE stands for Identify, Discover, Enhance, Anticipate, Target, Evaluate. IDEATE can be used as an approach for any entrepreneurial effort but has been used successfully for a number of technology start-ups. It was originally developed by Dan Cohen, Gregory Pool and Heidi Neck, and has been successfully implemented at Wake Forest University and other university entrepreneurship programs (see Figure 16.6).[5] The IDEATE approach is essentially a combination of Design Thinking and a modified Canvas Board with a focus on finding and solving "migraine" headache problems. "Migraine" headache problems are the key significant problems confronting customers. The IDEATE approach then provides a formalized process of designing a solution to these "migraine" problems by defining the steps and posing questions.

IDEATE Model of Technology and Entrepreneurial Thinking	
Identify	• Identify a "migraine headache" problem worth solving. • Distinguish between high-quality, "exemplar" opportunities and low-quality, uninspired ideas. • Begin to develop a sense of what makes ideas valuable. versus ideas that are not worth the time and effort to explore.
Discover	• Actively search for opportunities in problem-rich environments. • Leverage your passions and areas of extreme curiosity to spot problems. • Explore current trends that are getting a lot of attention.
Enhance	• Add innovation and novelty to enhance existing opportunities • Develop a "value for all" mentality to ensure all stakeholders are invested in your opportunity. • Experiment with alternative business models to increase value.
Anticipate	• Use the four sources of change to anticipate new opportunities: social and demographic, technological, political, and regulatory. • Examine how these changes affect existing markets and create new markets. Anticipate customer needs that are likely to emerge as a result of future changes.
Target	• Identify target customers and understand their unmet needs. • Explore and connect with early adopters to better understand why they are buying and what resonates most with them. • Personify your ideal or typical customer.
Evaluate	• Practice scoring, selecting, and defending high-quality ideas. • Circumvent confirmation bias and other cognitive biases to avoid falling in love with bad ideas. • Avoid the excessive optimism trap and use critical thinking to evaluate ideas.
Source: Cohen, Pool and Neck	

Figure 16.6: The IDEATE Framework. Source: Cohen, Pool and Neck.

I-Corp Training: A Model for Technology Start-Up Training

The I-Corps™ program was originally developed by the U.S. National Science Foundation to accelerate basic research projects toward commercialization. The success rate appears impressive, with a claim that 50% of the teams participating in I-Corp programs have resulted in actual start-ups.

The I-Corps™ model is to have 20 or 30 teams as a training cohort, which are then hosted by specialized I-Corps™ Hubs within different geographical areas. Many of the hosting organizations are university entrepreneurship programs that have been certified by I-Corps™. Teams participating in I-Corps™ training include private organizations and government agencies, with a focus on scientist and engineers that are developing technologies in university laboratories. The I-Corps™ focus is to identify "Deep

Technologies" with high potential impact and move these deep technologies toward commercialization.

The training model used by I-Corps™ tends to be a somewhat standard entrepreneurship model, utilizing many of the topics covered in this book. The key focus is on customer discovery and then developing a path toward commercialization.

The core modules include:

a) Lean LaunchPad Methodology
b) Business Model Canvas
c) Customer Discovery (particularly using Voice of the Customer tools)
d) Developing an Entrepreneurial Mindset
e) Understanding the Commercialization Process

In addition, I-Corps™ incorporates other training topics including communicating with customers and industry stakeholders, identifying opportuning, and applying for SBIR/STTR grants.

The LeanLauch Pad is the foundational framework to establish entrepreneurial thinking in the I-Corps™ program. The LeanLauch Pad process was invented by Steve Bank with a focus on three components: first, using the business model canvas to organize and challenge the thinking process (discuss earlier); second, an aggressive Voice of the Customer process which involves establishing untested hypotheses about the customers and then testing these hypotheses with customers; and third, making sure the design and engineering process is highly agile and can quickly adapt to new ideas and pivoting.

Technology Accelerator Programs: A Model of Immersive Development

Technology accelerators programs are designed to immerse technology developers and early-stage start-ups in an environment that encourages effective and synergistic progress toward commercialization. The actual designs of accelerators are wide and varied. Large and small, accelerators number in the thousands. Almost all major universities have at least one accelerator program. Local start-up companies can become involved. Some universities also have accelerator programs focused on student and faculty developed technology. The design of these accelerators varies in nature, but they often offer a common space for discussions and information exchange, as well as a focused sequence of training and coordination to encourage commercialization effort. These accelerators also offer access to prototyping and fabrication labs, and an opportunity to pitch to investors and technology system integrators.

There are also thousands of private or independent accelerator programs. Some of these accelerators are associated with large venture capital firms. Many of the independent accelerators have a strong international presence and offer programs around the globe. The most well-known accelerators are Techstars, Y Combinator, 500 Global,

PURDUE INNOVATES

Purdue University is one of the world's leaders in commercializing early technologies. Purdue University's accelerator is called the "Purdue Innovate" or PI Accelerator. It is a 3-month program where "participants will gain tailored strategic support and access to a powerful network of world-class mentors, corporate partners, investors, and alumni, empowering them to reach key business milestones and scale their companies". The PI Accelerator involves three phases

Phase 1: **Mentorship & Strategy Development**. Cohort sessions where participates start to refine their business plan.

Phase 2: **Customer Discovery & Validation.** Period of intense effort to understand the voice of the customer.

Phase 3: **Investor Readiness & Demo Day:** Opportunity to design an effective pitch deck, and actually pitch the business to investors and system developers.

Plug and Play, AngelPad, and Seedcamp. There are many other well recognized accelerators. Some accelerators specialize in certain industry segments, such as FinTech or biotech, while others are more generalized. Some accelerators are small, focused on one geographical area, while others are global in reach. Typically, these accelerators take applications, select applicants that have good potential, and then form a cohort. As part of the accelerator process, many of the largest accelerators also provide initial seed money in exchange for a small equity position in the start-up. These independent accelerators are known for intensive mentorship, access to funding, and working with strong networks of investors and industry experts that can assist early-stage technology businesses. These types of accelerators are often built around a 10 to 13-week experience. Some accelerators require residency in a high-tech hub, such as Silicon Valley, while other accelerators have their own co-working spaces. Some of the most well-known tech start-ups have benefited from these accelerators.

Governments around the world have also realized the importance of tech entrepreneurship accelerators. In the United States, for example, the National Oceanic and Atmospheric Administration (NOAA) supports accelerators that focus on developing technologies in ocean and related industries of the blue economy. There are government-sponsored accelerator programs that focus on historically under-resourced populations and communities. Some large government laboratories, such as Los Alamos National Laboratories in New Mexico, now also have accelerator programs. Almost all developed countries have similar government-supported accelerators. Germany, for example, has a number of government-sponsored accelerators, such as Start2 and the German Accelerators. Since these accelerators are government-funded, they generally provide seed funding or development grants, but don't take any equity in return – just a contractual promise to make the best effort to commercialize the technology. In addition, several cities have sponsored accelerator programs to encourage technology and entrepreneurial development within their communities.

Simply put, there is a huge variety of technology-oriented entrepreneurship support programs, ranging in the level, type, length, and format of training offered. The sponsors of these support programs can be quite creative in their names, such as the University of California San Diego's "Basement" for student start-ups and San Diego State Universiy's "Zip Launchpad" during the summers. Some programs, often called "incubators", tend to focus on a physical co-working space for early-stage technology firms. Incubators are usually associated with, or in the proximity, of research universities. While focusing on coworking, incubators might also offer various types of on-site commercialization training programs. Other programs, such as the accelerators discussed above, focus on the immersive training, networking, and funding aspects. The opportunities to obtain commercialization support, advice, and training are endless in the modern world.

System Failure Analysis

Systems are interconnected combinations of other systems. Some of these subsystems might be essential, where a failure will have catastrophic impacts, while other subsystems may be less critical. Almost everything in the world can be considered a system. Humans, animals, and plants are organic systems. Organizations and societies are systems. All technologies are systems. Some systems can be quite complicated, such as a commercial aircraft or space station, while other systems, such as a ball-point pen, might involve only a few parts. But all systems have the potential for failure.

A full discussion of system analysis is well beyond the scope of this book. However, system failure must be considered an important part of any technology development process. This is particularly true during the prototyping phases. But system failures can also certainly happen after a technology has been fully commercialized. System failures in technology development are not always strictly due to design problems. Organizational issues can lead to outcomes such as a well-functioning technology that is uncompetitive, fails to gain market traction, isn't supported sufficiently by post-sale service departments, or is too expensive to produce.

Some types of system failures can be mitigated through insurance and other methods described earlier in this book. However, insurance and other risk management processes need to be combined with an understanding of system failure analysis. In addition, organizational failure in technology development needs to be closely examined in order to make sure it does not happen a second time.

The following discussion just touches on some important topics of analyzing system failure. These techniques can be applied to a technology, but perhaps more important for this topic, can also be applied to the technology development process to see where things got messed up.

This potential for failure is well illustrated by the "iceberg model" of systems thinking, where visible events are just above the surface, while deeper structures and patterns often remain hidden – and like an iceberg, most of the iceberg and its dangers can't be seen (see Figure 16.7). A technology fails to reach the final commercialization stage, or it fails after launch. These are events. But like an iceberg, events are only a small part of the picture. Unseen at first glance, there is much more information. When

Finding the Hidden Forces: The Iceberg Model

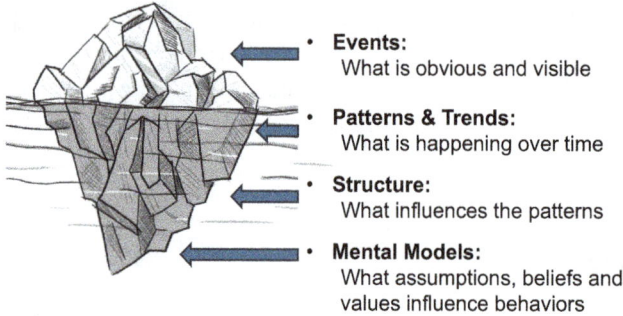

- **Events:**
  What is obvious and visible

- **Patterns & Trends:**
  What is happening over time

- **Structure:**
  What influences the patterns

- **Mental Models:**
  What assumptions, beliefs and values influence behaviors

Figure 16.7: The Iceberg Model for systems thinking.

Source: Systems thinking: what, why when, where and how ~ by Michael Goodman 1997.

DFMEA
Design Failure Mode and Effects Analysis

1	Outline all system functions and design specifications	6	Note detection methods and assign a detection effectiveness score
2	Determine how each component could potentially fail	7	Compute the Risk Priority Number (RPN) using severity, occurrence, and detection
3	Explain the possible consequences of failure and rate the severity	8	Develop and assign recommended corrective actions
4	Identify the root causes behind each potential failure	9	Track implemented actions with actual completion timelines
5	List current prevention measures and rate the likelihood of occurrence	10	Reassess RPNs and decide on follow-up steps based on updated risks

Figure 16.8: The Design Failures Model and Effects Analysis.

a negative or failure "event" occurs, it is important to dig deeper in order to understand the cause. This is going below the waterline of an iceberg.

The next section discusses some of the most commonly used methods to determine why a system failed.

Design Failures Model and Effects Analysis (DFMEA)

In our earlier discussion on project management, we discussed risk assessment and risk management. These are typical tools to analyze, identify, and hopefully mitigate risk during the technology development process. System failure analysis, the topic of this section, is essentially an after-the event analysis, to figure out what when wrong and try to fix it. Hopefully proper risk management will decrease the need for a system failure analysis, but one must always be prepared. Also, even when a technology might be successfully launched, perhaps it just doesn't meet the original pre-commercialization expectations and hopes. A system failure analysis would still be a best practice management tool in this case.

The DFMEA is a commonly used protocol for examining system failure. There are 10 steps in the full DFME protocol. Each of these steps has its own tools that can be used. Many of these tools involve a probabilistic or risk assessment (see Figure 16.8). One of the most important steps for determining why something failed is the root cause, or step 4 in the DFMEA protocol.

Root Cause Analysis (RCA)

Determining the root cause of any system failure, whether the organization failed at something or the actual technology failed in its workings, is critical to any system failure analysis. There are a number of tools that can be used in a root cause analysis (RCA), but the most relevant that we find being used in practice are the "5 Why" tool and the "Cause and Effect Tree".

RCA Tool: The 5 Whys. The "5 Why" tool is a formal process of just asking "Why" to each answer as to why something failed. Keep asking "Why" for at least five times, or until you get to something that is fundamental or completely outside your control. For example, suppose a technology was commercialized into the marketplace, but failed to achieve sufficient traction among customers. The technology adoption rate is so low that senior management is considered withdrawing the product from the market. A lot of time, effort, and resources have been wasted at this point. You, as a team leader, want to know what can be done to improve the technology development process, so this does not happen again. But to make improvements, you need to identify the root cause of the failure.

Your first "Why" might be, "Why did the technology fail?" – the response from the team might be, "Customers didn't like it". The second "Why" will be, "Why didn't the customers like it?", the response might be, "the customers did not like the color of the technology", the third "Why" might be, "Why didn't we know the customers would not like the color" . . . the questions continue, and after five questions you might find out that the technology was not properly tested in the targeted market through a beta-test. It is widely recognized that asking five levels of questions is often sufficient to uncover the root cause of a problem.

RCA Tool: Cause and Effect Trees/Map. A "cause and effect" tree or map graphically depicts a root cause analysis. Oftentimes the content of the "cause and effect" tree comes from a 5 Why analysis, but other results from testing and expert opinion can also be entered into the tree. The idea of a "cause and effect" tree is to graphically show the cause and the effect of each step, until the root cause is found. The following example in Figure 16.9 presents a "cause and effect" tree for a failed clothes dryer example. This can also be used in examining organizational failures.

Cause and Effect Tree: Finding Root Causes

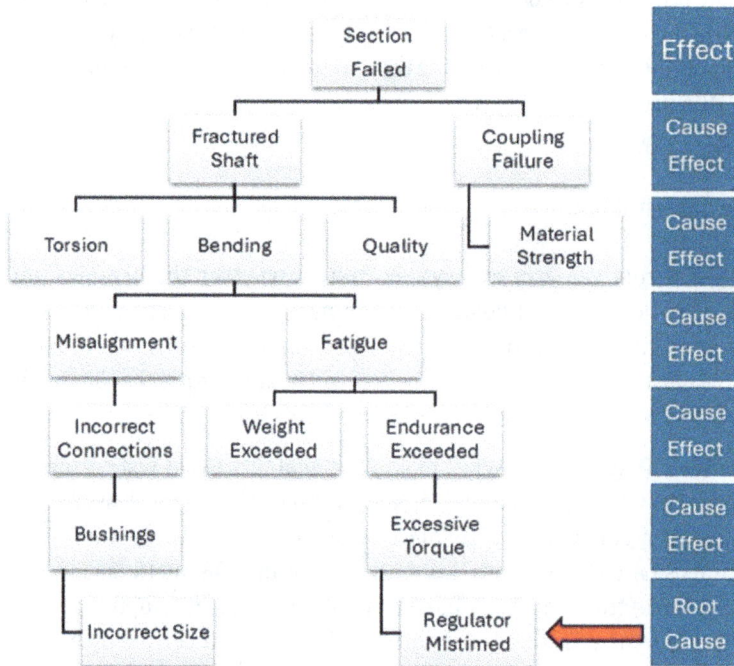

Figure 16.9: The Cause and Effect Tree for a failed clothes dryer.

Failure Analysis: Some Thoughts

Failure analysis is a hugely important part of understanding technology development. It is equally important to understand why a technology failed at different points in the development process, as well as why the organization failed in properly managing the process. We have only touched on the topic of failure analysis. There are a number of other tools that are also available such as Fishbone Diagrams and Pareto Charts that are also used in best practices failure analysis.

Concluding Insights

This chapter has explored three important management-oriented, best practice approaches that support successful technology development and commercialization: lean development, design thinking, and system failure analysis. While each topic draws from a much broader body of literature, the tools and models discussed here have been selected for their practical relevance to real-world technology challenges.

Lean development emphasizes efficiency, customer engagement, and rapid learning through tools such as the business model canvas, minimum viable products, and split testing. Design thinking brings a human-centered approach to solving complex problems and is particularly useful for technologies aimed at end-user or consumer markets. System failure analysis encourages a deeper understanding of why technologies or development efforts fall short – and how to avoid repeating the same mistakes.

Each of these frameworks offers a different lens for managing the uncertainties and complexities of innovation. They can be used independently or in combination, depending on the nature of the technology and the organization. Together, they provide technology developers and their support teams with actionable insights and practical tools to move from idea to impact – and when needed, to reflect and recalibrate after failure.

For readers interested in exploring these topics further, there is a wealth of books, training programs, and online resources available, including certification opportunities and specialized consulting support.

While this and the previous chapter have focused on internal management practices, the next chapter shifts the lens outward to examine strategic approaches for positioning and commercializing technologies in competitive markets.

Chapter Example: Los Alamos National Lab – External Acceleration as a Strategy for Advancing Deep Tech

For many early-stage deep technology developers, particularly those working in university labs or small research teams, the path from concept to commercialization can be slow, uncertain, and under-resourced. Even with access to basic infrastructure, researchers often lack the broader support systems needed to validate their ideas, connect with markets, and secure follow-on funding.

One strategy for addressing this gap is to participate in an external accelerator or residency program specifically designed for "deep tech". The term "deep tech" has become popular, meaning that the technology being developed may have significant scientific or technological impact. A new scientific method to develop a cure for cancer, or a technique that could double the efficiency of solar panels, for example, would be considered deep tech. These technologies often require substantial resources, investment, and support to develop and ultimately commercialize. They are the kinds of innovations that have the potential to transform society.

Some accelerator programs are independent efforts, but increasingly, such programs are being developed in conjunction with universities, government laboratories, and major technology-oriented corporations. These programs not only immerse participants in technology entrepreneurship concepts and methods, but they also provide access to funding, technical infrastructure, and credibility. These elements are often critical in moving a technology from mid-stage technical readiness levels (TRLs 3–5, which represent lab validation and early proof of concept) to prototype development and early commercialization (TRL 6+).

Deep Tech Commercialization in a National Lab Setting: The LEEP Program at Los Alamos

While programs like NSF's I-Corps™ and IDEATE help early-stage entrepreneurs and university researchers validate market needs and develop business models, other initiatives have emerged specifically to support deep technology ventures facing longer development cycles and higher technical complexity. One such model is the Lab-Embedded Entrepreneur Program (LEEP) at Los Alamos National Laboratory, which embeds entrepreneurs directly into the national lab environment.[6] LEEP combines technical collaboration with structured commercialization training, offering a distinctive pathway for deep tech start-ups to move from scientific discovery to investor readiness.

The Challenge

Deep technology ventures – especially those emerging from university research or national labs – often encounter a major gap between scientific innovation and commercial success. Researchers may have breakthrough ideas but lack entrepreneurial experience, infrastructure, and access to the funding networks necessary to move from concept to commercial readiness. Recognizing this persistent gap, Los Alamos National Laboratory created LEEP to embed entrepreneurs within its scientific ecosystem, providing both technical collaboration and comprehensive business training to accelerate technology maturation.

The LEEP Model

LEEP offers a two-year fellowship to three entrepreneurs per cohort. Each fellow receives a personal stipend and a technical budget ranging from $100,000 to $150,000 to collaborate with Los Alamos scientists. Participants gain access to the lab's specialized capabilities across sectors such as AI, quantum computing, materials science, space technologies, and energy systems.

In addition to technical support, LEEP delivers a robust business curriculum covering a wide range of commercialization topics – including intellectual property strategy, market validation, fundraising preparation, start-up boards, team building, and go-to-market strategies. Fellows pitch regularly to venture capitalists through quarterly VC roundtables and receive real-time feedback to improve their investor readiness. CEO roundtables provide further peer learning and mentorship from more experienced entrepreneurs. One of the program's ultimate goals is to ensure that by the end of the fellowship, each venture is not only technically advanced but also "investable".

Unlike traditional accelerators, LEEP tightly integrates each fellow's venture with Los Alamos' research infrastructure. This ensures mutual benefit: fellows advance their technologies while contributing to lab research priorities, all without generating conflicts over intellectual property ownership.

Entrepreneurial Mindset Development

Recognizing that many fellows come from academic or government research backgrounds, LEEP places special emphasis on mindset development. Fellows complete assessments using the Habit Story tool, a behavioral analysis platform that identifies the attitudes and habits associated with entrepreneurial success.

LEEP is intentionally designed to help participants shift from the perfection-driven culture of academia to the iterative, market-oriented mindset of start-ups. As Program Manager Molly Cernicek explained, "We do a tremendous amount of market analysis and due diligence to understand if there's a 'there there'". Throughout the two-year residency, fellows are challenged to rethink how they approach problem solving, value creation, and business-building.

Program Outcomes and Challenges

LEEP's early cohorts have demonstrated positive results. Space Kinetic, a company from an early cohort, raised $3 million in venture funding during the program and recently is in the process of closing a Series A round. Their propulsion technology is currently being evaluated for use in national space defense initiatives.

Nevertheless, the program faces challenges. Recruiting fellows to relocate to Los Alamos, far from traditional innovation hubs, can be difficult. Ensuring alignment between entrepreneurial projects and the lab's dual-use national security mission also requires careful screening and expectation setting. Despite these barriers, all ten companies supported through LEEP to date have remained in New Mexico, contributing to the growth of the state's innovation ecosystem.

Strategic Insights

Several strategic insights emerge from the LEEP experience. First, commercializing deep technology requires not just technical advancement but a parallel shift in mindset from scientific inquiry to entrepreneurial execution. Second, successful commercialization depends on alignment between a start-up's technical needs and the infrastructure available to support them. Third, programs like LEEP illustrate that building investable start-ups means developing both the business model and the founder. Finally, even in technically intensive environments like national labs, early engagement with customers and investors remains central to successful commercialization.

By embedding entrepreneurs within a national lab and supporting them through both technology maturation and business development, LEEP offers a compelling model for accelerating the path from science to start-up.

Chapter 17
Technology Strategies

This Chapter

- Introduces two foundational theories of competitive strategy: the Structure-Conduct-Performance (SCP) model and the Resource-Based Theory (RBT).
- Explains the VRIO framework and its application to developing effective technology strategies.
- Describes various market-based technology strategies, including licensing, strategic partnerships, contracting, and mergers.
- Outlines the key elements typically found in a technology licensing agreement.
- Emphasizes the importance of comprehensive strategic planning and the activities it must incorporate to support commercialization.

Key Management Tools and Best Practices

- The VRIO model of resources
- Technology licensing principles
- Strategic Partnerships and Mergers

! **INSIGHT**

Strategic management is what brings everything together. Not only do technology developers need to design and implement the best strategy for competitive advantage upon commercialization, but they also need to get to the final point of commercialization.

Technology development and commercialization does not happen in a vacuum. There are many steps along the way that need to be properly managed. This is where planning comes into focus. A good technology strategy will utilize the many tools and concepts discussed in this book, from IP protection, to project management, to communicating technologies. Above all, being able to effectively transition a technology from one stage of development to the next, all with an eye toward final commercialization, becomes critical.

Some large organizations can effectively internalize the whole process. Other organizations might only combine certain stages of development and pass the technology off to other players. But no matter what the business model is, it should always be well planned and implemented.

Introduction

While the previous two chapters focused on the idea of organizing and coordinating the technology development process in order to obtain maximum benefit, our final chapter will focus on technology strategy. What is strategy? The word "strategy" is derived from the ancient word "strategos". Strategy, as used in more modern times, would be equivalent in ancient Greece to the term "strategike episteme" or "strategon sophia" or the general's knowledge and wisdom.

https://doi.org/10.1515/9783111684420-018

There are several different approaches to understanding competitive strategy taught in business schools and used by strategy consultants. One approach, often labeled the Structure-Conduct-Performance (SCP) approach, focuses on the structure of industries. The SCP approach is grounded in traditional Industrial Organization Economics that dates back to the early twentieth century when economists started to really investigate how industries and firms work. The argument in the SCP approach is that industry structure drives the strategic conduct of firms, which in turn results in performance. This is certainly important to understand, since any strategy needs to take place within the competitive and economic structure of the developing technology. Understanding how technology-based industries are structured and evolve over time was the emphasis of the first several chapters in this book.

However, when it comes to understanding technology strategy, most experts tend to focus on an organization's ability to develop, nurture, manage, and exploit organizational, financial, and intellectual "resources". This leads to the second major theoretical approach to understanding competitive strategy, commonly known as the "resource-based theory", or RBT. RBT focuses more on how firms identify, develop, allocate, and organize their key strategic resources in order to be successful in the market. Both approaches are certainly relevant in understanding competitive strategy, but the RBT framework is now probably considered more relevant for high technology environments than the SCP approach since the structure of the industry is constantly evolving, as new technologies create new industries and sub-industries. Under the RBT approach, managing resources is key.

Any discussion of strategy also needs to discuss the planning process. A good strategy does not develop in a vacuum. Rather, organizations need to plan and manage for success. In fact, planning and managing for successful technology development and commercialization is the focus of this book – what are the most important tools and topics that need to be addressed in order to develop a strategy for successful technology development and commercialization?

This final chapter provides a high-level perspective, often referred to as a "20,000-foot overview", to address two important themes. First, we introduce the resource-based theory to explore how competitive decisions are shaped in technology-driven industries. Second, we look at the broader challenge of developing and implementing a coherent strategy, which has been a central focus throughout this book.

Resources: The Basis of Technology Strategy

Within the RBT, or resource-based approach to understanding competitive strategy, "strategic resources" are specialized investments that an entity develops, acquires, and holds. Strategic resources are assets, either tangible in nature, such as lab equipment, a manufacturing plant, and cash, or intangibles, such as knowledge and intellectual property. Understanding, acquiring, and managing strategic resources are the key to success.

True strategic resources have four characteristics. They are Valuable, Rare, Inimitable, and ultimately Organized to create a competitive advantage. This is often called the VRIO model of strategic resources and capabilities.

Valuable Resources: A valuable resource is a tangible or intangible asset that helps an organization deliver meaningful benefits to its customers. An efficient technological design might be considered a valuable resource, as successful commercialization often depends on how well the technology is developed and engineered. However, valuable resources, while necessary for success, are not sufficient to create a competitive advantage, especially if those resources are widely available. For instance, if other competitors are developing similarly effective technology designs, the advantage may be diminished. This is why additional dimensions of resources are critical for achieving success.

Rare Resources: In order to create a true competitive advantage, valuable resources must also be rare. In technology strategy, patent protection around an important piece of IP would be an example of a rare resource. Not everybody can get IP protection around the relevant technology. This is why IP protection has become so important. IP protection creates a legal "rarity" if enforced. There are, of course, other critical rare resources, such as having the top scientists or engineers with unique knowledge, or possibly even a strong network of connections. If a valuable resource is easily available to all competitors, it is not rare and does not create a strong advantage.

Imitability of Resources: One of the most critical characteristics of a strategic resource is that it is difficult for competitors to imitate. Resources that are hard to replicate, whether due to intellectual property protections, specialized know-how, or unique organizational capabilities, can provide a sustained competitive advantage. However, even rare or protected resources are sometimes vulnerable. For example, a company may hold a patent, but if that patent is weak or competitors can easily develop "workarounds", the protection offers little strategic benefit. Intellectual property theft is another concern. Trade secrets, by nature, are designed to be difficult to imitate, but if they are stolen, they can be exploited by competitors. Similarly, top talent, such as a leading scientist or engineer, can be poached by another organization, diminishing the uniqueness of the original firm's capabilities.

Organization of Resources: A technology development firm may possess valuable, rare, and hard-to-imitate resources, but without the ability to organize and integrate them effectively, these assets can be underutilized and may fail to contribute to a competitive advantage or lead to successful commercialization. This is clearly a management problem. The problem of organizing strategic resources is why entrepreneurs will license a technology from a university lab for further development and commercialization. Entrepreneurs may not have the scientific skill to invent IP, but the entrepreneurs will then attempt to effectively organize the various valuable strategic resources to take the technology further, once they bring the IP in-house – that is really the entrepreneurial expertise.

This, ultimately, is the central strategic challenge in technology management: how to effectively organize and align all of the firm's key resources. This includes everything from managing intellectual property and prototype development to coordinating manufacturing, distribution, and funding. Entrepreneurs, in particular, must skillfully orchestrate a wide range of external and internal resources. Larger organizations, meanwhile, often manage these elements through dedicated internal systems, all with the goal of guiding the technology successfully to market.

VRIO Importance Change over the Development Cycle: The VRIO model provides a useful framework for understanding how resources contribute to a technology strategy. But the importance of certain resources can change over time. That is one of the unique characteristics of the technology development and commercialization process – strategic resources are always a moving target. Consider the likely evolution of typical resources and skills over the development cycle, from TRL1 to TRL9 (See Table 17.1).

Table 17.1: Critical resources over the technology development cycle.

Resource Category	TRL1-TRL2 Invention	TRL3 Patent	TRL4-TRL6 Prototyping	TRL7–TRL8 Alpha/Beta Testing	TRL 9 Final Market
IP Development and Scientific Skills	High	High	Medium	Low	Low
Design Skills	Low	Medium	High	Medium	Low
Engineering Skills	Low	Low	High	High	Medium
Networking	Low	Low	Medium	High	Medium
Marketing Skills	Low	Low	Low	Medium	High
Distribution System	Low	Low	Low	Medium	High
Manufacturing Capabilities	Low	Low	Low	Low-Medium	High
Risk Capital	Low	Low	High	High-Medium	Medium
Later Phased Funding	Low	Low	Low	Low-Medium	High

Understanding both a) the VRIO nature of resources for technologies and b) how the nature of critical resources change over the technology development cycle becomes an important part of developing a coherent strategic orientation toward technology development and commercialization.

Toward a Theory of Vertical Technology Development Strategies

Other than the speed of innovation, perhaps one of the most unique characteristics of technology industries is how fragmented they are over the technology development cycle.

Different organizations are typically involved in different TRL stages. University and R&D labs, both public and private, generally work in the TRL1 to TRL4 stages. Many early-stage entrepreneurial firms tend to license technologies and then organize the necessary resources to move technologies to perhaps the TRL6 or TRL7 stages. Later-stage development firms then move the technologies from prototyping, through final beta testing at TRL8. In some cases, the final commercialization into an end user market, TRL9, might be managed by specialized technology marketing and distribution firms. Of course, some firms will combine these different phases internally. A few firms, such as large technology firms might attempt to internally manage the whole development process, from the earliest invention stages through design and prototyping, to the final commercialization introduction.

Another interesting aspect of technology industries is that a product in its final, TRL9 development stage, might simply become a component in a larger system that might be in a much earlier, prototyping phase. This intermediate system, in turn, might then be a component in an even larger system, at an even different stage of development. The whole development structure of technologies resembles a cascading waterfall. The end user for one technology developer may be the input for another technology. Thus, the definition of what constitutes a "successful commercialization" changes dramatically depending on where a technology fits in a larger system, or if the final product is being sold to the actual end user.

Likewise, funding also tends to be cycle specific. For entrepreneurial firms, the earliest development stages are often internally funded from family, friends, and the entrepreneurs themselves. Funding in the early-middle stages focuses on angel investment and seed funding from early-stage venture capitalists. In later stages, larger private equity investments, such as venture capital or partnership/merger funding, become more important. In addition, many government grant programs, such as the U.S. Small Business Innovation Research (SBIR) grants, will focus on specific technology development stages with their different phases of grants.

How can we think about the optimal vertical strategy. Valuable, rare, and imitable resources can be acquired in basically one of two ways. A firm can develop these resources internally through its own efforts, or a firm can acquire these resources from the marketplace, such as an in-licensing agreement.

From a theoretical point of view, which is the best strategy will always depend upon a trade-off between transaction costs and organizational costs. The notion of focusing on transaction and organizational costs when thinking about technology strategy is key. From a foundational view, two economists stand out in framing this way of thinking, Ronald Coase, who won the Nobel Prize in Economics in 1991, and Oliver Wiliamson, who received the Nobel Prize in 2009. This is cost-benefit analysis a key part of understanding successful technology strategies.

Transaction Costs: The Key to Understanding Markets

Both Ronald Coase and Oliver Williamson focused on the key differences between markets and organizations, and why sometimes markets appear to work better while other times organizations work better. Markets tend to be relatively efficient, but in any market transaction, there are always various costs associated with the transaction. Transaction costs involve search costs (such as finding an appropriate technology to license), communication costs (the time and effort to contact a potential license partner), negotiations and exchange costs (negotiating a deal), informational costs (not having full information about the technology or market, such as licensing a technology when a better one was available), and one of the most important costs, the cost of "opportunism".

Opportunism costs are when the partner to the market exchange takes advantage of the exchange. Opportunism costs tend to be very high in technologies. A license partner might violate the license agreement by selling their product in other markets, they might design a work-around technology in order to not pay royalties or design their own product, or they might steal trade secrets even though they have a non-disclosure agreement.

All of these transaction costs work both ways in the market – sellers of technology might suffer from opportunistic behaviors of buyers, while buyers of technology might incur other types of transaction costs in their desire to access available technologies.

When transaction costs are high, or at least higher than the costs of organizing the process of technological development internally, then companies will internally organize that stage of development, or at least bring in house the critical resources required in that stage of development as described in the table above.

For example, small entrepreneurial firms will often license technology. Some research suggests that over 90% of technology oriented entrepreneurial start-ups actually license their technologies from universities or R&D laboratories. Why? – because these small firms are generally founded by entrepreneurs skilled in business and networking. It is far easier for entrepreneurs to use the marketplace and license technologies and IP, than internally operate high-level R&D labs. Then the entrepreneur will often hire good design engineers and software developers in order to internally develop a licensed technology through the prototype phases. Entrepreneurs might also bring their extensive network connections to the table.

Likewise, small entrepreneurial firms will seek risk capital from private equity investors, using the marketplace, since it is almost impossible to develop the necessary funding internally within a small organization as the technology advances to later stages of development.

However, it should be noted that an important concept in the entrepreneurship field these days is enhanced self-funding, then speed to market to quickly generate sales, or "revenue-funding". This way one doesn't need to get tied up with external private equity firms. Private equity funding, particularly from some larger VC firms, has become known for aggressive demands on the company once invested. Recognizing this, many entrepreneurial firms try to avoid external private equity funding and develop a strategy of quick technology launches. Lean technology development techniques, discussed in the prior chapter, are a critical part of this strategy in order to minimize the financial "burn-rate" before generating sales.

Larger firms might attempt to perform all of these functions internally. But even larger firms almost universally recognize that they must often acquire technologies from the marketplace, particularly when developing complex systems. These larger firms will use a number of market mechanisms, such as licensing an early-stage technology if they feel they can further develop the technology internally. Larger firms can acquire or merge with small development firms to incorporate not only their technologies but also the development team if additional development needs to be done.

There is also a tendency for firms to internalize, through acquisition or internal development, any specialized investments that are "firm-specific". A firm-specific resource is something that is highly specialized to that particular firm. Specialized resources can be organized by certain firms better than others to create a competitive advantage. Clearly, if a resource is really a key success factor at a particular stage of development, then well-managed firms will attempt to internalize that resource in order to properly organize those resources in order to gain a strategic advantage. This discussion provides the underlying theory and model for understanding how firms and other entities strategically operate along the development cycle, from TRL1 to TRL9.

We now explore some of the most important strategic exchanges in this process. In general, there are four market-based strategies – licensing, partnerships, contracting, and mergers/acquisitions.

Licensing as a Technology Strategy

Licensing is a strategy. It is also one of the most common strategies in technological industries. Licensing is a contractual arrangement in which the licensor's patents, designs, trademarks, copyrights, trade secrets, or other intellectual property may be sold or made available to a licensee for compensation that is negotiated in advance between the parties.

Licensing is always a two-way street. Donor entities "out-license" their technology, while recipient entities "in-license" technology. While licensing can occur at any time during the technology development cycle, it typically occurs during three stages.

The first period when licensing is common is after a patent has been developed by universities and R&D labs. The second period is after a working prototype has been developed, where functionality can be established, initial performance data is obtained, and market acceptance can be more accurately assessed. The third period when licensing is common is the final stage, when companies may not have the marketing, distribution, manufacturing capabilities or scale to bring a technology to the mass market. This also might occur in global markets that require specialized distribution networks.

There are five key components to any license agreement.

Definition of Technology/Players. This is all the legal stuff, such as carefully defining the technology and IP that is being licensed, and the entities involved in the contract

Field of Use. The field of use defines what the licensed technology can be used for. This may include 1) a narrow or broad set of uses. For example, a platform technology can be used for many different applications. Thus, the "Escortin" transport molecule that can move other molecules through a cell wall described earlier in this book, could be used for any pharmaceutical application (a broad application) or just for dermatological applications (a narrow application). A narrow application reserves the right to license to other developers with different applications. 2) the regions or countries that the licensee can use or sell the product in (such as worldwide, a particular region such as the European Union, or just for one country), and 3) whether the license is exclusive (only the licensee has the rights to that particular application or market) or non-exclusive (the licensor can license the technology to competitive firms). The field of use decisions needs to be carefully considered and often relies upon the findings of a technology commercialization or feasibility study.

Payment. How does the licensee make money on the deal? The normal payment for technologies in later stages of development is a "running royalty". Running royalties are based on a percentage of the sales the licensee generates with the technology. Running royalties are usually in a range of 3% to 8%, but can range as high as 18%. Very high running royalties, however, discourage future funding efforts since few investors will want to fund something where perhaps as much as 18% of any revenues is taken off the top. Running royalties only make sense if your technology is being incorporated into another product that will start generating revenues in the near future, or if the final product is currently in the market and your technology will enhance the existing product.

For technologies not likely connected to immediate revenue generation, there are some other options. For example, license payments can also specify a lump sum royalty paid up front. In some cases, a license agreement will use a combination of a lump sum and running royalty. For early-stage technologies where commercialization is still distant, payment schedules may be structured around key milestones, such as the development of a lab prototype, the securing of specific funding, or the initiation of beta testing.

Occasionally, a license agreement might also allow for payment in equity. This is particularly common for early-stage technologies being licensed by smaller entrepreneurial firms. The licensor might agree to receiving a small percentage of equity from the firm wishing to license the technology.

Milestones. License agreements should also incorporate hurdles or milestones that need to be met. A problem can occur when an entity licenses a technology and then sits on it. The licensor is losing out on possible income from other potential partners. Milestones will identify important progress that needs to be met. Milestones can be varied, such as the speed of technology development, entering the market at a certain time, or obtaining certain levels of funding. If not, then the technology can revert back to the original IP holder. Remember, generally IP has a certain shelf life that is much shorter than the legal patent time length. IP typically loses value over time if not used due to emerging new technologies in the market.

Relicensing and IP Grant Back Clauses. In some cases, the licensee may seek to advance a promising technology to the next stage of development and then relicense the improved version to another party. Relicensing clauses will define what happens in this case. Another problem often seen is when a large company licenses a technology, then gives it to their engineers to develop a "work-around" design, then they file for their own IP. A grant back clause will define that any new IP developed from the licensed IP will grant back, in some percentage, to the original IP holder. This really needs to be negotiated, since many potential licensees will balk at this request.

Caveats for International Technology Licenses. Technology licensing from one country to another can present problems. Every country has its own set of rules that govern licensing agreements. Most developed countries leave it up to the transacting parties; however, many countries have other rules. Some countries require certain language in a license agreement, while other countries such as China and India might require licenses for many industries to be registered and approved by the government before it goes into effect. Some middle-eastern countries, such as Saudi Arabia, UAE, and Qatar, use a combination of Islamic law and modern contract laws to regulating license agreements. Other governments also prohibit royalty payments that exceed a certain rate. In addition, some governments prohibit contractual provisions barring the licensee from exporting products manufactured using the licensed technology to third countries

License agreements can be highly complicated documents, and it is important that well qualified legal experts are involved in crafting an appropriate license agreement. But any developer, and licensee, needs to thoroughly understand the license agreement carefully, even if the final document is crafted by a qualified legal expert.

Contracting as a Technology Strategy

In addition to licensing, technology firms, both large and small, often rely on a variety of contracted services to support different phases of the development and commercialization process. Within the RBT theoretical model, this happens with the cost of internally organizing these resources exceeds the cost of accessing these resources in the external market. These external partnerships can provide critical expertise and capabilities across a wide range of functions, including:

1) The legal team involved with protecting IP, developing license agreements, or other important legal functions.
2) Consulting firms who perform technology commercialization and feasibility studies.

3) Specialized design engineers and software developers who can work on early-stage design issues.

4) Prototyping companies. These specialized firms will use modern technologies, such as 3D printing, laser cutting, and multi-dimensional CNC machining to create early-stage prototypes. These companies can also produce limited run manufacturing for beta testing.

5) Pharmaceutical and biotechnology development firms will typically contract out clinical testing.

6) Alpha and beta testing are contractual agreements with certain users.

7) Final manufacturing and distribution.

8) Marketing and advertising firms for targeting consumer markets.

While these important activities may represent valuable resources to a successful technology development and commercialization effort, they tend not to be rare resources. There are many entities that can perform all of these activities, some perhaps better than others, but not uniquely. In these situations, it can make economic sense to obtain a market solution through contracting than attempting to organize these activities internally.

Larger technology corporations, of course, might have more internal capabilities in these areas. Due to their size, scale, and ability to spread these costs among a number of different technology programs, they might find the cost of internally organizing these resources more beneficial and thus do not need to sub-contract as many of these activities.

Partnerships as a Technology Strategy

Technologies are frequently acquired not through licensing, but through strategic partnerships. Strategic partnerships in technology spaces tend to be one of three types, a technology joint venture, a corporate venture capital investment, or a merger/acquisition.

Technology Joint Venture. A technology joint venture is when two parties, each needing resources that the other partner provides, create a separate entity for the partnership. Joint ventures are normally formed for the purpose of either developing the technology or marketing the technology. This separate entity will then establish the ownership structure, governance, and how profits are shared. IP assets will then be transferred, typically by either a license agreement or an assignment of the IP, to the joint venture. Other requirements will also be defined in the joint venture agreement. As a separate entity, the joint venture can solicit its own funding. The joint venture remains a separate entity, with its own governance, until the parties agree to dissolve the joint venture.

Corporate Venture Capital. Many large technology firms have realized the importance of supporting early-stage technologies that are being developed by small, entrepreneurial firms. Rather than just licensing a technology, larger firms may decide to act as a venture capitalist, providing corporate funds for an ownership stake in the smaller firm. As part equity owners, the larger corporation will then have certain managerial and board of director rights. Some corporate venture capital deals will also involve engineering and management support for developing the technology. An important part of almost all corporate venture capital arrangements is that the larger firm has early, and possibly exclusive, access to the technologies being developed by the smaller, entrepreneurial enterprise. Almost by definition, corporate venture capital groups focus only on technologies they believe will contribute to their core business mission.

The amount of corporate venture capital has increased dramatically in recent years. Companies with well-known, large corporate venture capital funds include Google Ventures, Intel Capital, Qualcomm Ventures, Johnson & Johnson Innovation, Cisco Investments, and Samsung Venture Investments. Qualcomm Ventures, for example, which concentrates on wireless ecosystem technologies, has over 150 active companies in its corporate investment portfolio.

Mergers and Acquisitions as a Technology Strategy

Larger technology companies may sometimes decide that it is better to simply acquire the technology and the supporting assets and development team. Mergers and Acquisitions (M&As) have been increasing globally in terms of both the number of deals, and the dollar volume. Annually, the overall M&A market is normally over $1trillion globally. The United States accounts for about half of the M&A deals, with developing nations in the Asia-Pacific region, such as China, South Korea, and Japan becoming more aggressive. Many of the M&A deals are in the financial and materials industry sectors, but an increasing number are in the technology sectors, particularly in information, communication and pharmaceutical development. The idea of a M&A versus either licensing or corporate venturing is to acquire and internalize 100% control of the technology, as well as the other skills and resources that the firm might have. This often includes the R&D and engineering team.

As an example, M&A has been a common strategy in the pharmaceutical industry for decades. A strategy often seen is for small, entrepreneurial drug-development enterprises to perform much of the early drug discovery, particularly in the advanced biotechnology spheres. These smaller biotechnology firms, generally supported by early-stage private equity funding, will develop the potential drug through various generic engineering methods and then take it through the pre-clinical stages of development. Pre-clinical development generally means testing the drug *in vitro* (test-tube testing), then early *in vivo* testing to determine the efficacy and toxicology of the drug. Early *in vivo* testing is often done with animal studies, such as with mice or monkeys. However, once a drug gets to the human testing phase, the expense is often so great that it makes more sense to merge with a "Big-Pharma" firm, who will then take the technology through the human testing phases, and ultimately to the final market.

Significant premiums are often paid to these smaller firms that are acquired by larger firms through an M&A process. This strategy makes sense given the different valuable and rare resources that each party brings to the deal.

Case Example. Technology Acquisition. One of the authors of this book co-founded a small biotechnology firm called "Biolife Technologies, Inc." Part of the firm's RD efforts included a drug delivery technology that was essentially, at the time, the "world's largest pill" that also had excellent taste masking, bonding, and shelf-life characteristics. This combination was obtained by certain proprietary technologies, some licensed and some internally developed (trade secrets). This allowed integrating a number of generally bad tasting molecules such as the key amino acids of protein, many vitamin groups such as B-complexes, and essential minerals, such as Iron, into a good tasting matrix with very few calories or added ingredients, such as sugar or sweeteners to hide the taste of the nutritional ingredients. Since this was technically a "large pill", it was not cooked, so the ingredients maintained their pharmaceutical nutritional standards. This final technology also looked like a wafer and came in different flavors, such as chocolate, which were developed through a series of focus groups. The product was then branded and packaged as xCEL and was beta tested in a number of California health food stores, where it received high reviews (see Figure 17.1). Soon afterward the technology/IP was subsequently acquired by a large South Asian pharmaceutical firm. This firm then repositioned the technology as a way of feeding poor and undernourished individuals. The technology is still in the market for this purpose years later.

Figure 17.1: Final product: Biolife Technologies, Inc.

Concluding Insights

A successful technology development and commercialization strategy inevitably involves a systematic approach in order to implement. To be successful, this must encompass all the typical components of a business plan, with a recognition that technology markets often require a somewhat unique orientation. The idea is to properly manage the transformation of innovations into the marketplace by transitioning through the various technology readiness levels (TRLs).

Technology strategy is fundamentally about alignment – between vision and execution, invention and market need, resources and opportunity. This chapter has highlighted the frameworks and tools that help organizations develop coherent strategies to move technologies through the complex journey from concept to commercialization.

We explored how the resource-based view and VRIO framework help firms evaluate their internal strengths and determine how to create sustainable competitive advantage. We also examined how resource needs shift over the technology readiness lifecycle, and how these changes influence whether resources should be built internally or acquired through the market.

Technology firms operate in dynamic and often fragmented environments. Strategies like licensing, contracting, partnerships, and mergers and acquisitions are not just transactional – they are strategic decisions that shape the firm's long-term positioning. These decisions are best made through a careful assessment of transaction costs, organizational capabilities, and the evolving structure of the marketplace.

Finally, strategy is not just about choosing a path – it's about managing that path over time. From resource planning to project management to customer communication, successful technology commercialization depends on integrating strategic thinking across every stage of development.

As you move forward, remember: a good strategy is not static. It evolves with the market, adapts to new insights, and reflects the careful coordination of people, tools, and vision. That, ultimately, is the essence of strategic thinking in technology development.

Technical Appendix: Technology Forecasting

Key Tools Discussed In Appendix
- Logistic Diffusion Model
- Gompertz Curves
- The Bass Model of Adoption
- Fisher-Pry Technology Substitution Model
- Experience Curve Estimation
- Trend Impact Analysis
- Signal Scanning
- Normative Forecasting and Backcasting
- Judgmental Forecasting and the Delphi Method
- Technology Roadmapping

Introduction: A Forecasting Scenario

Nothing in the natural world is simple, nor does the natural world create linear, straight lines. With perhaps the exception of a distant ocean horizon, the world, with all of it's natural forces, is both complicated and non-linear. Forecasting the nature, performance, and adoption of new technologies is no different.

Consider the following real-life scenario. As a doctorate student, one of the authors of this book worked as a consultant for a highly successful firm that specializes in developing and manufacturing sensors, actuators, switches, and other electronic components for a variety of OEMs in the aerospace, medical, industrial, communications, and transportation industries. The firm is vertically integrated from R&D to final component production and distribution, with plants around the globe. As in any technology industry, new technologies were constantly being introduced that threatened the firm's core product base. At the time of this author's involvement, this happened to one of the firm's most profitable products.

After spending years developing a strong reputation and a 40% market share for this particular component, a radically new solution was being offered from an Asian firm. The new solution, which everybody recognized was a long-term better design, was still much higher priced. Due to its higher price, the new design had only captured about 5% of the total market. But everybody knew it was just a matter of time. The chief engineer thought it might be 5 years before the new technology would get to a 20% or 30% market share, so he was not worried. The firm's Vice President was not so sure, so he asked two questions. How long before the new technology likely reached this 20% or 30% share of the market (so he knew how much time he had to start converting his technology to the newer design), and how many units did he need to produce of the new technology to be price competitive with the Asian firm? To answer these two questions

https://doi.org/10.1515/9783111684420-019

requires a combination of forecasting techniques – in particular, a forecast of the total market revenues, a technology substitution model to examine when the new technology was likely to get to a 20% or 30% penetration of the total market, and an experience curve estimate to figure out the rate of cost reduction over time once the firm started producing the new design.

In this book many different models have been presented. Concepts such as S-curves, technology substitution, experience curves, envelope and penetration curves, and the fact that innovations take place at lightning speeds in the modern world all underlie the nature of technology development and commercialization. Well-managed firms often need to forecast some of these issues, particularly when developing their future competitive strategies. That is the focus of this technical appendix.

While this appendix is not critical to the concepts in this book, it is designed for readers wanting a conversational understanding of technology forecasting as part of their knowledge portfolio. Sometimes we present the mathematical equation, but we do not go into the estimation of the equation, or the variations that are often proposed. It should be noted that each of these topics could be a book in itself. This appendix is really designed to only introduce the key technology forecasting concepts in a basic form, and to provide the critical terminology of the different methods. Much more detail on all of the methods, including software designed to implement these models, can be found online.

Forecasting Market Adoption: S-Curves and Trend Extrapolation

Market S-curves or technology adoption models were presented in Chapter 2. Market S-curves have two dimensions. One dimension is total industry sales or market share. The other dimension is time. Over time, more and more adoption takes place until a plateau is reached. In marketing, models depicting market adoption of a technology are known as cumulative penetration models. Market S-curves all represent a form of "trend extrapolation". But with these models, the trend is not linear or a straight line; rather, they all follow some type of a non-linear, S-looking shape. The differences between these extrapolation models are based upon assumptions regarding customer and market behavior.

Logistic Diffusion Model

One of the most popular formulas to model an S-shaped adoption model is the logistic diffusion model, also called a "Pearl Curve". The logistic diffusion model is a symmetric model, where the inflection point is in the middle of the chart. The logistic model assumes the acceleration prior to the inflection point is the same as the deacceleration after the inflection point. The basic equation for the logistic model is shown in Figure A.1:

$$Y(t) = L/(1+\exp^{-a(x-b)})$$

Figure A.1: Equation for the Logistic Diffusion Model.

$Y(t)$ represents the market share (market penetration) at a particular time period. L represents the limit, such as 100% if we are calculating market share penetration; α is the growth rate, and β is the inflection point (halfway up on the logistic curve). The value for α and β are what determines the shape of the curve and are estimated based upon the historical data we enter.

The logistic diffusion model, like most of the S-shaped models, utilizes the "Euler function", which creates the S-shaped curve. The Euler function simply means "e" raised to the power of "something". It is relatively easy to model the logistic diffusion equation, that is estimate α and β, on spreadsheets such as Excel using the "solver" tool, or with specialized statistical programs. The idea is the estimate an α and β that best fits the historical data and then use the equation for forecasting the future market penetration rate. If we are trying to estimate the total number of sales, rather than a penetration rate, we also need to estimate "L". In these cases, "L" can also be estimated using different programs such as Excel's "solver" function.

Gompertz Curve

Another basic mathematical model used to estimate S-curves is the "Gompertz curve". Unlike the logistic function, for the Gompertz curve the acceleration of growth before the inflection point can be different than the deacceleration after the inflection point (see Figure A.2).

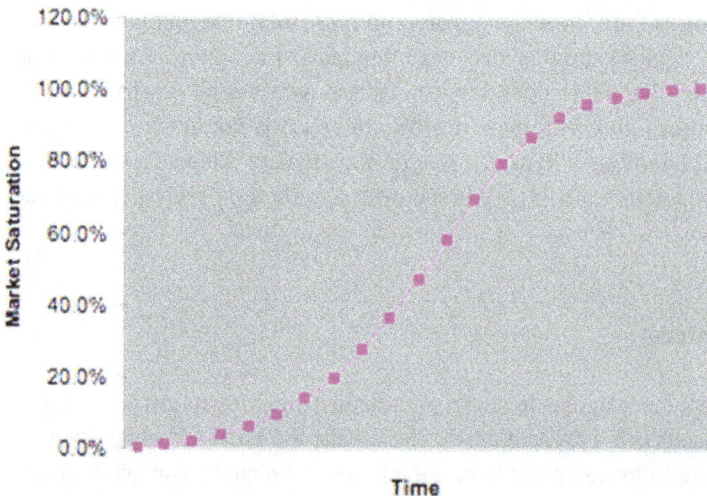

Figure A.2: The Gompertz Curve.

The Gompertz equation is illustrated in Figure A.3.

$$y(t) = L * \exp[-\alpha\ \exp^{(-Bt)}]$$

Figure A.3: The Gompertz Curve equation.

where y(t) is the market share at time "t". Again "L" is the upper limit (such as 100 for market share), and α and B again are parameters that can be estimated based on historical data. The Gompertz curve uses two Euler functions. Like the logistic model, it is also relatively easy to model the Gompertz model on spreadsheets such as Excel. It can also be estimated with specialized statistical programs. As with the logistic model, the idea is to estimate an α and B that best fits the historical data and then use the equation for forecasting the future penetration rate.

There are several theoretical reasons to choose one over the other, but generally it is based on how well each of the models fits the historical data. The Gompertz curve is used primarily for more consumer product adoption.

Bass Model

Another commonly used model to predict product adoption is the Bass model, named after Frank Bass, who was a marketing professor at Purdue University; Dr. Bass noted that in consumer products, adoption was influenced by a combination of both word of mouth and mass media. He developed the Bass model to use when there are both innovative and imitative components at play, typical in consumer products and technologies.

There are a number of other proposed model, many of which are quite complex; however, the logistic diffusion model, the Gompertz curve, and the Bass models are by far the most popular for estimating adoption of products and technologies, particularly among end user or consumer markets.

Technology Substitution Models: Fisher-Pry

Technologies are constantly being replaced by newer technologies. Sometimes it is important, such as the scenario described above, to forecast the rate of technology substitution. These models are called technology substitution models. The most popular technology substitution model is the Fisher-Pry model. With only a few data points, representing 5% or less market share penetration by a new technology, the Fisher-Pry model does a remarkably good job at forecasting what the future rate of substitution will be, and how fast the new technology will take over the market. The Fisher-Pry model is also based on an S-curve foundation.

The Fisher-Pry model is best used when the technologies are not impacted by other events, or by consumer advertising such as retail products. It is a very powerful tool for intermediate products and component technologies, such as the electronic sensors mentioned in the above scenario, when the new technology is seen to be superior in the long-term.

The Fisher-Pry model is defined by the following equation in Figure A.4:

$$y(t)=1/(1+e^{-b(1-a)})$$

Figure A.4: The Fisher-Pry Model equation.

where y(t) is the fraction of the potential market served by the new technology at time t. The parameter a is the time the new technology reaches 50% of the total market. The parameter b governs how fast the adoption proceeds. The Fisher-Pry curve is not symmetric and changes are based on the early rate of adoption.

As with all of the models discussed in this appendix, there is specialized software available to estimate the Fisher-Pry model.

Technology S-Curves

As mentioned in Chapter 2, technology S-curves plot how the performance of a technology changes over time. The measurement of performance differs depending on the technology. Performance could be speed of computing, density for hard drives, or conversion rates for solar panels. The performance dimension can be almost anything. In early stages there tends to be rapid performance; then over time the performance improvements start to slow down, ultimately reaching a limit defined by the laws of physics, design, or science that is associated with that technology. This creates the S-shape. At this point, another new design may enter the market and start a new S-shaped performance curve. Thus, technology S-curves tend to focus on the performance of a particular technology over time.

Like market adoption curves, technology S-curves are often estimated by the logistic equation. However, unlike the market S-curve, where the limit is 100%, if we are attempting to measure market share, for the technology S-curve we also want to estimate the performance limit in addition to the parameters that define the shape of the curve.

With some historical datapoints, various statistical programs can estimate these parameters and then plot a forecast of future technology performance as well as defining the limits of performance with that technology. Thus, the basic mathematical formula is the same,

$$Y(t) = L/(1+exp^{-a(x-b)})$$

Figure A.5: Logistic equation to estimate technology S-curves.

But now we don't want to set the limit L, but rather have the statistical program esti-mate L by finding the best fitting line through the early data points. There are several different programs that can find the best fit.

People often refer to technology performance increasing exponentially. For a par-ticular technology, this is unlikely due to the limits created by the technologies design. However, new technologies will generally replace old technologies, and it may appear that the overall performance of sequential technologies, each with different and better solutions, almost seems to increase exponentially. But here we are talking about the "envelope" curve created by a sequential series of technology S-curves, with each S-curve describing the performance of new and better technologies. In modern times, sometimes the envelope curve of sequential technologies that solve a problem is start-ing to look almost exponential.

Experience Curve Estimation

The strategic importance of understanding experience curves in many technology industries was discussed in Chapter 2. But experience curves are also useful in forecast-ing future productivity measures, such as unit cost, or production quality measures, such as yield rates.

The basic experience curve formula is illustrated in Figura A6.

$$Y=ax^b$$

Figure A.6: Experience curve non-linear formula.

where y=a measure of productivity and x=cumulative production experience. The parameters "a" and "b" are estimated from the data. In this formula, b is negative when the measure of productivity decreases with more experience such as unit cost and b is positive when the productivity measure increases with experience such as yield rates. Experience curves can be estimated at the technology level at a particular firm, or when examining trends at the whole industry level.

While the equation above is non-linear, the experience curve formula can be easily converted to a straight line by talking the log of both sides. Taking the log of both sides results in the equation below (Figure A.7):

$$Log(Y)=Log(a)+bLog(x)$$

Figure A.7: Experience curve linear (log) formula.

This equation becomes a straight line when the data is plotted on logarithmic paper. It also can be easily estimated by using a linear regression estimation on the logged historical data. The regression procedure will then estimate the coefficients. Once the parameters are estimated, from the data it is simple to plug in a future cumulative production experience and get a forecast of future productivity. Or one can plug in a future productivity target and then determine how much more production experience is needed to obtain the target.

The chart below shows the actual relationship between the price ($ per Watt) of photovoltaic (PV) modules and the cumulative sales of photovoltaic (PV) modules in megawatt hours (MW).

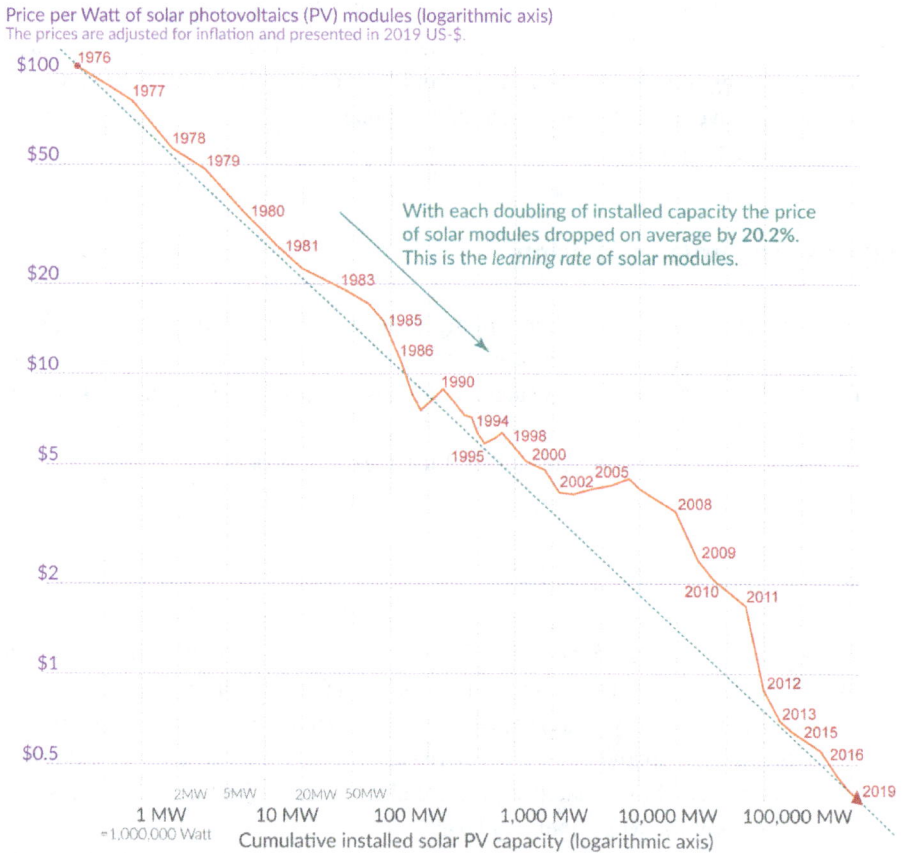

Price per Watt of solar photovoltaics (PV) modules (logarithmic axis)
The prices are adjusted for inflation and presented in 2019 US-$.

With each doubling of installed capacity the price of solar modules dropped on average by 20.2%. This is the *learning rate* of solar modules.

Cumulative installed solar PV capacity (logarithmic axis)

Figure A.8: Declining cost of PV modules with increasing market adoption.

Experience curves are a powerful tool when analyzing future productivity targets as well as tracking productivity improvements, such as costs and prices over time, and whether there is deviation from the expected improvements.

Many large technology companies have a long history of producing a wide variety of components. With this history, these firms often calculate the expected experience curve for a new technology using the estimates from prior production processes even before production starts for the new technology. They simply apply prior experience curves to the new technology and then use that as a standard for estimating the future productivity of the new technology. They can also use the experience curves of prior technologies as a baseline to see if their early productivity levels of the new technology are meeting expectations – this creates clear productivity targets for the production team.

Trend Impact Analysis

While the Gompertz, Bass, and logistic models are very powerful, they are still trend extrapolation models with time as the primary component. But events can often impact a trend. Impacts might include an election where the new administration might remove or increase incentives to purchase certain technologies. This is common for many environmentally related technologies such as solar panels or electric vehicles. Major military conflicts can also impact technologies, such as defense related technologies. COVID-19 was an event that impacted the adoption of technologies. Trend impact analysis is a forecasting technique that combines trend extrapolation with the impact of likely events.

Trend impact analysis starts with a trend, such as a simple straight line or a more complicated trend such as an S-curve. Then certain critical events are identified, and a team of experts could be asked the question – if this event occurs, what is the impact (given by a probability of the event occurring and the impact). These impacts are then plotted on a graph. In the example illustrated in Figure A.9, we assume that there is a 50% chance a new administration might be elected, and if the new administration is elected, then there will be a 50% increase in sales due to new incentives that have been promised during the campaign. Thus, the overall impact would be a likely 25% increase in sales over the base trend line for the first impact. This type of analysis would then be done for other potential impacts.

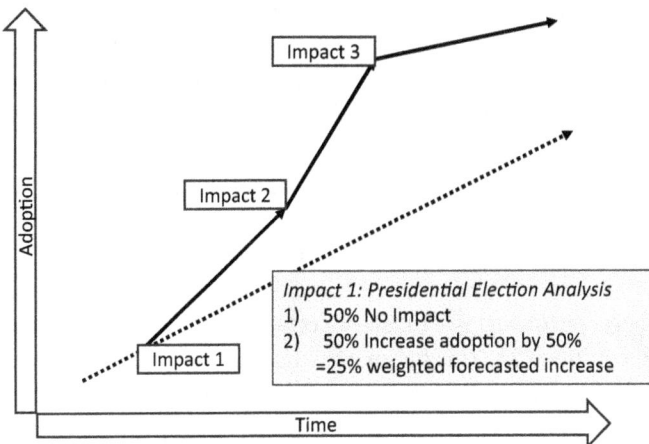

Figure A.9: Trend impact analysis.

Forecasting by Monitoring and Technology Scans

Technology monitoring and scanning is not a formal forecasting technique, but rather a process. This technique has many different titles, including "Horizon Scanning" and the "Foresight Method". Government agencies and larger corporations often have formal teams assigned to this technology scanning process. The idea is that technologies are always being developed by governments, corporations, and universities all over the globe. It is simply impossible for anybody to know all of the developments all of the time. But there are always "signals" about different technology developments. These signals might be product announcements, a patent application, a news report, presentations at a technical conference, laboratory personnel hires, a statement in an interview or blog, a review in a technology podcast, or an application for a grant. Signals are everywhere.

Technology scanning and monitoring is not trying to predict the future, but rather a formal process focused on the early detection of signals. After signals are detected, they need to be classified in importance levels, often called "weak" or "strong" signals. Strong signals will then be investigated in more detail, while weaker signals will be tracked in the future. There are formal recording methods for this type of scanning and monitoring that assist the manager to organize their constant scanning of signals. Before the internet, technology scanning often required subscribing to hundreds of papers, magazines and journals. Now web signal tracking is primarily keyword-oriented, with AI-supported searches becoming particularly powerful for monitoring and scanning.

Normative Forecasting and Backcasting

Normative forecasting, often called "backcasting", starts with a future event and then works backward to the present time to determine what technological advances need to be made, and when they need to occur, in order to obtain that future event. Essentially, these techniques assume that the future event will occur, and thus, by going backward these intermediate steps and their related technologies will also occur. Then this itemized path to the future becomes the technology forecast.

Backcasting only works when there is high certainty about the future event. For example, in a 1962 speech, President John F. Kennedy announced that the U.S. would put a man on the moon by 1970 and was willing to commit the resources to make this happen. This target, however, required a whole set of advanced technologies and systems, including new rocket technologies, a lunar spacecraft, and deep space communications that did not exist at the time. This became the target, and backcasting then determined all the technologies, and when they needed to occur in order to make this moon landing happen. These technology phases and requirements then became the forecasts. In 2025 President Donald Trump made a similar target of putting a man on

Mars. To achieve this target goal, will also require a sequence of new technologies and advancements (see Figure A.10).

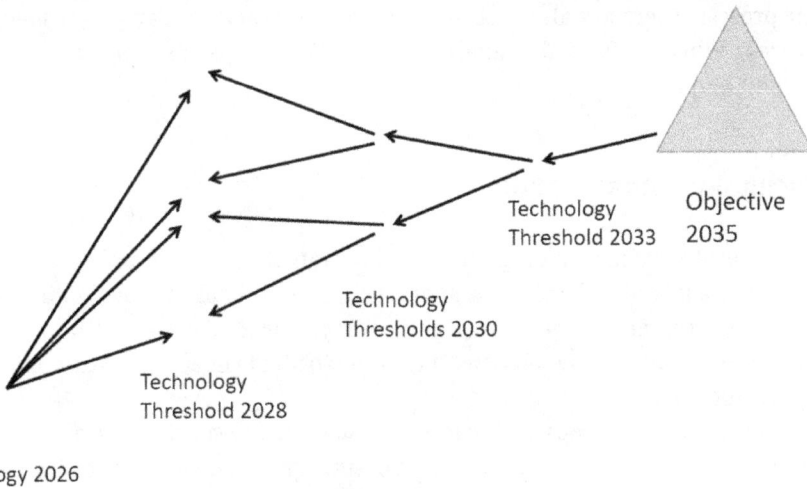

Figure A.10: Backcasting the technical requirements to put a man on Mars.

Judgmental Forecasting

Judgmental forecasting is a qualitative technique. The most commonly used judgmental forecasting technique is the Delphi method. The Delphi method is designed to overcome the problem of groupthink and the biases of just asking people about the future. The Delphi method has a number of characteristics.

1) It is anonymous, nobody knows who is in the Delphi group, or at least, what their answers are to questions
2) The Delphi panel is interdisciplinary, made up of experts from different fields.
3) The process involves four steps
   a) Ask a question about the future, such as "when do you think electric cars will obtain a 50% share of the total automotive market?
   b) Everybody provides a date.
   c) The facilitator then combines the results and calculates averages plus quartiles.
   d) This information is then returned to the Delphi members, and they are asked to reconsider their forecast based on the feedback. However, if anybody provides a forecast that is outside the inner quartile, they have to provide a reason why they believe this. This forces people to move more toward the center if they don't have a strong argument.
4) This process is run for several rounds, until some form of consensus is obtained.

The key in the Delphi method is getting consensus, with built-in incentives to encourage movement of people's positions. Delphi techniques are somewhat time-consuming, but now they are often performed online which dramatically shortens the process. There are also specialized Delphi programs that automate much of the process. When performed online, or with smaller groups of people, it is often called a "mini-Delphi".

Technology Roadmapping

A technology roadmap is somewhat like the Gantt Chart used in project management but focuses more on the short-term and long-term technologies that go into a future technology. Essentially, the technology roadmap matches the goals of the organization to the specific technology solutions. It identifies both the internal and external technology requirements.

Technology roadmaps tend to be very visual and are generally used to understand larger system requirements for purposes of strategic planning. They are also becoming more popular in IT and software system development. Technology roadmaps are also used extensively by governments responsible for different areas of technology development, such as developing spacecraft or defense systems.

Technology roadmaps not only forecast future technology events but also provide a visual framework for management to coordinate and plan for technology development. Developing a technology roadmap has several steps.
- Identify the technology system that will be focus of the "map"
- Identify the critical system requirements and their targets
- Specify the major technology areas
- Specify the technology drivers and their targets
- Identify the technology alternatives and their timelines
- Recommend which technologies should be proposed
- Write the technology roadmap report

There are several different methods used to present a technology roadmap, but the most common is a time-related chart that identifies and "maps" the critical systems, sub-systems, technologies, and drivers. Due to the desire to capture a lot of different components, technological roadmaps can become very complicated with larger systems. Figure A.11 represents a NASA technology roadmap as part of their vision study published in 2014 titled: *CFD Vision 2030 Study: A Path to Revolutionary Computational Aerosciences*. This road map also identified the technology readiness levels (TRLs) of the different technologies they are looking at.

As with all of the techniques described in this appendix, there are a number of external programs and resources available for developing technology roadmaps.

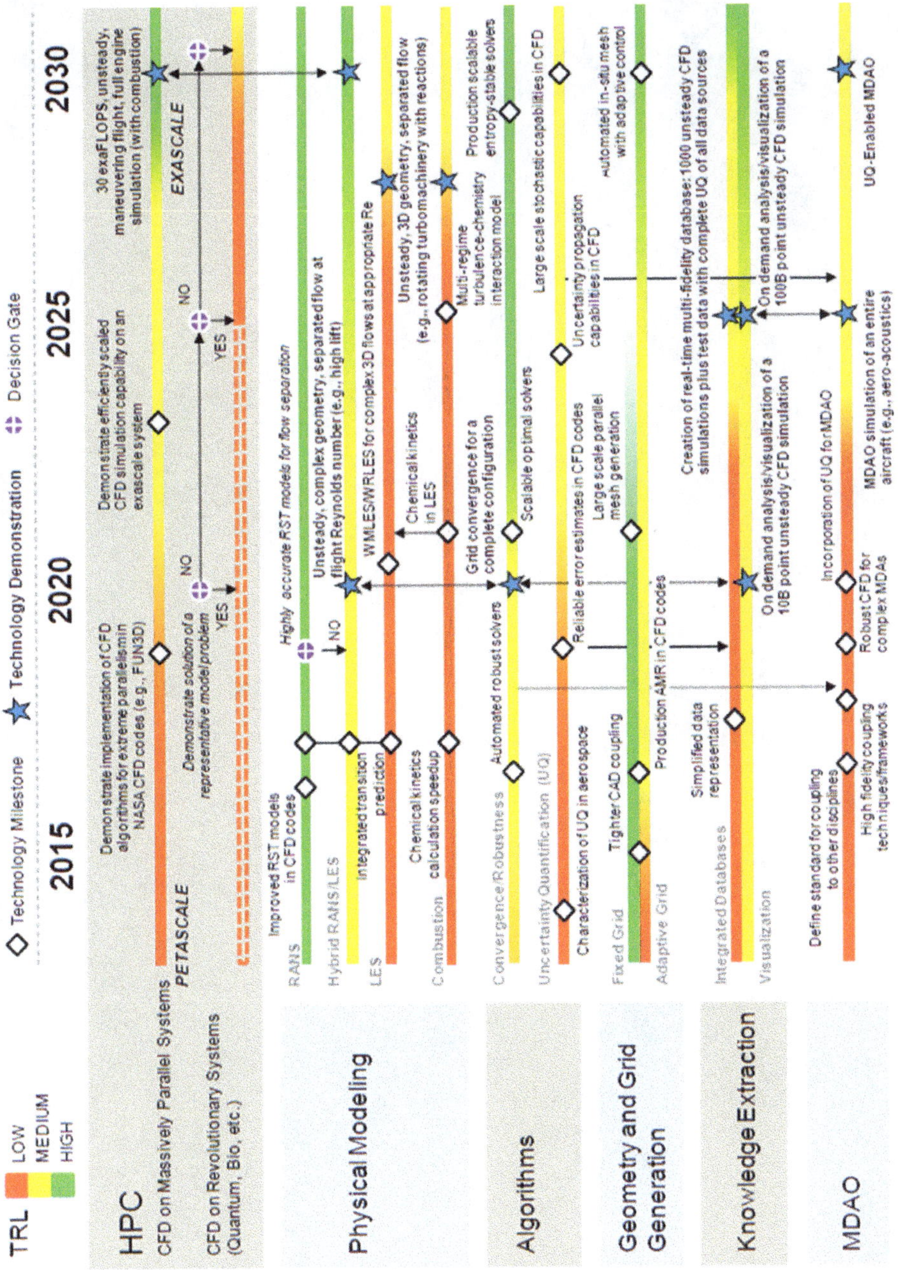

Figure A.11: Example technology roadmap: Computational Aerosciences.

Endnotes

Introduction

1 Wisconsin Historical Society. (n.d.). *First Practical Typewriter*. Retrieved March 25, 2025, from https://www.wisconsinhistory.org/Records/Article/CS2697

2 Henard, D. H., & Szymanski, D. M. (2001). Why some new products are more successful than others. *Journal of Marketing Research, 38*(3), 362–375; Troy, L. C., Szymanski, D. M., & Varadarajan, P. R. (2001). Generating new product ideas: An initial investigation of the role of market information and organizational characteristics. *Journal of the Academy of Marketing Science, 29*(1), 89–101.

3 Stevens, G. A., & Burley, J. (1997). 3,000 raw ideas = 1 commercial success! *Research-Technology Management*, 40(3), 16–27.

Chapter 1

1 Anderson, A., & Tushman, M. (1990). Technological discontinuities and dominant designs: A cyclical model of technological change. *Administrative Science Quarterly*, 35(4), 604–633; Taylor, M., & Taylor, A. (2012). The technology life cycle: Conceptualization and managerial implications. *International Journal of Production Economics*, 140(1), 541–553.

2 World Intellectual Property Organization. (n.d.). About intellectual property. *WIPO*. https://www.wipo.int/en/web/about-ip

3 See the Doug Engelbart Institute for a full and fascinating discussion of the various steps in developing the computer mouse. https://dougengelbart.org/content/view/162/. The develop of the computer mouse largely correlates with the stages of technology development discussed in this chapter.

4 Computer History Museum. (n.d.). The mouse and graphical user interface. *Computer History Museum*. Retrieved February 16, 2025, from https://www.computerhistory.org/revolution/input-output/14/350

5 NASA still extensively uses the technology readiness level, or TRL, model in their system development efforts. https://www.nasa.gov/directorates/somd/space-communications-navigation-program/technology-readiness-levels/

6 Department of Defense. (2022). *Manufacturing Readiness Level (MRL) Deskbook*. https://dodmrl.com/MRL_Deskbook_2022_20221001_Final.pdf

7 Sauser, B., Verma, D., Ramirez-Marquez, J. E., & Gove, R. (2006). From TRL to SRL: the concept of systems readiness levels. *Conference on Systems Engineering Research*, 1–10.

8 The authors adapted this IRL model from Eder, C., Mazzuchi, T., & Sarkani, S. (2017). *Beyond Integration Readiness Levels (IRL): A Multidimensional Framework to Facilitate the Integration of Systems and Systems*. U.S. Department of Defense.

9 Technology Innovation Agency. (2019). *TRL Descriptions for Biomedical Applications*. https://www.tia.org.za/core/uploads/2019/12/TRL-1.pdf

Chapter 2

1 Oftentimes people think the hard drive industry is declining due to modern web-based and "cloud" storage technologies, but actually local data storage systems are still a critically important component of

https://doi.org/10.1515/9783111684420-020

any standalone computer-based technology. https://www.marketresearchfuture.com/reports/hard-disk-market-8306

2 Griliches, Z. (1957). Hybrid corn: An exploration in the economics of technological change. *Econometrica,* 25(4), 501–522.

3 Rogers, E. (1962). *Diffusion of Innovations.* Free Press: New York.

4 Christensen, C. M. (1992). Exploring the limits of the technology S-curve. Part I: Component technologies. *Production and Operations Management,* 1(4), 334–357.

5 A number of studies have examined various psychological and cultural characteristics associated with adoption behavior for technology-based products. For example, see Davis, F. (1989). Perceived usefulness, perceived ease of use, and user acceptance. *MIS Quarterly,* 13(3), 319–340. See also Roberts, R., Flin, R., Millar, D., & Corradi, L. (2021). Psychological factors influencing technology adoption: A case study from the old and gas industry. *Technovation,* 102, for a good discussion of different psychological dimensions that are often used to examine technology adoption behaviors.

6 Hofstede, G. (2001). *Culture's Consequences: Comparing Values, Behaviors, Institutions and Organizations Across Nations* (2nd edition). Sage Publications.

7 For example, see Lee, S., Trimi, S., & Kim, C. (2013). The impact of cultural differences on technology adoption. *Journal of World Business,* 48(1), 20–29.

8 Many of these studies use Geert Hofstede's dimensions of culture to investigate the impact of culture on technology adoption. For example, see Alamrik, J. (2025). Antecedents of generative artificial intelligence technology adoption: Extended innovation of diffusion model with cultural dimensions and risks perceptions. *Journal of Ecohumanism,* 4(1), 1718–1738.

9 https://www.millioninsights.com/industry-reports/global-positioning-systems-gps-market

10 Fisher, J., & Pry, R. (1971). A simple substitution model of technological change. *Technological Forecasting and Social Change,* 3, 75–88.

11 Henderson, B. D. (1968). *Perspectives on Experience.* Boston Consulting Group.

12 https://fred.stlouisfed.org/series/IIAI

Chapter 3

1 Utterback, J., & Abernathy, W. (1975). A dynamic model of process and product innovation, *Omega,* 3(6), 639–656.

2 The discussion of the dominant design history of CubeSat is based upon a presentation by Yue Song and Rahul Kapoor, "How complements influence the variation, selection and retention of dominant designs" at the 2025 California Entrepreneurship Educators Conference.

3 Roghavachari, R. (2022). *Lifecycle Management of Approved Drug Products – FDA Perspective.* U.S. Food & Drug Administration.

4 Sethy et al. (2013). Product life cycle management in pharmaceuticals: A review. *Pharmatutor.* https://www.pharmatutor.org/articles/product-life-cycle-management-in-pharmaceuticals-review

5 For a more detailed discussion of the typical life cycles in pharmaceutical product development, see the PharmaMarketer. https://www.thepharmamarketer.com/knowledge/pharmacetuical-product-life-cycle

Chapter 4

1 Taylor, N. (2019). *LASER: The Inventor, the Nobel Laureate, and the Thirty-Year Patent War.* Simon & Schuster.

2 American Chemical Society. (n.d.). High-performance carbon fibers. *National Historic Chemical Landmarks.* Retrieved January 26, 2025, from http://www.acs.org/content/acs/en/education/whatischemistry/landmarks/carbonfibers.html

3 Engineering Product Design. (n.d.). Types of sensors in smartwatches, fitness trackers, and bands. *EngineeringProductDesign.com.* Retrieved January 26, 2025, from https://engineeringproductdesign.com/sensors-in-smartwatches-fitness-trackers/

4 Dovetail. (n.d.). What is feature creep and how can you avoid it? *Dovetail.com.* Retrieved February 4, 2025, from https://dovetail.com/product-development/what-is-feature-creep/

5 Millán, J. D., Rupp, R., Müller-Putz, G. R., Murray-Smith, R., Giugliemma, C., Tangermann, M., Vidaurre, C., Cincotti, F., Kübler, A., Leeb, R., Neuper, C., Müller, K. R., & Mattia, D. (2010). Combining brain-computer interfaces and assistive technologies: State-of-the-art and challenges. *Frontiers in Neuroscience, 4,* 161. https://doi.org/10.3389/fnins.2010.00161

6 Many pivots involve overlapping changes across product design, market segments, business models, and distribution strategies. Throughout this chapter, we focus on different categories of pivots for clarity, while recognizing that real-world cases are often more complex.

7 GoPro Zone. (2023). *Mapping the GoPro user's journey: Insights and transformations.* Retrieved from https://goprozone.com/mapping-the-gopro-users-journey-insights-and-transformations/

8 Romano, J. P. (October 4, 2023). 12 years of SIRI: A look back at its evolution and impact. *Medium.* Retrieved February 9, 2025, from https://medium.com/@Adviters/12-years-of-siri-a-look-back-at-its-evolution-and-impact-d6cefb0d7646

9 Background material on the Relaxin story was obtained from Dovey, B. (2023). *The Idea Is the Easy Part: Myths and Realities of the Startup World.* Matt Holt Books.

10 Loten, A. (May 30, 2019). The origin of Slack. *TechCrunch.* Retrieved February 12, 2025, from https://techcrunch.com/2019/05/30/the-slack-origin-story/

11 Butler, D., & D. Button. The Netflix story: From mail box to mega-cap. https://www.thestreet.com/technology/history-of-netflix-15091518

12 Wallingford, P. (September 12, 2024). How old is Duolingo and what's its history? *Duolingo Guides.* Retrieved February 13, 2025, from https://duolingoguides.com/how-old-is-duolingo/

13 United States Patent and Trademark Office (USPTO). (n.d.). Moondust and marketing magic. *USPTO.* Retrieved February 16, 2025, from https://www.uspto.gov/learning-and-resources/journeys-innovation/historical-stories/moondust-and-marketing-magic

14 Galbraith, C. (1990). Transferring core manufacturing technologies in high-technology firms. *California Management Review, 32*(4), 56–70.

15 Material for this case study came from an interview one of the authors conducted with the developer, Brad Chisum, on February 12, 2025.

Chapter 5

1 Brennan, J. A. (December 7, 2021). *The Battle of Cúl Dreimhne (Battle of the Book).* The Wild Geese. https://thewildgeese.irish/profiles/blogs/the-battle-of-c-l-dreimhne-battle-of-the-book-1

2 https://www.wipo.int/en/web/wipo-magazine/articles/ip-and-business-launching-a-new-product-freedom-to-operate-34956

3 Quote, Steve Fontana, Fontana International, May 9, 2025.

4 Material for this case study came from an interview one of the authors conducted with the Kirsten Leutke, a partner with Osage University Partners, on July 2, 2024.

Chapter 6

1 The Escortin technology is also an example of the IP problems that occur with prior publications. While several patent applications were made for the Escortin technology, a prior academic publication by the inventors made it difficult to obtain full patent protection. However, there are still trade secrets involved with the process. Thus, some commercial licenses were obtained.

2 Kay, N. (2013). Rerun the tape of history and QWERTY always wins. *Research Policy*, 42(6/7), 1175–1185.

3 Galbraith, C., & Kay, N. (2025). Hidden in plain sight: QWERTY, the search for optimality and IP complementarity. *Business History*. https://doi.org/10.1080/00076791.2025.2458052

Chapter 7

1 Material for this case study came from an interview one of the authors conducted with the founder, Darrel Drinan, on March 6, 2025.

Chapter 8

1 This VoC study was performed by one of the authors and is the basis for this real-life example.

2 This VoC study was performed by one of the authors and is the basis for this real-life example.

3 This VoC study was performed by one of the authors and is the basis for this real-life example.

4 For example, Trivedi, V., Chauhan, A., & Trivedi, A. (2021). Analysing consumers' smartphone adoption decisions using qualitative dimensions: A multi-criteria decision approach. *International Journal of Technology Marketing*, 15(1), pp. 48–65.

5 This VoC study was performed by one of the authors and is the basis for this real-life example.

6 https://www.ashokcharan.com/Marketing-Analytics/~bs-perceptual-maps.php#gsc.tab=0

7 Janik, E., Ceremuga, M., Saluk-Bijak, J., & Bijak, M. (2019). Biological toxins as the potential tools for bioterrorism. *International Journal of Molecular Science*, 20(5), 1181. doi: 10.3390/ijms20051181. PMID: 30857127; PMCID: PMC6429496.

8 *Annual Mail Security Reports* published by RaySecur.

9 This commercialization study and VoC analysis were completed by one of the authors.

Chapter 9

1 Belasco, J. (1990). *Teaching the Elephant to Dance: Empowering Change in Your Organization*. Crown Publishers.

2 Robert Cooper, the inventor of StageGate®, and his partner Scott Edgett have created a consulting group, *StageGate® International*. The website for this organization provides a number of resources and ideas related to this topic. https://www.stage-gate.com/

3 There are a number of firms that offer technology portfolio programs. One of the more popular is the "Planview" solution (https://www.planview.com/). Other firms also offer similar products. These solutions all attempt to present portfolios in a dynamic manner, over time.

Chapter 11

1 https://angelcapitalassociation.org/angel-funders-report/

2 This is a very simplified description of the difference between enterprise and equity value. In reality, there also needs to be adjustments for cash (since cash is generally not transferred in the sale of a business) and other small adjustments. However, debt and other business obligations represent the primary difference between equity value (or capitalization) and enterprise value.

3 With a business valuation, the discount rate includes components for equity premiums, small firm premiums, and industry premiums. In many cases of a well-established business, the discount rate can be calculated from the weighted "cost of capital".

4 Early-stage private equity investors often speak of wanting a 10× return on their investment in 5 years. This is like turning $100 into $1,000 in 5 years. This type of return requires an annual cumulative return on investment of approximately 60%. Obviously, this does not happen a lot, but it is a typical target for private equity investors when analyzing the risk of investing in start-up firms developing early-stage technologies.

5 Professor Damodaran from New York University, for example, publishes average betas (a measure of risk) for publicly traded firms in different industries. https://pages.stern.nyu.edu/~adamodar/New_Home_Page/home.htm

6 For an example of international equity premium adjustments, see Damodaran equity risk calculations. http://www.stern.nyu.edu/~adamodar/New_Home_Page/data.html

7 Villiger, R., & Nielsen, N. (2023). Discount rates in drug development. Report, AVANCE. http://biostrat.dk/financialvaluation-methods-for-biotechnology.pdf

8 Adapted from Valuation & EBITDA Multiples for Tech Companies: 2025 Report – First Page Sage.

9 Material for this case study came from a series of detailed interviews that both of the authors conducted with several Tech Transfer Officers in late 2024 and early 2025.

10 Heartland Forward. (2022). *Research to Renewal: Advancing Tech Transfer*. https://heartlandforward.org/case-study/research-to-renewal-advancing-university-tech-transfer/

11 COGR (2022) *Technology Transfer in U.S. Research Universities: Dispelling Common Myths.*

Chapter 12

1 https://www.businesswire.com/news/home/20240918316822/en/Almost-40-of-Small-Business-Owners-Hit-By-Employee-Litigation-In-The-Past-Year

2 https://amtrustfinancial.com/blog/insurance-products/top-trends-employment-practices-liability-claims

3 Material for this case study came from interviews with Napoleon Monroe and Michael Mesa on multiple occasions in January and February 2025, along with the supporting background material from Brian Dovey's book *The Idea Is the Easy Part* (2023). We wish to recognize the many personal discussions we had over the years with Brian Dovey on this and many other topics before his untimely passing in 2023.

4 Lockey, S. D., Sr. (1980). A new method of administering aqueous epinephrine: The Epipen, an automatic syringe. *Journal of Asthma Research*, 17(4), 165–168.

5 Neffy webpage, Neffy.com (accessed May 2025).

Chapter 13

1 Galbraith, C., Merrill, G., & Cambell, K. (1991). The vertical transfer of technological know-how in the Navy research and development community. *Journal of High Technology Management Research*, 2(10), pp. 15–33.

2 Galbraith, C., McKinney, B., DeNoble, A., & Ehrlich, S. (2014). The impact of presentation form, entrepreneurial passion, and perceived preparedness on obtaining grant funding. *Journal of Business and Technical Communication*, 28(2), pp. 222–248.

3 https://www.buyapowa.com/blog/88-of-consumers-trust-word-of-mouth/

4 Chaffey, D., & Ellis-Chadwick, F. (2019). *Digital Marketing* (7th ed). Also, much of this section was adopted from the RACE framework described by Wright, G. (2023). Technology product marketing lifecycle strategies for your IT/High tech business, https://www.smartinsights.com/digital-marketing-strategy/the-internet-of-things-iot-is-here/

5 https://upg-cd-ncus.kantar.com/north-america/inspiration/technology/same-brand-device-ecosystems-drive-consumer-loyalty--and-revenue-growth

6 Material for this case study came from an interview one of the authors conducted with Omitron Co-Founder, Eric Aquilar, on March 5, 2025.

Chapter 14

1 https://www.allbusiness.com/97-percent-of-all-patents-never-make-any-money-15258080-1.html

2 The 30% commercialization rate (defined as earning income) is based upon a study completed by the authors of this book on over 300 technologies that were reviewed by a granting agency and then tracked over a 3-year period. The majority of these technologies were in the TRL 5 to TRL 6 stage of development.

3 Galbraith, C., DeNoble, A., & Ehrlich, S. (2009). The use and content of formal rating systems in Angel Group investment initial screening stages, *Journal of Small Business Strategy*, 20(2), 61–79.

4 For example, Galbraith, C., Ehrlich, S., & DeNoble, A. (2006). Predicting technology success: identifying key predictors and assessing expert evaluation for advanced technologies, *Journal of Technology Transfer*, 31, 673–684.

5 https://www.universitylabpartners.org/blog/understanding-the-sbir-review-process

6 This percentage is based upon the R^2s of regression models predicting future technology success using the CCAT 4-dimensions. Other than the published research using the CCAT data, there are very few studies that use "ex ante" information to predict future success.

Chapter 15

1 Green, K. C., & Armstrong, J. S. (2015). Simple versus complex forecasting: The evidence. *Journal of Business Research*, 68 (8): 1678–1685. https://kthinnovationreadinesslevel.com/#:~:text=The%20KTH%20Innovation%20Readiness%20Level,idea%20status%20across%20key%20dimensions

2 Measuring the progress of a technology – RCNDE.

3 Lucia Tian, Jacob Mees, Vanessa Chan (Office of Technology Transitions); William Dean (Office of Clean Energy Demonstrations) (2023), Commercial Adoption Readiness Assessment Tool (CARAT). U.S. Department of Energy, Commercial Adoption Readiness Assessment Tool (CARAT)_030323.pdf.

Chapter 16

1 Ries, E. (2011). *The Lean Startup: How Today's Entrepreneurs Use Continuous Innovation to Create Radically Successful Businesses.* Crown Business.

2 Osterwalder, A., & Pigneur, Y. (2010). *Business Model Generation: A Handbook for Visionaries, Game Changers, and Challengers.* Wiley.

3 Osterwalder, A., Pigneur, Y., Bernarda, G., & Smith, A. (2014). *Value Proposition Design: How to Create Products and Services Customers Want.* Wiley.

4 Buchanan, R. (1992). Wicked problems in design thinking. *Design Issues,* 8(2), 5–21.

5 Cohen, D., Pool, G., & Neck, H. (2020). *The Ideate Method: Identifying High-Potential Entrepreneurial Ideas.* Sage Publications. Cohen, D., Hsu, D. K., & Shinnar, R. S. (2020). Identifying innovative opportunities in the entrepreneurship classroom: a new approach and empirical test. *Small Business Economics,* 1–25.

6 Material for this case study came from an interview one of the authors conducted with Molly Cernicek, Los Alamos' NM LEEP Program Manager, and Richard Sudek, member of NM LEEP's Strategic Advisor Leadership Council, on April 7, 2025.

List of Figures

https://doi.org/10.1515/9783111684420-021

About the Authors

Craig Galbraith, Ph.D. is currently the Duke Progress Energy/Betty Cameron Distinguished Professor of Entrepreneurship and Technology Management at the University of North Carolina Wilmington. He has taught graduate and undergraduate classes in technology commercialization, technology management, and entrepreneurship for decades. He holds a Ph.D. in strategic management and economics from Purdue University, an M.Sc. in molecular biology from the University of Nebraska, and an M.B.A. in manufacturing management from San Diego State University. He has also been on the full-time faculties of the University of California Irvine and Purdue University.

He has extensive personal and professional experience at all levels of technology commercialization. He has been the director of his research university's Technology Transfer Office, responsible for patenting and licensing technologies across a range of sectors. He has been the co-founder and Chief Operating Officer of an early-stage biotechnology firm that successfully developed and commercialized a drug platform into the retail market, a technology that is still in use today. More recently, he was appointed a vice president for a small medical instrument development firm and has been a consultant to many technology-oriented corporations, large and small.

For two decades, he was also a contract senior project manager responsible for performing commercialization and feasibility studies for highly advanced U.S. Department of Defense dual-use technologies, as well as various "green" technologies from several national and state government programs. He has been an active angel investor in early-stage technology enterprises, heading a number of due diligence committees for private equity investors. Additionally, he is a Certified Patent Valuation Analyst (CPVA). In this role, he has valued over 300 early-stage companies, including various IP components such as patents and trade secrets, for purposes of investment, acquisitions, and various court hearings. He has published over 100 academic articles and 8 books.

Alex F. DeNoble, Ph.D. is an Emeritus Professor of Entrepreneurship after a 40-year career at San Diego State University in Southern California, one of the hotbeds of technology development. As a recognized leader in the field of entrepreneurship, he served as executive director of the University's Lavin Entrepreneurship Center. Throughout his career, he has been deeply engaged in technology commercialization, particularly through his work with the Center for the Commercialization of Advanced Technologies (CCAT). As a co-principal investigator on numerous Department of Defense (DoD) grants, he played a pivotal role in creating market research teams tasked with finding commercial applications for dual-use technologies, originally developed for military applications. Additionally, he worked with technology developers seeking to adapt innovations for government and military markets.

For many years, he collaborated with Los Alamos National Laboratories, where he created a graduate technology commercialization course. Through this course, students gained experience in the commercialization process by evaluating potential market pathways for technologies supplied by Los Alamos National Laboratories. This initiative provided students with direct exposure to real-world technology commercialization challenges, preparing them for roles in industry.

Prior to retiring from SDSU, he also served as one of the instructors in the University's CSU I-Corps™ program, where he worked with engineering and science faculty and students on projects to commercialize lab technologies.

He has consulted for numerous corporations, including Qualcomm, San Diego Gas & Electric, Siemens, and NEC, applying his expertise in innovation and strategic management. His leadership has also extended to roles with the United States Association for Small Business and Entrepreneurship (USASBE), where he served as a prior president, and the International Council for Small Business (ICSB), where he has held board positions. He recently published a book entitled *The Entrepreneur Within: You Don't Have to Quit Your Day Job to Experience Entrepreneurship*.

https://doi.org/10.1515/9783111684420-022

Index

https://doi.org/10.1515/9783111684420-023